Good Fridays Aug 18/89

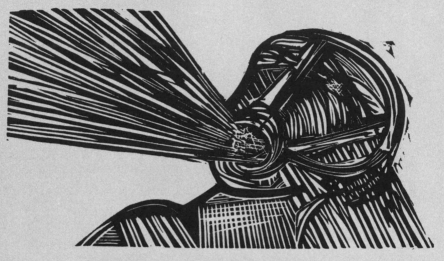

Woodcut by Cecil Skotnes.

FROM SOUTH AFRICA

New Writing, Photographs, and Art

Edited by David Bunn and Jane Taylor
with Reginald Gibbons and Sterling Plumpp

The University of Chicago Press
Chicago and London

The University of Chicago Press, Chicago 60637
The University of Chicago Press, Ltd., London

© 1987 by *TriQuarterly*
All rights reserved. Published 1987
University of Chicago Press edition 1988
Printed in the United States of America

97 96 95 94 93 92 91 90 89 88   5 4 3 2 1

Library of Congress Cataloging in Publication Data

From South Africa: new writing, photographs, and art / edited by
    David Bunn and Jane Taylor, with Reginald Gibbons and Sterling
    Plumpp.
        p.   cm.
    Bibliography: p.
    1. South African literature (English)—20th century.   I. Bunn,
David.   II. Taylor, Jane, 1956–   .
PR9364.9.F76 1988   88-10739
820'.9—dc19   CIP
ISBN 0-226-08035-8 (cloth); 0-226-08036-6 (paper)

Contents

A Note on the Art in This Issue

*Generally, biographical notes on artists and photographers
appear with their work. Artists whose work does not appear in
separate sections include:*

Cecil Skotnes—born in the Cape Province in 1926; graduated in fine arts from the University of the Witwatersrand. At the Polly Street Art Centre in Johannesburg in 1952, he trained and worked with some of the first major black artists to emerge in South Africa. Since 1955 his main medium has been the woodcut, which he has developed as an important art form. He has exhibited extensively in Europe and the U.S. and has received many major commissions. His awards include a major prize at the Third International Biennale of Graphic Art in Florence in 1972. Well-known for his illustrations, Skotnes provided superb woodcuts for Stephen Gray's The Assassination of Shaka (Johannesburg: McGraw-Hill, 1974). The woodcuts which appear in this volume are from Ek Sing Waar Ek Staan, and accompany the Afrikaans poems of Phil du Plessis, translated in the same volume by Patrick Cullinan.

Gavin Younge—born in Zimbabwe, studied fine arts at the Johannesburg College of Art and subsequently obtained a B.A. in philosophy and the history of art from the University of South Africa. In 1975 he accepted a position teaching sculpture at the University of Cape Town. He helped establish the Community Arts Project (CAP), and has won a number of significant awards, such as the Institute of Race Relations award in 1971 and the Afrox Award (Professional category) in 1979. His work has been exhibited in many countries, including South Africa, the U.S., Germany and Australia. He was invited to exhibit at the Valparaiso Biennale in Chile but refused in protest against the brutal and murderous campaign of General Pinochet against artists, students and academics in that country. His most recent solo exhibition has been "Crossing the Cunene" (Market Gallery, Johannesburg, 1981). He has also made a number of films and videos, including Abaphuciwe—The Dispossessed (1981), which has been seen in the U.S.

René Weideman—grew up in South Africa and presently lives and works in Canada.

Billy Mandindi, David Hlongwane, Sipho Hlati, and Eunice Sefako are students at the Community Arts Project (CAP), an independent art and culture project. Hamilton Budaza is teaching in Guguletu and working for CAP. Sydney Hollow studied at CAP and now works at the Nyanga Art Center; he is also a musician. All of these artists' work was included in an exhibition called "Township Artists," held in February 1987 at the Akademie Der Bildenden Kunste in Munich.

The editors wish to thank Manfred Zylla for his help in making available to us the work of the CAP artists.

Editors' Note

Foreign words—from African languages, Afrikaans, or idiomatic South African English—are generally footnoted only at their first occurrence in this volume. Where works have been previously published in South Africa or elsewhere, we have indicated this in the biographical headnotes; all other works came to TriQuarterly in manuscript and are here published for the first time anywhere; all works are here published for the first time in the U.S. Please note that a chronology of important events in South African history, glossaries of place names and of acronyms, and a map of the country may all be found in the appendices, beginning at page 487.

Photograph by René Weideman. (This graffiti commemorates the 1986 police slaying of five youths in Guguletu, a black township on the outskirts of Cape Town.)

11

Linocut by Hamilton Budaza.

Editors' Introduction

David Bunn and Jane Taylor

David Bunn and Jane Taylor live together in Cape Town, and both lecture in the English Department at the University of the Western Cape. From fall 1979 to spring 1985 they lived in Chicago, where Bunn was completing a Ph.D. at Northwestern University and Taylor worked for McDougal Littell, an Illinois publishing company. They returned to South Africa in 1985, and are presently both involved in academic research and alternative education.

> *Almal het gedog dat apartheid on the way out is, en hier het ons hom weer in so 'n nuwe gedaante, met a splinternuwe army-jas aan.**
> —Breyten Breytenbach

It seems quieter now, but nobody is being fooled.

Almost a year after the introduction of the second State of Emergency in June 1986, the Botha regime, in announcements by its propaganda arm, the Department of Information, claims to have reduced violence in the country to a minimum. Yet even the most servile government newspapers speak of an "uneasy calm" and continue that Manichean style of rhetoric which habitually depicts white dread in terms of looming black clouds on the horizon.

For progressive South African writers and activists, however, this is not the time to brood on images of peace before the storm. In the past twelve months almost 35,000 people have been detained, including much of the leadership of democratic extra-parliamentary organizations and trade unions. Journalists, artists and writers have also been severely affected, and rank among the lists of "disappearados" or those brutally murdered by unknown assailants.

---

*"Everyone thought that apartheid was 'on the way out,' yet here he comes again in new guise, wearing a spanking new army greatcoat."

This special issue of *TriQuarterly* appears at a time when a wave of state repression has virtually eliminated the effectiveness of certain mass organizations. Moreover, in the past twelve months there has been an unprecedented, unexpectedly direct assault on the freedom of writers to express themselves openly. Represented in this issue are some of the most innovative and articulate new voices from South Africa; yet each one of these is haunted by the echo of another in solitary confinement, or another who has felt called upon to stop writing and start organizing.

The "South Africa" which emerges from the combined evidence of these various stories, speeches, articles, poems and political documents is structurally different from versions of the same land suggested by texts five years ago. This is now a country at war, or intent on its liberation struggle, or in the initial stages of a revolution which has so far forced the white military state to show its first line of defenses against the people: a new generation of riot-control vehicles called Casspirs, Buffels, and Hippos; water cannons that shoot purple dye with an irritant chemical; rubber bullets, birdshot, buckshot and 7.62-mm bullets; and the widespread use of vigilante squads. This is to say nothing of the systematic violence against detainees under police care. Naturally the public consciousness of violence is noticeable in a way it was not five years ago. Texts being produced in this country today are conscious of their contribution to a struggle for cultural hegemony. It is our privilege to report to you some of the stories from this battlefront.

In December 1986, in the last stages of gathering manuscript material for this issue, we were cheered at the prospect of the biggest cultural festival in South Africa's history due to be held in Cape Town. More than 600 artists, writers, actors, dancers and musicians were gathering to celebrate *Arts Festival '86*, under the slogan "Towards a People's Culture." That this event nearly took place is in itself remarkable. The rhetoric associated with the festival was strongly populist, and yet a wide variety of politically progressive artists aligned themselves with the principles behind it. Consider the following list of aims set out in a pamphlet produced by one of the organizing subcommittees:

● to give momentum to a long term process in which the conscious and concerted building of a people's culture occurs;
● to further the struggle for political liberation ... i.e., facilitating the creation and expression of emerging cultural forms, content and creative method;

14

● to foster relationships across certain ideological differences through cooperation and working together in the cultural spheres. Participation will be limited, however, to those who agree with the basic non-profit, anti-apartheid (including non-collaboration with apartheid structures), anti-militarist, and anti-sexist principles of the festival.

To those unfamiliar with the terms of the cultural and ideological struggle in present-day South Africa, such statements may ring with utopian hollowness. Nevertheless, there have already been many extraordinary sacrifices in the name of cultural liberation. To call for a "people's culture" is not as vacuous as it might seem, for in large sections of this country there are in effect already "people's" education, government and justice. In over forty townships, last year, there was an almost total rent boycott which, according to some estimates (*Weekly Mail*, September 29, 1986), cost the government a million rands* a day. Spurred on by the example of areas in the Eastern Cape which were virtually self-governing in 1986, a network of street committees—linked to consumer boycotts—spread throughout the country. In an interview given shortly before he was detained, Zwelakhe Sisulu, editor of the *New Nation*, asserted confidently: "The advent of mass action and people's power is weakening the organs of the State, day by day. The organs of control in the townships have all but collapsed" (*Leadership*, Vol. 5, No. 4, 1986, p. 90). Faced with this sort of assessment, it should come as no surprise to learn that the government, responding with increasing anger to notions such as "people's culture," banned *Arts Festival '86* the day before it was due to start. Zwelakhe Sisulu is still in detention.

Though we hope this issue of *TriQuarterly* does not privilege any one progressive group, it is especially difficult to ignore the important cultural influence exerted by organizations such as the United Democratic Front (UDF) and the End Conscription Campaign (the ECC, under whose auspices the recent Festival was planned), together with the Congress of South African Trade Unions (COSATU) and its affiliates. These groups have played a fundamental role in unifying artists against apartheid. In a recent speech, Menán du Plessis—one of the new generation of writers represented in this collection and herself a member of the UDF—addressed the question of the artist's commitment to the popular struggle:

It's clear that the struggle for cultural freedom is perceived as one aspect of, and indivisible from, the general struggle for national liberation. And if ordinary

---

*About $490,000

15

CANCELLED

The programme of the Arts Festival '86 in Cape Town was booked to run in this space.

Unfortunately the festival was banned on Thursday afternoon.

The organisers regret that they cannot provide any details.

WEEKLY MAIL, December 12 to December 18, 1986

people, often heartbreakingly young people, are prepared to make terrifying sacrifices for the sake of these freedoms, it seems almost incumbent on artists—in their turn—to stand up and declare themselves willing to fight shoulder to shoulder with the people.*

In the past, many South African writers complained about the pressure of the political, yet in the last decade a majority have come to accept the interrelatedness of literary representation and the liberation struggle. This has not been easy, nor should we mistakenly think that *agitprop* is now the preferred form of expression in this troubled state. By aiming to produce, through cultural work, a "liberated zone" in which the oppressed command the means by which they represent themselves, artists reveal the extent to which materialist theories such as those of Gramsci have been popularized in South Africa. Yet the average white South African, starved of news, is unaware of how far this transformation has advanced.

The new cultural dynamic emerging in South Africa today is at its most visible in the streets, at mass gatherings and at union meetings. Furthermore, the character of the ideological struggle has changed markedly since the latest phase of conflict began in Sebokeng in 1984. Since then, largely through the influence of union federations such as the Federation of South African Trade Unions (FOSATU) or, more recently, COSATU, older elements of oral performance poetry and worker's theater have been adapted to produce a significant new political art.

Of course the performative directness in cultural productions of the past decade has left its mark on established writers such as Mtutuzeli Matshoba, Mongane Serote, and even Nadine Gordimer. Across a wide front, in fact, there is a formidable public consciousness of art and its use value. Paging through a magazine such as *Staffrider* (one of the most important journals of new writing in South Africa), one often finds advertisements such as the following:

---

*Speech given at a "Jews for Justice" forum on "The Right to Know." (Unpublished.)

Translation: "*Amandla Ngawethu [Power to the People],* a first volume of Afrikaans poems by Patrick Petersen, made its debut appearance on 11 September 1985 at the Genaadendal printing office. This is a relevant collection with a politically relevant message. There are thirty poems in the book, and they will be of particular interest to the black reader. This volume can be profitably used at mass meetings, during school boycotts, and at protest marches, funerals, etc."

This changing emphasis has also been reflected in certain sectors of the publishing industry. Editorial collectives are a far more common phenomenon, since to rely solely on an individual editor spells disaster if he or she is arrested. (This is the pragmatic reason for the practice; the ideological reason is based upon a democratic impulse to distribute and share the task of selection.) Freedom of access to books has also become a charged issue (especially so, now that the grip of the academic and cultural boycott is being felt). Some progressive publishers have gone so far as to include this sort of notice on the copyright page: "You are free to reproduce all or parts of the book for educational and nonprofit purposes. Please mention the source."

Academic fashions over the past decade have come gradually to prefer theories of "textuality" rather than literariness. This trend has taken on a particular political character in South Africa, however, because of the increasing desire to match what has been written with community needs. Consequently, there has at times been a very sharp focus on the accountability of the artist. Many whites, for instance, shuddered at the recent spectacle of the Department of Information sponsoring a "peace song," featuring a variety of local artists, to the tune of 4.3 million rands.* It seemed a grotesque exercise in propaganda and fiscal excess. Community organizations took the project far more seriously, and went so far as to warn artists that they could expect reprisals. Soon after the song was released, there was a series of petrol bombings aimed at those black musicians who had collaborated in the production, prompting many of them to apologize and return their earnings.

A very different type of accountability (of a kind usually associated with Verwoerdian apartheid) was recently revealed in the squabble over *Standpunte*. *Standpunte* is the preeminent journal of Afrikaans letters, synonymous with the Afrikaner academy. Last year, following the withdrawal of all its funding, *Standpunte* suddenly ceased functioning. Various rumors circulated about the reasons for the collapse, but it is clear that the liberal editorial program instituted by André Brink, the new editor, became too much for the sponsors to stomach. It is precisely this sort of reactionary high-handedness that causes more *verlig* (enlightened) Afrikaners to look sympathetically at the path of action chosen years back by exiles such as Breyten Breytenbach.

The demise of *Standpunte* was a shock for Afrikaner culture in a way that overseas readers may have trouble understanding. Some writers had become complacent about the state's relatively liberalized censorship procedures, and the *Standpunte* episode seemed a return to the bleak practices of the sixties when most of this nation's talented artists were either banned or driven into exile. Now, the demise of this Afrikaans journal is of little consequence to the liberation struggle; it is, however, a sign of a government growing increasingly nervous as it watches the disintegration of ruling-class alliances.

Overseas viewers and readers were bombarded with news about South Africa in 1986. However, despite the intensity of the coverage, overseas analysis of political events in this country is sometimes determined by stereotypes of South Africa common in the sixties. American analysts, for instance, studiously avoid making connections between capitalism and apartheid's labor practices. In similar fashion, writing in this country, to many overseas, is forever associated with severe state censorship and Calvinist paranoia. Looking back at 1985, though, it is difficult to comprehend how a regime such as the present one could tolerate as

---

*About $2.1 million

much incendiary internal criticism as it did. We must confront this apparent paradox if we are to understand the writers in this issue.

In 1985, one could attend a mass rally, or funeral, with relative freedom, joining hands with those gathered together to mourn for the victims of apartheid. Speakers at such gatherings would often call for mass, united action against exploitation, and the event would usually be punctuated by poetry, theater, liberation songs and other gestures of cultural defiance. During that year it was also possible to attend, say, End Conscription Campaign rallies which sometimes featured video footage of police shootings and rousing jazz performances dedicated to Mandela. Many of the photographers featured in this issue of *TriQuarterly* have exhibited at such gatherings, and the unifying theme behind such exhibitions was usually protest at police and security force violence.

Until recently, the state pretended to tolerate such events, for it believed it could control the spread of seditious opinions. Contrary to popular belief, the Botha regime had traditionally been sensitive to the accusation that South Africa treated its writers worse than Chile did; and in any event intellectuals had been seen as an ineffectual class who could be allowed their liberal catharsis. Over the past few years, however, the audience for political writing has broadened considerably and government censors have reacted, focusing less on examples of blasphemy and obscenity and more on the political.

Weekly Mail statistics for the period June 1985 to December 1986 show that 813 books, publications and objects were banned in South Africa. Of these, 371 were banned for political reasons, and the political emphasis of state control is more clearly apparent when one looks at the targets of the banning: the United Democratic Front leads the field, followed by the African National Congress (ANC), and then, distantly, the South African Communist Party. State censorship, in other words, is being massively concentrated on *organized* internal dissent. Today's novelists, playwrights and poets, unlike writers of previous generations, are only really seen as dangerous when they align themselves with political organizations.

Symbolically, the current State of Emergency in South Africa represents the Botha government's crisis-riddled attempt to control the uncontrollable: the historical imperative moving this country towards a new social order. The present struggle to forge a new, oppositional South African culture clearly is based upon long-term objectives. The oppositional model of self-definition and artistic explanation is one designed for a post-revolutionary, nonracial South Africa. To the state, such an imperative is both insulting and deeply seditious, and it has responded with the most repressive legislation in the history of this country. Even certain conservatives now admit cautiously that we are living in a police state, and unusual fractures are also appearing in the enameled surface of white working-class solidarity.

At no other time in South Africa's history has the printed word, or textual representation, been viewed with such suspicion, and this is a grimly fascinating phenomenon for students of literary theory. Even allowing for the delay in worldwide intellectual fashions reaching the southern hemisphere, local academics have for some years now been drawing on European notions of the interdetermination of ideology, the subject and language, and it has been fruitful to examine the discourse of apartheid in these terms, especially when one considers the Manichean rhetorical habits which reinforce attempts by the white ruling class to separate blackness from whiteness and barricade the former in the homelands. Such theories, however, cannot do justice to the way the state is now responding to the revolutionary Word. Failing to stem the revolutionary fervor or activism, it has fallen back on an attempt to control the means of representation. This aspect of government strategy is most directly enforced by the catch-all definition of "subversive statements" in the emergency regulations:

Definitions

1. In these Regulations, unless the context otherwise indicates—

(i) "Act" means the Public Safety Act, 1953 (Act 3 of 1953);

(ii) "Force" means the South African Police referred to in the definition of "the Force" in section 1 of the Police Act, 1958 (Act 7 of 1958), the South African Railways Police Force established under section 43 of the South African Transport Services Act, 1981 (Act 65 of 1981), the South African Defence Force referred to in section 5 of the Defence Act, 1957 (Act 44 of 1957), or the Prisons Service established by section 2 (1) of the Prisons Act, 1959 (Act 8 of 1959);

(iii) "Minister" means the Minister of Law and Order;

(iv) "print" means to produce by printing, typing or by any other method of reproduction;

(v) "prison" means a prison referred to in section 20 (1) of the Prisons Act, 1959 (Act 8 of 1959), including a police cell or lock-up;

(vi) "publication" means any newspaper, book, magazine, pamphlet, hand-bill or poster, writing, letter-press, picture, photo, print, engraving, lithograph, painting, drawing or other similar representation, any record or other object in or on which sound has been recorded for reproduction, and also any film as defined in section 47 (1) of the Publications Act, 1974 (Act 42 of 1974);

(vii) "statement" means also any publication;

(viii) "subversive statement" means a statement which contains anything which is calculated to have the effect or is likely to have the effect —

(a) of promoting any object of any organisation which has, under any law, been declared to be an unlawful organisation;

(b) of inciting the public or any person or category of persons to —

(i) take part in any unlawful strike;

(ii) take part in or to support any boycott action;

(iii) take part in any unlawful demonstration, gathering or protest procession;

(iv) take part in any acts of civil disobedience; or

(v) discredit or undermine the system of compulsory military service;

(c) of inciting the public or any section of the public or any person or category of persons to resist or oppose the Government or any Minister or official of the Republic or any member of a Force, in connection with any measure adopted in terms of any of these Regulations or in connection with any other measure relating to the safety of the public or the maintenance of public order or in connection with the administration of justice;

(d) of engendering or aggravating feelings of hostility in the public or any section of the public or any person or category of persons towards any section of the public or person or category of persons;

(e) of weakening or undermining the confidence of the public or any section of the public in the termination of the state of emergency, or of encouraging the public or any section of the public to commit any act or omission which endangers or may endanger the safety of the public, the public order or the termination of the state of emergency; or

(f) of encouraging or promoting disinvestment or the application of sanctions or foreign action against the Republic;

and the expression "subversive nature" shall have a corresponding meaning:

(ix) "writing" includes any mode of representing or reproducing letters, figures, signs or symbols in visible form.

What is surprising, though, is not the severity of these measures (infractions can be punished with up to ten years' imprisonment), but the Orwellian manner in which they attempt to control not only public but also private utterances. Having rendered virtually equivalent, for legislative convenience, the words "subversion" and "representation," and behaving as though symbolic subversion is a kind of poison gas drifting across the country, the government now seeks to prevent every subversive representation. At the far edge of absurdity, the press was informed in June 1986, for instance, that even deliberate blank spaces in newspapers—spaces that indicated where articles had been censored—constituted a form of subversion.

This sort of neurotic fascism turns the most delicately ironic and ephemeral forms of resistance into major propaganda victories for the left. Many examples spring to mind: members of the End Conscription Campaign building sand-castle models of the Cape Town castle (the symbolic headquarters of the South African Defence Force) close to the low-tide line; residents of townships all over the country blacking out whole suburbs to hold candlelight vigils for detainees. In the face of fascism, a language of subversion develops which is at once intricate, resilient and inventive.

These, then, are some of the specific cultural and political contexts for this special South African issue of *TriQuarterly*. Each of the poems, stories and essays in this volume, however, also addresses itself to local debate. Though we cannot hope to provide a critical introduction to all the pieces published here, some literary trends and themes need to be highlighted.

II

TriQuarterly #69 represents an unusual moment in the annals of South African writing, for it brings together new work from within the country and new stories, poems or translations by writers who have lived in exile for many years. Let us not pretend this is an easy association, for the strain of separation has left its mark on the most progressive South African art. It has been difficult for us too, as editors and individuals with firm political opinions, to reconcile the perspectives on South Africa from outside and from inside. Thus the literary problem imitates the urgent problem confronting all opponents of apartheid: the question of a united front.

The most famous moment in Jeremy Cronin's collection *Inside* is his assertion that we have to "learn how to speak / with the voices of this land." Learning how to speak this ever-present language, both new and forgotten, is an ideological as well as personal project, and it involves writers who are exiled from this country as much as those at home. So it is with some pleasure that we have included work by writers living overseas. The lot and determination of South African exiles is still a living issue in this country, epitomized by the local wave of mourning for the recent deaths of Alex la Guma in Cuba and Bessie Head in Botswana. We support, too, Christopher Hope's rebuttal to the claim that the only "authentic" South African writing is produced by residents: "This is another of those declamatory statements that sound very pious and mean nothing at all. And it is the old business of separatism in another guise" (*Leadership SA*, Vol. 5, No. 2, 1986). Over and above this question, though, there is the sheer variety of what we have collected in this volume. Let us consider some of its features.

The three essays in this volume are important statements by increasingly important critics. In general, they provide a corrective to that popular version of the South African reality which hovers somewhere between *Cry the Beloved Country* and *Out of Africa*. Njabulo S. Ndebele's address, first of all, needs to be seen in the context of an increased local anticipation that English will be the post-revolutionary *lingua franca*. His article warns against complacent acceptance of the language, highlights its imperialist legacy and criticizes the liberal tradition which advertises its advantages.

Ndebele has been at the center of critical controversy recently, especially after his 1984 article "Turkish Tales" (*Staffrider*, Vol. 6, No. 1). At one point in this essay, for instance, he argues that African writers have been denied access to the means of literary production. He then goes on to make the following claim:

> The point of the matter is that the average African writer . . . produces an art of anticipated surfaces rather than one of processes: processes in character development or in social evolution, for example. He produces an art that is grounded in the negation of social debasement, where scenes of social violence and a host of examples of general social oppression become ends in themselves. As a result very little transformation in reader consciousness is to be expected. . . .

Now this statement is obviously directed against oversimplification and stereotyping in overtly political fiction. Yet Ndebele's statements appear to some to favor an unproblematic theory of "character" and subjectivity which stands in sharp contrast to his own provocative comments about process and ideology in the literary text. The debate around this essay has been rich.

Ndebele's statements about writing and resistance should remind us of the continuing influence of Black Consciousness theory on South African writers, though now often combined with more materialist forms of analysis. Whether to explain the South African reality in terms of racial domination or class conflict; whether the struggle ahead will be determined by a popular, nationalist movement or working-class leadership: these are the perennial questions still plaguing writers in this country. Problems of explanation such as these are clearly manifested in late

1970's works such as Mtutuzeli Matshoba's *Call Me Not a Man* (Cape Town: Ravan, 1979). In one of the stories in that collection, Matshoba's narrator speaks of "an army for the defence of the rights of man":

> When I thought of an army I did not necessarily have a belligerent force in mind. I was thinking of that army of men and women of our world who see the outrage being perpetrated on mankind by an insane ideology and resist it in different ways. This army is also not necessarily black, should not be. To define it along these lines is to make true sons and daughters of the soil of other shades believe that they have no place in the ranks of the army of justice. (pp. 126-27)

For Matshoba, in this story, the liberation struggle has taken on a popular, nonracial dimension. Since the late 1970's, many black writers have consciously addressed their work to healing divisions that exist within mass organizations.

In December 1985 the Congress of South African Trade Unions (COSATU) came into being, uniting into one federation thirty-three previously distinct trade unions. COSATU's effect on the constitution of anti-apartheid forces in this country has already been profound, and through it and active affiliates such as the National Union of Mineworkers the workers' cultural movement has gained new life. This is the terrain of Kelwyn Sole's probing essay on black South African literature, charting the way recent forms of cultural expression are often politicized transformations of older, frequently rural genres such as the praise-poem. Some of the most famous worker poets mentioned in this essay are included in *TriQuarterly*, and we would like to thank Ari Sitas and the COSATU Workers' Cultural Local for permission to reprint these examples. As Sitas explains in his introduction to that section, many of the poems reproduced here are in translation and suffer from being wrenched out of their context: "They lose much of their oral power: the songs, the chants, the ululations, their improvisatory nature and of course, the popular responses that accompany their oration."

Nevertheless, the political and cultural brilliance of these works overrides the problem of context. They are also a direct challenge to the whole notion of a "South African" literature as it is commonly understood, for what has been fixed in texts over the past few centuries represents but a fraction of the singing that has sustained the culture and the sacrifice of the majority of South Africans.

If the two essays by Ndebele and Sole enrich our sense of the diversity of South African culture, then Hein Willemse's remarks on politics, identity and the black Afrikaans writer will shatter certain preconceptions. Willemse is himself a poet and activist of note, a leading figure—

together with Donald Parenzee, Jeremy Cronin, James Matthews and others—in the politicized cultural forum associated with the Cape Flats area. A new generation of radical little magazines is being supported in this region, including *Vakalisa*, *Ekapa*, *Realities* and, most recently, the weekly *South*.

The question of Afrikaans and an Afrikaner culture tainted by fascism is of particular importance to a future South Africa. Until recently, this was a question outsiders immediately associated with the lone, brilliant voice of the exiled poet Breyten Breytenbach. Take, for instance, his angry address to a group of Afrikaner academics while on a lightning visit to this country last year:

> *Ek moet nou sommer dadelik antwoord op 'n vraag wat seker in ieder geval later gestel sou geword het. Probeer ek nou die denkorde ondermyn? My antwoord moet wees: Ja Baas. (Die Suid Afrikaan, 6, 1986)*

> [I must turn immediately to a question that would have been put to me later anyhow. Am I attempting to undermine establishment thought? There is only one answer: Yes Boss!]

But Hein Willemse's essay discusses the way the cultural struggle has also been carried forward in Afrikaans writing by blacks. He reminds us that Breytenbach and André Brink are not the only Afrikaans writers to outspokenly criticize the government. The community of writers Willemse explores has a formidable history of resistance. Since the avant-gardism of the *Sestigers*, however, a whole new marginal tradition of white Afrikaans writing has sprung up. This new wave advanced on the flood of the old: fine new contemporary voices such as Antjie Krog's obviously owe much to Breytenbach, and because her work, too, depends heavily on neologisms, it is extremely difficult to translate. Recent trends in Afrikaans fiction shed light, as well, on internationally acclaimed novelists such as J. M. Coetzee. Tendencies that are strongly parallel to his work can be found in Karel Schoeman (*'n Ander Land*), Wilma Stockenström (see her *Expedition to the Baobab Tree*, translated by Coetzee), and the excerpt in this issue from Klaas Steytler's apocalyptic *Die Walvisman*.

There is one feature of contemporary, progressive Afrikaans writing which is well represented in *TriQuarterly*: a new wave of feminist, politicized work by writers such as Ingrid Scholtz, Welma Odendaal, Jeanne Goosen and Antjie Krog. Clearly some of these writers have been influenced by European post-structuralism; like its European counterpart, progressive Afrikaans writing is sharply focused on questions of identity and authority.

There is, finally, a crucial recent development in Afrikaans writing that can only be hinted at in this introduction: the new genre referred to somewhat elliptically as "grensliteratuur" ("border literature"—an English-language story which reflects very similar tendencies is Andrew Martens's "The Fly"). Put simply, "border" literature is that emergent genre associated specifically with the experience of young white conscripts forced to defend apartheid in the various wars on the borders of Namibia, Angola, Zimbabwe and Mozambique. Some of the more famous representatives of this new corpus include Jaap Steyn (*Diary of a Traitor*), Étienne van Heerden (*To A.W.O.L.*) and Alexander Strachen (*A World Without Frontiers*). Works such as these emerge from a particular set of material circumstances: the contradictions experienced by the apartheid state as it faces escalating conflict in the townships and on its borders, on the one hand; and on the other, increasingly reluctant white conscripts, more and more of whom are failing to report for military service.

According to critics such as Phil du Plessis, Afrikaans border literature can only be explained with reference to the history of violence as it is popularly understood by the Afrikaner nation. In an unpublished essay, du Plessis writes of "the emotional struggle that the Afrikaans writer has to cope with, to break free from the traditional cultural values and prejudices. . . . " Himself an Afrikaans poet of note, du Plessis recalls how his early childhood was charged with stories of violence perpetrated against his Afrikaner ancestors. Later in his life came a different revelation:

> As I grew older, I heard the other side, how Bushmen had been hunted like game, how blacks had been flogged to death on farms into recent times. I saw the baptismal register from the chapel at Schloss Duwisib near Helmeringhausen in Namibia. Page after page, the entries read like this: "Johannes / Buschmann / Getauft und erschossen" [Johannes / Bushman / baptised and shot]. Then the escalation in violence and the deaths in detention started, like the tragedy of Steve Biko.

As *TriQuarterly* goes to press, virtually the only remaining journal of any note for Afrikaans writers is *Stet*, a deeply ironic, satirical, sometimes *angst*-ridden magazine which regularly features work that is critical of the South African Defence Force.

III

As editors for an overseas audience, we have found we have had to gloss one word more often than any other: that word is "Casspir." It is this armored, troop-transporting combat vehicle, with its characteristically hunched, high-gaited step (designed to withstand land-mine blasts) which hunts through so many of the linocuts, stories and photographs. Faced with such persecution, and fleeing it, life can fragment. And what we have collected here, in this issue is also fragmentary and interrupted; it is jagged pieces of a larger cultural picture, a picture which can only be hinted at through these selective images. No single volume could hope to be representative of the variety of violence and creativity in this country, yet the task of gathering manuscript material has been rendered particularly difficult by the State of Emergency. There are gaps everywhere in the fabric of our daily dealings with artists and writers, holes left by the disappearance of people, and of course by their detention. The homes of activists, and buildings housing progressive publishing companies, are routinely shot up or petrol-bombed.

Some other aspects of our editorial task have also been disturbing: in particular, occasional stories submitted to us can only be described as attempted talking cures, obsessive rewritings of an original and profound hurt suffered under racial capitalism. Finally, there is an ever-increasing psychological attrition felt by writers who live in the township war zones, trying to balance precious moments of concentration against nights torn by bullets and arc lights.

You will notice, as you scan these narrative reworkings of our struggle here, that certain images appear over and over again with dreamlike persistence. In Njabulo S. Ndebele's new short story, and in the poems by Ingrid Fiske, Donald Parenzee and Chris van Wyk, the figure of the child maimed, tortured or wounded is held up for our scrutiny. Poems such as these are responding directly to material conditions. Conservative official figures for October 1986 show that in that month 2,677 children aged seventeen or younger were being detained. A total of 2,280 children — 1,880 of whom were black — were imprisoned with their mothers last year. Then there is the slow procession of funeral images through many of the poems and stories, with Sipho Sepamla's "Heroes of the Day" exemplifying the manner in which mass gatherings work the names of the dead into the living fabric of history. Ghastly pictures of South Africans burning and dying have appeared with awful regularity in overseas newspapers and on television. The visual texts brought to you in this volume are, however, very different. For instance, the photographs are not intended to be illustrations for the written texts. Rather, the works by Santu Mofokeng, David Goldblatt, Paul Weinberg, Omar Badsha, Paul Alberts and various members of the Afrapix collective should be seen as distinct essays, each with an internal coherence and narrative logic of its own.

TriQuarterly #69 also contains a variety of graphic art, ranging from the crowded, visionary and often witty linocuts by John Muafangejo to the Community Arts Project linocuts and Manfred Zylla's distorting moral fables. Though it is true that much South African art, including Gavin Younge's sculptures, William Kentridge's drawings and Billy Mandindi's prints, all travel fairly well, we want to remind readers that inside South Africa their power is far greater. There is also the danger of some of these images being read, in pseudo-ethnographic style, as "primitivist" or "naïve," whereas their very power depends on an ability to confront directly a ruling-class discourse in South Africa which itself has imposed exactly those sorts of terms. (One obvious reason why linocuts are a significant art form in this country at the moment is the ease with which it is possible to produce the image, reproduce it and use it politically. A similar political impetus sometimes produces in South African writers a greater concern for the performance of their work than for the publishing of it.)

Thus the State of Emergency, although intended as a repressive influence, ironically renders fixed a certain theory of representation: the belief that images are indeed mimetic and that they narrate, have intention and can therefore subvert an audience. In terms of the regulations we have already quoted, the most ephemeral of representations, the most private whisperings, can be deeply menacing. To some, the State of Emergency has meant that their work is imbued with explosive potential; others have simply found their creativity severely restricted. Our conversations with press, documentary and social-realist photographers have often been unhappy ones; for many, the last year of restrictions has meant a forced return to somewhat neutralized landscapes.

TriQuarterly #69 is one version of South Africa—an active statement and a series of pointed productions rather than a mirror image of life under apartheid. To live in this state now, under worse repression than ever before, is to run the risk of profound disillusionment. An immediate effect that one has to consciously control is the sense that there are only two types of text—those which make a daily difference and those which do not. Each day brings yet another pamphlet which sharpens the nerves and sets the adrenaline pumping. From a sea of examples, one floats up at random:

FIRST AID GUIDELINES

THIS PAMPHLET IS A GUIDE TO THE EMER-
GENCY TREATMENT OF INJURIES CAUSED BY
POLICE. INJURED PEOPLE ARE OFTEN AUTO-
MATICALLY ARRESTED WHEN THEY GO TO
HOSPITALS FOR TREATMENT. SO, MANY PEO-
PLE DO NOT GO TO HOSPITAL OR SEE A DOC-
TOR AT ALL. THIS PAMPHLET WILL HELP PEO-
PLE TREAT SMALL INJURIES IF THEY ARE
REALLY NOT PREPARED TO GO TO HOSPITAL. . . .

Some may argue that the texts included in this issue of *TriQuarterly* do *not* make a daily difference. To say this, though, is to ignore the fact that much of what is published here has already been tested in a public, deeply political context. Many of these narratives are active cultural reinterpretations, and they are going to enable South Africans to rede-fine themselves and their affiliations in a post-apartheid society. Despite the difficulty in which we find ourselves, the last ten years have already freed a South African culture which is truly alternative, and a real foreshadowing of future liberation.

Acknowledgements

We would like to express our deep indebtedness to the following indi-viduals and institutions for their assistance in putting together *Tri-Quarterly* #69: Fred Shafer, who originally conceived the project; Chris van Wyk and other editors at Ravan Press; Marie and David Philip of David Philip Publishers; the University of the Western Cape, and, es-pecially, Professor Stan Ridge and Professor Jakes Gerwel, the university rector; Ari Sitas; Kelwyn Sole; Keith Gottschalk; and Omar Badsha, David Goldblatt, and Paul Weinberg of Afrapix. Furthermore, we would particularly like to thank the Cape of Good Hope Foundation and Flor-ence Feiler for their financial support and Jennifer Sorrell of *ADA* mag-azine, for putting us in touch with some fine artists. We extend also our warm thanks to Phil du Plessis for his generous advice about contemporary Afrikaans writing. Finally, we would especially like to thank Reginald

Gibbons for his enthusiasm, compassion and extraordinary talent for understanding new art.

Dedication

This special issue is dedicated to those writers, artists, and cultural workers among the approximately 33,000 people detained between June 1986 and May 1987.

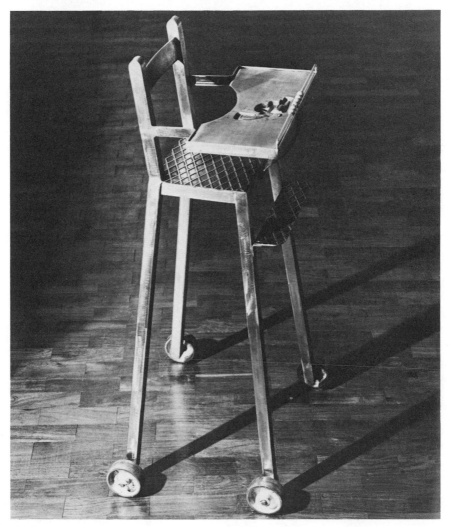

"Botha's Baby" / sculpture by Gavin Younge, now in the University of South Africa art collection.

Death of a Son

Njabulo S. Ndebele

Njabulo Simakahle Ndebele is a lecturer in African, Afro-American and English literature at the University College of Roma, Lesotho. He holds an M.A. from Cambridge and a Ph.D. from the University of Denver.

In 1984 Ndebele won the Noma Award for his collection of short stories, Fools *(Johannesburg: Ravan, 1983). These stories are complex and compassionate tales set in Charterston Location, a township where Ndebele grew up.*

Ndebele is an articulate critic of the cultural oppression which succeeds colonialism. Kelwyn Sole (see page 267) has called Ndebele "possibly the most influential figure in South African literary studies." Ndebele's essay on the colonial legacy of the English language begins on page 217.

At last we got the body. Wednesday. Just enough time for a Saturday funeral. We were exhausted. Empty. The funeral still ahead of us. We had to find the strength to grieve. There had been no time for grief, really. Only much bewilderment and confusion. Now grief. For isn't grief the awareness of loss?

That is why when we finally got the body, Buntu said: "Do you realize our son is dead?" I realized. Our awareness of the death of our first and only child had been displaced completely by the effort to get his body. Even the horrible events that caused the death: we did not think of them, as such. Instead, the numbing drift of things took over our minds: the pleas, letters to be written, telephone calls to be made, telegrams to be dispatched, lawyers to consult, "influential" people to "get in touch with," undertakers to be contacted, so much walking and driving. That is what suddenly mattered: the irksome details that blur the goal (no matter how terrible it is), each detail becoming a door which, once unlocked, revealed yet another door. Without being aware of it, we were distracted by the smell of the skunk and not by what the skunk had done.

We realized something too, Buntu and I, that during the two-week effort to get our son's body, we had drifted apart. For the first time in our marriage, our presence to each other had become a matter of habit. He was there. He'll be there. And I'll be there. But when Buntu said: "Do you realize our son is dead?" he uttered a thought that suddenly brought us together again. It was as if the return of the body of our son was also our coming together. For it was only at that moment that we really began to grieve; as if our lungs had suddenly begun to take in air when just before, we were beginning to suffocate. Something with meaning began to emerge.

We realized. We realized that something else had been happening to us, adding to the terrible events. Yes, we had drifted apart. Yet, our estrangement, just at that moment when we should have been together, seemed disturbingly comforting to me. I was comforted in a manner I did not quite understand.

The problem was that I had known all along that we would have to buy the body anyway. I had known all along. Things would end that way. And when things turned out that way, Buntu could not look me in the eye. For he had said: "Over my dead body! Over my dead body!" as soon as we knew we would be required to pay the police or the government for the release of the body of our child.

"Over my dead body! Over my dead body!" Buntu kept on saying.

Finally, we bought the body. We have the receipt. The police insisted we take it. That way, they would be "protected." It's the law, they said.

I suppose we could have got the body earlier. At first I was confused, for one is supposed to take comfort in the heroism of one's man. Yet, inwardly, I could draw no comfort from his outburst. It seemed hasty. What sense was there to it when all I wanted was the body of my child? What would happen if, as events unfolded, it became clear that Buntu would not give up his life? What would happen? What would happen to him? To me?

For the greater part of two weeks, all of Buntu's efforts, together with friends, relatives, lawyers and the newspapers, were to secure the release of the child's body without the humiliation of having to pay for it. A "fundamental principle."

Why was it difficult for me to see the wisdom of the principle? The worst thing, I suppose, was worrying about what the police may have been doing to the body of my child. How they may have been busy prying it open "to determine the cause of death"?

Would I want to look at the body when we finally got it? To see further mutilations in addition to the "cause of death"? What kind of mother would not want to look at the body of her child? people will ask. Some will say: "It's grief." She is too grief-stricken.

"But still . . . ," they will say. And the elderly among them may say: "Young people are strange."

But how can they know? It was not that I would not want to see the body of my child, but that I was too afraid to confront the horrors of my own imagination. I was haunted by the thought of how useless it had been to have created something. What had been the point of it all? This body filling up with a child. The child steadily growing into something that could be seen and felt. Moving, as it always did, at that time of day when I was all alone at home waiting for it. What had been the point of it all?

How can they know that the mutilation to determine "the cause of death" ripped my own body? Can they think of a womb feeling hunted? Disgorged?

And the milk that I still carried. What about it? What had been the point of it all?

Even Buntu did not seem to sense that that principle, the "fundamental principle," was something too intangible for me at that moment, something that I desperately wanted should assume the form of my child's body. He still seemed far from ever knowing.

I remember one Saturday morning early in our courtship, as Buntu and I walked hand-in-hand through town, window-shopping. We cannot even be said to have been window-shopping, for we were aware of very little that was not ourselves. Everything in those windows was merely an excuse for words to pass between us.

We came across three girls sitting on the pavement, sharing a packet of fish and chips after they had just bought it from a nearby Portuguese cafe. Buntu said: "I want fish and chips too." I said: "So seeing is desire." I said: "My man is greedy!" We laughed. I still remember how he tightened his grip on my hand. The strength of it!

Just then, two white boys coming in the opposite direction suddenly rushed at the girls, and, without warning, one of them kicked the packet of fish and chips out of the hands of the girl who was holding it. The second boy kicked away the rest of what remained in the packet. The girl stood up, shaking her hand as if to throw off the pain in it. Then she pressed it under her armpit as if to squeeze the pain out of it. Meanwhile, the two boys went on their way laughing. The fish and chips lay scattered on the pavement and on the street like stranded boats on a river that had gone dry.

"Just let them do that to you!" said Buntu, tightening once more his

34

grip on my hand as we passed on like sheep that had seen many of their own in the flock picked out for slaughter. We would note the event and wait for our turn. I remember I looked at Buntu, and saw his face was somewhat glum. There seemed no connection between that face and the words of reassurance just uttered. For a while, we went on quietly. It was then that I noticed his grip had grown somewhat limp. Somewhat reluctant. Having lost its self-assurance, it seemed to have been holding on because it had to, not because of a confident sense of possession.

It was not to be long before his words were tested. How could fate work this way, giving to words meanings and intentions they did not carry when they were uttered? I saw that day, how the language of love could so easily be trampled underfoot, or scattered like fish and chips on the pavement, and left stranded and abandoned like boats in a river that suddenly went dry. Never again was love to be confirmed with words. The world around us was too hostile for vows of love. At any moment, the vows could be subjected to the stress of proof. And love died. For words of love need not be tested.

On that day, Buntu and I began our silence. We talked and laughed, of course, but we stopped short of words that would demand proof of action. Buntu knew. He knew the vulnerability of words. And so he sought to obliterate words with acts that seemed to promise redemption.

On that day, as we continued with our walk in town, that Saturday morning, coming up towards us from the opposite direction, was a burly Boer walking with his wife and two children. They approached Buntu and me with an ominously determined advance. Buntu attempted to pull me out of the way, but I never had a chance. The Boer shoved me out of the way, as if clearing a path for his family. I remember, I almost crashed into a nearby fashion display window. I remember, I glanced at the family walking away, the mother and the father each dragging a child. It was for one of those children that I had been cleared away. I remember, also, that as my tears came out, blurring the Boer family and everything else, I saw and felt deeply what was inside of me: a desire to be avenged.

But nothing happened. All I heard was Buntu say: "The dog!" At that very moment, I felt my own hurt vanish like a wisp of smoke. And as my hurt vanished, it was replaced, instead, by a tormenting desire to sacrifice myself for Buntu. Was it something about the powerlessness of the curse and the desperation with which it had been made? The filling of stunned silence with an utterance? Surely it ate into him, revealing how incapable he was of meeting the call of his words.

And so it was, that that afternoon, back in the township, left to ourselves at Buntu's home, I gave in to him for the first time. Or should I say I offered myself to him? Perhaps from some vague sense of wanting to heal something in him? Anyway, we were never to talk about that event. Never. We buried it alive deep inside of me that afternoon. Would it ever be exhumed? All I vaguely felt and knew was that I had the keys to the vault. That was three years ago, a year before we married.

The cause of death? One evening I returned home from work, particularly tired after I had been covering more shootings by the police in the East Rand. Then I had hurried back to the office in Johannesburg to piece together on my typewriter the violent scenes of the day, and then to file my report to meet the deadline. It was late when I returned home, and when I got there, I found a crowd of people in the yard. They were those who could not get inside. I panicked. What had happened? I did not ask those who were outside, being desperate to get into the house. They gave way easily when they recognized me.

Then I heard my mother's voice. Her cry rose well above the noise. It turned into a scream when she saw me. "What is it, mother?" I asked, embracing her out of a vaguely despairing sense of terror. But she pushed me away with an hysterical violence that astounded me.

"What misery have I brought you, my child?" she cried. At that point, many women in the room began to cry too. Soon, there was much wailing in the room, and then all over the house. The sound of it! The anguish! Understanding, yet eager for knowledge, I became desperate. I had to hold onto something. The desire to embrace my mother no longer had anything to do with comforting her; for whatever she had done, whatever its magnitude, had become inconsequential. I needed to embrace her for all the anguish that tied everyone in the house into a knot. I wanted to be part of that knot, yet I wanted to know what had brought it about.

Eventually, we found each other, my mother and I, and clasped each other tightly. When I finally released her, I looked around at the neighbors and suddenly had a vision of how that anguish had to be turned into a simmering kind of indignation. The kind of indignation that had to be kept at bay only because there was a higher purpose at that moment: the sharing of concern.

Slowly and with a calmness that surprised me, I began to gather the details of what had happened. Instinctively, I seemed to have been gathering notes for a news report.

It happened during the day, when the soldiers and the police that had been patrolling the township in their Casspirs began to shoot in the streets at random. Need I describe what I did not see? How did the child

36

come to die just at that moment when the police and the soldiers began to shoot at random, at any house, at any moving thing? That was how one of our windows was shattered by a bullet. And that was when my mother, who looked after her grandchild when we were away at work, panicked. She picked up the child and ran to the neighbors. It was only when she entered the neighbor's house that she noticed the wetness of the blanket that covered the child she held to her chest as she ran for the sanctuary of neighbors. She had looked at her unaccountably bloody hand, then she noted the still bundle in her arms, and began at that moment to blame herself for the death of her grandchild. . .

Later, the police, on yet another round of shooting, found people gathered at our house. They stormed in, saw what had happened. At first, they dragged my mother out, threatening to take her away unless she agreed not to say what had happened. But then they returned and, instead, took the body of the child away. By what freak of logic did they hope that by this act their carnage would never be discovered?

That evening, I looked at Buntu closely. He appeared suddenly to have grown older. We stood alone in an embrace in our bedroom. I noticed, when I kissed his face, how his once lean face had grown suddenly puffy.

At that moment, I felt the familiar impulse come upon me once more, the impulse I always felt when I sensed that Buntu was in some kind of danger, the impulse to yield something of myself to him. He wore the look of someone struggling to gain control of something. Yet, it was clear he was far from controlling anything. I knew that look. Had seen it many times. It came at those times when I sensed that he faced a wave that was infinitely stronger than he, that it would certainly sweep him away, but that he had to seem to be struggling. I pressed myself tightly to him as if to vanish into him; as if only the two of us could stand up to the wave.

"Don't worry," he said. "Don't worry. I'll do everything in my power to right this wrong. Everything. Even if it means suing the police!" We went silent.

I knew that silence. But I knew something else at that moment: that I had to find a way of disengaging myself from the embrace.

Suing the police? I listened to Buntu outlining his plans. "Legal counsel. That's what we need," he said. "I know some people in Pretoria," he said. As he spoke, I felt the warmth of intimacy between us cooling. When he finished, it was cold. I disengaged from his embrace slowly, yet purposefully. Why had Buntu spoken?

Later, he was to speak again, when all his plans had failed to work: "Over my dead body! Over my dead body!"

He sealed my lips. I would wait for him to feel and yield one day to all the realities of misfortune.

Ours was a home, it could be said. It seemed a perfect life for a young couple: I, a reporter; Buntu, a personnel officer at an American factory manufacturing farming implements. He had traveled to the United States and returned with a mind fired with dreams. We dreamed together. Much time we spent, Buntu and I, trying to make a perfect home. The occasions are numerous on which we paged through *Femina, Fair Lady, Cosmopolitan, Home Garden, Car,* as if somehow we were going to surround our lives with the glossiness in the magazines. Indeed, much of our time was spent window-shopping through the magazines. This time, it was different from the window-shopping we did that Saturday when we courted. This time our minds were consumed by the things we saw and dreamed of owning: the furniture, the fridge, TV, videocassette recorders, washing machines, even a vacuum cleaner and every other imaginable thing that would ensure a comfortable modern life.

Especially when I was pregnant. What is it that Buntu did not buy, then? And when the boy was born, Buntu changed the car. A family, he would say, must travel comfortably.

The boy became the center of Buntu's life. Even before he was born, Buntu had already started making inquiries at white private schools. That was where he would send his son, the bearer of his name.

Dreams! It is amazing how the horrible findings of my newspaper reports often vanished before the glossy magazines of our dreams, how I easily forgot that the glossy images were concocted out of the keys of typewriters, made by writers whose business was to sell dreams at the very moment that death pervaded the land. So powerful are words and pictures that even their makers often believe in them.

Buntu's ordeal was long. So it seemed. He would get up early every morning to follow up the previous day's leads regarding the body of our son. I wanted to go with him, but each time I prepared to go he would shake his head.

"It's my task," he would say. But every evening he returned, empty-handed, while with each day that passed and we did not know where the body of my child was, I grew restive and hostile in a manner that gave me much pain. Yet Buntu always felt compelled to give a report on each day's events. I never asked for it. I suppose it was his way of dealing with my silence.

One day he would say: "The lawyers have issued a court order that the body be produced. The writ of *habeas corpus.*"

On another day he would say: "We have petitioned the Minister of Justice."

On yet another he would say: "I was supposed to meet the Chief Security Officer. Waited the whole day. At the end of the day they said I would see him tomorrow if he was not going to be too busy. They are stalling."

Then he would say: "The newspapers, especially yours, are raising the hue and cry. The government is bound to be embarrassed. It's a matter of time."

And so it went on. Every morning he got up and left. Sometimes alone, sometimes with friends. He always left to bear the failure alone.

How much did I care about lawyers, petitions and Chief Security Officers? A lot. The problem was that whenever Buntu spoke about his efforts, I heard only his words. I felt in him the disguised hesitancy of someone who wanted reassurance without asking for it. I saw someone who got up every morning and left not to look for results, but to search for something he could only have found with me.

And each time he returned, I gave my speech to my eyes. And he answered without my having parted my lips. As a result, I sensed, for the first time in my life, a terrible power in me that could make him do anything. And he would never ever be able to deal with that power as long as he did not silence my eyes and call for my voice.

And so, he had to prove himself. And while he left each morning, I learned to be brutally silent. Could he prove himself without me? Could he? Then I got to know, those days, what I'd always wanted from him. I got to know why I have always drawn him into me whenever I sensed his vulnerability.

I wanted him to be free to fear. Wasn't there greater strength that way? Had he ever lived with his own feelings? And the stress of life in this land: didn't it call out for men to be heroes? And should they live up to it even though the details of the war to be fought may often be blurred? They should.

Yet it is precisely for that reason that I often found Buntu's thoughts lacking in strength. They lacked the experience of strife that could only come from a humbling acceptance of fear and then, only then, the need to fight it.

Me? In a way, I have always been free to fear. The prerogative of being a girl. It was always expected of me to scream when a spider crawled across the ceiling. It was known I would jump onto a chair whenever a mouse blundered into the room.

Then, once more, the Casspirs came. A few days before we got the body back, I was at home with my mother when we heard the great roar of truck engines. There was much running and shouting in the streets. I saw them, as I've always seen them on my assignments: the Casspirs. On five occasions they ran down our street at great speed, hurling tear-gas canisters at random. On the fourth occasion, they got our house. The canister shattered another window and filled the house with the terrible pungent choking smoke that I had got to know so well. We ran out of the house gasping for fresh air.

So, this was how my child was killed? Could they have been the same soldiers? Now hardened to their tasks? Or were they new ones being hardened to their tasks? Did they drive away laughing? Clearing paths for their families? What paths?

And was this our home? It couldn't be. It had to be a little bird's nest waiting to be plundered by a predator bird. There seemed no sense to the wedding pictures on the walls, the graduation pictures, birthday pictures, pictures of relatives, and paintings of lush landscapes. There seemed no sense anymore to what seemed recognizably human in our house. It took only a random swoop to obliterate personal worth, to blot out any value there may have been to the past. In desperation, we began to live only for the moment. I do feel hunted.

It was on the night of the tear gas that Buntu came home, saw what had happened, and broke down in tears. They had long been in the coming. . .

My own tears welled out too. How much did we have to cry to refloat stranded boats? I was sure they would float again.

A few nights later, on the night of the funeral, exhausted, I lay on my bed, listening to the last of the mourners leaving. Slowly, I became conscious of returning to the world. Something came back after it seemed not to have been there for ages. It came as a surprise, as a reminder that we will always live around what will happen. The sun will rise and set, and the ants will do their endless work, until one day the clouds turn gray and rain falls, and even in the township, the ants will fly out into the sky. Come what may.

My moon came, in a heavy surge of blood. And, after such a long time, I remembered the thing Buntu and I had buried in me. I felt it as if it had just entered. I felt it again as it floated away on the surge. I would be ready for another month. Ready as always, each and every month, for new beginnings.

And Buntu? I'll be with him, now. Always. Without our knowing, all the trying events had prepared for us new beginnings. Shall we not prevail?

40

Law and Order

Douglas Reid Skinner

Douglas Reid Skinner was born in 1949 in the arid and sparsely populated northern Cape Province in the town of Upington. He worked on and off in drilling, mining, trucking, acting and insurance, followed by twelve years in computer systems in Cape Town, London, New York, San Francisco and Johannesburg. He has published two collections of poetry, Reassembling World *(Cape Town: David Philip, Mantis Series, 1981) and* The House in Pella District *(Cape Town: David Philip, 1985). At present he lives in Cape Town and works in the field of publishing.*

There is a great commotion. Men and women
run back and forth, in every direction, shouting,
"Who is the enemy? Where are they? What are
they doing?" It is summer. There are days
of flooding and pain, and days of exultation,
warmth and possibility solidly in the air.

And the men and women who dress in the
long robes and the language of life and death
sit in the solemn rows of doing and undoing.
Their lips move, and their hands also, yet
nothing happens. The walls crack open and let
light in, but their eyes are empty, they do not see.

Elsewhere it is the same as it was before.
A mother leaves in the darkness before dawn
to work for too little. A man stands waiting
in a forest of hands, and is not seen, and

only his hunger informs him that he is real
and must continue to breathe out and in.

The body of a child only six years old becomes
the body of a child only three years old.
Soon she will exchange that for the body
she had before the world became houses
and trees and fingers and years. And there is
no miracle in this. It happens on every day.

In an emptied harbor the last ship rocks
in water trembling with waves of expectation.
On deck the captains rush in every direction
pointing and yelling, "Here he is. There they are.
She's the one. That's them. There, over there."
And purple veins stand out on their temples.

Elsewhere, on the high land that lies beyond
a ridge of blue mountains, the heat increases
and the short green stalks turn into wheat.
Everyone sits an afternoon on the veranda,
half in sleep and half out, dreaming of
death and dying. The grass dries and turns

the color of sand, the grapes and seeds
ripen and fall to earth, and burst. Everything
melts, and from the ocean with salt a wind
comes hurrying to rub out people and trees.
In the narrow kitchen of a house the radio
whines and crackles and loses the station,

and only the long sounds of distance remain.
The listeners look in every direction, asking,
"What happened? Where is it? Where are we?"
and see only themselves and the room they are in.
Time passes. They walk in circles making
gestures and signs. The room darkens steadily.

Elsewhere a man walks out into an empty field
and raises his arm, and does not return.
A woman sighs as she feels the delicate bones

of her wrist dissolve beneath the weight
of a blow that falls from behind. And a child
out walking stumbles and falls as a bullet

that glances from a wall of scrawled words
enters her chest; and she cries out in pain
to her father, but he does not hear, and she
does not rise again. The cameras click and whirr.
And the men and the women who dress in the long
robes of life and death and sit in solemn rows

are startled from sleep, sit up and wonder,
"Is this it? Is it now done? Is this the end?"
Their lips move, and their hands also, yet
nothing happens. Elsewhere it is the same.
Days of flooding and days of pain, and days
of exultation. Warmth and possibility solidly

in the air, unstoppable brightness to come.

"Crossroads" / linocut by Sydney Hollow.

From *A State of Fear*

Menán du Plessis

Menán du Plessis, who is in her mid-thirties, has published literary criticism and political writing in addition to her novel, A State of Fear *(Cape Town: David Philip, 1983), which in 1985 won for her the Olive Schreiner Prize, and from which the following excerpt was taken. The book was published in England by Unwin Hyman Ltd.*

Currently a teaching assistant at the University of Cape Town and working on a Ph.D. in Linguistics, she is also a member of the United Democratic Front and writes for one of its publications.

A State of Fear *is set in the Cape Town of 1980 and depicts the widespread unrest that has characterized the past decade. Resistance is expressed on a number of different fronts, and once again two of the most significant strategies are the consumer and educational boycotts. Anna Rossouw, the narrator, is a white teacher at a so-called "colored"* high school. As the excerpt opens, she has just given refuge to two of her students, Felicia and Wilson. The two are engaged in some kind of political activity; exactly what that entails is unclear to Anna.*

I

It's been two days now. Two days, or is it nights, they've been here. When the knocking came, I thought calmly, At last; as though I'd been expecting it.

But as I got up to answer the persistent tapping I felt the strength seep away till there was nothing left inside me, under the skin: except some internal honeycombing of dried bone and tissue. I wanted to call out, No. No, let me stay as I am. There was no choice, though. The typewriter keys had been falling back stiff under my fingertips for more than an hour in any case—clammy as an iron grate in the morning.

I unlatched the door. Stared at them for a second only: they seemed

---

**colored:* racist designation for South Africans of mixed descent numb with exhaustion, hardly able to speak coherently. I saw how the streetlight was casting a dull, pewtery gleam across the boy's cheekbones.

Once I'd let them in, once I'd shown them to my room—I didn't know what else was expected of me. They were speechless, wanting only a place to sleep. Foolishly I toyed with the blankets, trying to cover their stiff limbs: but they were heavy almost immediately with sleep, the girl's knee jutting defiantly out from under the rug.

I went and made two cups of cocoa—the proper way, warming the milk till the bubbles were just rising at the rim of the saucepan. Carrying the cups slowly along the dark passage, I spilt some: the tremors in my hands magnified by the china and the liquid. The kids were too far plummeted into sleep, though. I could only gaze at them, after putting down the chinking cups. And then I began to see that they weren't properly resting, despite the low, steady hush of their breathing. I think it was that that left me more helpless than anything. I could see a sporadic jerking of Felicia's shoulder: fitful. And I heard the boy half cry out once. It wasn't words, but muffled, smothered chunks of pure sound that might have been trying to tear themselves a way out from nightmare.

I came back here into the study, although I'd lost all my heart for letters. I just wanted to lie down on the spare divan.

When once we could lie on our bellies in the warm, sweet grass, discovering the microfauna—ants, beetles, leaf-hoppers, millipedes.

I don't know how long they're going to be here: it's been two days already, and they've given me no indication. They're not very talkative—with me, I mean. I find myself lapsing into brooding, irrational doubt, wondering whether children ever simply go away again, once they've come to you stricken with tiredness in the small hours.

They slept until noon yesterday. Yesterday? Yes. I wasn't sure whether to wake them: spent the morning tiptoeing up and down the passage, peering in at them uncertainly. All I could discover was a whitish flickering of nervousness in my own wrists and ankles, and the burning ache in my chest; while the children remained an enigma. Even waking, they keep to themselves—they spent the whole of the afternoon yesterday reading in the sitting room. I think now that they were resting themselves, consciously working for a calmness of mind. Because they were going out again: Felicia came to the study door to tell me, politely, that they'd want a light meal at eight. The boy doesn't speak to me at all.

It's no good, is it, succumbing to emotion. I keep explaining that to myself, trying to wrench the words around to make them face me. We're going to be all right, after all. I spent that night on the divan worrying minutely over a domestic inventory, with an insistent belief in my mind that each new detail, each careful specification would restore a sense of realness to my thin blankets and the darkened study. There was powdered milk, sugar, half a loaf of bread that I could think of, and a sack of onions in the vegetable rack, mouldering slightly, with bright shoots beginning to stick out through the plastic mesh. I had the calm detachedness of that person in the corner of one's skull, the one who witnesses dreams. The jars were well stocked with lentils, split peas, soya beans, brown rice. "Realism, this is realism," I tried at one point to whisper: but the words were small and hard as seeds. "Rice." I remember how the word lodged itself under my tongue, against the ridge of my teeth. In the museum there is that ancient pottery—earth-colored, but incised with patterns and fire-smudged: made by the early nomads here, then smashed by a child perhaps, or some animal, or simply time, and reconstructed by modern scientists. The form is there still—perfect really: except that the meaning of that earthenware, its wholeness, its use remains in those shards that were littered in the dust, underneath the crystalline leaves of mesembryanthemums. And I continued with my small catalog: there were raisins left, and a packet of masala.* Tomato paste somewhere, there had to be.

Perhaps it's all a fiction. I feel tempted to believe that none of this is real, that the outside world, our invisible Revolution, the children—that none of these exists at all, but rises up out of my own sleeplessness, blazing chaotically at night behind my own burning eyelids: nothing more than fantasies of light pressing against my own retinas. If that were true, though, then it might be correct to speak about despair. If there were no one else, then where would I be?

They came in at four again this morning: and it was uncannily similar to the scene before. The way the children huddled in the doorway, as if embarrassed by the spill of light from the streetlamp. But this time I was perfectly calm, knowing what to do. To grow accustomed so swiftly? I have an uneasy feeling that it's almost immoral: yet it's a flair I've always had. An ability to change in an instant, in response to someone else's whim or some new situation. Slip into the next gossamer costume, quick: before they notice the naked flesh of the actress. How else should I try to be. Natural? Just myself? When you need to be knotted in, I think, bound up into some social existence before you can forget the absence of your own being. . .

I don't know what it is they're involved in and I daren't ask them

---

*masala: a spice used in making curry

anything—sensing that I have no right. Or maybe I'm unwilling to take a snub. Wilson has such a frozen, bitter-faced method of ignoring me. It's easy to speculate; appallingly easy to conjecture some shadowy, glamorous venture. People keeping on the run all night, hunched low but moving rapidly from street to street to street. Easy to imagine kids taking the terse words of a code from someone who waits for them in the backroom of a shanty, where the iron walls gleam in the darkness—hinting at illuminations of old mattress springs and empty bottles on a dirt floor. Easy to guess at kids being picked up and taken out by car, hidden under earth-stained hessian sacks: perhaps to those long, inconspicuous buildings low in the dunes near the coast. Munitions factories, aren't they? I can almost see a supple, slight figure being hoisted up towards the tiny squares in a window frame. Both of the children wear dark clothing—indigo denim, black jerseys. Perhaps it is fighters' clothing? But no. No. Because you can paint almost anything if you allow yourself. And I don't want to give in to a deluded, wistful, tremulous, rushing kind of imaginary anarchy.

Whatever it is, this mission of theirs, it seems unlikely that it should have anything to do with my own sickly presentiments of disaster. These children are bright, unsentimental; they know what they're doing. "Children." Ought I to say something else then? Soldiers, perhaps. Feel certain they're working to some thought-out, highly organized major plan. I must be only a small part of their scheme: irrelevant even, only the actualized version of some cipher for the person who would come up with shelter and food. And that's all right. I think I can be that for the time being—this alpha or delta.

They're sleeping now—not going out tonight. It's begun to drizzle again and there's a small, sharp hint of cold under all the wet, subtle as tungsten wire.

Supper was such a stupid affair of noncommunication. Everything I murmured, trying to be sociable, was left unanswered—and ended up as an exposed banality. When Felicia offered, conventionally only, I thought, to help with the supper, I waved her away, smiling and flustered. But it was just a curry, there was really nothing for her to do. And I was afraid of the small talk we'd have to make—both of us pretending a curiosity about the silvery-thin sheath between the onion layers, or admiring the deft edge to the steel blade of my kitchen knife. Then when we ate, neither of them would speak. I pressed things on them with a growing sense of anger: salt, chutney, more rice.

Felicia got to her feet at the end of the meal and said hurriedly,

"Thank you for the supper; that was very nice." Started to recover myself after that, wondering whether the original formula hadn't ended with the word "Mommy."

I remember Felicia in *Romeo and Juliet*. I'd seen the production in dress rehearsal and also disjointedly from the wings—helping backstage on the two previous nights. But watching it from the front on the final night, with the lights down in the hall . . . all my academic notions of the play seeped slowly away. Each time Felicia stepped out on to the proscenium and her eyes flickered shyly upward, there was a long shaft of amber light that brightened the darkness in them. You forgot about the latent imagery of the flower still budded, a sun not yet fully risen, the ascending flight of stairs still be scaled, a duke not sufficiently possessed of his own strength to govern. Of course, the lighting had a part in it. The two kids in charge were—well, gifted. Those effects they managed, deep umber shadows and muted light spilling over the cheap, dyed muslin of the costumes. And it wasn't only the designing: those same boys did all the wiring. One of them has a dad who owns a small electrical supply company, I think. They must have organized the PA system for the music as well. But Felicia. The way she could carve out a perfect stillness at the heart of the audience, leaving a deep, echoing hollow that she could whisper into, and still be heard at the back of the hall. How do actors do that? Something in their tone, or is it in their faces, or their posture? She didn't overplay either. In that tiny pause before she swallowed the sleeping draught there was desolate fear in her face—behind its pinched, blank mask all the imaginings that billow up gigantically in the mind of a child.

It hurt her badly, I think, that her father never saw the play. He's skipper of a fishing trawler and often has to spend days, even weeks at sea. It must be one of those factory ships. Wonder what kind of fishing it is, though. Pelagic? Do they go after pilchards and anchovies from Hout Bay, I wonder. Maybe it's mid-sea trawling, for whitefish. Cape hake. And they still take tunny, don't they, and snoek, in the season? And haarders and kabeljou, John Dory, squid and maasbankers?

It must be hard for Mrs. Moodie too. I've only met her once or twice, at PTA meetings. Hardly spoken to her, really; but I've liked her. One thing I remember, a facial trick: as she is speaking to you a slight frown sometimes starts to set in across her forehead, but almost immediately smoothes itself out again—as though a conscious self-correction has forgotten about itself and turned into a habit itself.

I remember something now. It was at the end of last year that I spoke to her. Her husband's name had finally come up on the waiting list for a house at Mitchell's Plain—but it was troubling them that Felicia would have to travel all the way to Athlone to get to school. Mitchell's Plain is right out at the coast, near Strandfontein, way on the other side of all those flattened dunes and the Port Jackson wattle. No proper public transport for the place yet. There are a few schools but I think they're still struggling to build up reputations for themselves; and parents don't want to take their kids out of the better-known schools, especially once they're halfway through already. Some children, I know, are boarded with relatives in Athlone.

The parents. At least they're supporting the kids this time. I remember those mordant satires in the popular poetry after 1976. About parents glassily watching their television screens—anything to avoid seeing what their children were fighting for; parents sick with fear, and warning their kids bitterly to get back to school and stop their troublemaking.

There was a story in last week's paper. Well, impressions collected from people in the street—asked how they felt about the students carrying on the boycott. One mother afraid that her kids will be sent back to Transkei unless they settle down next term; and another, obviously convinced of the political rightness of the movement, but nonetheless despondent that while it drags on and on her child is learning nothing, except new habits of crowding a pavement in a jostling group of friends, or sneaking into matinee shows at the cinema.

I can't help wondering whether there aren't two different schools' movements. It's treacherous to think that. But can it really be the same for our kids and their parents as it is for the people who live out at Crossroads and Philippi and Guguletu? I know it is a common struggle. I know, I know that. But when we object to a ludicrously conceived technical course, and the parents back up that protest—perhaps it's partly because these kids have the potential to enter the economy at some fairly rich nodes. Everything is supposed to be shooting and blooming. Well, you can see it in the advertisements for jobs. Secretarial, managerial posts with salaries starting at 700 rands* sometimes, for young people. I think that there are some people, maybe even some of the parents, who still suppose our kids would be content if they just had the same education that the white kids get. Separate but equal: the way apartheid was meant to work.

So many people still seem to think that the issue here is race—whether they're conservative or liberal, I mean. The same newspaper story quotes

---

*About $350

a teacher who is tiredly angry because some of her best students have dropped out of school and gone to work in a factory. The editor even takes that up—talks about "tragedy." "Tragic" because those kids might have gone on to university, or even straight into commerce. Could have joined the establishment, and instead they've been reduced to a working-class life. Well, maybe there are some kids at our school who'd want to perpetuate the bourgeois life-style their parents have struggled to create for them.

But what about the kids who can't even hope to come near that? There are a few thousand who might matriculate and then go on to a teachers' training college, or bush university. But for most of them, even if they stay on till standard six,* there's no future in anything except the lowest kinds of manual, semi-skilled work. For the kids from those single- and two-roomed, low-roofed brick cottages that each hold several families. Hok** in the backyard with perches and sack-draped nesting boxes for a half-dozen spattered, grimy chickens; strip of gray sand in the front, with cabbage plants, or a stand of virus-infected mealies, with yellowed, streaked leaves; and at the side of the house, diagonal, tense streaks of whipping light and wires, where the wind tugs at shirts and blouses and children's vests. Those areas that we learned about as children—seen remotely through car windows, and beyond tall fences that seemed eternally semi-plastered over by a decoupage of litter and newspaper scraps that the wind held adamantly up against the mesh.

I used to suppose that those kids must be moving towards change with a much more profoundly sustained anger than anything our kids could possibly feel. But now I understand how arrogant it was to think that. After all, the students at our school worked out for themselves that their cause was allied to the struggle of the meat workers who're on strike. Because we also have children from petty bourgeois backgrounds—kids who are thin and fiery with imagination. Who understand that the rites of oppression in this country call for a double-bladed axe—racism on one cutting edge, and capitalism on the other. Children who are young enough still to sneer at comfort and material security, and old enough to be taut-faced already from the strain of responsibility.

It's still raining. I was looking at the night through the bathroom window: not a darkness really—more the shapes of rain and misty cloud; and there's glinting everywhere, coming off the guttering across the

---

*Standard six is equivalent to eighth grade.
**hok: shack

50

alleyway, from the telephone wires, from the snail tracks on the bricks outside.

That strike is still on—did I mention? Would like to support it, but then I never buy meat anyway. Wonder about people that have no consumer power—because they have no money. Plenty of people living mainly off bread, beans and samp, or mealie-pap.* Sometimes get a sheep's head, I suppose.

Ought to go to sleep. Perhaps just lie down on the divan for a while, listening to the water: still get some rest that way. But it's more than that. One has to dream. That's what they say. More important, perhaps, than a respite for the muscles. Perhaps it's the dreams my body wants to ward off: whatever they are—remembrance of meaning. Can't be a physical fear? Of losing one's hold; slipping back into a chasm of guilt.

No.

II

Wilson has still not spoken to me. He brought a book with him into the kitchen and kept it open next to him on the table throughout the meal. Not really reading; but it made the silence easier to endure, for all of us. Beginning to wonder why they came here, if he trusts me so little. Perhaps it was Felicia's idea. She offered to wash the dishes afterwards. There were only a few plates, frying pan, saucepan: but I couldn't refuse her, remembering my stupid rejection of her last offer to help. I fussed in the background, making the tea. Coffee for Wilson. Even made some squares of cinnamon toast with the last of the stale loaf. He ate some of it too. Considerate, perhaps: but how could he know the extent of my dependence—that his refusal, even of a bit of sugared bread, would have left me feeling forlorn? And perhaps he simply has a liking for sweet things.

I've begun to place him: he's one of the matric students, an orator, I think.

I remember one occasion when I saw him in action. It was the day the students swept out of the grounds on that spontaneous protest march down towards Klipfontein Road. Just before the real momentum of it began I'd been called out into the foyer. Well, not called out, perhaps. I was sitting in the staff-room, trying feebly to read. Marianne was in a slumped, introverted mood, with a book on her lap. I happened to look

---

*mealie: ear of corn—hence, corn mush

51

up suddenly, sensing something—and saw that it was Cynthia, wistfully hovering at the staff-room door. The kids aren't supposed to come in, you see, and the shy ones never conceive of themselves as special cases. I could see even across the room that her face had taken on that dangerous, bleached look, and went out to her immediately, trying not to make my hurry seem too wild. I didn't want any of the gym teachers to get to her. They're the ones that cope with sprains and cut fingers; and they've decided that Cynthia's an irritating malingerer. ("That child gets on my nerves. It's just attention. You must leave her. She's just seeking attention.") It's true that she's annoyingly vague when she's in that condition—she'll stand in front of you helplessly, avoiding your gaze, with her fingers working at a pleat in her dress. All she can tell you usually is that she feels "funny." But I think she's grown used to being abused for her attacks: and now she puts half her thin, listless self into placating people who want to grab her roughly by the shoulders and bring her to her senses.

Apparently the students' meeting inside the hall had turned into a crashing, rowdy, dinning rebellion of excitement. A few hundred children from another school had swarmed in across our fields to join the assembly, and something was beginning to stir. People leaping up to speak, shouting at each other, and the whole hall stiflingly packed with close on fifteen hundred kids, all on their feet, swaying and cheering. Some of the tougher boys were trying to clamber forward to speak, shoving through the crowd, without caring much where they put their feet or their elbows. I think Nicholas was inside there, somewhere, watching it all with Hennie.

Cynthia's own halting account was almost inaudible against the noise. I could see her on the verge of collapsing into a faint. Partly she may have wanted the fit, I suppose: at least it would release her from the intolerable demands of consciousness. Thank God she had the presence of mind to get herself out of the hall. What if she'd fallen in there? She could have been horribly trampled by people in flight, in panic.

Got her to lie down on the bench in the foyer. Luckily I know where she keeps her tablets, top right-hand blazer pocket; and know how many to give when she's having an attack. The clamor inside the hall seemed to recede suddenly, but to replace it there was a more concentrated noise: one person speaking, insistently. The sound was badly distorted, so we could only hear hiss and bellowing, and that eerie, high-pitched electronic screaming. And then that got drowned out when the kids began pouring out of the hall. Cynthia went very quiet for a few minutes, but she didn't seem to be having a full-blown attack. All I could do was to hold her hand

and try to shield her from the buffeting of the kids streaming out through the foyer. Didn't want to suffocate her with my own presence either. When she came round she was shivering badly. Her shoulders and upper chest began to jerk slightly, and then she was crying. Feebly pushing her hand through her hair; whimpering. The kids just kept coming, hundreds of them flying through those swing doors.

I began to feel shivery myself, sick with a double apprehension. What if Cynthia began to hyperventilate: I wouldn't know how to control it. And I was worried about the kids, so many of them, straining towards the foyer doors—plate glass, set into metal frames. You could feel the rough, shoving excitement. There was a welter of dark blue gabardine. Striped ties were flung back over shoulders. People were trying to free themselves from the press by holding up their satchels and rucksacks over their heads. Underneath the pushing and shrill giggling, and the fragmentary protest chants, you sensed a somber awareness that the whole experience was something alive, rich with significance. Finally some of the prefects must have managed to push open the side doors of the hall, because the flow suddenly lessened and we began to see the crowd moving past outside, as the kids came out in tributaries now, and smaller groups.

Nicholas came out of the hall with Hennie. He was grinning, burning almost with excitement. Made some waving, perhaps beckoning gesture in my direction and then shouted something hoarsely, with the other hand cupped around his mouth. I couldn't make out what he was saying. Most of the staff was packed around the staff-room doorway—but not more than four or five people could really see anything, of course. Mr. Naidoo was standing to one side of the main entrance, speaking to Rachied with an expression on his face of totally absorbed, intense concern. Rachied's head boy, and universally popular with the students. His face still has a kind of delicate, silvery gleam along the jawline, although he's begun a beard. And he has a hugely generous, crooked grin. I suppose that Debbie in my class is not the only child who's announced, ingenuously at large, that she thinks he's "fantastic." I doubt though that he's any sort of skillfully driving rhetorician on a platform.

The streaming of children through the foyer had ended by then: most of the kids were out in the grounds, or already beginning to rank up and march down the road. A boy came out into the foyer carrying a megaphone. I'm certain now that it was Wilson: that same thinness; slightly stooped, bony shoulders; the pallor of the face; the tense, unsmiling look about the eyes and mouth. He must have been the speaker just before the shouting in the hall changed into a more dynamic energy. He'd stopped trying to deliver his exhortations by then and looked emptied of all his strength. I saw him meet Rachied's glance and they nodded curtly to one another, as though acknowledging some sort of failure.

Gavin suddenly appeared next to me, rather breathless. "Miss, is Cynthie all right, Miss?" They're cousins, and I think he feels it his personal responsibility to look after her. A bit dazedly I promised him that Cynthia was fine. "Did she take her tablets, Miss?" I reassured him again. He seemed to be at a loss. Noticed he was flushed in the face. He had his school rucksack with him, trailed over his shoulder by a single strap. "What must I do, Miss?" he said eventually.

"It's O.K., Gavin, there's no need to . . ." Then I began to wonder what he was really asking me. The schoolgrounds were steadily emptying. We could hear the chanting and singing of the kids out in the road, even though the vanguard must have been at least a kilometer away by then. Some of the staff had gone out to escort them, disturbed at the thought of real danger if the kids began moving out onto the busy highway at the top of the road.

Tentatively I said, "If you want to go with your friends, I think Cynthie will be all right here with me. I'm going to ask Mr. Abrahams if he'll drive her home just now."

I could see the anxiety tightening the skin across his boyish cheeks. When Cynthia is sick he has to stay with her. I don't think it's purely his family's insistence either: it seems to be his own private rule. His small face seemed to turn coppery with unhappiness.

"But some of the other boys, Miss, they say we mustn't go, because it's irresponsible. That what they say, Miss: the action hasn't got a planned motivation." And he looked at me, fixedly.

I made up a kind of solution for him then. Perhaps it was wrong: but I couldn't bear his tremulous uncertainty. "Perhaps, Gavin, if you don't mind . . . maybe you could stay here. I'd like to get some tea for Cynthie, and she might feel better if you stay here while I'm gone? Also, Gavin, I wonder if I could ask you to go home with Cynthie in the car: so she won't be alone at home, you see." He put his rucksack down and settled himself next to his cousin, resting his hand instinctively on her shoulder. When I came back with a cup of tea for each of them, that dark, disquieted flush was still there on his face.

The wind outside is racketing. Such a dry sound. The neighbors' dog is upset; and that iron gate in the alleyway keeps fighting and listing against its own hinges. Wish it would rain again.

III

Felicia came to ask me for a few more books. Caught a glimpse of myself drawn up into a thin earnestness as I was trying to decide. Wanted to give them something "educative," I suppose. Embarrassed then: fumbled at the first things I could find. Had *The Social Contract* and *The Coloniser and the Colonised* on my desk anyway, so I held out those. I wished I'd had some Brecht for Felicia. Took down half a dozen books of protest poetry, and piled them in her arms.

There's a whispering feeling inside me that they're planning to go out again tonight. Wish I had some way of stopping them. I know, I know: I'm behaving like a fussing parent. And even if I dared speak to them, there's nothing I could sensibly point to. The sky is dark, but I don't think it will rain.

I saw Wilson reading in the sitting-room. Well, both of them: they sprawl on the giant cushions, wedging the scatter pillows under their tummies or their elbows to make themselves more comfortable. I was standing in the kitchen, waiting for the kettle to boil—couldn't help glancing in their direction from time to time. Wilson seems to have a knack of centering all his concentration, without his body showing any angularities of tension. Think he was oblivious of me; all his energy had gone into holding the sense of the text in his mind. He shifted one arm lazily before turning the page. It's a calmness he has, as though his thoughts are grayish crystals he can turn over and over, peacefully, in the palm of his hand—like frankincense or myrrh.

And it suddenly seems a fatuous proposition that he should ever return to school. To be examined on the syllabus as it stands now?

I know that I'm not apart from it all. I'm beginning to understand what teaching English literature is about. Why the examination format makes it inevitable that I have to provide the kids with model character analyses. Why I have to teach them a sophisticated repertoire of eulogisms for the novels they study. It's really the form they're being asked to commend. The kind of society that gives rise to such a peculiarly intense, personal ownership of a cultural act. Almost a contradiction in terms. And there's an insidious side effect. If the prescribed literature really has no living meaning for them and yet it's invested with so much apparent value—they begin to feel there's something lacking in themselves. Remember being discomforted myself, as a teenager. Why on earth they set us those dreary books? *Moonfleet. Mr. Polly.* Used to feel a physical ache as I tried diligently to "enjoy" them.

I wonder if it's different for Afrikaner kids. Afrikaans literature is

55

genuinely their possession, and maybe reading it really does instantiate for them that notion of an eie kultuur.* There's a kind of beauty that you find in young, educated Afrikaners—something in their faces, their bearing. Assuredness, I suppose it is. Self-pride. Knowing that you belong to a community. Or rather *not* knowing it: taking it for granted.

And I'm going to go back and teach. Am I? All this vacillating: surely it's false. I wonder what real alternatives I have. It makes me feel old-fashioned, almost prim to confess this, but teaching is my vocation. You long to teach, so you work at a school: where you end up not teaching at all, but preparing kids for examinations. Where despite your best intentions you help to instill the values that will keep the ruling class in power.

Wonder about Marianne. What turbulences her teaching might set up. Because she's teaching Afrikaans literature to kids whose home language is Afrikaans, who're ostracized by the English-speaking students—and who probably detach themselves the more woodenly from that prose and poetry written by people like Anton Rossouw.

If I wrote to Papa, perhaps, asking for advice. He's always had that conscientious, gravely concerned side to him, as an educationist.

If it comes to that, why haven't I chosen him all along to act as my remote confessor? But this is almost the nub of things. There's a last, perhaps saving feeling that Papa is the one person I must never begin writing to. What I've wanted from him all my life is The Answer, I think. And I know, without really wanting to believe it, that writing out the endlessly insistent question on paper is one certain method of warding off response.

I've been directly to him a few times. Gauche with my abrupt demands that he never seems to have understood. Demands I've never understood myself.

The time I went to him about the protest meeting, and all he could tell me was that I should decide for myself what I wanted. When I was wanting him to tell me what my own desire was.

In the end I decided that I did want to go and help make posters. About fifty of us arrived that Saturday afternoon: meeting at a colossal, intimidating house in Kenilworth. (It must have been owned by some corporation: perhaps someone's dad was managing director of a big company.) The kids who were setting up the protest had arranged free cool drinks for all of us, and there were cellophane packets of salty, papery chips being passed around. I remember the neatly stacked sup-

*eie kultuur: own culture

56

plies of poster-size cardboard and different-colored koki chalks:* you took your requisition and wandered off to find a working area. We all drifted across the pale, cropped grass of the lawns and let ourselves into the high-fenced tennis court. Because of the spacious surface, covered with smooth asphalt, the green kind. The other kids all seemed to know one another. They couldn't have been any older than I was—fifteen or sixteen—yet some of them had a kind of élan: something in the casual way they kicked off old, broken sandals and then strolled across the tennis court in their bare feet; or perhaps it had to do with their small, intense voices that sang and called and commanded incessantly. Still clutching my sheets of cardboard, I could feel the tendons in my upper arms beginning to stand out in an ugly rigidity. I was scared, suddenly, that I would be sick. Too young then to know that anxiety is always transient: a seizure that has to grapple for itself and struggle, until it slowly dies.

I began to have a glimmering of something about myself then, for the first time. I'd always been passionately excited about schoolwork—and I think I imagined that my classmates shared in precisely the same delight. The bliss that crowded my thoughts when we read Catullus. Listening to the small hops and chirrupings of Lesbia's sparrow. Or else the feverishness that would come during a lesson on electron orbitals. I mistook my own hectic state for communication: and it never occurred to me that I never confided in any special schoolfriend. Used to spend so much of my time reading in the afternoons and evenings that I fully believed I was talking endlessly—superbly gregarious in a void of silent pages.

Michael Bernstein saved me that afternoon. He came up with a box that held some small white cards, and squatted down next to me as I pretended to be gazing purposefully at the blank sheet on the tarmac. I was sitting cross-legged, but huddled, clasping my ankles. He introduced himself, and took my name and address to write down on one of his cards. When I told him which school I came from, he grinned and flopped down in front of me. "Same as—," he said. "Are you in the same class? She's up at the house with Pete and Helen and the other guys. You know them? You know Dave? Mike Newman?" The panic was beginning to seep back into me and I almost cried out, trying to stop that cheerful streaming of assumption. Perhaps he noticed then that I was feeling out of place. He squinted at my poster and I blushed for the few timid guidelines I'd dared to rule in pencil. I mumbled that I didn't know how to letter and Michael responded with energetic kindness. "Yeah, I'm not

---

*koki chalks: felt-tip pens

so fantastic. But look it doesn't have to be perfect." He did have the knack, though. He took over the central parts of the posters, lettering the key words with dashing streaks of color – and then passing them to me to fill in the less-conspicuous details about the date and time of the meeting. Forget what it was we wrote. I suppose PROTEST MEETING and FREE SCHOOL BOOKS FOR SOME, perhaps UNEQUAL EDUCATION – that sort of thing.

He went off again later, to get names and addresses from the rest. Explaining that they wanted to draw up a mailing list – to keep in touch with everybody who was interested. About half an hour later he came back, though: with two bottles of Coke and a packet of sharp, salty chips. "Hey, Anna, break time." He passed me one of the bottles and glanced at the dozen posters I'd managed to color in – carefully imitating his first designs. "Hey, those are great," he said. And I had a handful of chips to cope with suddenly as well. I asked him then about the other kids – that indefinable feeling of "groupiness" that they had. I remember he began chuffing and giggling, and then the Coke in his bottle started to fizz up and spill. "Yeah you could call it that," he agreed. He explained that most of them belonged to the Young Progressives: knew each other from working on election campaigns. "Hey, wouldn't you like to see what we do sometime?"

I noticed that both of us had small flakes of broken potato crisps clinging to our jerseys. Michael wore glasses – little round, gold rims, with astonishingly thick lenses. Yet his eyes shone so vividly. They were beautiful, I thought: a deep black-gold.

I helped him afterwards, once all the finished posters had been collected together. Most of the other kids had begun to gather their things, retrieving shoes and sweaters and jackets from the lawn or the periphery of the tennis court. Felt slightly on edge, because the afternoon had grown late already and the bus stop was at least twenty minutes' walk away. "You going to the bus stop, Anna? Why don't you hang on just for ten minutes, then I'm going that way too." He was busy punching holes into the posters. I took each one from him and threaded lengths of coarse sisal string through them. So that they would be ready for tying up to the streetpoles. "Lucky we managed to get the permit yesterday," he said. My hands were beginning to feel stiff, reddened by the rough fiber: I couldn't make sense of what Michael was saying. "Ja, permit. You've got to get a permit from the city council, you see, before you can put up posters." We'd nearly finished our trussing of the posters by then. "Anyway, now we can start to put them up. We're going out tomorrow night, cause Dave's got his dad's combi.* Hey, if you want to come and help you're welcome."

It would be foolish to pretend that no one ever made overtures, that I wasn't urged, generously, to join in.

---

combi or *kombi*: Volkswagen minibus

Mummy Let Me Go

Text and linocuts by David Hlongwane ("Uhuru")*

For a biographical note on David Hlongwane please see page 10.

Mummy let me go
To the battle
On the 21st March
Our heroes have been killed
By the Boere

Mummy let me go
To the battle
On the 16th June
Our students fell like animals
They have been killed
By the Boere

Mummy let me go
To the battle
In 1985
They have killed
Our heroes like animals
In their Land of Afrika

Mummy let me go!!
Mummy let me go!!
Mummy don't stop the children

---

*Uhuru, which means "freedom" in Swahili, was the "freedom cry" of the Mau-Mau.

Three Poems

Chris van Wyk

Chris van Wyk was born in Johannesburg in 1957. In the seventies he worked for the South African Committee for Higher Education (SACHED), an independent educational trust, writing material for students learning to read English. He is at present an editor of Ravan Press, one of the most progressive publishing houses in the country today.

In 1979 Van Wyk's first collection of poetry, It Is Time To Go Home, was published by Ad. Donker. In it, he frequently uses his verse to explore the linguistic manipulations which prop up the apartheid structure. Van Wyk has also published a novel for teenagers, A Message in the Wind (Cape Town: Maskew Miller, 1983).

He is married and has two sons.

The Road

I was hardly four and living at my granny's
when the news came
as it does to all four-year-olds
from the overhanging vines of the adults,
through the eaves of the wise who suddenly
are not so wise.
Cooking stopped.
Panic shattered the eardrum of the cup of peace.

All was not well,
not only two miles down the road
from where an out-of-breath boy
had brought the news
in short telegram gasps.

Quickly Granny wrapped me in a blanket as cold
as the flag of a sad country,
took me away to my mother
whose tears by now were warmer, had more salt
than the dead child, brother, grandchild.

Along the rough road, cobbled with the dirges of beer cans,
tremulous with stones and filled with more people
than children born to the world that day,
my grandmother walked, and for her the road grew shorter.
For me staring over her shoulder, longer and longer.

Helping My Father Make a Cupboard

My father for the moment
thinks in forty-five degrees,
the sun in twenty-eight or so;
and we wipe our brows
in the knowledge of both.

A festival of sawdust
begins to burgeon
under the persistent drill and saw.

Holding a plank fast,
passing on a hammer,
I descend into childhood.
My mother is tugging at my dirty hand.
We wade through sawdust
up to the butcher's cold counter.
He negotiates;
first with Mum,
then with his scale.

Planks marked bottom
and planks marked top
are fitted on and nailed together.

Everyone's opinion is heard
under the noise of the flailing hammer.
Except my father's:
his mouth is stuffed into silence with nails—
enough, at least, to crucify a man
or build a long coffin
for one with half a conscience.

The Ballot and the Bullet

The ballot.
This means voting.
There's this big box.
It has a slot.
Ja, like a money box.
You're given options.
Do you want a cruel government
or a kind one?
A lazy one
or one that works?
You have to make an X
on a square sheet of paper
to decide who is to be
the custodian of the people.
But first you have to identify yourself.
This is easy.
All you need is an I.D.
This looks like a passbook;
It has your photo and signature.
Only difference is
you can leave it at home
and not get caught.
That's a ballot
Not a bullet.
Ag now, surely you know
what a bullet is.

To Whom It May Concern: Linocuts on a Poem by Sipho Sepamla

Billy Mandindi

For a biographical note on Billy Mandindi please see page 10. The poem is from Sepamla's Hurry Up to It! (Johannesburg: Ad. Donker, 1975). For a new poem by Sepamla and a biographical note, see page 485.

Bearer
Bare of everything but particulars
Is a Bantu
The language of a people in Southern Africa
He seeks to proceed from here to there
Please pass him on
Subject to these particulars
He lives subject to the provisions
Of the Urban Natives Act of 1925
Amended often
To update it to his sophistication
Subject to the provisions of the said Act
He may roam freely within a prescribed area
Free only from the anxiety of conscription
In terms of the Abolition of Passes Act
A latter-day amendment
In keeping with moon-age naming
Bearer's destination is Reference number 417181
And (he) acquires a niche in the said area
As a temporary sojourner
To which he must betake himself
At all times
When his services are dispensed with for the day
As a permanent measure of law and order
Please note
The remains of R/N 417181
Will be laid to rest in peace
On a plot
Set aside for Methodist Xhosas
A measure also adopted
At the express request of the Bantu
In anticipation of any faction fight
Before the Day of Judgement

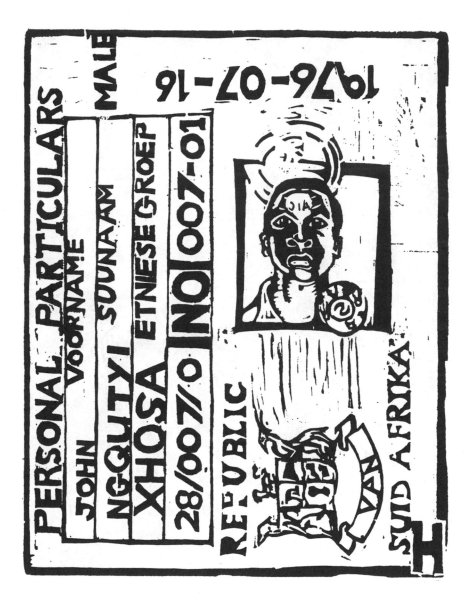

Nine Poems

Jeremy Cronin

Born in 1949, Jeremy Cronin went to school in Rondebosch and completed his studies at the University of Cape Town and at the Sorbonne in Paris. On his return to Cape Town he lectured in philosophy and political science. He was arrested in July 1976 and charged under the Terrorism Act for having carried out ANC (African National Congress) activities for a number of years. He was sentenced to seven years' imprisonment. His term was spent in various prisons, including three years amongst the death-row prisoners in the notorious Pretoria Maximum jail. During his stay in prison, his wife died unexpectedly.

In May 1983 Cronin was released from jail. He now serves on the Western Cape executive of the United Democratic Front. He and his second wife live in Cape Town.

In 1983 Ravan Press published his collection of poems, Inside, which won the Ingrid Jonker Prize. The following poems are from Inside, which Ravan will be reprinting early in 1987.

Cronin has, with Raymond Suttner, written and compiled Thirty Years of the Freedom Charter (Johannesburg: Ravan, 1986) a document on the history of the ANC and its charter.

The Naval Base (Part III)

I cannot disclaim that string-thin, five-year-old boy
with big ears and bucked teeth from thumbsucking late,
who woke to dockyard hooters on mornings of mackerel-green
    sea
that cast up sea-eggs, argonauts, unexplained white rubber
    balloons.
A soft sea full of cutting things, of sharkstooth, barnacles, and
    ultramarines.
Who polished with envy and Silvo his pa's ceremonial sword.
Who dreamt of mama and the ocean's lap-lap,
and that one day the tide would ride out,

yes ride oh right out, uncovering bedclothes.
That boy, that endless earache, who knew at five,
because learnt by heart, the naval salute, the sign of the cross,
the servant's proper place, and our father who art.
—This five-year-old boy, this shadow,
this thing stuck to my feet.

Photograph by René Weideman. (Walter Sisulu, at present serving a life
sentence, was arrested with Nelson Mandela and other African National
Congress leaders in Rivonia in 1963. His son Zwelakhe Sisulu, editor of
the outspoken newspaper *New Nation*, is at present also in detention.
Oliver Tambo is the longstanding president of the ANC in exile.)

Motho Ke Motho Ka Batho Babang (A Person Is a Person Because of Other People)

By holding my mirror out of the window I see
Clear to the end of the passage.
There's a person down there.
A prisoner polishing a doorhandle.
In the mirror I see him see
My face in the mirror,
I see the fingertips of his free hand
Bunch together, as if to make
An object the size of a badge
Which travels up to his forehead
The place of an imaginary cap.
      (This means: A *warder*.)
Two fingers are extended in a vee
And wiggle like two antennae.
      (He's being watched.)
A finger of his free hand makes a watch-hand's arc
On the wrist of his polishing arm without
Disrupting the slow-slow rhythm of his work.
      (*Later.* Maybe, later we can speak.)
*Hey! Wat maak jy daar?**
      —a voice from around the corner.
*No. Just polishing baas.***
He turns his back to me, now watch
His free hand, the talkative one,
Slips quietly behind
      —*Strength brother*, it says,
In my mirror,
      A black fist.

---

*"What are you doing?"
**baas: boss

Group Photo from Pretoria Local on the Occasion of a Fourth Anniversary (Never Taken)*

An uprooted tree leaves
    behind it a hole in the ground
But after a few months
You would have to have known
    that something grew here once.
And a person's uprooted?
Leaves a gap too, I suppose, but then
    after some years . . .
There we are
    seated in a circle,
Mostly in short pants, some of us barefoot,
Around the spot where four years before
When South African troops were repulsed before
    Luanda**

Our fig tree got chopped
    down in reprisal. — That's Raymond
Nudging me, he's pointing
At Dave K who looks bemusedly
Up at the camera. Denis sits on an upturned
Paraffin tin. When this shot was taken
He must have completed
    seventeen years of his first
Life sentence.
    David R at the back is saying
Something to John, who looks at Tony who
Jerks his hand
    So it's partly blurred.
There we are, seven of us
    (but why the grinning?)
Seven of us, seated in a circle,

---

*Pretoria Local is a jail where political detainees are held.
**In November 1975 South African troops crossed the border into Angola.

The unoccupied place in the center
    stands for what happened
Way outside the frame of this photo.
So SMILE now, hold still and
    click
        I name it: Luanda.
For sure an uprooted tree
    leaves behind a hole in the ground.
After a few years
You would have to have known
    it was here once. And a person?
There we are
    seated in our circle, grinning,
    mostly in short pants,
    some of us barefoot.

Labyrinth II

. . . and Ariadne, her beautiful erotic thread unwinding, guiding him in the stone darkness. . . .
— Yannis Ritsos

I'm unravelled by day, at night
I weave now and weave
with the fading scent
of soap, following its thread down
to another time, another bed
to where a-hooked and kicking we
ssshh — wildeye, like
two katonkel,* made love.

Or awoke, a-tangled
androgyne, twice-fourlegged:
— us and the bed.
Laden with scents of voyages made
of voyages still to become
its pine frame solid enough to take
a mattress of foam, being
not too wide, being
                    — just so.

It had sheets that knew creases,
a pillow once swollen,
in daytime it became
a settee, where the back
of a knitting needle purled
at my upper left arm
as you knit and knit
the far end of this twine.

---

katonkel: a barracuda-like game fish

76

As I Remember

As I remember
these things are ribbed:
   a sanddune
untouched:
   a fishing boat
on a slipway:
   the roof
of your mouth.

Woodcut by Cecil Skotnes.

Your Deep Hair*

Remember the meerkat's**
footfall down the inner-sleeve of night,
under the milkbush, under the curdled
star clouds of galactic semen
spilled across the sky, you turned in sleep and
from your deep hair tumbled
aromatic buchu and the wide veld.

Three months now.
Scalp shaved,
you died, they say,
your head encased in wraps.

---

*Cronin's wife died while he was in jail.
***meerkat*: a small rodent, similar to a prairie dog

White Face, Black Mask

Thoughts
    concerning the person
    named Who:
Who is naked beneath his clothes,
Who is black in the night,
Who is
    unwashed before his bath,
and you mustn't suck cents
    you never know
Who might have touched them last.
Who is mask.
Who is beyond
    mask, lock, yale, bolt, chain, electric alarm.
Who,
    son of Who,
Who's Who, when the dog barks
there also is Who.
Who peeps through windows.
Who desires my mother, without a pass.
Who wields
    a double-edged knife.
Who entertains
    my darkest
desires.
Who,
    a temporary permanent
sojourner in my dream's backyard.
Who walks through our night.
Who stalks our women.
Who looks at my sister
    with longing.
        Yes,
Who.

Lullaby

But who killed Johannes, mama . . . ?
Sssssssshhh! now close your eyes.
    Mama . . . ?
Only a bar of soap, they said.
So *thula, thula*, now quiet my child.

But who killed Solomon, mama . . . ?
Sssssssshhh! your blanket's tucked in.
    Who?
Only a length of rope, I suppose.
So *thula, thula*, now quiet my child.

But who killed Ahmed, mama . . . ?
Sssssssshhh! we must get up early.
    Please?
Only the tenth floor, I heard.
So *thula, thula*, now quiet my child.

But who killed Joseph, mama . . . ?
Sssssssshhh! tomorrow's work is hard.
    Mama . . . ?
Only a flight of stairs, I read.
So *thula, thula*, now quiet my child.

But who killed Steve, mama . . . ?
Sssssssshhh! it's a long walk to the bus.
    Mama . . . ?
A brick wall, the magistrate said.
So *thula, thula*, now quiet my child.

But who killed Looksmart, mama . . . ?
Sssssssshhh! sleep and grow strong.
    Who, mama . . . ?

His own belt, that's what was blamed.
So *thula, thula*, now quiet my child.

But who. . . .
Thula! Thula! Thula! my child.

To Learn How to Speak

To learn how to speak
With the voices of the land,
To parse the speech in its rivers,
To catch in the inarticulate grunt,
Stammer, call, cry, babble, tongue's knot
A sense of the stoneness of these stones
From which all words are cut.
To trace with the tongue wagon-trails
Saying the suffix of their aches in -kuil, -pan, -fontein,*
In watery names that confirm
The dryness of their ways.
To visit the places of occlusion, or the lick
in a vlei-bank** dawn.
To bury my mouth in the pit of your arm,
In that planetarium,
Pectoral beginning to the nub of time
Down there close to the water-table, to feel
The full moon as it drums
At the back of my throat
Its cow-skinned vowel.
To write a poem with words like:
I'm telling you,
Stompie, stickfast, golovan,
Songololo, just boombang,*** just
To understand the least inflections,
To voice without swallowing
Syllables born in tin shacks, or catch

---

*-kuil: -pool; -pan: flat place; -fontein: fountain (common Afrikaans suffixes for place-names)
**vlei: a small, inland body of water
***stompie: cigarette butt or short person; stickfast: a type of flea; songololo: millipede; boombang: anything quick, unpremeditated

the 5:15 ikwata bust fife
Chwannisberg train,* to reach
The low chant of the mine gang's
Mineral glow of our people's unbreakable resolve.

To learn how to speak
With the voices of this land.

---

*Here Cronin imitates the black township pronunciation of the "quarter-past-five Johannesburg" commuter train.

Five Drawings

William Kentridge

William Kentridge has provided the following note on his life and art: "I have spent all my life in Johannesburg. School, university, my studio, are all within a three-kilometer radius of where I was born. So even when my pictures are set in Paris or New York, in the end they are about Johannesburg—that is to say, a rather bewildered provincial city. The pictures are not all little morals or illustrations of apartheid life. But they are all provoked by the question of how it is that one is able to construct a more or less coherent life in a situation so full of contradiction and disruption."

THE GENERALS OF DERBY ROAD

Four Poems

Ingrid de Kok

Born in 1951, Ingrid de Kok has published her poetry in magazines in Canada and South Africa. Her work also appears in LIP, an anthology of South African women's writing (Johannesburg: Ravan, 1983). Her first collection of poetry is due to be published by Ravan in 1987.

De Kok completed a B.A. in politics and English at the University of the Witwatersrand, followed by an honors degree at the University of Cape Town. She obtained an M.A. from Queen's, Kingston, for her work on Hardy's poetry. At present she works for Khanya College, an independent, progressive educational institution, a project of SACHED Trust.

She lives in Cape Town and has a son.

Dolphin Eater

There was nothing else to eat.
So I ate the dolphin
and asked my friend
never ever to tell.

Like lightning
that night
sea struck me
and I screamed in my sleep
for a boat to take me back
to the first shore
where I had eaten no dolphin.

In my eyes dolphins dancing
in the bay close to shore
a gift of the evening tide
to the strollers on the beach.
In my mouth, dolphin.

I tricked the silent ferryman,
gave beads for land,
and the silver cargo of the dhow
discharged into my palm.

Nothing will save me now
in the waves off the cliffs.
I will not be brought home
on the leeside of a dolphin's fin.

Small Passing

For a woman whose baby died stillborn, and who was told by a man to stop mourning, "for the trials and horrors suffered daily by black women in this country are more significant than the loss of one white child."

1

In this country you may not
suffer the death of your stillborn,
remember the last push into shadow and silence,
the useless wires and cords on your stomach,
the nurse's face, the walls, the afterbirth in a basin.
Do not touch your breasts
still full of purpose.
Do not circle the house,
pack, unpack the small clothes.
Do not lie awake at night hearing
the doctor say "It was just as well"
and "You can have another."
In this country you may not
mourn small passings.

See: the newspaper boy in the rain
will sleep tonight in a doorway.
The woman in the busline
may next month be on a train
to a place not her own.
The baby in the backyard now
will be sent to a tired aunt,
grow chubby, then lean,
return a stranger.
Mandela's daughter tried to find her father
through the glass. She thought they'd let her touch him.

And this woman's hands are so heavy when she dusts
the photographs of other children
they fall to the floor and break.
Clumsy woman, she moves so slowly
as if in a funeral rite.

On the pavements the nannies meet.
These are legal gatherings.
They talk about everything, about home,
while the children play among them,
their skins like litmus, their bonnets clean.

2

Small wrist in the grave.
Baby no one carried live
between houses, among trees.
Child shot running,
stones in his pocket,
boy's swollen stomach
full of hungry air.
Girls carrying babies
not much smaller than themselves.
Erosion. Soil washed down to the sea.

3

I think these mothers dream
headstones of the unborn.
Their mourning rises like a wall
no vine will cling to.
They will not tell you your suffering is white.
They will not say it is just as well.
They will not compete for the ashes of infants.
I think they may say to you:
Come with us to the place of mothers.
We will stroke your flat empty belly,
let you weep with us in the dark,
and arm you with one of our babies
to carry home on your back.

Al Wat Kind Is*

"They took all that was child in the house."

—resident of Victoria West, reporting on
police action in the town

They took all that was child
and in the dark closed room
visions of a ripe split melon
were at the tip of the knife
they held to the child's dry tongue.

All that was child
lies on the tarmac;
the intestines spill
like beans from a sack,
seaweed from the winter sea.

The bird of state has talons
and shit that drops like lead.
Its metal wings corrode the streets,
it hatches pools of blood.

A stone against a tank is a stone against a tank
but a bullet in a child's chest rips into the heart of the house.

But when in time the single stones
compact their weight and speed together,
roll up the incline towards the lamvanger's** lair,
crushing sand into rock, rock into boulder,
boulder into mountain, mountain into sky,
then the lungs of the bird will choke,
the wings will blister and crack,
at last the eyes will glaze, defeated.

---

*"All That Is 'Child'"
**lamvanger: literally "lamb catcher," but used idiomatically to mean "vulture" or "bird of
prey"

And this torn light,
this long torn light
will repair itself
out of the filaments of children,
and all that is child will return to the house,
and will open the doors of the house.

Our Sharpeville

I was playing hopscotch on the slate
when the miners roared past in lorries,
their arms raised, signals at a crossing,
their chanting foreign and familiar,
like the call and answer of road gangs
across the veld, building hot arteries
from the heart of the Transvaal mine.

I ran to the gate to watch them pass.
And it seemed like a great caravan
moving across the desert to an oasis
I remembered from my Sunday-school book:
olive trees, a deep jade pool,
men resting in clusters after a long journey,
the danger of the mission still around them,
and night falling, its silver stars just like the ones
you got for remembering your Bible texts.

Then my grandmother called from behind the front door,
her voice a stiff broom over the steps:
"Come inside; they do things to little girls."

For it was noon, and there was no jade pool.
Instead, a pool of blood that already had a living name
and grew like a shadow as the day lengthened.
The dead, buried in voices that reached even my gate,
the chanting men on the ambushed trucks,
these were not heroes in my town,
but maulers of children,
doing things that had to remain nameless.
And our Sharpeville was this fearful thing
that might tempt us across the well-swept streets.

If I had turned I would have seen
brocade curtains drawn tightly across sheer net ones,
known there were eyes behind both,
heard the dogs pacing in the locked yard next door.

But, walking backwards, all I felt was shame,
at being a girl, at having been found at the gate,
at having heard my grandmother lie
and at the fear her lie might be true.
Walking backwards, called back,
I returned to the closed rooms, home.

Woodcut by Cecil Skotnes.

From *The House Next Door to Africa*

Denis Hirson

Denis Hirson left South Africa in 1973 with his family when his father, who had been a political prisoner for nine years, was released from jail and went into exile. He has lived in France since 1975, working as a teacher of English, and as an actor with the Atelier du Chaudron. He has previously published a collection of translations of Breyten Breytenbach's poetry, In Africa Even the Flies Are Happy.

The House Next Door to Africa is Hirson's first novel; it was published in South Africa by David Philip, and in the U.S. by Carcanet Press.

The school crest: is divided into four colored quadrants. Red backs a crown with three gold branches, yellow an open book; blue, a scroll of parchment about to eat a plume; green, two tapes running under an archbishop's mitre: Alfred, Bede, Caedmon and Dunstan, who came from England a long time ago.

There is one crest sewn to my navy-blue cap, another to my navy-blue blazer. Blazer and pants pockets, if not burst, are fat with marbles, the odd coppery pupa that wiggles at the tip, jumping bean, lump of pink sweet.

My eye is out for beetles and other passersby; watching, always watching, with silence for a tower. The skin down my legs is tattooed by mosquitoes, scratched to blood before I know it.

On the road in the morning: the mulberry tree where I dream of letting all my silkworms loose; ivory seeds in spongy canna pods, good for peashooters; a few nannies walking Grade One's and Two's, in icing-colored aprons and crimped white caps that bring out the chocolate of their skins. They have names like Regina, Patience, Angelina, Evelina.

Morning glories thread through the fences, tender violet-tongued trumpets that fit over the nose. Breathe in and the petal flesh plugs the nostrils, bringing fragrance up behind the face, cutting out air.

In garden after garden swimming pools blow wobbly bubbles up through cool blue depths. Men with smooth jowls snooze down driveways in low-slung highly waxed motor cars. Their elbows jut out of the windows, voices address them over the radio. The men are soon lined up along the road, with their windows closed and the voices raised.

One driver doesn't edge forward fast enough for the driver behind him, who reaches down into his glove compartment and pulls out a gun. A gray angel watches from an archway, bees swarming underwing.

*   *   *

Brenda's house: has at least two immaculate storeys, with no tree or creeper to encumber the salmon-pink walls. The tall split-pole fence around it stinks of pitch, the palings let no light through. A sign screwed to the gatepost bears the legend "Pluto Alarm Systems" below the head of a dog with black spots and a flat eye.

From the garden comes a sound of water falling in gouts. Sometimes, leaves rustle. Just once a gray limousine slides out, without Brenda. Behind it I glimpse fluted cream columns, tar chips and a few rose bushes whose branches make cracks against the sheen of the walls. Then the gates close, and someone crunches slowly away.

Brenda arrives at school by unknown means, freckled and quiet and smiling with her eyes. She plays netball, for Bede. We don't notice each other at all.

*   *   *

Marbles: alies malies ghoens glassies puries smokies ironies twos castles tens twenties shy up it's not counted if you don't toe the line toe the line! Right. Everything under the sun and nix for you. Pockets biscuit-tins cigar-boxes bank-bags grimy hands full of marbles and the glass chatter of marbles you're too crack give me my marbles back I never said you could shy give them back! Drops? Tish? O.K., ghoen-ghoen tish.

Four paces for a castle fifteen for a twenty little bits of grit strewn strategically in front of the glittering prize. Paul Salko sits in a line of others before the library bushes fat legs forked open a ten of bright ironies between them, everyone raining marbles at him all at once from miles away, backs almost against the hall wall. Meanwhile Paul Salko's gang is in the bushes, hunting down whatever his bulk of body fails to stop.

A marble snicks the pyramid but glances off leaving it intact and the gang advances, pushing everyone away. A second marble topples half the pyramid but no one can decide whose marble it was. Wild fists and scuffles are interrupted by the bell.

We run across the marble patch pounding powdery bottoms, stamping sandals as our cooped-up marbles collide. Clouds of dust accompany us to class. And there in line are Leonie Hofmeyr and Karen Waldman, Naomi Beneishowitz and Merle Korp. There is Brenda. They are standing calmly, polished all the way down to their white socks. Not even ink spots seem to get them.

*   *   *

The wagons: are on the move as first light breaks and the mountains climb down from the sky. Their wheels leave dark slots in the mercury grass, steaming dung and hullabaloo come from the cattle and sheep pressing about them.

The people in the wagons test their whips between the horns of the oxen, adjust their bonnets, and wash their eyes in the new air. It is going to be another brilliant day on their way north. Someone begins to sing:

> *Janpierewiet, Janpierewiet, Janpierewiet staan stil,*
> *Janpierewiet, Janpierewiet, Janpierewiet draai om.*
> *Goeie môre my vrou, hiers 'n soentjie vir jou,*
> *Goeie môre my man, daar is koffie in die kan.*

Behind the wagons is the wild green sea, and at the sea stands Jan van Riebeeck, his luxuriant hair flowing out in the breeze. There is goffered lace down his breast, his calves are molded by gleaming boots, his palm rests lightly on the pommel of his sword. Around him are all the carrots and tomatoes and cucumbers that he came to plant in 1652.

There are also stinkwood trees, yellowwood trees, spittoons and slave-bells, white gables and white grapes and brown people whose bellies stick forward and whose bottoms stick backwards and who have arrived from just the other side of the mountains to meet Jan van Riebeeck, the first man at the Cape.

Then the British land, and hand out Bibles, and get everyone to speak English and be free. So the people in the wagons, who were Dutch but are now Voortrekkers, load up with concertinas and coffee and rusks and muskets and Bibles of their own, yoke their oxen and head north.

They stop at nothing. They slit up lions for shoes and trousers, and festoon their wagons with drying meat. With pangas they hack through thorn and scrub. When a mountain appears the wagon wheels roll off, the canvas roofs flap up like sails and bit by bit everything drifts over the peaks. On the other side the wagons fit together again, and buckle down to the business of getting further away from the British.

There is no one else on the land they cross, though every now and then they come across a kraal with a black king in it who has a lot of wives lying on floors made of dung and ox blood. Meanwhile, tribes are marauding their way down Africa, trampling on all the thorns and scorpions with their bare feet and advancing in the form of ox-heads.

Horns of warriors curve across the land with assegais and giant shields, as quietly as grass. Against their onslaught the Voortrekkers hitch all wagons into a laager, cramming the gaps with branches of thornbush and mimosa. While the women and children ram powder down muskets and sing hymns, the men fire at the black breasts of the enemy.

When it is all over the rivers run red with blood and the Voortrekkers, who are slowly becoming Boers, pick assegais out of their wagons. They make pledges and vows and covenants. The leaders give their names to mountains and cities and public swimming pools.

Each year the wagons rattle and strain out of the Cape, led by intrepid men whose wives wear coal-scuttle bonnets to keep their cheeks pink and whose children are born with nerves of steel. Each year we follow them until they are white dots in the distance, becoming Afrikaners while the British—now known as the English—wage a small war on them and then everyone becomes European.

The marauding tribes, who are the cause of Kaffir Wars* and later become Natives and Bantu, line up for health inspection and go down to work in the mines. Finally there is a Republic, and the whole school gets bronze medals and flags and sings about blue heaven with kranses in it.

Our class goes down to the museum in the middle of town, to find out a bit more about the story. There is an ox wagon whose thick wooden frame is charred and pocked under its beeswax. There are Chinese dice, and pictures of Chinese miners wearing headbands and looking sullen. There is a stuffed Bushman with a shrunken leathery skin standing in some sand in a glass case.

Just before lunchtime Eleanor Lambeth has an epileptic fit. She lies on the floor next to the ox wagon, ice-white and triangular with her eyeballs working under their lids, kneecaps protruding. Every now and then her body shudders. Her tongue has slipped down her throat, and our teacher and the librarian hunt everywhere for a soupspoon so they can fish it out.

* * *

The Duplessis's: are all orange. They slip out of bed in uncreased orange pyjamas, and arrive simultaneously at the breakfast table neatly dressed for the day. They smile at each other and tuck into a steaming orange breakfast. Afterwards, Meneer Duplessis drives off in his car, and Hennie and Sarie wheel their bicycles to the gate, while Mevrou Duplessis in an orange polka-dot apron waves Totsiens to them all from the front door.

Meneer Duplessis walks into his orange office, where he has an iron filing cabinet, an orange secretary, a clock and a window with an orange cloud in it. Meanwhile, Hennie and Sarie are in class. They have taken off their blazers, and lean cool as cucumbers over their exercise books. Then the bell rings, and they dive into the orange school pool.

By evening the Duplessis's are together again, waiting for supper as orange as ever. They are there every time our teacher, Mrs. M, unrolls them, clearing her throat and tapping at them with her cane so that they dimple and sway a bit. This is the signal for us to strike up a frame-

---

*kaffir: equivalent of "nigger"

by-frame commentary, in Afrikaans, which we do with a lot of vigorous rhythm and a few shaky phrases that trail in the wake of Mrs. M's booming cues.

Mrs. M is puffy and stout. Her hair is red, and her pets in the front desks have to go up and tease it every now and then. Heaving under a sunset skyline frieze of ox wagons, kranses, umbrella trees and women with clay pots on their heads, she conducts us through the Duplessis day.

Several lessons later, after we have thankfully seen Hennie and Sarie off to bed, Mrs. M sends the class monitor off to fetch a fresh roll of Duplessis. She pulls on the ring at the end of the string and there they are again, only this time they are all blue, and it is Saturday morning.

We get no more than a glimpse of Hennie, who is helping an old blue lady across the street, when Mrs. M realizes with a start that Afrikaans should be over, it is time for Hygiene. Tomorrow we will have to go faster, to catch up with the syllabus.

*　　*　　*

Ronald: has trouble easing into his desk and trouble easing out of it, trouble with his buttons and trouble with the stairs. He gets both feet onto one step before attempting the next; flesh trembles along his tapering legs till he stops to dab the sweat from his brow.

He takes no part in marbles, bullfights, knifey-knifey, red rover or king stingers. All break he is out on the gray slate patio, chewing on sandwiches and jam doughnuts and surveying the chaos.

Only once does he bring his costume and towel with him when the class goes down to the swimming pool. Hot-faced he emerges from the changerooms into the unsparing sunlight, his breasts gazing down at the pinkness that swells up under a faint blue net of veins. The next time he brings a note, gets scowled at and is allowed to go and sit on the stands.

We are in the hall one afternoon after school helping to set chairs out for a meeting when, through the pandemonium, a deliberate series of bangs is heard coming from the direction of the stage. The stage curtains jerk apart and an apparition drifts into view, swaddled in heavy plum-colored curtain cloth and topped by a school cap, inside out so that only the shiny black lining shows.

In the middle of the stage it comes to a stationary position, turns, and waits for silence. "In my native village in Johannesburg," it announces at length, "there is a song that we always sing when a young girl gets married. It's called 'The Click Song' by the English, because they cannot say 'Qongqothwane.'"

It sweeps its way forward, curtain rings in tow, face burning with purpose. Under the row of shields, red for Alfred, yellow for Bede, blue for Caedmon and green for Dunstan, it pauses, hauls in a breath, and begins:

*"Igqipa lendlela nguQongqothwane . . ."**

Sweat twinkles from under the black cap, arms hitch the slipped curtain up a few times and otherwise sway this way and that, holding the song out towards us. Everyone is motionless and remains so. Then the apparition sweeps off, and neither foot-stamping nor cheers will bring it back. Those who go to investigate find Ronald already unwrapped and on his hurried way home.

Next day he is out on the gray slate patio again, munching sandwiches and jam doughnuts, surveying the chaos that reigns all break.

*   *   *

Miss Ilse von Pfluck-Hartung: lives in a little old house squashed between honey-brick flats, with a thick, lush jungle for a front garden and an Alsatian called Kaiser in a kennel round the back. She comes to the door with a pack of Pekinese dogs snuffling and woofing and weeing their way past her ankles to investigate any newcomers.

The whole house smells of marrowbones that are simmering on the stove and lying under the piano; the nose is also met by flea powder, wet carpet, freshly rubbed resin and the box-files of yellowing sheet music that lie in wait all along the passage.

In the music room someone is usually just finishing a lesson, suspended over the edge of the piano or a violin. In this case I can glibly listen out for mistakes while deciding whether I should break the news to Miss von

---

*"The healer of the road, he is the dung-beetle. . ."

102

Pfluck-Hartung that I haven't practiced, again, or let her discover this grinding bit of information for herself.

Miss von Pfluck-Hartung is very broad. She has got broad, burly shoulders and broadness where her hips would be if her tubular dresses disclosed them. She has got aluminium-pale hair cut short and square around her broad face, a baby mustache, and a delicate crackling light in her gray eyes.

She sits with her tough fingers on the keys, pressing out a few chords while waiting for me to step over the pekes and set my music on the stand. "Come on, come on," she urges, while I stall for time. "Well, how did it go this week?"

Her words come out precisely tooled by her German diction, but her voice is not unkind. I look down at the mauled, stained, hair-strewn carpet that must once have been brown. I cannot tell a lie, but the truth is somewhat extreme.

I hand her the violin, mentioning a peg which is always slipping and needs to be chalked. Then, when there seems no hope of doing anything else, I begin to bow my way desperately through a forest of smooth-headed, skinny-tailed notes which all squawk at my approach. Miss von Pfluck-Hartung stops me in the middle, and asks if I am not perhaps having problems with my eyesight: I have been screwing up my eyes at the notes as if I had never seen them before.

The lesson continues, and I am in the middle of a rousing if not immediately identifiable rendering of "Oh for the Wings of a Dove" when the pekes pick themselves up from the carpet and herald in the next victim.

Sometimes, I go with Miss von Pfluck-Hartung down the passage into the spare-room or her bedroom in search of chalk, or resin, or an E-string to replace the one which has fortunately just snapped. There is more of the plastic beechwood wallpaper that lines the music room, framed by deep-stained wooden panels and skirting boards; more of the smoky, tapering ice-cream globes that must be switched on because honey-brick wall blocks the light from the windows.

There are dog leashes, hat boxes, crates topped with rubber drums, rattles, tambourines, triangles, clay cuckoos and castanets for Miss von

Pfluck-Hartung's boisterous and unbashful Saturday morning toy orchestra. There are birdcages, one containing a lonesome blue budgie and a cuttlebone; a few back numbers of *Stern* magazine with women lifting big stiff breasts out of the front covers; dog bowls filled with water or mush at the feet of music stands in various states of collapse.

Stranded in the clutter, backs to the walls, there are bedsteads, commodes and grand wardrobes, carved with flowers and shields and curlicues. They stand foursquare, glimmering darkly out of the dust, forgotten messengers from another world.

*   *   *

At the end of the year, when Miss von Pfluck-Hartung's pupils give their concert, the double-doors down one side of the music room are opened out to reveal her immaculate salon. In cram grannies, grandpas, aunts, uncles and other proud and unsuspecting music lovers, along with disabused mothers and fathers who have all year been caught between the desire to get their children to practice and the consequences for the household when they do.

Afterwards, when everyone is recovering over tea and cake, I go into the salon. There is polished woodwork and plate silver, there are wide shallow bowls planted with cactuses, glazed bridges and pagodas. Opposite the bay windows that look out onto the jungle hang two sepia photographs, stamped with a family crest.

In one there is a castle seen from a distance, shingles, turrets and dormers hoisted above oak trees into the air. In the other there are three children. The little big-boned girl holding her hands over a velvet dress has Miss von Pfluck-Hartung's face; nothing from the ribbons in her hair to the buckles on her shoes has not been starched and pleated into place.

At the end of the afternoon, when it is time to go home, we walk down the steps while Miss von Pfluck-Hartung waves goodbye from the porch, her recently liberated pekes jumping up and down and woofing till they squeak.

I watch the jungle rise up and swallow her, ferns, vines, tendrils taking her body away. Behind a screen of greenery the little girl is left, with one big hand raised, and suffused light settling on her soft helmet of hair.

*   *   *

The Sunday city: is already laid out on the kikuyu grass, away from the shade of the trees, when we get there. Barbers with silver Figaro clippers and slices of mirror apply themselves to bent heads. Photographers pace around rings of gilt-framed portraits, disappear under black cloths and embrace their tripods. In the midst of the city, mountainous blazing green men beat the sky with wickerwork crosses. Heaped against them is their congregation.

There are no walls, no gates, no roads to the city. The nearest sign says "No Ball Games" and is some way down the kikuyu slope. There are few children, no one who is not black; everyone is dressed up in Sunday best and melted together till the last of the grass-blades goes under.

Men tilt their heads back, take a pinch of snuff, swig at a brown-paper bag. Women with giant thighs cluck and sigh as they thread needles through intricate embroidery. One man strokes a river out of a guitar, another jives into it. Someone holds a head wrapped in a rag. Someone digs cautiously at a corn on a toe.

We wander on down to the Lake, one-eyed peacock feathers shimmering out of Robert's grimy hand, a fat bag of bottle-tops slung over my shoulder. We pass iron white men on the bowling-green who make their balls curve perfectly.

We pause at the ponds, where tree roots go red and dip into the pitch-thick water, and crabs glimmer like distant headlamps along the bottom. Everywhere couples walk around on three legs, or stop and squeeze each other till they have no strength left and must lie down. "Love stories," says Robert, and rolls his eyes knowingly.

At the Lake, families fit themselves into wobbly wooden boats, and retire to the shaded restaurant for milk shakes and varnished wedges of tart. Ducks waddle out of the weedy goo of the water, barking for crusts.

When the light weakens, the spray of the fountain in the Lake turns mint green, pink and cherry red. There are still a few boats on the water. The cormorants glide in to roost in the trees that throng the island. They flap their wings out before folding them up, and hook their dark throats into the sky.

It is time to go home, dribbling pine cones, keeping an eye open for rare bottle-tops. At the bowling green we slow down and look about. There is nothing left of the Sunday city, nothing but a large area of squashed grass and a few empty snuff-tins.

Further on we see some of the inhabitants of the city, in aprons or overalls, crimped hats, tackies. It is nearly Monday, and they have begun leading their other lives.

*   *   *

The blacks cross the field to the wire fence, tens of hundreds of them, line it, lean over it, wince into the sunshine. There are broad ladies under parasols, young men punching the air, an old man punting himself along on a walking stick. They wait. They have got all day. Someone should be arriving at the police station any second now to address them, a man from the government.

Saracen tanks roll down the road. A policeman manning one waves from the hatch. Blacks wave back. The tanks roll into the police-station grounds.

The blacks are running. Youths, women, breasts swung to one side, doeks* gone skew, one man mounting a bicycle, two boys together, arms intersecting in flight. Some twisted round in interest, some in laughter, some in disbelief, one doing a dance step, they advance across the stubble and the clumps of long grass.

At their backs, behind the fence, policemen stand on tanks, Sten guns and revolvers lengthening out of them. One bends to reload.

In the road: bodies, fallen, feet towards the fence, clothes blotting up blood; a litter of shoes, bags, hats, bicycles. Some of the fallen prop themselves up, a priest holds a jar of water to the lips of a man soon dead. In the background: two horses and a foal, heavy old cars with narrow windows.

Further down the road: survivors, looking over their shoulders. White policemen in peaked caps and blacks in topis leave the confines of the

---

*doek: scarf worn on head

106

fence. They carry Sten guns, revolvers, a sjambok.* The survivors walk on.

Heaped against the wire fence: hats, soft felt hats, slouch hats, a Stetson, a beret, crushed, upside-down, filled with sunlight; a Basotho hat, a sun hat, coats, a blanket, a punctured parasol, odd shoes, one with eyelets up to the ankle. A policeman stands there, bare burnt arm down past holster to rifle butt.

Sharpeville, 21 March 1960: "The tree of freedom is watered with blood."

Again I sit at the bookshelf, locked in the images: death reaches among the bright-eyed runners, dead and living still together. Next plate, the pick has been made. The holes in the backs of the fallen are clean, blood seeps from their stomachs into the ground.

*   *   *

The book is wrapped in the dustcover of Stendhal's *The Red and the Black*, wedged two rows behind a stout cordon of tomes; it is, not surprisingly, overlooked by the Special Branch men when they come round for a visit.

Rarely does my mother find the time to read about anything but microbes or glands or hermaphrodites; each night she raids books full of them, taking rapid notes in her insect scrawl while chewing on apples and nuts for fuel.

My father, on the other hand, can sit for hours with a book, shifting his eyes across it while his brow stretches and shrinks. He goes from upright to sliding, from there to eased out, and lands up snoozing, the roof of the book open over his chest. He wakes up and carries on. Upright, sliding.

Books are where my father lives, where he digests and gets excited and receives his visitors. When the men from the Special Branch take him away he leaves his life behind in his books, pressed smooth and waiting to loom up from between the covers.

------

*sjambok: quirt or short whip

He smells of old trees and must, and creaks when opened. His domain is all slits and keyholes and notches of ink sunk into pages, reaching through the creamy silence of the frames.

Between the floors and the moulded-steel ceilings he ambles, from cover to cover, from shelf to shelf, making arcane jokes, wise prognostications, equations beyond dispute.

In my long gray school flannels, on tiptoe, leaning over, chin down between my knees, I keep a periodic eye on the titles. One by one I will come to know his ways, page by page, sentence by sentence; at the commas I will pause inside him. He is everywhere, waiting. One by one, I will become him.

*   *   *

The house is so quiet, after classes and the blunder and crunch of the rugby field. Nothing moves bar dust in the angled yellow shafts at the window; down the road, a dog. The tin roofs tremor, white-hot, the blood is still wet on the ground; backwards and they are all up, running without a sound.

*   *   *

The two men in the front seats are staring at the windscreen. Their hair is shaved to bristle, sideburns clipped. The napes of their necks come clean as a whistle out of safari-suits. My father and I are sitting behind them, holding on to each other by the eyes.

He has lost weight and looks jaded, leaning into the corner of the seat. His cheeks are flushed. He keeps his voice down low and deliberate, but everything he says is hunger.

The two men in the front seats don't flinch. Past the windscreen, heat waves warp the bonnet of the Volkswagen.

It is my thirteenth birthday, special visit. I receive the khaki of my father's clothes, the chocolate of his corduroy jacket, the grizzled warmth of the hairs on his chest. I receive the singleness of his glance, the multitude of what he wants; the finality of his surmounted will.

I bear witness before him in the back of the Volkswagen, bring to him word of my mother his wife, my brother his son, my sister his daughter.

So high, I show him with the flat of a hand. Crawls. I speak, and go numb. One clean nape twists around and announces that time is up.

My father presses my hands in his gout-studded hands. I close the car door, leaving the three of them inside. Behind me is the blunt horizon of the Fort, planted with broad-bladed aloes; in front of me, the clinic, steam shooting from a grill in the pavement. I cross the tarmac stone-cold, composing myself for my mother and a cup of tea.

"Menace" / linocut by Eunice Sefako.

The Other Side
of the Family

Welma Odendaal

Welma Odendaal was born in July 1951 in a small mining town in the southern Transvaal, South Africa. Her father was a gold miner and eventually became a used-car salesman, traveling from town to town, taking his family with him. The writer grew up on the road, in small towns and highveld villages, attending eight schools between the ages of six and twelve and settling eventually in Pretoria, where she lived with her family until graduating from high school. In her young adult life she attended a film school for three years, married, gave birth to twins, a boy and a girl, and in 1974 published her first volume of short stories, Getuie vir die Naaktes (Witness for the Naked). Her second volume, Keerkring (Tropic), was published in July 1977 and banned by the government six weeks later. The book stayed on the banning list until 1985 and has not been republished.

Welma Odendaal has been a journalist for the past twelve years and is presently working in Cape Town on an English-language newspaper.

I grew up on stories. Tales told from then the present and now the past. Listening quietly as children were told to be from the lap of my mother, the crook of my father's arm, the comfort of my grandfather's shoulder, the bosom of Grandma, forbidding matriarch who remembered all. Tales of those who trekked across the hinterland, those who fought the war against the English—starving brave burghers, hensoppers* and joiners and those who died in the concentration camps; those who refused to fight the Englishman's war in Europe and were interned in camps, those who supported the Nazis, those who formed the party and those who became the ruling class.

At times I believed in the enemy as much as they did. Understood what it was like to be poor, a downtrodden people, oppressed in your

---

*hensoppers: literally, "handsuppers"—derogatory slang for Boers who surrendered to the British

110

country of birth, treated with contempt, bloody Boer. To hate, to be hated . . . such a fragile division. In this country our lives are sodden with bloody tales of the past. The story is no different now.

Mid-year '85, the winter is turning harsh. State of emergency, state of panic, state of control. The rain came late this year. Burning barricades on the highway, strange and lonely in the mist. A message comes from upcountry, your father is dead. Outside the ground is like sponge.

My father was a kind and funny man. He drove around with a short piece of hosepipe* in the back of his car and when someone asked him about it he pulled a grotesque face, "Oh, you know, things can get a bit much sometimes . . ." and they all laughed. Two weeks later he took a quiet turnoff off the eastern bypass, parked under the bloekoms** and killed himself.

From all over the clan on both sides of the family came with their grief and condolences; my father was a well-liked man. The clergyman was hired for the occasion, he had a solemn face and read from a piece of paper. My mother wept and blamed herself. My sister's fat husband, who pawed me when I was younger, thanked me for coming from so far and the police for doing their duty. My sister handed out checks and tranquilizers. My father didn't want any flowers or fuss. My father's was a hard act to follow.

In the early evening the family gathered at the house of a cousin. Mother, children, aunts and uncles, cousins, more children. In the kitchen the women prepared the feast: frikkadel,*** steamed carrots, sweet potato and boer-pampoen,**** apple tart fresh with cream. And later when night had settled, the provincial rugby match had ended on TV and the windows and doors had been shut against the chill, out came the bottle of Cape brandy. The teasing started, bickering, laughs and arguing. Langjan took up where we had left off as kids: ". . . *Do you still write such shitty books?*" Someone wondered what had become of some other lost relative: "*. . . have you heard . . . do you know . . . he's decided to sell the farm . . . she went and married among the black Maritz clan . . .*" And later, not much later, out came the stories.

Aunt Baby and Kita and old Maans Merwe's wife Magriet were thrown together in the same concentration camp. Kita says old Baby was already

---

*hosepipe: garden hose
**bloekoms: Australian blue gum tree
***frikkadel: meatballs
****boer-pampoen: pumpkin

something else. Lord Aunt Letta, but you know Baby. She probably never gave the khakis* a moment's peace. The food in the camp was vile, that's why the children all died like flies from stomach diseases even after the Englishwoman, who was she again? Emily . . . yes, that's the one, Hobhouse, thanks, Aunt Letta, yes, even after this Emily came from overseas with a program of reform and white nightgowns for the womenfolk. Totally useless in the Free State winter, according to Kita. That's why Aunt Baby always waited till the very last minute before she visited the outhouse, there was only one, up against the hill, and they had to share it with the khakis too. One evening Aunt Baby was scurrying up there in extremis, you know, and the way Kita tells it, old Baby takes the turn on the hill at a moer** of a speed, sorry Aunt Letta, and as she runs she already pulls down her bloomers, and my God Aunt Letta, just as she collapses gratefully, she goes and sits on a Tommy's lap. Can you imagine it? Smack on a Tommy's lap.***

Baby was just fourteen and her brother, my Oupa Willie, just a tiny baby when they fled from the farm a few steps ahead of the English, who came with guns and fire and threat of the camps. They say he was in a chest at the back of the ox wagon and in their haste to get away from the British the chest fell off and landed in a ditch with baby grandfather still inside. Later they detoured back and found him there, quiet as a little mouse. When I was a child and Oupa Willie and I made boats from acorns and matchsticks to sail in the leivoor**** in front of his house, I insisted he tell this story again and again. I remember thinking how brave this little baby was to have lain there so still while the murderous khakies thundered overhead.

"Weren't you scared, Oupa?"
"Scared to death, but a Boer-child mos knows when it's time to lie quiet as a little mouse."
"But weren't you ever a fighter, Oupa Willie?"
My grandpa laughed his shy laugh, "No, man, your Oupa Wilhelm, he was the fighter of the family."

And as many times as the story was told, I made my little brother lie in the dry water canals under the fruit trees of my grandfather's house as I

---

*khaki: metonym for "British soldier"
**a *moer* of a speed: a hell of a speed
***This and other italicized passages were translated from the Afrikaans by Lynne Bryer.
****leivoor: irrigation ditch

thundered overhead a stick trailing in the dust shouting, *"Jo! Jo! Die kakies kom!"* Did I even then identify with the enemy? My brother never lay quiet for very long and these games usually ended with grandfather intervening, dusting of a screeching little boy and reprimanding me with a puzzled look on his face. I think he secretly thought I took after Oupa Wilhelm's side of the family.

I never knew my Oupa Wilhelm; he died when I was a few months old of a sickness in the lungs, they said. Oupa Willie died quietly in his house on the banks of the Vaal River when I was at school one day and I wasn't allowed to go to the funeral. I'd never been to a funeral until my father died this year, and that was more of a service, really, with no church music and songs, no pallbearers or flowers, just a quiet service before the cremation. In his father's time things were different, funerals were big affairs, there were marches and banners and songs, as the stories go, funerals then were often political affairs.

I've seen pictures of my father's father, a tall man, straight, with a bushy mustache and wild eyebrows above pale eyes. I did not know Oupa Wilhelm, but I knew him by the stories my grandmother told.

As a preschool child I spent many days with her on her smallholding outside the town in which we lived then. There I wandered and dashed and hid among the kosmos* and tall winter grass, making up games based on the past. Ouma was fairly easy about most things. Once I had caught a butterfly and tried to keep it captive in those round Smarties** boxes you used to get. She made me let it go and said I should never try and catch one again. But they're so pretty. Yes, she said, because they have free spirits, insects, butterflies, birds, should be free to roam and never be held captive.

> *"But what about your fowls, Ouma, you keep them in a hok?"****
> "Enough of your smartness, little miss."*

And Oupa Wilhelm, why was he held against his will? That's a long story. Tell me again. About Oupa? Yes, and Sister Maggie, and the marches. And the funeral? Yes, everything. She laughs and draws me closer. You have his eyes, they were like chipped glass. And her own eyes become soft, misted with memories of the past. Her voice digging deep at times almost a whisper, and at times harsh and angry as she remembers the general strike of 1913.

---

*kosmos: a spring wild flower
**Smarties: multicolored candies
***hok: shack

The miners' strike was called in May that year, Kleinfontein was the first mine to go out, Apex soon joined in sympathy and before long the others—Modderfontein, Modder B, Van Rhyn—all came out on strike. Tribal workers at a few mines attempted to join the strike effort and at Modder B black workers refused to go underground until the white men came back. Their general demand was for higher wages, although, according to the *Illustrated Star*, "they were liberally paid . . . during the period of the strike the natives received 15s. 7d.* a day . . ."

In June 1913 the union was negotiating with the mine managements but talks broke down and other miners were hired to fill the positions of those who had gone on strike.

There were many fights between strikers and scabs; it was a time without pity. One man died when his car was overturned and set alight, bricks were thrown at houses, children taunted at school . . . *scab scab scab . . . Jou pa is 'n scab*. On the twentieth, the strike leaders were arrested; Wilhelm was one of them but grandmother didn't know him then. The state banned all political meetings. Eight days later the ban was lifted and the leaders released, but a meeting defying the ban had already been arranged for that night.

All of the men and women workers in the factories in Johannesburg and the Rand had received invitations to come to Benoni where the meeting was held. Grandmother went, and her younger sister Maggie. People were angry—"Come armed," the pamphlets said. At the meeting the call came for a general strike to support the miners. All the delegates agreed—the factories too would come out. It was there grandmother met Wilhelm the first time.

The hall was packed, a babel of mankind. Some were shouting and heckling the speakers, others stood quietly to the side and listened. People from the strikers' newspaper The Worker *handed out badges with the motto: "Workers unite. Unity is strength." It was then that your oupa stood up from the crowd, the tall fair man with the pale eyes. He announced himself as New Modderfontein's representative. Said his men and the people from Modder B and Van Rhyn would refuse to come out unless "The Worker" printed: "Werkers verenig. Eendracht maakt Macht"** on the other side of the badges. Hear! Hear! cried the Afrikaner workers and the man from* The Worker *had to give his promise there and then. Later I went over to your Oupa Wilhelm and pledged my factory's support. He smiled shyly and shook my hand.*

---

*A trifling amount
**"Workers unite. Unity is strength."

114

*The time had come. Friday, Fourth of July, the Americans' day of indepen-
dence, the day of the general strike of 1913.*

Friday, Independence Day, was the day set apart for the declaration of
the general strike, and things moved rapidly . . . (*Illustrated Star*, July 12,
1913)

*Market Square crawled with people. The women were marching down from
Fordsburg, Sister Maggie and I were together, our arms firmly linked. By two
o'clock anyone who could move was there in the throng at the trade hall in the
city center. On one side stood the police and the dragoon guards, stolidly,
armed with batons and rifles. "Oh, come ye prisoners of starvation . . ." we
sang deafeningly, our feet drumming as we marched in formation across the
paving stones, down Commissioner Street, westward towards the market
square. Women in the vanguard, Maggie at my side, westward the multitude
streamed. From every side fresh wings of women joined us until we formed a
force so large and loud no one would have been able to hold us.*

*At Rissik Street a group broke away yelling: "To the station! To the station!"
Rissik Street, Hoek Street, North Street . . . on to Park Station. People pushing
and shoving, how we screamed and sang and surged together. Wherever you
looked there were workers who had come out on strike, come out in support of
the miners. Then, suddenly, there was the reek of petrol and fire. North Street
is burning, the station is burning— "Come, come to Park Station!" Over the city
the black smoke rose into the sky.*

*"Quick!" yells Maggie and grabs my arm: "Here come the police." Panting
from the smoke, the women swarm about, regroup, jeer at the policemen:
"Scab! Scab! Scab!" Gunfire reverberates. Here lies a motorcar, overturned
and smoldering, there a riderless horse gallops away. An official is trumpeting
orders: "All citizens must disperse at once . . . all citizens disperse . . ." But it's
too late. Park Station is burning.*

*In the deadly pall of smoke, the air a bitter fog of ash, no one notices that the
western sky is growing bleaker, darker.*

The events on Saturday form the blackest page in the history of the
strike and its appalling incidents . . . (*Illustrated Star*, July 12)

*Black Saturday, people people, everywhere you looked the streets of Johannes-
burg were a seething mass of people. In the morning there was a deceptive
lightheartedness in the air. Spectators crowded every balcony, some of them
staring silently, others waving and cheering the strikers on. Here and there
hung a banner: "Workers Unite. Up the Miners." The crowd was roaring*

115

incitement in the dawn. Come on, people, come! Maggie and I were in the group round the San Toy Bar. Our numbers had swelled since the previous day, we had smelled fire and blood, nothing could stop us now. "Awake! Arise! Arise!" On went the army of strikers, on to the Rand Club, haunt of the mine bosses.

And, my child, no one would admit to it, no one would say, but someone pulled the trigger, someone cried out, and all at once the people broke rank and scattered in all directions. More shooting—clack, clack, clack—shots raining thick and fast in the hour of panic. And quietly beside me, as if she were lying down for a moment's brief rest, Maggie fell. "Maggie . . . ag, come now Maggie . . . little sister? Ease your head against my breast, don't turn your face away like that, there, there, come, let's rest awhile." I drag her a short distance out of the way of the fierce hoofs of the police-horses, people are running and jumping over her sprawled limbs. "Where, oh where, little sister, did you get so much blood?" I pull her dress down modestly over her legs, which are lolling into the street; I close the empty, hurt eyes . . . Hands together and say "amen."

I wasn't there when the police and dragoon guards stormed the crowd at the Rand Club and the column of workers fled home, tails between their legs, bruised and sore from the baton blows, dragging the wounded and dead.

Sunday morning arrived with the weather in harmony with the general feeling of the Johannesburg people . . . the gloomy overcast sky and the cold wind . . . (*Illustrated Star*, July 12)

White-faced, eyes shadowed, we stand in a dense throng, listening to the preacher's words in the weak wintry sunlight. He begs the Lord to let this cup pass from us, to cleanse us from violence and anger. He prays for the day when our people will return in droves to the mines, when the women will go back to their homes and children. He prays that we will wash the ash of North Street and the soot of Park Station, the reek of sweat and blood, from our bodies. But can we ever forget the cries of our wounded comrades?

Most of us are exhausted, children are hungry. Twenty dead, more than three hundred wounded in the massacre of the twelfth of July. Blue baton weals on the bodies of our men. But the women say, "No, no, don't give in now, don't turn back." Mrs. Fitzgerald, who's been in the forefront for so long, speaks out with hoarse fervor: "Don't turn back, workers, the power is in your hands . . . Stand up, onward march! Stand firm in the struggle . . . die stryd duur voort, Yes, the struggle continues, for ourselves and those who have perished." Somewhere a group begins to sing the words of the "Red Flag"—

116

"dum-dum-de-dum"—faintly the sounds carry on the chill of the wind. In the grayness and the cold, once more night falls.

With unease, the people return home. But no one sleeps and in the confusion of those times, the Quinlan Opera cancels its performance of Verdi.

Half-past nine a shockwave rocks the city. The streetlamps are out but in the shadows there is life. The railway line this side of Jeppe has been blown up and the silences fill swiftly with the hoofbeats of horses. Far away the bells of the fire wagons wail.

That night I stood vigil over Maggie while we prepared her for the morrow. And early in the evening Wilhelm came to pay his respects. Our hands met briefly as our eyes but I would not forget him.

A wearied and exhausted Johannesburg tramped to work on Monday morning in nervous expectation . . . (*Illustrated Star,* July 12)

In rows six deep we walked carrying the dead in their swaying coffins down Bree Street to the new cemetery. Ahead of us the band played, "Lead us kindly light." There were six or seven thousand of us. Some carried red banners, some sang softly. In rows of six deep we came to bury our dead.

That day my grandmother buried her sister Maggie. Wilhelm and the others returned to the mines; they got married and later had a daughter and a son. Her beloved Wilhelm died a sick and wheezing man at the age of fifty-five and she saw him too to his grave. She was not present this year when we buried my father. Chipped glass, do you know the color I mean?

Ouma died in a little house in Benoni while we were on holiday in December at a summer place on the east coast. We drove through the night to be back in time for her funeral. I was twelve and not allowed to go. It was a solemn drive although they had all expected her to die soon. I was sad about cutting short the summer holiday, leaving that place of warm days and long evenings. The place of wooden shacks scattered along the beach the latrines in a row against the scrub, smells of sea and disinfectant, summer evenings hiding behind the dunes watching the older children explore each other by the light of beach fires with hands and mouths. I was not so sad about Ouma dying; I remembered too well her sickbed, the overpowering smell of urine, her mouth limp and her hands cold, her face gray and strange. No smiles, no lightness, no stories being told. But afterwards I went to her grave and took her some flowers, those morning glories she used to say she liked. Poor purple flowers for my dead ouma. I imagined then the dead to lie piously in row upon disinfected row, arms neatly folded waiting patiently for God to come and unlock them from their slumber.

Last night I dreamt my father came into my house. He was big and bear-like and wore a suit and tie. He had come, he said, to say goodbye.

"Man Going to Exile" / linocut by David Hlongwane.

THE WEEKLY MAIL

PRICES: JOHANNESBURG, PRETORIA & REEF R1,00 (plus 12c GST) — ELSEWHERE IN SA R1,12 (excl. GST)

Volume 2, Number 24, FRIDAY JUNE 20 to THURSDAY JUNE 26, 1986

THE PAPER FOR A CHANGING SOUTH AFRICA

WE'RE BACK ON THE STREETS!
The paper that was seized last week will be on sale as usual from today

The EPG report: An extraordinary document made ordinary by our extraordinary times **8**

A leaf-munching plan to beat malnutrition **7**

FRONT PAGE COMMENT

Our lawyers tell us we can say almost nothing critical about the Emergency

But we'll try:

P IK BOTHA, the Minister of Foreign Affairs, told US television audiences this week that the South African press remained free.

We hope that ▆▆▆▆▆▆▆▆▆▆▆▆▆▆, ▆▆▆▆▆▆▆▆▆▆▆▆▆▆▆▆▆▆▆▆▆▆▆▆▆▆▆ ▆▆▆▆▆▆, was listening.

They considered our publication subversive.

● If it is subversive to speak out against ▆▆▆▆▆▆, we plead guilty.

● If it is subversive to express concern about ▆▆▆▆▆▆, we plead guilty.

● If it is subversive to believe that there are better routes to peace than the ▆▆▆▆▆▆, we plead guilty.

● To PAGE 2

● To PAGE 2

RESTRICTED Reports on these pages have been censored to comply with Emergency regulations

On the Front Line:
A Portrait of Civil War

Paul Weinberg and Afrapix photographers
Guy Tillim, Dave Hartman and
Steve Hilton-Barber

Born in Pietermaritzburg in 1956, Paul Weinberg attended Natal University where he earned a B.A. in political science and economic history. In 1977 he obtained a certificate in photography from Natal Technikon.

In 1979 Weinberg taught photography at the Open School, a nonformal education program in Johannesburg. He has worked for the Institute of Race Relations as a media worker, and in 1980 and 1981 made two super-8 documentaries, one on Alexandra Township and one on Page View, an Indian community outside of Johannesburg which was systematically destroyed because of the Group Areas legislation.

Weinberg set up Afrascope, a community film project, and in 1982 was co-founder of Afrapix, a photographic collective. This photo-essay was compiled by Weinberg, using Afrapix photographers. He has worked as a free-lance photographer since 1983. His work can be seen in South Africa: The Cordoned Heart, *edited by Omar Badsha and commissioned by the Second Carnegie Inquiry into Poverty and Development in Southern Africa (Gallery Press, 1986) and in* None But Ourselves, Masses vs. Media in the Making of Zimbabwe, *by Julie Frederikse (Johannesburg: Ravan, 1982).*

A photo-essay entirely by Weinberg, "A South African Photographer in Zimbabwe," begins on page 468.

"I don't take sides. I take pictures" was Nick Nolte's classic throwaway line when confronted by a revolutionary when they land up in a police cell together.

South Africa is not Hollywood and the heroes that are laid to rest are almost never photographers. Yet as we find ourselves caught in the midst of a civil war the question begs itself with more pertinence than ever before.

This essay is presented at a time when the restrictions of press freedom have never been greater in our history. We are precluded by law from photographing unrest situations, illegal strikes, funerals, street-committee organizations, boycotts or strikes. It seems that the government is intent on blotting out a phase of resistance politics in the struggle against apartheid.

The resistance that has taken place has transformed the country. We live in a state of emergency. Thousands have died in the unrest of the last two years and many thousands more have been detained. Just about all aspects of "normal" life have been affected—from transport to education. We have witnessed the emergence of a culture of resistance.

This collection of photographs in no way attempts to cover all areas of struggle but is an edited version of a greater picture we have not even seen. They are images from a collective called Afrapix.

—*Paul Weinberg*

Victoria Mxenge funeral, Durban, August 1985. Photograph by Paul Weinberg/Afrapix.

Squatters salvage their possessions as Crossroads burns, June 1986. Photograph by Guy Tillim/Afrapix.

Soweto, July 1985. Photograph by Paul Weinberg/Afrapix.

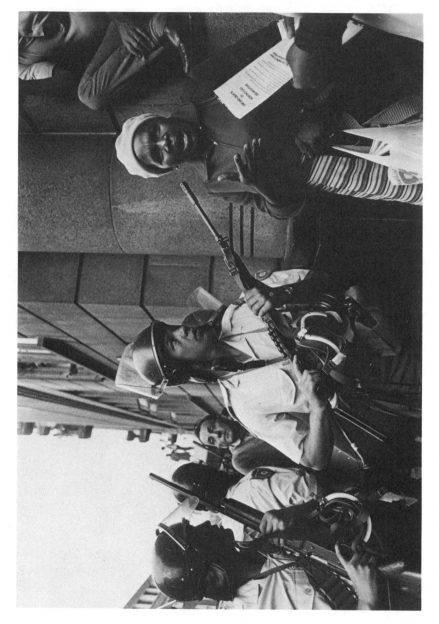

May Day 1985, Khotso House, Johannesburg. Photograph by Paul Weinberg/Afrapix.

Daduza township, July 1985. Photograph by Paul Weinberg/Afrapix.

People build burning barricade, Belgravia Road, Athlone, Cape Town, November 1986. Photograph by Dave Hartman/Afrapix.

Vigilantes attack, in Leandra, February 1986. Photograph by Paul Weinberg/Afrapix.

"Comrades" defend themselves against a vigilante attack, in Leandra. February 1986. Photograph by Paul Weinberg/Afrapix.

Young boy shot, Eastern Cape, March 1986. Photograph by Steve Hilton-Barber/Afrapix.

Funeral, Eastern Cape. Photograph by Steve Hilton-Barber/Afrapix.

A pallbearer at a funeral for a squatter killed in Crossroads violence winces as the procession is teargassed by police. Crossroads, June 1986. Photograph by Guy Tillim/Afrapix.

Funeral for a squatter killed in Crossroads violence. Crossroads, June 1986. Photograph by Guy Tillim/Afrapix.

African National Congress flag at funeral of a person killed by police,
Guguletu, December 1985. Photograph by Dave Hartman/Afrapix.

From *Die Walvisman*

Klaas Steytler

Nicolaas (Klaas) Steytler was born in Ladybrand, Orange Free State, in 1922 and was educated at the University of the Witwatersrand and the University of Cape Town. He has worked as a journalist, magazine editor and as a publisher with Tafelberg. His five novels, which range from the comic to the apocalyptic, have been published by Human and Rousseau. The most recent, Die Walvisman *(The .Whaleman, Cape Town: Human and Rousseau, 1986), a work based on the Jonah saga, has already received considerable critical acclaim and is at present being translated into English. A previous work,* Die Wonderwerke van Judas Iskariot *(Cape Town Tafelberg, 1977), explores biblical motifs. He also has a collection of short stories,* Zap Zap *(Cape Town: Human and Rousseau, 1975).*

Steytler, who lives in Cape Town, is married to Elsa Joubert, whose celebrated documentary novel Die Swerfjare van Poppie Nongena *is available in the U.S., in translation, as* Poppie Nongena *(W. W. Norton).*

Letter to a Friend

[Jonah came to Nineveh, the most sophisticated city on earth, and told the inhabitants, pursuant to YHWH's* instructions, the simple truth: "In forty days Nineveh will be destroyed."

He had found lodgings with a widow and on the eighteenth day after his arrival he sat in the small, cramped living room of the woman's flat, paging through his pocket diary. The widow's eleven-year-old daughter, Rachel, entered and sat down next to him.]

"What are you looking for?" the child asked. A naive, inquisitive girl with an unwitting sense of hurting with the truth. She placed her hand between his and looked at him searchingly. This kind of unsolicited affection touched him. It filled a need, made empty rooms habitable.

---

*YHWH: *Yahweh,* or Jehovah

"What are you looking for?" the child asked again. She had seen him paging through his diary.

"A thought, a memory. I am looking for a memory," he answered.

With outstretched arms she took his head between her hands. "Oh, that is easy," she said, "you open this up—you open the door."

"Inside is only darkness and death. You won't be able to see anything. There is very little light, and it is rapidly becoming impenetrable, quite black."

"Then I will enter, open it up and let in light. With a small candle. You will see."

"Is that so?"

"Oh, yes. But you won't open the door. You do not open up to anybody. One opens doors to one's friends. I do not think you have any friends."

He stood up in a surge of emotion, smarting. He did not care for the drift of the conversation, especially under the watchfully inquisitive eyes of the widow.

"Where are you going?" the girl asked.

"I must leave," he answered. "I still have a lot to do tonight. Until midnight."

Outside he walked to the nearest metro station. He still had three meetings to attend, but would be through by ten. The lie had been quite unnecessary, an overreaction easily explained. But he could not dredge up the real reason why it had come out so effortlessly by itself.

On the twenty-third day Rachel rushed up to him when he came home at about seven. There was a letter for him, she announced in excitement. A letter posted locally, in Nineveh. A bulky letter, she said, somebody surely who had a lot to tell. A friend?

He took the letter, but did not answer the girl, went to his room and closed the door. He could see that she was disappointed, stung, by his not sharing the letter and its contents with her. A mysterious friend. The barb she had left in him a few days ago had started festering.

The address was typed. He sat down at the table and tore open the envelope. It contained a few sheets in a fine but closely written hand, to get as much on a single sheet as possible. There was no address at the top of the page, only a date, that of three days ago.

"Dear Friend," it began.

Jonah looked at the handwriting, held it some distance away from him, then moved it closer and squinted, trying to form a mental picture of the author's personality and character.

He smiled wanly.

It was a mean trick to have played on the girl. To post a letter to himself. If the envelope had been filled with blank pages he would have had to take stock of himself immediately for symptoms of an inflammatory neurosis or some form of paranoia. But he knew that there were any number of other factors which relegated worries about neuroses and paranoia into insignificance.

He took up the long letter and realized full well: he was busy paying the price of a promise.

Jonah read:

"Dear Friend,

"I possibly owe you some form of communication. What leaves, what goes out from the self, must return. The truth of the matter is that since my arrival here, life, thought, words, have left me. The outcome is loneliness, There has been no reply, no answer, no return.

"In place of some form of reply it might be useful if I told the story of a man whom I met yesterday at a sidewalk café in the city. But that is not the truth either. I only lightly touched his soul, in my usual supersensory fashion, as you know, to give warmth and constraintlessness to a casual meeting. Let us dispense with my reasons for wanting to talk to this stranger.

"The man I met was called Ivan; his surname has slipped my mind. A retired civil servant, 77 years of age. His namesake was a great uncle, but apart from this the Russian stock in his lineage is minimal. He said he was a Christian, but not of the reborn type. He partakes in the religious rituals of his faith as an outward subscription to the process of civilization. Also because he finds it necessary for the support of his inner realms. He was also quite insistent that his faith's mysteries, although completely submerged and possibly wholly lost to the congregation, still fortify him.

"I remember him as a spare man, rather tall, with thin sandy hair, a somewhat bulbous nose, a good and not very wrinkled skin but pale. His smile over a good set of false teeth was urbane.

"A civilized person of the old sort, one who maintained a central position and devised a form of existence which suited him, he explained. The realities of his life at this stage were such that the inevitability of death was not something to be taken into consideration at all. He added, not without pride, that all the vital organs in his body were completely healthy and functioning normally.

"He was by profession a teacher of linguistics, he said, but it so happened that for the major part of his career he taught literature, first in public schools and, after his retirement, for some time in private schools and night classes. His father, a civil servant in the department of internal revenue, died at a fairly youthful age. This left his mother struggling with a very small pension and a bit of money of her own until he could support her. Thereafter she focused her life on good works in the world at large and upon vodka in the privacy of her bedroom, an arrangement that worked well for quite a number of years. She became bedridden and he was forced to engage a daytime nurse until her death in her eighty-seventh year. He misses her a great deal, especially her incessant complaints during the last few years of her life. It provided permanence to his existence, although in its own perverted kind of a way.

"As far as he himself is concerned, Ivan said in his reserved but well-articulated sentences, he loves a fine turn of phrase. It is a sign of the civilized human being. Coarse and slovenly talk, as an indication of urban sophistication and an urge to make common cause with the vulgar masses, presages devolution and the disintegration of society and eventually civilization. He loves a well-clothed thought, the play in poetry of honed ideas, standing in juxtaposition to each other, giving promise of new perspectives. A density between words, so to speak. Actually, though, he must confess that his preference, and his love, is for prose. A sense of character—that is what he possesses, and what he always stressed while still teaching. Character is the central driving force in life. Therefore it should be observed and studied. All other claims to the contrary beg the question.

" 'But talking about a sense of character, sir,' he said, 'please forgive my brashness. You obviously belong to one of the old and influential families in Nineveh. A man with the wisdom of our world without its weariness, and the self-assurance bred on achievement and ancestral wealth, good breeding and education. Live and let live, without the present-day propensity to harm or denigrate your fellow human being. And if I may say so, your apparent somberness is merely subterfuge. In the right company you would be expansive, even witty in a lightly ironical vein.'

"Mr. Ivan was enjoying his indulgence in analysis.

" 'Sir, please pardon me these few stray remarks,' he continued, 'but I am a judge of character. And do not regard this as in any way forward, but I feel as if we have known each other for a long time. We operate on the same wavelength, it is pleasant to meet a kindred spirit. At this stage of my life my needs are few and relatively simple—I enjoy good company the most, apart from the orderliness of a regular life. And I enjoy what this Great City of Nineveh has to offer, although the quality of life has coarsened considerably during the past few decades.

" 'It is a case where the bad life drives out the good life, to use an analogy of Gresham's Law. There are no limits in an open license to gross excesses.

" 'In any case, there is enough worthwhile left to savor to keep me satisfied. Nothing will come to an end, whatever the prophets of doom — or *the* prophet—predict. Life just does not stop by itself, and not suddenly, full stop, as is being alleged during these past few weeks. Creation—the Creator—has seen to it that life regenerates itself; we live within a self-regulating system. Nothing collapses finally, becomes dust. In any case, degeneration will finally regenerate itself to rebirth and life. The phoenix will always emerge from the ashes. Hiroshima and Nagasaki were isolated, single events, done with a view to economy. But not to be repeated. Come Christmas I will buy a few candles to light in the cathedral, in memory of my mother, and remembering a Savior.

" 'I am not overly intellectual or acute,' he continued, 'I like order, I keep to myself in an ordered society to which I contribute taxes. My opinions—my vote, to put it more bluntly—has lost its importance to me during these past few decades or more because our life has become one of universal manipulation. I am on the way to becoming eighty, I enjoy good health, I have small and insignificant hobbies, I do not have much religious faith because it is unnecessary, I am a human being.'

"My friend, imagine yourself in my position. I, YHWH's messenger, the hangman of the Great City of Nineveh, am sitting next to a man who does not know with whom he is conversing. I, the Supreme Being's sheriff, am being provoked by a rentier of this civilization. A harmless, disciplined and even charming old man with an inviolable right to his own opinions. Why would I have fallen in with his meandering conversation? As you know I have the choice and the duty to converse, to talk to whomsoever I wish in this Great City. I experience everything, I can home in on whatever pitch of the conscious or every layer of the unconscious to hear what he or she is saying—and conversely and of supreme importance—to make them hear and understand completely what I am telling them. I move within each person's personal and collective unconscious, I can open the hidden doors to the spirit so that my voice is heard and they will understand what I am saying, so that my words will have effect. That is why I endured the whale.

"I must and I will fulfill my promise.

"I ordered a glass of *vin blanc* for each of us and Mr. Ivan smiled. 'You are most kind,' he said.

" 'And what, sir,' he asked, 'do you do?'

" 'I, my friend, am an announcer of death.'

" 'What an strange sort of profession. Somewhat like this Jonah that everybody is talking about lately. A strange kind of a man, don't you think? And to whom do you announce death?'

" 'Oh, to everybody. Also to you, Mr. Ivan.'

"He looked at me nonplussed, as if I had found a weak spot in his armor.

" 'Have we met each other previously?' he ventured as if looking for a way out, a way to discontinue a conversation casually started.

" 'Oh, of course we have. I had an appointment with you. For this afternoon. To tell you the truth, right now, with the sun lying red and dry over the rooftops over yonder.'

"I immediately felt sorry for this small and rather melodramatic sentence. He, as a widely read man, would have recognized its source in any case.

" 'But please don't be disturbed, Mr. Ivan. I have need of conversation,' I said by way of apology. 'It is not something I have indulged in a lot lately; quiet, desultory conversation.'

"He smiled, relieved. He took a visiting card from his inside pocket and gave it to me. A sign of appeasement, possibly.

" 'If you do announce death, you would surely know what it looks like.'

" 'Oh, yes, I know him,' I said. 'He has already crossed my path once or twice.'

"My friend, you must realize that I was not playing games, fooling with a defenseless old man. My instructions are quite clear: I am to spare no one. No man or animal, nothing that draws life in this Great City of Nineveh. Everything must perish. If you do not have monolithic belief, you fail. Right? So I told him a few facts, because he had asked me.

" 'What does he look like?'

" 'He wears a colorless kind of hat and a dun raincoat, his face is of sand and his eyes lack brightness. I do not know whether he has a mouth that he can open to talk, to warn people that he is approaching. He walks noiselessly; also those that operate with him. They look alike because I have seen them. They react to instructions because I have seen them emerging from an operations room, taking their overcoats from pegs in a passage, to go out on their business.'

"Mr. Ivan's face lit up because he had seen a gap for himself.

" 'They are then on their way to gather in the harvest—whether ripe or still green and growing. The harvest is alive and well and the men, or the man, in the dun coat, is on his way. But now, what happens, say, if he were to stumble, or if the original instructions were changed or canceled and him on the way to his victim?'

" 'It is rare, as far as I know. Because if they leave their base, all the signs are there. For them to see and for those to be harvested. The signs are present for the operatives and the harvested to know that the time has come.'

" 'What are the signs?' he asked very quietly.

" 'The signs, Mr. Ivan . . . The red glow in the west, as you see growing on the rooftops. The air is dry and dust is suspended in the sky like a luminous sheet of muslin, and the sun is setting and one becomes aware of a sense of breathless anticipation. Because something unnameable and irrevocable is about to happen. It is a moment in the heavens, a small sliver of a second, the quiet before the storm breaks. Actually it is a classical phenomenon. I grant you that it is a stereotyped image, but it is a recognizable silence to those who still know nature.'

"And if he comes, what happens then, sir?'

"He has a peculiar kind of vibration, a taste of his own. Quite neutral, neither evil nor dark, and completely distinguishable from the stream of life that most of us accept unwittingly and without analysis or question. Death has its own kind of music, it has no color, it manifests itself in the back of the skull, it leaves a coating on the tongue, the mouth dries out and the muscles of the body relax so that the bodily fluids leave by themselves. It creates a kind of fear that is possibly greater than death itself, a kind of fear that causes the seed to burst forth from the pod at birth, or that allows the wind to blow away the husk at the time of death.

"You know how these things happen, friend. A syndrome develops within you, you feed it every day. I came to announce death in this Great City, not life. Therefore I must have unconsciously opened up the gates within me and hit this man directly. Like the time on that first day when I addressed the investment congress. At times you do not know when the power leaves you. When I looked up I saw that the pale man of 77, Mr. Ivan, was chalk-white.

"Could I have done something to rectify matters? I do not know. I am a simple-minded man. In life I have only one direction in which I move: forward.

"I pushed the glass of cold white wine with my fingertips to touch his hands resting on the table.

" 'Drink,' I said softly.

"Naturally I had it within me to project to him calmness and the conviction that he had nothing to fear. But that possibility did not even occur to me because it was not part of my brief. Put in another fashion: I did not even think of it.

"It appeared as if he had not heard what I had said—to drink.

" 'And when is he coming?' Mr. Ivan asked.

" 'In thirteen days' time, Mr. Ivan. Then it will be the end of this City. But you can, of course, break out. Take a bus or a train, or leave by plane,' I added apologetically.

"Mr. Ivan shook his head.

" 'I know that old Sufi tale very well, sir. When I arrive at my destination, death is there waiting, saying that I had come sooner than he had expected. An extremely cynical story, if you take into consideration the masses of fear that we drag along all the way through this life. Extremely cynical.'

"He looked desperate. 'And what certainty have you that the end, that death, will arrive on the fourteenth day? You sound very much like this much discussed and notorious Jonah.'

" 'I am he, Ivan.'

"You must realize, my friend, that I was, that I still am exhausted. Since my arrival in Nineveh I had given my task everything humanly possible. I dare not make null and void that which I have done by looking at the other side of the coin, to listen to other voices, to the counter-argument. The other side is of no importance to YHWH. What applies in this case is simply the Kabbalistic precept of *Gevurah*, the *Sefirah* of stern judgment.

"Ivan stood up without drinking his wine. I said goodbye. His hand was icy cold, he said nothing, he walked away and disappeared among the crowds on the pavement.

"I could have commanded him to remain seated, implanted other thoughts and feelings in the poor man. It was a simple, even an automatic procedure. But would it have made any sense? Many people had died as a prelude to my coming, many more have died since my arrival. Would one solitary old man affect the totality? What is the value of a single hair on the head of a man who is fast growing bald?

"I signaled the waiter and ordered a glass of schnapps. I tossed the whole lot in the back of my throat and could feel my eyes smarting with tears. I took out my handkerchief and wiped my eyes. I told myself it was due to the potent spirits, the fire that burned inside of me.

"I was boundlessly sad and depressed. I took Ivan's visiting card lying in front of me and looked at the address, then asked the waiter where it was. The old gentleman is a regular customer, he said, he always comes at this hour for his customary sundowner, he never skips a tip, but he did so today.

"I gave the waiter a treble tip, took the card and walked in the direction in which the waiter had intimated the address was. On the way I stopped a city policeman and asked him to accompany me; I feared that something serious had happened at this address.

"The front door was not locked. We found him in the bathroom. Ivan had used an old-style cutthroat razor and severed his jugular veins with one mighty stroke. They must have gushed like fountains — the bath and white-tiled floor were covered with a glistening red carpet. An unusual amount of blood for such a pale old man, I thought.

"I could not understand this violence, almost as if a samurai had decapitated his friend with a single stroke in *seppuku*. An act of defiance? Ivan was so filled with fear, he wished to drive out death with a single stroke. Does not death live next door to survival?

"I will pay that that I have promised.

"Shalom,

"Jona ben-Amittai.

"PS The style and sentiment expressed in the letter, I find on rereading it, is timid and slightly oldfashioned, somewhat like nineteenth-century Russian fictional confessions. How strange. I wonder where it comes from."

Translated from the Afrikaans by the author

Mamlambo

Bheki Maseko

Bheki Maseko lives in Phiri, a township of Soweto. He is in his thirties, a factory worker, and is married.

Maseko is a regular writer for Staffrider *magazine. His informal, popular style has won him a wide reading public, and his firsthand knowledge of township life and the workplace make him a powerful communicator of the urban experience. However, Maseko is also familiar with traditional structures and values, and as such can record the ambivalent experience of the South African worker.*

This story first appeared in Staffrider.

Mamlambo is a kind of snake that brings fortune to anyone who accommodates it. One's money or livestock multiplies incredibly.

This snake is available from traditional doctors who provide instructions regarding its exploitation. Certain necessities are to be sacrificed in order to maintain it. Sometimes you may have to sacrifice your own children, or go without a car or clothes. It all depends on the instructions of the doctor concerned.

The duties involved are so numerous that some people tend to forget some of them. A beast must be slaughtered from time to time, and failing to comply with the instructions results in disaster. It is said that this monster can kill an entire family, always starting with the children and leaving its owner for last.

Getting rid of this fortune snake is not an easy task when one has had enough of luck and sacrificing. Some say a beast must be slaughtered, then the entire carcass must be enfolded with the skin and thrown away. This is done in the presence of an indigenous doctor who performs the necessary ritual to the end.

Someone will come along, pick up a shiny object, and Mamlambo is his. There are many things said about this monster.

143

Here is an account of how Sophie acquired Mamlambo and what happened to her:

Sophie Zikode was a young, pretty, ebony-faced woman with a plump and intact, moderate body. Ever since she came to stay in the Golden City to work as a domestic servant, she never had a steady boyfriend. The man who lasted longer than any other was Elias Malinga, who was from Ermelo. He was the first man she met when she came to Johannesburg and he was the only man she truly loved.

She was so obsessed with love that she readily abandoned any possessions or habits that Elias disliked. In spite of the priority his children and wife in Ermelo enjoyed, she was still prepared to marry Elias Malinga without the slightest intention of disrupting his marriage during their love affair.

One day, after a quarrel, Elias went away and never came back again. She phoned his place of employment to be told by a friend of Elias that he (Elias) had had enough of her. She never heard from him ever again.

After Elias, Sophie never again had a steady boyfriend. They all deserted her after two or three months. But it no longer hurt. The only name that haunted her day and night was Elias.

Ever since Elias left her she had never loved anybody else. All she wanted now was a husband she could be loyal to. But she just could not find one. Then along came Jonas, a tall, well-built Malawian who was much more considerate than any of the other men.

For the first time in her young life a thought came into her mind: She must consult a traditional doctor for help. She wanted to keep Jonas forever. She must see Baba Majola first thing in the morning.

The following morning Sophie visited Baba Majola, who was a street cleaner. The old man listened sympathetically to her problem while he swept rubbish out of a gutter. He told her to return at four in the afternoon. Sophie was there on time.

Baba Majola gave her some smelly, sticky stuff in a bottle. He told her to rub her whole body with it before the boyfriend came, and to put it under the pillow when they sleep. The poor girl agreed amicably.

She did exactly as she had been told to do. She felt guilty as the atmosphere became tense in the little room.

They ate in silence as the clock on the small table ticked away, disturbing the deep silence. Jonas was not his usual self today. He was quiet in a strange manner.

They were sleeping for some minutes when Jonas felt something peculiar under the pillow. It felt cold and smooth.

"Sophie, Sophie," he called, shaking her gently. "What is this under the pillow?"

Sophie had felt the strange object soon after they had climbed into bed. But she had been scared to ask Jonas what it was.

"I don't know," she replied, pretending to be sleepy. "Switch on the light, let's have a look."

With a trembling hand Jonas fumbled for the switch. "Gosh, what a big snake!"

Jonas was the first to jump out of bed. Sophie followed. They fiddled with the door until it was open and ran into the brightly-lit street.

Semi-naked, they knocked at the servant's room of a house in the neighborhood to wake up a friend of Sophie's. Sophie's friend was very stunned to find them in that manner.

Quickly they explained the situation and together they went back to Sophie's room. Through the window they could see the snake, lying across the bed. Sophie was very scared, but Jonas—Christ!—Jonas, he could hardly speak.

Realizing that things were bad, Sophie decided to tell the whole truth. She told Jonas she did it "because I wanted to keep you forever." They decided to go to a traditional doctor who stayed a few streets away.

They knocked and, after waiting awhile, the doctor answered. He opened the door but quickly closed it again. They heard him say: "Wait outside there. I can sense something melancholy."

They could hear the indigenous doctor saying something in a strange language, and the smell of burning muti came to them in full force.

He began to moan, as if speaking to gods in a faraway land. He then opened the door and inquired what their problem was. Sophie retold her story.

"Oh, my girl. What you have in your room is Mamlambo," he shuddered.

"What? Mamlambo!" cried Sophie. "Oh God, what have I done to deserve such punishment? What big sin have I committed to be punished in this manner?" Tears streamed continuously down her cheeks.

"Crying won't solve the problem, my dear girl," intervened the doctor in broken Zulu. "The only solution is to get rid of the snake, and I need your cooperation to do that. I'll give you a suitcase to take to your room, and the snake . . ."

"What!" cried Sophie. "Must I go back to that room again? Oh, no, not me, I'm sorry."

"The choice is yours, my girl. You either keep it or get rid of it. The sooner the better, because if you don't it will be with you wherever you go. It is your snake. The witch doctor was tired of it, so he transferred it to you. So you are duty bound to transfer it to someone else or keep it."

"Transfer it to someone else! Oh no! Why don't we throw it into the river or somewhere?" Sophie grumbled.

"You can't. Either you transfer it, or you keep it. Do you want my help or what?" asked the doctor in a businesslike manner.

"Yes." Sophie agreed, in a tired voice, eyeing her friend, Sheila, and the timid Jonas, with the "I hate to do it" look.

The traditional doctor took a large suitcase from the top of the wardrobe, put some muti inside and burnt it. He moaned again, as if speaking to gods they could not see. He chanted on in this manner for what seemed like ages.

"You'll take this suitcase to your room and put it next to your bed. The snake will roll itself into the suitcase." He saw that Sophie was doubtful so he added: "It's your snake. It won't harm you." He continued: "You will then go to a busy place and give it to someone. That you will figure out for yourself."

They all went back to Sophie's room. The big snake was still there. Having told herself to "come what may," Sophie tiptoed into the room and put the suitcase next to the bed.

Slowly, as if it were smelling something, the snake lifted its head, slid into the suitcase and gathered itself into a neat coil.

Her mind was obsessed with Johannesburg Station, where she would give Mamlambo to someone for good. She walked quickly towards the taxi rank, impervious to the weight of the suitcase.

She did not want to do this to anyone, but she had no option.

Remembering that taxis were scarce after eight, she quickened her pace. She saw a few police cars patroling the area, probably because of the high rate of housebreaking, she thought.

It was while she was daydreaming at the bus stop that she realized the car at the traffic lights was a patrol car headed in her direction. Should she drop the suitcase and run? But they had already seen her and she would not get far. How will she explain the whole thing to the police? Will they believe her story? The news will spread like wildfire that she's a witch! What would Elias think of her?

"What are you doing here at this time?" asked the passenger policeman.

"I'm waiting for a taxi, I'm going to the station," answered Sophie, surprised that her voice was steady.

"We don't want to find you here when we come back," commanded the policeman, eyeing the suitcase. The car screeched away.

She was relieved when the taxi appeared. The driver loaded the suitcase in the boot asking what was so heavy. She simply told him it was groceries.

There were two other passengers in the taxi who both got off before the taxi reached the city.

"Are you going to the station?" inquired the driver inquisitively.

"No, I'm going to the bus terminus," Sophie replied indifferently.

"I know you are going to the station and I'm taking you there," insisted the man.

"You can't take me to the station," said Sophie, indignant. "I'm going to Main Street, next to the bus terminus."

Ignoring her, he drove straight to the station, smiling all the way. When they reached the station he got out of the car and took the suitcase from the boot.

Sophie paid him and gestured that she wanted her suitcase. But the man ignored her.

"To which platform are you going? I want to take you there."

"I don't want your help at all. Give me my suitcase and leave me alone," she urged, beginning to feel real hot under the collar.

"Or are you going to the luggage office?" mocked the man, going towards the brightly-lit office.

Sophie was undecided. Should she leave the suitcase with this man and vanish from the scene? Or should she just wait and see what happened? What was this man up to? Did he know what was in the suitcase, or was he simply inquisitive? Even if she bolted, he would find her easily. If only she had brought someone with her!

Suddenly she was overwhelmed by anger. Something told her to take her suitcase from the man by force. He had no business to interfere in her affairs. She went straight into the office, pulled the suitcase from between the man's legs and stormed out.

Stiff-legged, she walked towards the station platform, feeling eyes following her. She zigzagged through the crowds, deaf to the pandemonium of voices and music blaring from various radios. She hoped the taxi driver wasn't following her but wouldn't dare look back to see.

"Hey you, girl! Where do you think you're going?" It was the voice of the taxi driver.

She stopped dead in her tracks, without turning. She felt a lump in her throat and tears began to fall down her cheeks. She was really annoyed. Without thinking, she turned and screamed at the man.

"What do you want from me? What on earth do you want?"

With his worn-out cap tipped to the right and his hands deep in his khaki dustcoat pocket, the smiling man was as cool as ever. This angered Sophie even more.

"You are running away and you are trying to erase traces," challenged the taxi driver indifferently, fingering his cap time and again.

"What's the matter?" asked a policeman, who had been watching from a distance.

"This man has been following me from the bus rank and is still following me. I don't know what he wants from me," cried Sophie.

"This woman is a liar. She boarded my taxi and she's been nervous all the way from Kensington. I suspect she's running away from something. She's a crook," emphasized the taxi driver looking for approval at the crowd that had gathered around them.

"You are a liar! I never boarded your taxi and I don't know you. You followed me when I left the bus rank." Sophie wept, tears running freely down her cheeks.

"Let her open the suitcase—let's see what's inside." Sheepish Smile went for the suitcase.

"All right. All right." The policeman intervened. "Quiet, everybody. *I* do the talking now. Young man," he said, "do you know this woman?"

"I picked her up at Kens . . ."

"I say, do you know her?"

"Yes, she was in my taxi . . ."

"Listen, young man," said the policeman, beginning to get angry. "I'm asking you a straightforward question and I want a straightforward answer. I'm asking you for the last time now. I-say-do-you-know-this-woman?" He pointed emphatically at Sophie.

"No, I don't know her," replied Sheepish Smile reluctantly, adjusting his cap once again.

"Did she offend you in any manner?"

"No," he replied, shamefaced.

"Off you go, then. Before I arrest you for public disturbance," barked the policeman, pointing in the direction from which the man had come. Then he turned to Sophie.

"My child, go where you are going. This rascal has no business to interfere in your affairs."

Relieved, she picked up her suitcase, thanked the policeman and walked towards platform fourteen, as the policeman dispersed the people and told them to mind their own business.

* * *

Platform fourteen. The old lady grew impatient. What's holding him? she thought. She came bimonthly for her pension pay and each time the taxi dropped them on the platform, her son would go to the shop to buy food for the train journey home. But today he was unusually long in coming back.

These were the thoughts going through her mind when a young, dark, pretty woman approached her.

"Greetings, Gogo," said the young woman, her cheeks producing dimples.

"Greetings, my child," answered the old lady, looking carefully at this young pretty woman who was a symbol of a respectable makoti.

"When is the train to Durban departing?" asked Sophie, consulting her watch.

"At ten o'clock."

The conversation was very easy with the loquacious old lady. The cars and people on the platform increased.

"Excuse me, Gogo, can you look after my luggage while I go to the shop? I won't be long."

"O.K., O.K., my child," agreed the old lady, pulling the suitcase nearer.

She quickly ascended the steps. By the time she reached the top she was panting. To her surprise and dismay, here was Elias shaking hands with another man. They chatted like old friends who hadn't seen each other for a long time.

Sophie stood there confused. Fortunately Elias's back was turned on her and the place was teeming with people. She quickly recovered and mingled with the crowd. Without looking back she zigzagged through the crowded arcade.

She was relieved when she alighted from the bus in Kensington. She had nearly come face-to-face with Elias Malinga. Fortunately he was cheerfully obsessed with meeting his friend. She was scared all the way to the bus terminus, but more so for the taxi driver. Now something else bothered her. The old lady? Who was she? Sophie felt as if she knew, or had at least seen the woman somewhere. She searched into the past, but couldn't locate it.

What will happen to the suitcase? Will the old lady take it?

And Elias? What was he doing there? She suddenly felt hatred for Elias. He had never pitied her, and it was worse when she phoned his place of employment, to be a laughingstock to his friends. She became

149

angry with herself to have allowed her life to be dominated by love that brought no peace or happiness, while Jonas was there giving all the love and kindness he possessed. For the first time she fell in love with Jonas. But will he still accept her? If only he could ask her to marry him. She would not do it for the sake of getting married. She would be marrying a man she truly loved.

Jonas and the Nyasa doctor were seated on the bed when Sophie came in. Sophie was surprised to see all Jonas's belongings packed up.

"Are you leaving me, Jonas?" Sophie whispered in a shaky voice.

"No, darling. My father wants me back in Malawi because he can no longer handle the farm by himself. And I would be very happy to take you along with me."

"But I don't have a passport. How can I go to Malawi without one? And besides, my parents won't know where I am."

"We are in fact not going today. We will negotiate with your parents next Saturday," said Jonas, pointing at the doctor who sat quietly on the bed, nodding time and again.

*　　*　　*

It was a cool, sunny Saturday when the doctor took Sophie and Jonas to Jan Smuts Airport in his small car. Sophie was going to board a plane for the first time in her life. Jonas had made many trips to see his ailing father, who wanted him to take over the farm. For a long time Jonas had ignored his father's pleas for him to take over the running of the farm. But now he had finally relented.

Through the car window Sophie watched the people moving leisurely in and out of shops. The trees lining Bezuidenhout Valley Avenue and the flowers in the Europeans' gardens looked beautiful and peaceful as they fluttered in the cool morning air. It was as if she were seeing this part of Johannesburg for the first time.

They couldn't identify Baba Banda (the doctor) among the crowd that stood attentively on the balcony, as they stared through the plane window.

The flying machine took off and the crowd waved cheerfully. Sophie felt that it was taking her away from the monster that had terrified her a few days ago.

The buildings below became smaller as the airplane went higher, until the undersurface turned into a vast blue sky.

She wondered where, in one of those houses, was Mamlambo. But could never guess that it had become the property of Elias. Yes, after Elias had chatted to his friend, he went back to his mother.

"Whose case is this, Mama?"

"A young girl's. She asked me to look after it for her until she returned. But I don't know what's happened to her."

"Well, if she doesn't come back, I'll take it."

"Struggle Continues" / linocut by Hamilton Budaza.

Rhodes:
Some Women
Photographed

Text and photographs by Paul Alberts

Paul Alberts, born in 1946 in Pretoria, spent his youth in Botswana and the Northern Trans-vaal. He has worked as a writer and photographer on various South African newspapers, including a five-year period on the arts page of Die Burger *in Cape Town. In 1975 he turned to free-lance photography and in 1981 he founded The Gallery Press, dedicated to the publishing of social-documentary photography. Alberts lives in Cape Town and works as a free-lance photojournalist and as a director of the Gallery Press.*

Albert's photographs are published in major magazines in South Africa and overseas. He has published four photographic books, and his work is also included in South Africa: The Cordoned Heart, *edited by Omar Badsha (Cape Town: Gallery Press, 1986). Since 1975 Alberts has exhibited extensively in Cape Town and Johannesburg.*

It only takes about ten minutes to walk from one side of Rhodes to the other. The name first given by white people to the village was Rossville. The name first given to the village by black people was Zakhele; they still refer to it by that name. In English, freely translated, Zahlela means "to build with your own hands."

In the community there are five white people. If one adds to that the members of the South African Police who are there not out of choice, that number increases to eight (this includes the wife of the officer in charge). And if one adds to that figure the Drakensberg Divisional Council representative and his wife, then the community can be said to have ten white members. The small, one-star hotel in Rhodes caters mostly to passing tourists and the local farmers who gather in the hotel's historical bar.

There are two general-dealer stores in the village. The owners do not get on with each other and their feud is a blessing for the blacks because it tends to keep the prices of goods down.

I regard myself as living at Rhodes, but at present I do not count as a permanent inhabitant because smoke does not billow from the chimney of my house every day of the year.

In the community there are roughly five hundred black people. They live in the location on the hill. They are mostly women and children, since the men of the community are usually working in distant cities. Amongst the men that remain, there is a high incidence of alcohol abuse, out of which the hotel retail liquor sales make a profitable business.

These are some of the women of Rhodes. They are amongst the most dignified and courageous people that I have encountered in my life. They endure a great deal of suffering and deprivation, and they must make do within difficult limitations.

Theirs is the lot of millions of black women in this country.

Four Poems

Donald Parenzee

Donald Parenzee, born in 1948, grew up and was educated in District Six, a region on the edge of Cape Town city which was deliberately and systematically demolished after the introduction of the Group Areas legislation. Both of his parents were factory workers.

In the late sixties and early seventies, Parenzee studied architecture at the University of Cape Town, where he first became involved with democratic cultural organizations. He now teaches architecture at the Peninsula Technikon just outside of Cape Town. Because of his interests in design and in language, Parenzee has moved increasingly towards working in an interdisciplinary way. He is writing with less of a commitment to publishing and more of a commitment to performance. This is also an expression of his belief in a need to broaden and deepen a cultural and political front in South Africa. His one volume of poetry, Driven To Work, *was published by Ravan Press in 1985; these poems are from that collection.*

An Apparent Loss

Lighting the cigarette the man
cupped his hand around the flame,
held it like a world in his fleshy palm.

I watched, said nothing, the little world
flared up, paled and was gone.

For the rest of the night I tried to find it
with whispers, low shouts, songs of love,
extracts from profound texts. Analyses.

Some time, at dawn, I stretched out a hand
and found him there, not yet asleep.

Interview

for Megan, at ten years

At his home in the brilliant area,
casually slung between the parked cars
vacant on the peaceful driveway,
I pacify my indecision, stride

forward, press the bell; the room
invites like a lounge, another future
colleague who will also live like this
after the first red flush of discomfort.

The quiet, efficient public servant
tactfully takes my coat, my brief life
spreads its soft cloth
on the carpet: qualifications,

salary scales, fringe benefits;
ghostly pleats, tucks and hems
are planned for a new voice
in the college body politic.

Only to listen, perform a little snap
handshake and back out
into the warm suburban sun
scratching my itchy ignition finger

and be shaking again with the honest ecstasy
of our city's natural beauty,
spreading my weekend pleasures
guiltily through the week.

But your arms, as subtle as paper chains, fall
in the minutes before you leave
into sleep, lightly from my shoulders,
trusting that I shall never run, never desert to freedom.

And this interviewer, his childsface
distorted with horrific, secret lust,
I shall repay with portraits
of truths in children's minds.

Woodcut by Cecil Skotnes.

Pain Isn't Something

Pain isn't something
to be enjoyed;
only the torturer
sees it that way.

The politicians of our day
aren't sadists either;
our pain is something
they prefer not to see.

Therefore some see logic
in suffering publicly
even if nobody
applauds the eccentric

who feels his pain
like a favorite toy.
The manufacturer finds no real joy
in pouring products down the drain;

our poverty is necessary
to keep his prices alive.
Therefore some say thrive
on tragedy, anarchy

but they forget
the torturer's pleasure.

In the Morgue

Cold, cold the body at last
forgets its motherhood:

the sensitive child who was
meant to be gentle forever

begins his raging: not the first
metal drawer nor the last

stone eyes to be seen encased,
nor the mutilated

parent, but harsh
white light and coffin prices

press the condemnation
through to adulthood.

Three Poems

Kelwyn Sole

Born in 1951, Kelwyn Sole completed his schooling in Johannesburg, and subsequently obtained a B.A. with honors from the University of the Witwatersrand and an M.A. from the School of Oriental and African Studies in London. He has worked as a teacher in Botswana, an educationalist and free-lance journalist in Johannesburg, and was an editor of Donga. Sole also worked for SACHED, where he was involved in designing and writing an African History course. He is at present working on a Ph.D. on black South African literature, and is teaching at the University of Cape Town.

Sole worked for the Council of Churches, Namibia until he was deported in 1980 under the Undesirable Aliens Act. In 1976 he had his passport taken away by the South African authorities, and has still not had it returned.

Sole has had critical essays published in the journal English in Africa, and the South African Labour Bulletin. An essay is due to be published in Research in African Literatures. His poetry has appeared in Donga, New Classic and Staffrider. Ravan Press will be publishing his first collection of poetry within the next year.

Appointment

listen quickly
I can't talk for long
the lines are nearly down
don't trust me
from here to eternity

what was that I can't hear

164

I said

I can't hear
your voice is
unsound where are you
other than here

I want to tell you
blissfully I'd stay
with you forever
but

I said
the moonlit beach
in the tall forest
under the stars
forever

can't hear

I said

The Sunlight Has Moved

The sunlight has moved
to that other place where we don't live
either. Tasks of life

seem redundant now, drowning kittens,
weeding the lawn, the yellow dust
of pollen useless on your hand
after you have crushed a flower.

Listen, she says, a tape
I bought can play
our own voices back to us.
We move inside from room to room, heads cocked,
entranced. Magnetically
our feet squeak the thickening carpet.

Her head bobs in pleasure
like a lemon in a glass:
the room tips as I drink
around her.
The air bubbles, smothers.

Each day the horizons march closer.

As We Stop Loving

As we stop loving the window
admits buildings, bald and jagged,
that loom over us. Retrograde Orion
fades towards the west
wheeling, wheeling —

a clotted sky
full of the unremoved reek
of chemicals hangs
from a nail above our heads.
You turn

away from me
spattered by the avatism
of moonlight, now choked with glass,
refracting through your body.
The globes of your buttocks
themselves rise like waning moons.

Unknown, in you, by us
atoms begin to nucleate.

I shudder: place
a thin-boned hand in yours
seeking comfort. Plead
that we, just us, may not
like all the others too
be dying?

How do I love you?

Let me count the ways —

in the caverns under your flesh
where the blood sea surges, where mucus
thinly pearls, where the bones

rub and jig
as you move

a tiny cell, future
made of our love, no longer needful,
opens its fish-mouth forming
to laugh at me.

Eight Photographs

Omar Badsha

Omar Badsha started out as an artist, and won a number of awards for his painting. It was only in 1976 that he turned to photography and began documenting the social conditions and political upheaval of South Africa over the past decade.

A founding member of Afrapix, a photographers' collective (see page 120), Badsha has been involved in a number of significant photographic projects and exhibitions. He is the editor of the recent publication of the Gallery Press, South Africa: The Cordoned Heart, *commissioned by the Second Carnegie Inquiry into Poverty and Development in Southern Africa (1986).*

Textile workers on strike. Clemont Stadium, 1981.

A minute before police charged demonstrators protesting the assassination of United Democratic Front executive member Victoria Mxenge. Durban, August 1985. Mxenge was the defense attorney in the 1986 treason trial of five UDF leaders (the state later dropped all charges). She was gunned down by unknown assailants in her own driveway. Before her death, her husband, African National Congress attorney Griffith Mxenge, was killed by a hit squad.

Inkatha officials meeting in Inanda, 1982. (Inkatha is a Zulu organization less opposed to present South African institutions than UDF and ANC.)

Riot police dispersing crowd after the shooting of UDF (support) youth by Inkatha official. Berea Stadium, May Day 1986.

At mass rally to launch the militant trade-union federation COSATU. Kings Park Stadium, Durban, 1985.

"Shack lord" ("slum landlord") and Former Kwa Zulu M.P. Rogers Ngcobo. Meeting, Inanda District, 1982.

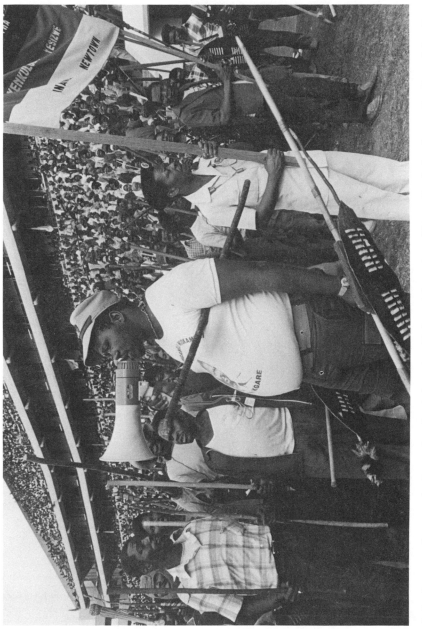

Inkatha members at the launch of a right-wing Zulu trade union. Kings Park Stadium, Durban, May Day 1986.

Meeting to commemorate the death by assassination of community leader
and ANC activist Msizi Dube. Lamontville, 1985

Two Excerpts from *Emergency Poems*

Keith Gottschalk

Keith Gottschalk was born in Cape Town in 1946. He taught for a number of years at the University of Cape Town, and now lectures in the Political Science Department at the University of the Western Cape.

Gottschalk has had his poems published in South Africa in literary magazines such as Contrast, New Coin, Staffrider *and* Upstream. *His work has also been published in the* Minnesota Review *in the United States, as well as in* Breakthru *in Britain, and* Transition *in Uganda. Several of his poems have been translated into German and are available in anthologies in both Germanies.*

Chairperson of the Civil Rights League, a human rights organization, and a member of the United Democratic Front, Gottschalk frequently performs his poetry at political rallies and concerts to raise funds for families of detainees. He was detained in solitary confinement for a period in 1985.

These poems are excerpted from a larger work about Gottschalk's prison experience, written for performance, hence the intercom voice between poems.

First Night

on my first night
i saw the moon.
Dennis Brutus only saw the stars
once in three years;
Breyten Breytenbach only saw the moon
once in seven years.

but on my first night,
through the six window slits of cell 250,
through the jailyard floodlights which lash

five orange weals on the left wall,
five orange weals on the right wall,
the moon anoints me with silver photons.

six silver banners,
night parade, half-mast,
slow march across the wall.

(intercom): *Luitenant van Greunen, kontak beheer**

---

*kontak beheer: contact Control

War Memorial

they probably don't know it yet,
but this place
has a calli-graphic,
a sort of war memorial,
to Jeremy Cronin
(marxist, seven years),
Breyten Breytenbach
(buddhist, seven & a half years).

go past the reception desk
graced by two delicious monsters,
manned by two undelicious monsters;
enter the contact visitors' room,
look at the wall on your right—
I mean the new Regulasie 4(f):

"no letter
containing a poem
shall be forwarded
from a prisoner
to the outside,
or from outside
to a prisoner."

(intercom): *Bewaarder Niemand, kom na dienskombuis**

---

*"Warder Nobody, come to the staff kitchen."

Poem

Hein Willemse

Hein Willemse, born in 1957, is a senior lecturer in Afrikaans and comparative South African literature at the University of the Western Cape. He is a member of Vakalisa, a progressive Western Cape artists' collective that compiles and publishes a wide range of new artistic materials, from poetry to graphics. Vakalisa's purpose is, in part, to give art a community base, by holding exhibitions in local halls instead of galleries and museums.

Willemse is important as a poet, as an academic and as a critic of Black Afrikaans culture. His first collection of poetry, Angsland (Land of Anguish) *was published in 1981, and a second volume,* Die Lê van die Land (The Lie of the Land) *is due to come out this year. He is co-editor of* Swart Afrikaans Skrywers (Black Afrikaans Writers, 1986) *and* Die Trojaanse Perd (The Trojan Horse, 1986), *a document which analyzes and records a notorious episode in which a young boy was shot and killed by police troopers.*

the stormtroopers are in the streets
the poets have buried their metaphors
the preachers are exiled prophets
the young boys are walled in
the young girls are violated

the stormtroopers are in the streets
the women wash dishes with their tears
the old women's knitting needles are broken spears
the men smash jugs of wine against panzers
the old men forget their front-stoop newspapers

the stormtroopers reign in the streets
they lob schoolboys from armored car to armored car
the streets are not empty
the stormtroopers reign in the streets

the writers die in exile
the preachers call to their gods in vain
the raped prime their barrels with thunder

the stormtroopers are in the streets
the youths carry spears

the stormtroopers are castrated in the streets
the girls carry spears

the stormtroopers are walled in
the children are in the streets

Translated from the Afrikaans by David Bunn and the author

"Khayelitsha" / linocut by David Hlongwane.

The Representative

Achmat Dangor

Achmat Dangor, born in 1948 in Johannesburg, was an influential member of the writers' group, Black Thoughts, and was himself banned for five years from 1973–78.

His work is interesting in its depiction of class conflicts within township communities, and also for its examination of the impact of apartheid on sexual relationships. His collection of short stories, Waiting for Leila (Johannesburg: Ravan, 1981), was recipient of the Mofolo-Plomer Prize. He has recently published an anthology of poetry, Bulldozer (Johannesburg: Ravan, 1983), and is at present working on a novel, from which the following excerpt is taken.

Soon after young Georgie DaCosta left the place they called Z-town and crossed the border, the rains stopped. A severe drought spread across the land. Newly planted crops withered in the fields, dams were drying up and dust storms that blinded people with fine red silt blew across what was once green and fertile cropland.

There were special days of prayer, when the country came to a standstill, while people filled the churches and prayed for rain. But the dry period carried on, and the drought spread, until there were dark whispers of mass starvation. Some said that God had brought a curse to the country for its "sinful ways." In their sermons, priests urged people to return to the ways of God.

In our township, very little else had changed. It was winter and the wind, merciless and dry because of the drought, drove clouds of white dust from the mine dumps through the streets.

And a new representative had been sent by the "Colored Parliament" to administer the township in place of Joseph Fischer, who had fled after his office had been attacked with petrol bombs.

Pieter Kock sat outside his house and watched Mr. Samson, the new representative, drag his luggage into the township office. Two armed soldiers stood guard, leaning leisurely against the walls of the office, protected from the wind by an unfurled canvas awning.

Samson was a slender man, with a dark, gleaming face. His curly hair was piled all onto one side, in the fashion colonial artists had created for Christianized slaves in the previous century.

"A real Hotnot-god!" Pieter muttered.

But the thing that struck him most was Samson's mouth. He had thin lips that pursed into a faint smile you would expect to see on the face of a wanton young woman. It seemed cruel and unnatural on the otherwise rugged face of Paulus Samson.

Pieter went indoors where he found his wife Sarah chatting with Elsa Da Costa.

"Morning, Elsa. Have you heard anything from Georgie?" he asked.

There was a flicker of fear on the woman's face.

"Nothing. Do you know, Pieter, the police are worrying me. The questions they ask me! How do I know where Georgie is? Ai, the things that young people get into today!" Elsa said.

"Ah well, they are doing what they believe in," Pieter said gently.

"Believe in! My foot! All that they are doing is making trouble for us. Joseph Fischer was a kind man, even if he worked for the guvverment. What do you think we will get now? Why did they throw petrol bombs at poor Mr. Fischer? To get someone worse in his place!" Sarah said harshly.

"They are young and don't think. But they *are* our children," Elsa said.

"Yes, look at the mess Georgie's got you into. You lost your job at the council, and poor Mario has to work all by himself. And he is ill on top of it all," Sarah answered.

The two were sisters, and Elsa, the younger one, accepted Sarah's harsh words without offense. That was her way of talking, anyway.

"Stop going on like a steam engine with nowhere to go," Pieter said. "Rather use all that steam and make us some tea."

"You must call *me* a steam engine! Ever since he retired from the railways he is full of cheek. But it does not work with me," Sarah responded good-naturedly, in spite of her harsh tone of voice.

"I was not retired. Only managers get retired. I was fired. 'Retrenchment,' they called it," Pieter said, seating himself by the window.

"It was because you joined the trade union. You want to mos* show you also know something about politics. A damn politician. All you got was a place in the unemployment lines. You know, Elsa, he should be

---

*mos: just

183

glad that his children are grown up and that he has only me to feed," Sarah said.

But Pieter did not respond; he was staring intently out of the window.

"You know, if something is happening in this township, trust Mr. Busybody Kock to know about it. Who is that, Pieter?" Sarah asked, looking over his shoulder.

"The new representative," he answered.

"Oh, he looks like a nice man," Sarah said.

"Everybody is nice, to you. Even the devil. And, Jurre,* you'll talk him dead too. Where is that tea we spoke about?" Pieter said, without taking his eyes off the activity outside the township office.

Workmen in gray overalls that bore the municipal emblem were erecting what appeared to be a large notice-board. Samson, his hands on his hips, was issuing instructions to the workmen. The two soldiers were still there, leaning casually on their rifles. In a little while the wooden structure, with two supporting pillars, was complete. The speed with which the work was done, and the sturdy way it seemed to have been designed, astonished Pieter. It also pleased his craftsman's eye to see such professional workmanship. But still Samson remained busy. Soon the notice-board was covered with white sheets of paper. There was one sheet that bore large letters, but Pieter's eyes were not that good anymore, and he could not read the words.

A small crowd gathered around the notice-board, peering at the notices with narrowed, intense eyes. Many of them were illiterate and could not understand what the notices said. Pieter saw Reginald Baaitjies scuttle across the empty lot towards the church, raising small clouds of dust in his wake.

"Where's Reggie going to?" Sarah asked as she handed Pieter the cup of tea.

"Where else? Off to see the priest. People in this township don't even go to the toilet without Father MacNally's permission," Pieter answered.

"Don't be disrespectful, Pieter. We all have our beliefs," Sarah admonished him.

"Listen, whatever it is that has made Reggie go running like a rat to the priest, I don't see what the priest can do about it," Pieter said. "We can't pray ourselves out of trouble."

Pieter finished the tea, gulping down the hot liquid with gasps of breath drawn between his teeth. He walked towards the door.

"Pieter, please—don't get involved," Sarah said.

Jurre is a mild expletive.

He smiled at her, and his craggy, somber face lit up with the expression of childlike innocence she had seen before.

Father MacNally awoke, trying to dispel the fragments of the dream he was striving to escape from. His eyes searched the darkness of the room, attempting to focus on familiar objects, but there, on the mantelpiece above the fireplace sat the tormentor of his dreams. A huge ape with grotesque, yellowed teeth bared, sat tugging at an enormous, rigid penis.

Father MacNally shut his eyes and prayed, and when his soothed mind felt ready to allow him to reopen them, the apparition was gone. He got out of bed, nevertheless, with a premonition of sorrow. He drew open the curtains, letting in the frail afternoon sun. The wind blew in cold gusts against the window, leaving a fine deposit of dust upon the windowsill.

How dry and desolate everything had become. The garden outside the vestry had shriveled, and even the tree, a once-magnificent, gigantic oak, had been stripped bare of all its foliage.

He saw Reginald Baaitjies running across the veld towards the church, raising clouds of dust behind him.

"Perhaps it is time to return to green Ireland to die," Father MacNally thought.

The doorbell rang, sharply, urgently.

"Hush, hush now, Reginald, calm yourself. You look like the devil is after you," Father MacNally said as he opened the door.

"Father, there is a new representative. New regulations. A curfew," Reginald gasped, still out of breath.

"Calm yourself, Reggie, and then we shall go and see," MacNally answered, his authority regained.

Paulus Samson stood at the window and observed the crowd milling around the notice-board. Some stared with blind, illiterate eyes at the bright pieces of paper. Even those who could read were puzzled by the pronouncements he had pinned up. But now was not the right time to go out and explain the rules and regulations to them. He would wait until the wind had become unbearable, and his arrival would provide a respite from the cold.

And until the priest was there. And some of the others whom the Security Police said were suspected of having incited the petrol-bomb attack on his predecessor.

He stared out at the crisscross of dusty streets, at the houses without electricity. The familiar, heavy curtains so laden with dust that they did not stir, even when buffeted by the ferocious wind. How many of the residents would recognize him? He too had grown up there, snot-nosed, with running sores on his skin.

"I am back here because it is my duty. And my destiny," he said resolutely to himself. From a house across the road a man emerged. He was tall and powerfully built, with short, graying hair. He had the patriarchal appearance that immediately commanded respect. Samson recognized him as the kind of man, so typical of this community, that retained the respect of everyone, even if he were a thief or murderer. Or a communist. He watched as the crowd stood back from the notice-board and allowed the man to step up and read the notices.

Now, from across the veld came another commotion. Samson saw the priest, Father MacNally, walking briskly towards the office, his hands clasped behind his back. The priest's face was pinched pink by the icy wind. Behind him shuffled Reginald Baaitjies, as if attached by an invisible chain to the priest.

Samson opened the door and walked towards the notice-board, just as Father MacNally reached the muttering crowd. Samson observed Pieter Kock quietly walking back to his house, not heeding the many calls from people to stay "and help with this issue."

By now the wind was howling, and already the township dogs were slinking away into the quickening dusk to search for shelter from the coming night.

Father MacNally, who had quieted the crowd, turned to face Samson.

"Now, Little Moses," MacNally thought, "why don't you just raise your hands and make the wind die down? Perhaps we'll believe in you."

They spoke of it later as a miracle, and called him a sorcerer, a toordenaar. Some regarded him with awe and fear. As Samson reached the crowd, a ripple of muttering erupted. He raised his hand to quieten them, and, miraculously, the wind died down. The clouds of dust settled like blood-reddened snow.

"Why, that's old Emma Samson's grandson—Paulus! Remember? They sent him away to a reformatory!" someone said.

The silence that followed the dying away of the wind remained in the township for quite a while. Pieter Kock listened to the familiar sounds that the screeching wind had muffled for so many days. Worn axes splintered wood for the fires that soon filled the sky with gray, acrid smoke. Cisterns gushed noisily in the backyard toilets. Even the children stayed out longer than usual, despite the bitter cold. He heard their voices echo in the darkness.

Despite the welcome respite from the wind, Piet was filled with foreboding. He had seen men like Samson before. Men with ambition so fierce that it destroyed everything that stood in its way. Pieter tried to recall Samson's family. All that he remembered was an old woman named Emma who died a few years after they had been removed from Albertsville. This Paulus Samson must be a grandson. An orphan who was taken away to be placed in a home. There must be hundreds of them from this township. Orphans who became wards of the state. Very few of them become as powerful as Paulus Samson.

There was a knock on the door. Pieter, somewhat resentful of the intrusion, let in their neighbor, Thomas Peet.

"Good evening, Pieter. Why are you sitting here all alone in the dark?"

"Waiting for Sarah to get back from church," Pieter answered and rose to light the lamp on the table. Thomas offered Pieter a cigarette made of pipe tobacco rolled in brown paper.

"God, Thomas, dried-up old zolls! Is that all you've got to smoke?" Pieter asked gently.

"And that is all we ever going to have until this Mister Representative decides to pay out our pensions," Thomas answered.

The harsh taste of the tobacco burned warmly in Pieter's lungs.

"What do you think of the new representative?" Thomas asked.

Pieter did not answer immediately, but stared contemplatively at the glowing cigarette.

"He is going to give us hell," Pieter said quietly.

"You always think the worst. Anyway, I think things may get better now that one of our own people is in charge," Thomas said.

Is he one of our people? Pieter thought to himself. Same color, yes, and he came from this township. But now he is from a different world. Educated to be different. You could see it in his eyes. He wouldn't stay in this dusty township forever. We are his stepladder to higher things.

"You know, I remember his family in Albertsville. His old man was a drunk, killed himself drinking. But he first killed his wife. Then old Emma brought up this Paulus until she too died. Maybe he'll remember how we suffered. Maybe he won't let us suffer," Thomas said.

Pieter allowed Thomas to ramble on, full of fearful hope and optimism. What else was there for Thomas Peet to do but hope? He was nearing seventy, and had been driven from township to township, from home to home, all his life.

"Do you remember what it was like in Albertsville?" Thomas asked.

Pieter did not answer. He knew that beneath Thomas's cheerful exterior a bitter recollection bubbled, a cauldron of acid that would soon erode his hopefulness.

Yes, Pieter remembered what Albertsville was like. A green and quiet place, narrow tarred streets lined by oak trees. Albertsville had real homes, not the shantytowns and filthy slums that so many people remember now with fondness. And it was ours. We owned it. Until the government called it a "Black spot," and told us to move.

We resisted, signed petitions, stood with placards in the streets. Like fools, without hope of victory. They had weapons. We were only in the right. They moved us, men in gray suits with sharp, blue eyes that burned into our souls.

Pieter remembered the peach tree in the yard where he had sat and sipped beer on Sundays while Sarah was in church. And her gentle admonishment at his "godless" ways, and the bad influence they had on their children. He remembered going back a few years later, and saw another family seated under this tree. A white family to whom the government had given the house. He remembered feeling hatred for the first time in his life.

Thomas had fallen silent, his cigarette dangling from his mouth. He opened the curtains and looked out.

"Hell, Pieter, the fucking wind is blowing again," Thomas said.

It was strange to hear Thomas use such a vulgar expression, but Pieter noticed that there was no bitterness in his voice. Thomas paused at the door.

"Hey, Pieter, do you remember when you got the lot of us to join the Communist Party?" Thomas asked, a mischievous twinkle in his eye.

"That was a long time ago. More than forty years," Pieter answered.

"Yes, that was a long time ago," Thomas said before closing the door behind him.

Pieter watched Thomas hurry through the darkness, the wind driving a cloud of dust, red with new silt it had acquired. Pieter wished that Sarah would come home soon; he felt a weariness overcome him.

"Blerry* church gatherings, talk and pray. And solve nothing."

The streets of the township were quiet, deserted. Dogs stirred in the shadows as he passed, and growled, but his calm, measured footsteps reassured them. This was the quietude that Samson enjoyed. Alone in

---

*Regional pronunciation of "bloody"

the darkness. The bright moonlight bathed the darkened houses in a dusty whiteness.

They sleep in the comfort of their hovels, huddled together like sheep. Warm and smelly refuge, the accidental stroking of a sister's sex. The incestuous claustrophobia of poverty.

I was once like that, an urchin of the ghettoes. Drunken father looming above, overshadowing the light from the lamp. Drunken wrath, the length of a leather strap that whined as it struck our cowering backs.

Believe in the Almighty. Alms for the poor. Soup from soup kitchens, meals on wheels, rotting teeth in the mouth of a smiling nun. We thank you, Lord, for what we are about to receive. The face of God, ikoned upon the wall above our bed. I saw it bleed with tears in the darkness.

You are your own salvation.

He stopped outside the house the "Occupants Register" had identified as being occupied by Mrs. Muriel Meraai, widow, thirty-nine years of age. Four children, none of whom were married. Samson smoothed his narrow mustache before knocking.

There was no reply. The sound of the wind and stirring dogs. Then, bare feet making splashing noises on the stone floor. The light of a candle advanced in the darkness of the house towards the front door.

"Who is it?" a woman's voice called out.

"Samson, Paulus Samson," he answered.

He heard the sounds of numerous latches being undone, and the door opened slowly. A young girl peered out of the darkness at him, the candle held in front of her so that he was visible in the arc of its flickering light.

"Who are you?" the girl asked.

"Is your mother home?" Samson responded.

Another face peered out from behind the heavy curtains.

"God, Janey, can't you see it's the new representative?"

"Open the door!" a woman's voice called out.

The young girl withdrew into the darkness, and her mother, Muriel Meraai, opened the door wide.

"May I come in?" Samson asked. His polite tone was as cold as the wind that blew in through the open door.

"Ma, close the door, everything is blowing away here," voices called from the rear of the house.

"Please, of course," Muriel said and stood aside.

A figure stirred on the floor of what was intended to be the living room.

"Please come to the kitchen, Mr. Samson, you know how it is with children. They know the house is small, but they still bring friends, strays, to come home and sleep over," Muriel continued, out of breath.

"Were you sleeping?" Samson asked.

"No, we were just sitting in the kitchen, having some coffee." Muriel was now speaking loudly, at the top of her voice, in a tone that was obviously intended to be a warning.

Samson heard the sound of scuffling feet and the low murmur of voices. A door shut, followed by an absolute silence.

"I see you've added on a room to the house," Samson said.

"Oh yes. Mr. Fischer, he was here before, he gave us permission," Muriel said.

Samson entered the bedroom, a corner of which was partitioned off by a dark curtain. The room smelled of burnt-out candles, carnality, of unwashed mouths.

He walked to the window, his shoes making crisp sounds on the greasy linoleum carpet. But he could feel the rotting floor underneath. Something made his stomach turn, and he had to suppress his nausea.

He recalled how his grandmother had made many wasted walks to that same blackened window. Nothing had changed. They have chained my memory to poverty. He followed Muriel to the kitchen where he was confronted by the smell of ash in the stove, and the pungency of cheap alcohol. The young girl who had opened the door and a sullen-faced young man sat at one of the long tables that crowded the kitchen.

Muriel, her fear and anxiety masked by an eager, over-friendly manner, introduced Samson to the two young people.

"This is my daughter Janey, the eldest. And this is a friend, John."

Janey nodded her head shyly and looked away. John half rose from his seat and extended a cold limp hand that Samson grasped with equal indifference. Samson's eyes roamed around the crowded kitchen, which was obviously the room most lived in. Unwashed dishes in the sink, and glasses hastily rinsed, were packed face-down on another table. Despite the appearance of chaos, the kitchen had an aura of businesslike order. Samson smiled to himself.

"Is there something wrong?" Muriel asked.

The clock ticked loudly and the fire was dying.

"No. Nothing. I used to live in this house," he said.

"Oh yes, this was Ouma Emmy's house!" Muriel said, relief in her voice. "Mind you, someone else lived here after she died. Can't remember for a moment who it was. Should have seen the mess they left behind. Mr. Fischer was kind to give us permission to fix it up like this," she added hastily.

Samson's nausea had subsided, and he fought to ward off the drug-like effect the smells in the kitchen had on him. I am rid of my past, he said to himself, continuously, almost like someone intoning a prayer.

When at last he spoke again to the fearful and mystified Meraai family, his voice was as cold and authoritative as before.

"Did Mr. Fischer also give you permission to run a shebeen?"* he asked. Muriel's face was perspiring, her eyes downcast.

"I have to make a living, I have to feed three children. Without a husband," Muriel said. Her voice trembled with the anguish of someone quite used to pleading with the authorities, but there was resentment in her eyes, almost scorn, that she should be pleading with someone like Samson. Someone who had come from this township, out of this very house.

Samson was smiling, a distant, detached expression on his face. He would need shebeens, and shebeen owners, like Muriel. They are the best sources of information. He had learnt that in other tours of duty.

"Well, here is a customer, aren't you going to serve me?" he asked.

"What do you drink?" Muriel asked.

"Whiskey," he said, almost wickedly. Township shebeens don't stock whiskey, he thought.

"Water and ice?" Muriel asked. Her voice was triumphant. Mr. Samson had weaknesses after all, she thought.

"Ice nog-all!** You really do it in style, Mrs. Meraai," Samson said mockingly.

Muriel motioned to Janey to get the ice from the fridge, and as she rose from the darkness of the corner in which she was seated, it was, to Samson, like a vision rising from the shadows and the squalor around him.

It was not the rustle of silk, but coarse cotton, lovingly cared for, and worn to a soft and faded smoothness. She was no more than nineteen, and had the dark, virginal look that endures in some women well after the years of experience should have made it fade away. To Samson, it was as if a king from Africa, endowed with extraordinary grace, had penetrated the squalor of the girl's beginnings and planted a magnificent seed. For her beauty was athletic, her face and legs shone with an incandescent health.

---

*shebeen: an illicit liquor store, sometimes associated with prostitution
**nog-all: as well

With a shock Samson realized that he was describing her beauty, in his own mind, as "African," that the health in her blackness was not robust but exquisite. For years he had been taught that anything of "African" origin was base and vulgar. He was mulatto, a "Colored" of mixed parentage. Perhaps it was the dim recollection, suppressed deep within his own memory, of his mother rising from the darkness to bring him something to drink and to comfort him, that so distracted him.

He heard Muriel rambling on about the fridge, that it was only gas-cooled and noisy, and that she hoped that Mr. Samson would bring changes so that they would get electricity. And not be disturbed by the hissing and chugging of that monster, the gas-cooled fridge.

Janey leant over as she handed the glass of whiskey to Samson. He smelled in her hair the same odor of soot and smoke, but her breath was cool, and there was another smell about her that he could not identify, but it heightened his sense of shock.

He gulped down a portion of the whiskey, which brought tears to his eyes. It was obvious to Muriel that Samson was not used to drinking. The vision of Janey disappearing into the darkness swam before his inflamed eyes. The astute Meraai observed the almost hypnotic effect that Janey had on Samson, and motioned to her daughter to leave the room.

Muriel encouraged Samson to have more whiskey, telling him that "she was inside, in the next room." He began to caress Muriel, running his hands over her face, touching her coarse, graying hair. At last, in the darkness of the room she led him to, Samson enjoyed the only pure joy he was capable of: communion with his own kind. Revelry in the shadows of the bizarre. Loins that reeked of unspeakable hunger, savage because it had been so prolonged. Finally, the smell of sweat, and of musty coldness, brought his body to a gasping, shuddering stillness. He lay quietly, watching Muriel's breath form frozen plumes in the air. He raised himself on his elbows and asked Muriel to light a candle. His mind and body were infused with the vision of a tender and vulnerable virgin who had acquired extraordinary sexual gifts in his arms. The stench of phosphorous and scorching tallow invaded his senses as Muriel lit the candle. She smiled at him, revealing in the flickering candlelight a face with only one eye. On a table beside the bed a glass eye floated in a cleansing fluid like some magical submarine animal.

A scream formed in his mouth, but Muriel held her finger to her lips in a gesture of silence towards the children sleeping in the enclosure behind the curtain. He rose and dressed hastily, then stepped out into the icy coldness of the night. The dogs howled and barked, but scampered out of Samson's path as he walked towards his office. He felt cold and desolate.

Samson returned to his quarters filled with shame and dread. He knew that by morning the story of his visit to Muriel Meraai's house, and the hour at which he left, would be spread throughout the township. But he could deal with that. He had dealt with blackmail before. It was the memory of her disgorged eye, and the glass eye that floated so calmly in the liquid by the bedside that disturbed him most. He could not shut his eyes without those distorted visions swarming all over his mind.

He had bathed himself upon his return, scrubbing his body harshly, but still the smell of her perspiration lingered in his nostrils. And oh, the sharp pang in his loins whenever he recalled the throb of her pulsating body beneath him. And above it all loomed the vision of the beautiful young girl, her faded cotton dress, her dark and shining complexion.

After a while, he gave up trying to sleep, and went to the office. He began paging through the Occupants' Register. He ran his finger down the columns, reading the names of various tenants, making a mental note of the names the Security Police had warned him about. There was, of course, the priest, Father MacNally, and someone called Pieter Kock, who had once been a member of the Communist Party and was a known troublemaker.

Finally, he came to the household of Muriel Meraai. Janet Louise, born September 26, 1967. She was only nineteen. He thought of his own mother. What was she like at nineteen? Her young and supple body in the slovenly embrace of a drunken husband. What evil there was in the loins of humans to bring together such beauty and such beastliness!

It was dawn before he shut the book and crawled into bed.

For a while life continued in the township without change. The wind blew mercilessly, and the drought continued. People spread scandal about Samson's visit to Muriel, saying that he had brought *her* long drought to an end. The story was woven and embroidered, until it became a tale of dark perversity. How the one-eyed woman had seduced the powerful new representative, with potions she added to her drink that made men forget her ugliness. For a while the wives in the township forbade their husbands from drinking in her shebeen, but Muriel allowed them to drink on credit, and they were soon forced to return to their custom, even at the risk of their wives' wrath.

Muriel listened to the scandal in silence. In her heart she knew that

193

Samson wanted Janey, indeed he was obsessed with her. She feared what he might do to get her. Samson was an aloof and lonely person who did not socialize with the rest of the residents. Old Juanity Fortuin, whom Samson hired to cook and clean for him, described him as a real queer fellow. He was obsessed with cleanliness and bathed at least twice a day.

He was also a creature of the night, who wandered about the township after dark, nodding curtly to the people he passed in the street. He shunned the community and they shunned him. Often he would stand outside the church and listen to the choir struggle through its practice under the inept guidance of Father MacNally. Whenever his presence became known, the choir would stop singing until he moved on. His nocturnal wanderings, however, always seemed to end up outside Muriel's house. He would stand there for a while, staring intently at the darkened windows. Muriel's customers began to fear him, for he scowled fiercely at them as they entered or left her house. Finally, about a month after he had arrived, he again knocked upon Muriel's door.

When he entered the house a silence fell upon all those seated in the kitchen. Many of the men finished their drinks and left, greeting in low, respectful voices. He sat there in silence, staring at the customers, until they all left. Only Muriel and Janey, who sat in her customary corner, remained. Neither John nor the other children were home.

Very little is known about what happened at the Meraai home that night. Perhaps Muriel conferred with Samson privately for a while, for a passerby later said that he had seen two figures, their whispering pose cast against the curtains by the lamplight.

People saw him leave a short while later, his thin lips pursed in a smile, like that of a cruel woman. Muriel stood at the door, staring at his figure disappear into the shadows. The next morning his car pulled up at the Meraai house, and to the astonishment of the residents, they saw Janey, shy and innocent Janey, the dark flower of the township, hand her suitcase, bulging with her clothes and held together by a leather strap, to Samson who loaded it into the boot* of his car.

"Is Janey going away, Muriel?" Aunt Suze asked.

"Yes, on honeymoon," Muriel answered. Her face was hard and cold.

The township buzzed with the news. Janey and Samson were married and were away on honeymoon. Others were less kind.

"Where the hell do you think you get instant marriages? Instant honeymoons, yes—but not marriages." The crowds that gathered in the backyards to talk about this astonishing event also took the opportunity

---

*boot: trunk

to celebrate a little. After all, life was like that. Full of surprises. You couldn't just talk about your troubles all the time. None of them noticed young John, who had been Janey's boyfriend since childhood, walk away with his head bowed.

The couple returned a few weeks later. Janey was dressed in a smart floral dress, and wore a hat and gloves.

"A real blerry madam," Sarah said.

Samson seemed like a changed person too. He beamed and waved at people, almost like he was part of the township, as if he belonged to the community. They moved into the little house adjoining the office, and hung curtains on the windows. That night they walked to church together, arm in arm, and went to sit in the front pew, like people accustomed to going to church and praying. Father MacNally conducted the mass with his usual reserve and detachment. But who could begrudge him the self-indulgent little twinkle in his eye? Love had transformed an enemy into a parishioner, perhaps even a friend.

Muriel Meraai did not appear in public. It was rumored that in an uncharacteristic drunken bout she confessed to a few of her customers about the cruelty of life. There were those who accused her of selling Janey to Samson in return for the license to continue her illicit business.

"What do you know about morality?" she was reputed to have said. "What do you know about life and beauty? I was married to beauty. Big, black, strong and beautiful. He was Janey's father. A Xhosa, perhaps he was a king, a chief at least. But so clean and pure. Then they took him away. Called him a Bantu. He had no pass. I never saw him again. And then I ended up here, with a man who tore my eye out in his drunkenness. And fathered two children in me. Oh my little legal bastards, that black man should have been your father. In any case, Janey is better off." She passed out, they said, with a moan of anguish, like a child in pain.

Outside in the cold, young John watched the bridal pair walk regally through the shadows. Janey was dressed in white lace, at the insistence of her husband. She would be, to him, virginal forever.

John's scream rent the air, and the knife in his hand flashed in the moonlight, like quicksilver.

"Whore!"

But he was young and uncertain, and the knife trembled near Janey's cheek, inflicting merely a small cut near her eye. It was more the tremble of his hand that cut her cheek. John dropped the knife and walked away weeping.

By now quite a crowd had gathered, those going home from church, others on their way to purchase their last drink at the shebeen. As John was walking away without haste, they saw Samson calmly draw a pistol from underneath his coat and shoot him in the back. His body lay crumpled in the dust, while Father MacNally bent over him. Aunt Suze began to wail.

"He has murdered my son!"

Muriel Meraai awoke at eight o'clock, much later than usual. Although the sun was quite high, her room was still cold and damp. She propped herself up in bed and listened to the bustle that separated her bedroom from the rest of the house. It was Saturday morning, and although she could hear the clink of glasses, the usual loud banter of early morning drinkers was absent.

The few loyal customers she still had, loyal only because they owed her money and had nowhere else to get a drink, sat solemnly around the fire and talked to each other in subdued voices. The radio blared out a tuneless popular song that no one listened to, but that nevertheless filled the air with sadness.

Muriel rubbed her empty eye socket. Suddenly she remembered how Mr. Samson, many weeks ago, had caressed that hollowed, scarred recess with blind and fevered hands. And his horror afterwards, when he saw her disfigured face in the candlelight. She often thought about her motives for luring Samson into her bed, and she had vaguely made up her mind that it was in order to deflect Samson's attention from her daughter Janey.

But she also admitted to herself that Janey "was better off now." Living with a man who had somewhere to go in life. She would not simply give herself to one of the township boys, in an alley, behind the toilet, like a bitch giving herself to the township dogs. It did not matter now that Samson had not bothered to marry Janey, but took her away to Durban, to honeymoon in a cheap hotel.

"It was by the sea, Mama," Janey had told her excitedly, like a child who had seen a magical new world for the first time.

Janey, who before her trip to Durban had never been out of Johannesburg, had been awed by the ritual of living in a hotel. The breakfasts in the large dining room, overlooking a smelly, stagnant river, drinking brandy and a Coke on a veranda overhung with green creepers. And Samson's man-of-the-world bearing, giving orders to the waiters in a sharp and haughty voice. All this gave her a sense of being special. How different she was upon her return to the township, arrogant, with the air of a person who had seen a world different and better than the one she had come from.

But Muriel feared for her. She was still a child, enjoying her new life as if it were a toy, and not understanding the world she had entered or the man she was with. Since Johnny's killing, Samson had become a lonely, reclusive man. He surrounded himself with soldiers, of whom another twenty had been drafted into the township. He had become ruthless with anyone breaking his rules. How often she had seen the soldiers clear the streets whenever it seemed that people were about to gather and talk about the situation in the township.

People hated him, and met secretly, mostly under the guise of prayer meetings at the church or at the house of Pieter Kock. He was a cunning and dangerous man, this Pieter Kock. A communist, people said. And she feared that he was stirring people up against Samson. They would harm Janey as well.

The door to Muriel's bedroom opened and her second daughter, Dorothy, entered, a steaming cup of coffee in her hand.

"Ma, are you feeling ill?" she asked.

"Just a bit chilled. Touch of flu, maybe—my back hurts," Muriel answered, reciting her litany of ills. Because they were so familiar, her daughter did not notice the puffy wariness in Muriel's eyes.

"Hell, Ma, you should see all the police in the Township! Why, they are only going to bury young John. Not as if he was somebody important or anything like that."

"What time is the funeral?"

"At eleven."

Muriel had a determined look on her face.

"Ma! You're not going to the funeral, are you?"

"I am."

"Mama, they will take it as an insult. Who knows what they'll do today!"

"We must show them that we are not afraid. That we have some dignity. Johnny was a fine young boy who got himself into things above his head."

"Ma, Samson killed John because of Janey. Because of us."

"He did not! He killed Johnny because Johnny had a knife and was threatening people."

"Oh, Ma, you don't listen to what people are saying in the township, do you?"

"What are they saying?"

"Mama—"

"Well, what are they saying?"

"That we are all Samson's whores. First you, then Janey. Some of them even ask when it will be my turn."

"Who said that? Why they want to make an enemy of me?"

But her daughter remained silent, her head bowed. Tears rolled down Muriel's cheek, streaking one side of her face with sorrow and anger. The other side of her face remained dry and untouched, her gouged-out eye unable to cry.

"Dorothy, bring me the tub—I want to bathe," Muriel said when she had regained her composure.

Her body slid into the steaming water, an envelope of heat that soothed the deep ache inside of her. Yes, she thought, Samson did awake something inside of me. Lord, forgive me, ten years without a man! She remembered Samson's hardness thrusting inside her, and a new ache awakened in her loins and in her breasts. She scrubbed herself vigorously. She had long ago stopped using the harsh, carbolic-based Blue soap so commonly used in the township. They washed dead people with that soap. There is always the stench of carbolic and incense at funerals, and I am not dead yet. How different are they, all those holy-holy people who talk about us? Yes, they are married, but they are also only objects to their men. Fuck-things to be used in the dead of night! To be fumbled at, a drain into which they pour their filthy passion.

Still seething, Muriel dressed herself. Black stockings that masked the varicose veins that lined her legs. She paused and stared at her stock-inged nakedness in the mirror. Thighs somewhat heavy as she entered her fortieth year. Not as agile as the bright young things that paraded in the streets with thin, spindly legs, more as a result of childhood malnu-trition than by design. It was also not the slim beauty of the women who lived across the line, who gorged themselves on rich food then spent hours in exercise, trying to overcome the results of their greed. No, her strength was the strength acquired in the streets, strength capable of receiving the lusts of men and of bearing children as hard as the streets. Or else they do not survive.

Muriel's rage was slowly receding, as she looked out at the still-deserted street, the wind raging in the dust. She felt at home, at one with its desolation. She slipped over her head a black dress, simple and austere, that had seen many funerals, and donned a hat with a lace veil that hid the bloodshot sorrow in her eye.

Into the street flowed the black-clothed mourners, faces masked by a chilly somberness. The church was already full, reeking of incense, sweat and carbolic, by the time Muriel arrived. In the street people nudged each other and pointed at her.

"Blerry hypocrite! Imagine her going to Johnny's funeral, praying and crying!"

As she entered the church, Muriel was struck by the smell that was so familiar, but that she still could not get used to. She held a handkerchief to her gagging mouth, and walked to the front of the church. She was unable to stop the tears from flowing from her smarting eye.

People in the church began to hiss, some whispered to her to get out.

"Maybe Johnny was her lover too! She likes to share with her daughters!"

"Nah—not young Johnny, he was too young. He wouldn't know where to find it among all the wrinkles."

The tepid circle of anger was broken, and laughter rippled through the church. Father cleared his throat, raised his arms for quiet and began to say the Lord's prayer. But Muriel knew that her ordeal was not yet over.

As the funeral cortege left the church and wound its way slowly across the veld towards the cemetery, Muriel walked along proudly, her head held high.

*"Muriel, wat soek jy hier? Meraai, Meraai, Samson soek n' naai!"** some-one whispered to her. The words, spoken in Afrikaans, were heard quite clearly, and despite the somber mood of the mourners, many burst into laughter.

She wheeled around at her tormentors, her black dress billowing in the wind, her arms akimbo. A dark and terrifying bird swooping down from the hot blue sky upon her frightened prey.

No one is sure, up to this day, exactly what happened. When what sounded like the flapping of great wings stopped, two of Muriel's tormentors lay still, blood oozing from gaping wounds in their throats, which seemed to have been slit by a sharp object, either a knife or the razor-like talons of a great bird. A bewildered cry went out from the crowd.

"Muriel has murdered Jan April and Clarence Meyer."

"You're playing the fool. Have you no respect?"

"Stroes God? Vrek!** Right there in the dust!"

"Necklace! Necklace! Necklace!" a group of youths began to chant.

Muriel was fleeing through the veld, her black dress contrasting starkly with the gray and desolately dry veld. Her dress billowed in the wind, and her strong legs raised clouds of dust as she ran. A group of young men were chasing her, and brought her down, like a hunted

---

*Muriel, what do you want here? Meraai, Meraai, Samson wants a fuck."
**Stroes God: dialect elision of "As true as God."/vrek: dead

199

animal, into the dust. They dragged her towards the waiting crowd, who had forgotten Johnny's burial and had set his coffin down, respectfully, upon a mound of rocks. Father MacNally, red-faced and frantic, was screaming at the crowd, in futility.

"Let us bury our dead and go home! Let us not also become killers!"

"Let the dead bury the dead," someone shouted back. Pieter Kock too was silenced as he tried to urge the crowd to "let justice take its course."

"Necklace! Necklace!" the crowd was chanting in unison.

A motorcar tire was passed from hand to hand across the crowd that encircled Muriel, doused in petrol and placed around her body so that her arms were trapped inside its circle. The fear in her face was white. A look of horror that Pieter would never forget. He saw death in her eyes, a living thing that breathed for one terrifying moment before Muriel shut her eye. The dead eyelid would not close over the glass eye, and he saw in its reflection his own graven image.

"No! No!" Pieter screamed. But he was shoved aside like some inconsequential hindrance.

"Voetsek!"* a voice whispered harshly.

As he lay on the ground with his eyes shut, he heard the distant sound of gunfire, of trampling feet, and finally he felt rough hands raise him to his feet. Pieter opened his eyes and stared into the face of a soldier. A pistol was pointed at Pieter's head, its hammer cocked. All around him people were fleeing, and bullets felled them as they ran.

"Leave him, he saved the woman," a voice said.

Pieter saw Muriel Meraai, her clothes soaked in petrol, the motorcar tire, which was to have been her necklace of death, lying at her feet. The sky had grown dark and cold. Pieter shivered and said:

"I want to go home."

Suddenly the winter was over. The wind died down, and the dust settled. Although the rains did not come, in the desolate gardens patches of grass struggled up through the dry soil. And the lonely trees, distantly interspersed along the dark streets, were tinged with green.

Samson ruled the township with ruthless authority. The dead were buried at night. The mourners found their way by torchlight and sang their hymns in a ghostly manner, their voices rising up into the darkness.

"Somebody is being buried in Zombietown," the people who lived

---

*"Fuck off!"

across the railway line said, as they heard the distant voices of mourning in the dark of night.

Meetings were banned and no one was allowed to walk the streets at night. The soldiers roamed about the empty streets shooting at shadows that seemed to flit from one darkness to the next.

Then, to everyone's astonishment, it was announced that an inquiry was to be held into the "situation in the township," particularly into the death of young Johnny. The community was invited to form a committee and to appoint a lawyer to represent its views at the inquiry.

"They are going to whitewash the whole affair," Pieter said.

"If we have a chance to send Samson to jail for killing Johnny, we must take it," Thomas Peet said.

"Thomas is right. How else are we going to make our grievances known?" Father MacNally said.

In all their discussions, no one mentioned the mysterious deaths of Jan April and Clarence Meyer at Johnny's funeral. Nor did anybody speak of Muriel Meraai, who had not set foot outside of her house since the day people had tried to set her alight. Even Janey had lost her arrogant attitude, and went about the township in secret, always under guard. Dark rumors circulated in the township that the third member of Muriel's family, her daughter Dorothy, had joined Samson in his concubinage. She, Dorothy, though not as beautiful as Janey, was young and sensual, and turned many heads.

"Someday, somebody will kill for her too," Sarah remarked.

Finally the Investigator arrived. A man in his late sixties, with white, crew-cut hair. He peered at witnesses over his bifocals, a quizzical look in his bright, gray eyes.

"I told you they'll cover this whole thing up," Pieter said. "That's why they sent this old man out here. He's not going to risk his pension by condemning a man like Samson."

"Listen, Samson's like a cornered rat. Look at the way his eyes shoot all over the room. Looking at people. He's afraid, I tell you."

"Cornered rats are desperate. Samson does not look like a desperate man to me," Pieter answered. He pulled on the cigarette and inhaled deeply. He looked appreciatively at the cigarette the lawyer had offered him. "Tastes good, a real cigarette. Somehow I don't think Samson even cares," Pieter added quietly.

At last it was Samson's turn to give evidence. He was intently questioned by the lawyer for the community, parrying answers with a skill that infuriated the lawyer. Finally he was questioned by the Investigating Officer.

"Why did you kill him?"

"He had a knife in his hands."

"Witnesses said that he dropped it."

"He cut the face of my. . . he cut Janey's face."

"Witnesses also said that he turned away. Turned his back to you."

"He was going to pick up a rock."

"How did you know that?"

"There was hate in his eyes."

"But he was walking away from you."

"Walking? He ran. He had hate in his eyes. His feet raised dust in the streets."

"You shot him in the back."

"He was a criminal. He stabbed a young woman. Then ran. There was dust. After I shot him the dust settled."

"Could you not have—"

"When the dust settled there was peace and quiet, just like you wanted."

Samson turned in his chair and addressed the last statement, looking not at the Investigator but at the crowd, at the priest and at Pieter Kock.

Finally the Investigator delivered his findings to the quiet and attentive audience in the large rent hall that was being used for the hearing. Flies buzzed and the electric fan whirred in the warm air.

He cleared his throat and read aloud from the piece of paper in front of him.

"I find that no one can be held legally responsible for the death of John Lepere."

He gathered his papers, placed them in his briefcase, nodded to his audience and then quietly walked out of the hall. Samson rose, took Janey by the arm and led her out of the hall. They were met by Dorothy, who slid her arm through Samson's. The three calmly walked out into the bright sunlight.

It began to rain soon after, soft incessant rain that hissed and surged against the windowpanes. It seemed to rain for weeks, until the dust and dirt was transformed into quagmires of mud. People stared out of the window and watched the water flow through the streets like dark and shimmering rivers.

It was during this time that the rumors were first heard. No one was certain that they had actually heard anyone saying that George Da Costa was seen in the township. Thomas Peet recalled that he first heard of George Da Costa's return from Pieter Kock. But Pieter had said it more as a prophecy than as a fact.

Footprints were found in the mud in the veld near the cemetery, and it was reported that dark figures stole through the streets at night, while the soldiers were in their quarters, not willing to venture out in the rain.

"We can't go out and chase every shadow the residents tell us they see."

The strange thing was that the residents did not report anything to the soldiers. They went about their lives as they had for many years, before Samson came. His rules were a nuisance, a terrible nuisance at times, and many people had died since Samson arrived, but he, they knew, would not ultimately change their destinies, whether he lived or died.

As soon as the rain stopped the soldiers were out in the veld, searching through the grass and the muddy pools, looking for arms and hidden insurgents. They also carried out house-to-house searches and questioned people. They kept a constant eye on the house of Elsa and Mario Da Costa, waiting to see whether their son would make contact with them.

Finally the rumors faded and life returned to normal.

Samson walked about again, inspecting houses and insuring that residents understood that he was in charge. One morning, as the residents were busying themselves with the needs of the day, a young boy came running in from the veld.

"They have found him. They found his body. He is dead!"

A coldness overcame Elsa's heart, as she saw the soldiers carrying a body, shrouded in the mists of the early morning. She saw the bright gleam of boots, too expensive to belong to a guerilla.

"It's Samson," Pieter said, as he stood next to Elsa. "He was shot in the head. One bullet."

Rumors and conjecture once again besieged the township. He had been stealing away from his house late the night before, and had walked briskly into the veld. A slim, girlish figure was said to have followed him. It must have been Dorothy, meeting Samson secretly in the veld, under the moonlight, in the thick mattings of grass, fragrant wild honeysuckle greeting their nostrils as they lay in each other's arms. . . .

As they hurried through rapidly disappearing mists towards the bus stations, many residents of the township wondered what their new Representative would be like.

The Soft Has No Durability

Jeanne Goosen

Jeanne Goosen's "The Soft Has No Durability" was first published in 1986 by HAUM in a short-story anthology. It forms part of a series dealing with the author's encounter with the emergency situation in a small town in the interior of South Africa. Goosen's fifth book, a novel entitled Lou Oond, *due to be published this year, continues to examine the violence in a society that proclaims itself democratic and peace-loving.*

Trained as a radiographer, the author has recently joined an alternative organization which provides medical services to the disenfranchised in South Africa's black townships.

Goosen has also published two anthologies of poetry (Cape Town: Tafelberg, 1971 and 1975), and was arts editor for a prominent Afrikaans newspaper for ten years.

"And on Wednesdays we break the tedium of the week at the Panorama Hotel," the doctor's wife said. "The usual, you know, a get-together, a few drinks and so on. And of course you are coming," she added with affected sternness.

". . ."

The BMW's window glided down. "What's the frown for? We'll pick you up just after eight. Sooner or later you'll have to meet the townsfolk. Besides, they're switching on the lights for the first time this evening."

"The lights?"

"Long story. I'll explain later." She smiled like a governess, exhibiting two gold flecks in her front teeth.

"See you later. And Dirk," she said, "we don't accept 'no' for an answer."

The wind swept a bundle of leaves down the street. A layer of fine red dust had settled on the porch. The furniture was arranged more or less as he wanted it. The house inside now looked almost identical to his previous home in Johannesburg. There was not much left to do. Everything was in its appointed place. A door slammed. Slowly he started opening the shutters. A few drops of rain streaked the dust against the windowpanes. Every particle had a future. It was part of an order which in turn obeyed a higher order. Since his arrival here he had often thought about Such Things.

He slipped a tape into the cassette player. Haydn. Every cadence ended perfectly. It was too correct, too transparent, too terse. A world of perfect order. What could Beethoven possibly have learnt at Papa Ponytail's knees?

What shall I do to get through this day and not die of boredom before bedtime?

In the bedroom he put on a warm coat and wound a scarf around his neck. He locked the door carefully and walked down the street to the museum. The woman in the foyer glanced up from her knitting, recognized him and nodded. He swung past her to the great hall on the left.

In the hall of about 100 meters, where the dead lived, their rise and fall as life-forms had been visually reconstructed. A region of marshes and swamps, glaciers and windswept deserts had been recreated and populated with massive flesh-eaters, plant-eaters, primitive amphibians, fishes and invertebrates. The migratory waves of life had apparently been dominated by reptiles.

If I start walking now and begin singing a hymn at the same time, I shall, before the song has even ended, have paced through a geological time span of 240 million years. And before the last note sounds, billions of organisms will each have had a turn at short-lived success before disappearing into the void of inevitable extinction.

A volcanic eruption and the detachment of ice plates lay two handbreadths from each other. Gondwanaland disintegrated in a split second. With each pace the crank handle of time swung round and placed a new group in power. Splinter by splinter, life coalesced: from a closed temporal region to temporal opening, from a dental maxilla to horned beak, from scale to feather, from landbound to free flight, from solid bone to hollow pipe and eventually from cold- to warm-blooded.

Outside, a siren wailed.

Is everything that lives in its present form today of any real significance in the greater history of Time and Space? Even man, evolving from some primordial phlegm? Rejoice thus, all ye living beings.

Before he exited, he paused and read the pamphlet: *In the absence of excessive microbial activity, the hard parts of the body, such as the bones and teeth, are preserved by gradual replacement of their chemical compounds by chemical substances present in the surrounding mud or clay medium.*

And further on: . . . *teeth provide the most important information* . . .

So. It was the teeth, then. Not the brain nor the feeling within the brain. No report of the howl, the sudden shudder in the center of the skin-bag of God and bones, the fear, vitality, restlessness. What is soft, decays, has no durability.

Outside, the street smelt of freshly-baked bread. His eyes stung from the dust. In front of the courthouse a soldier guarded several handcuffed men. A prisoner raised his fist, like a primitive black crab with a pincer.

It was cold and Dirk dug his hands deeper into his pockets. We are not adapted for life here. It's either too cold, or the wind blows too much, or the air is too humid. We cannot slip readily through a whirlwind. We cannot lie naked on a rock, assessing the prey, or, with the hard eye of a dove, discern danger. Will we bear testimony, over millions of years, standing reconstructed and stuffed between the whales and antelope, the geraniums and eucalyptus, to our small successes? *Homo sapiens*, the undisputed rulers of the earth that have possessed almost every available habitat. And destroyed it. Also one another. *Homo homini lupus.*

A Casspir stopped in front of the post office, a head-butting Cynodont, with a thickened skull-plate to protect the brain. With its uninterrupted respiration and fast metabolic rate, it would survive this zone.

Women on one side, men on the other. For the time being, anyway. The mayor's wife is wearing a fur coat and sipping a Bloody Mary. "If Jane doesn't come to work tomorrow, I'm going to get someone else. There are multitudes who are looking for work."

"We can afford oysters every night with the rand/dollar exchange as it is now," said Pat Duggan, the archeologist from Texas. He and his team had been busy for months researching the social interactions and migratory habits of the early Bushmen and Hottentots of the region.

"Things will sort themselves out again," the hotel manager said. "Gold will rise again."

"Of course," everyone agreed.

"My men are exhausted," said Major Pug du Toit, the chief of police. "The searchlights will put a stop to all this nonsense at night. If necessary, we can go into action from this very hilltop." He glanced at his watch. "About fifteen minutes to go and we'll surprise the bastards with the eternal light."

The women moved closer. "If one only knew what it is they want," the doctor's wife said. "Give them schools and houses, and they go and burn them down. I really don't know . . . " She lit a cigarette.

"If there's an outbreak of cholera, at least we'll know where to begin looking," Manie Bester, the district surgeon, remarked. "The municipality was in there three weeks ago. It's one fucking big, stinking mess. The sewage vans have all been overturned and set alight." He turned to Dirk: "And what have you got to say for yourself, my fellow?"

"Still waters . . ." the mayor's wife laughed.

Slowly they moved along to the hotel's glass-walled porch. Below, at the foot of the hill, on the other side of the national road, the black township lay in a depression. Here and there a weak light flickered.

"There's hardly any light," said Dirk. "Perhaps they're asleep already."

"Not a damn," said Major Pug du Toit, "they've got no paraffin. Or money." He laughed. "But we'll give them some light on the entire subject soon."

"How on earth are the poor devils going to sleep?" the doctor's wife asked. "It has to be absolutely pitch-dark before I can get to sleep."

"They're like battery chickens," the mayor's wife said. She giggled hysterically. "Imagine if the whole lot should start laying eggs!"

"Unfertilized, please," the district surgeon said drily.

"Do you really think spotlights are a solution?" Pat Duggan asked. "There'll never be an end to war. Our digs bear witness to continual warring, flight and return, plunder and annihilation. We've found caches of primitive arms stretching over a period of five hundred years to prove this. And to think that in all this time there was more than enough room to live peacefully together."

They all looked at him uncertainly. "That's interesting," they said. "Interesting."

"Five minutes to go," said the police chief. He winked the waiter nearer. "Another quick round, my boy!"

Dirk moved with the group of people as they went and stood in a neat row next to each other along the wide windows of the porch and waited.

Translated from the Afrikaans by E. J. Cloete

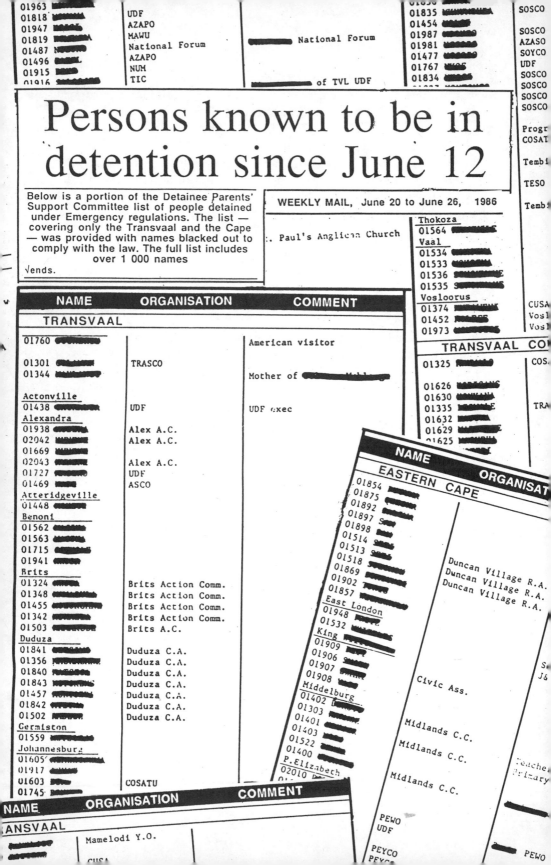

01963		
01818	UDF	
01947	AZAPO	
01819	MAWU	
01487	National Forum	
01496	AZAPO	
01915	NUM	
01916	TIC	

| | National Forum | |
| | of TVL UDF | |

01835	SOSCO
01454	
01987	SOSCO
01981	AZASO
01477	SOYCO
01767	UDF
01834	SOSCO
	SOSCO
	SOSCO
	SOSCO
	Progr
	COSAT
	Temb
	TESO
	Temb

Persons known to be in detention since June 12

Below is a portion of the Detainee Parents' Support Committee list of people detained under Emergency regulations. The list — covering only the Transvaal and the Cape — was provided with names blacked out to comply with the law. The full list includes over 1 000 names

/ends.

WEEKLY MAIL, June 20 to June 26, 1986

:. Paul's Anglican Church

Thokoza
| 01564 | |

Vaal
01534	
01533	
01536	
01535	

Vosloorus
01374		CUSA
01452		Vos
01973		Vos

NAME	ORGANISATION	COMMENT
TRANSVAAL		
01760		American visitor
01301	TRASCO	
01344		Mother of ...
Actonville		
01438	UDF	UDF exec
Alexandra		
01938	Alex A.C.	
02042	Alex A.C.	
01669		
02043	Alex A.C.	
01727	UDF	
01469	ASCO	
Atteridgeville		
01448		
Benoni		
01562		
01563		
01715		
01941		
Brits		
01324	Brits Action Comm.	
01348	Brits Action Comm.	
01455	Brits Action Comm.	
01342	Brits Action Comm.	
01503	Brits A.C.	
Duduza		
01841	Duduza C.A.	
01356	Duduza C.A.	
01840	Duduza C.A.	
01843	Duduza C.A.	
01457	Duduza C.A.	
01842	Duduza C.A.	
01502	Duduza C.A.	
Germiston		
01559		
Johannesburg		
01605		
01917		
01603	COSATU	
01745		

TRANSVAAL CO
01325		COS...
01626		
01630		
01335		TRA
01632		
01629		
01625		

NAME	ORGANISAT...
EASTERN CAPE	
01854	
01875	
01892	
01897	
01898	
01514	
01513	
01518	
01869	Duncan Village R.A.
01902	Duncan Village R.A.
01857	Duncan Village R.A.
East London	
01948	
01532	
King	
01909	
01906	
01907	Civic Ass.
01908	
Middelburg	
01402	
01303	
01401	Midlands C.C.
01403	
01522	Midlands C.C.
01400	
P.Elizabeth	Midlands C.C.
02010	
	PEWO
	UDF
	PEYCO
	PEYCO

NAME	ORGANISATION	COMMENT
TRANSVAAL		
	Mamelodi Y.O.	
	CUSA	
		PEWO

Kodwa Nkosana . . .
(And Yet, Master . . .)

M. T. Mazibuko

M. T. Mazibuko was born in 1946 and began attending school in 1959. The poem reprinted here is from his second collection, Iyezane *(Pretoria: Via Afrika Limited, 1972), and has been newly translated by Daniel P. Kunene (see page 406). Mazibuko's first collection, published in 1971, won the S. E. K. Mghayi poetry prize (Mghayi was an outstanding Xhosa poet and poetry reader).*

Whether the season be dry or wet or cold,
I am tired, I am hungry,
And I have no money, yet . . . master . . .
I work for you even though my reward
Is far below my needs.
Besides, the work you have assigned me
Burns scars upon my shoulders,
Though you will find me singing my song
As the pick and the shovel wrench
My arms. You did not call me with your voice,
Master, but with the nakedness that made me
Leave my children behind saying
I am going to work for you, my family, least realizing
I was coming to enrich you, yet . . . master . . .

Whether raining or cold, my feet sinking
In the mud as I go to school for education
To raise me to a higher status
So I can feel confidence in my step and know that
You are my brother in matters of intellectual awakening,
That both of us were given souls like eternal flames,

Yet . . . you master have no fellow-feeling, you shamelessly
Live on the sweat of my brow! You loathe me,
Yet you like to be served by me;
I have no place to eat in the hotels yet
I am the cook; to you I am like a donkey!
Yet you . . . master, receive high wages.
I have even studied and become a Professor like you,
And become a doctor like you, yet
Your reward always surpasses mine, though . . .
Master! The price of goods
Does not differ for you and me. Yet . . .
Master, bear this in mind, that your
Life of ease is due to the weariness of my limbs
Aching as if broken into fragments
Because I sacrifice all to serve you —
And yet . . . master . . .

Translated from the Zulu by Daniel P. Kunene

The Structure of Things Here

David Goldblatt

Born in Randfontein in 1930, David Goldblatt developed an interest in photography at an early age: he in fact wanted to be a magazine photographer but found that this was a profession unheard-of in South Africa. He worked as a shop assistant until the death of his father. In 1962, he sold the family business and since 1963 has directed all his efforts towards photography.

Goldblatt's professional work has been almost entirely outside of the studio, including assignments for magazines and corporations. The portraiture unfailingly has a distinctive quality because he chooses to photograph individuals within, rather than distinct from, their usual contexts. His personal work, spanning some thirty-eight years, has been directed towards critical explorations of South African society. His photographs have been widely published, and may be seen in many galleries and museums.

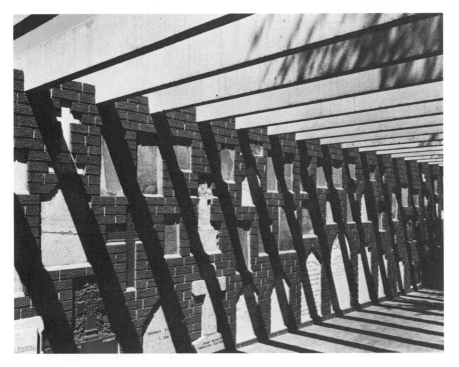

Gravestones of Boer Women and children who died in a British concentration camp in the Anglo-Boer War of 1899–1902. Volksrust, September 1986.

211

Dutch Reformed Church. Quellerina, Johannesburg, November 1986.

The home of Koos and Alina Mhlangu, farm laborers. Near Vrede, September 1986.

Garage wall of a house in Verwoerdburg, April 1986.

The Methodist Church of Magopa after the enforced removal of the Magopa community and the destruction of their buildings by the state in pursuance of the elimination of "Black Spots," October 1986.

Family on trek in the Great Karroo, near Colesburg, August 1986.

The English Language and Social Change in South Africa*

Njabulo S. Ndebele

For a biographical note on Njabulo S. Ndebele please see page 32.

The current political context in which this conference is taking place appears to have left its mark on the manner in which the conference itself was conceived and subsequently organized. I am thinking here of the attempts on the part of the organizers at making extensive consultations with varied individuals and groups so that, as the organizers had hoped, a diversity of interests can be accommodated in the various discussions that will take place in the course of the conference. Such conduct is, no doubt, fully in keeping with the demand of the oppressed of this troubled land for full democracy in the conduct of every aspect of the country's life.

Yet, well-meaning though these attempts may have been, it is essential, at such times, that we exercise such a state of vigilance that would enable us to express tactical reservations if only to ensure that all relevant issues have been brought to the surface so that we can make pure motives even purer. The point of the matter is that, viewed from the angle of those towards whom the hand of friendship is being extended, such democratic largesse can become an unintended trap. For example, it should never be forgotten that behind the hand of friendship is the presence of the Academy's solid institutional history: a history that has left its mark on habits of thought in the literary culture of this country. Consequently, when such an organization seeks urgently to respond to certain pressing exigencies of history, it will do so from the assumed

---

*Keynote address delivered at the Jubilee Conference of the English Academy of Southern Africa, September 4–6, 1986.

validity of its organizational base, and such a base would almost dictate a strategy of benevolent containment and encapsulation in order to maintain, expand and exert influence. Under such circumstances, the organizational base itself might even appear to be a negotiable factor, when in fact it is not. This is because it is usually so firm as to make it almost unthinkable for the organization to consider the possible strategy of self-sacrifice so that it could be absorbed into a new and necessary, if seemingly threatening, dispensation. This is to suggest that when a centipede curls itself into a protective stance, it still remains a centipede.

Now, the subject of central concern to this conference is the evolving place of English in Southern Africa. It makes perfect sense that, since the English Academy's central interest is the promotion of the English language, the Academy should devote special time to this matter just at that moment when South Africa finds herself compelled to seek new directions into the future. Indeed, it has become the sign of the times that any organization that regards itself seriously should engage in the mandatory exercise of reevaluation at this crucial time in our history.

In keeping with my opening remarks, it is pertinent to note what some renowned thinkers, who are native speakers of English, have observed over the years of the development of the English language around the world. Noting the spread of English throughout the world, and how that phenomenon has meant that with the advance of years from the times of colonialism, the development of English in various parts of the world has taken forms that have gone beyond the control of the native speakers, they have concluded that English is no longer the exclusive property of its native speakers. No less an authority than George Steiner commented back in 1965 that:

> The great energies of the language now enter into play outside England . . . African English, Australian English, the rich speech of West Indian and Anglo-Indian writers, represent a complicated polycentric field of linguistic force, in which the language taught and written on this island is no longer the inevitable authority or focus.[1]

In South Africa, our own Professor Guy Butler has remarked in a recent article that "Twenty million blacks will use English for their own interests and ends, without worrying much about the views of less than two million ESSA's (English-Speaking South Africans)."[2]

There are at least two possible responses of the native speakers of English to this seemingly inevitable process. They may celebrate, in the spirit of international linguistic democracy, the birth of new languages based on the English language; or, they may descend into fits of anxiety, firstly over the purported mutilation of their language with the possible attendant loss of intelligibility and, secondly, over the fear of the loss of influence.

Unfortunately, it is the latter response that has won the day. Beginning from a positive and open-minded acceptance of reality, this latter response has triggered concerted efforts by metropolitan English-speaking policy-makers to effectively stem the strong tide of history. This has entailed attempts to weave a web of containment around this spontaneous, worldwide transformation of the English language so that English can continue to serve various kinds of metropolitan interests, interests which may have very little to do with the concerns of those who, out of specific needs arising from their own forms of social interaction, have to fashion a new language for themselves.

Practically, this need to maintain control over English by its native speakers has given birth to a policy of manipulative open-mindedness in which it is held that English belongs to all who use it, provided that it is used correctly. It is assumed, of course, that it is the native speakers who will determine the standards of correctness. In other words, you really cannot control what will eventually happen to English in the hands of nonnative speakers; but then you can control it. This is the art of giving away the bride while insisting that she still belongs to you.

That this latter tendency predominates should not surprise anyone who attempts to ask some ultimate questions, for this tendency will then be found to be perfectly consistent with the history of English and, later, American imperialism. The much-vaunted traditions of English and American democracy have promised an attractive world of "freedom and opportunity" to all those who would enter that world. Yet, many of those who entered, mainly as colonial subjects, soon discovered that the newly-promised freedom was premised ultimately on the subject's *unfree-dom*. The colonial subject had to give up much of what constituted his own sphere of freedom. And so, the very concept of freedom came to be standardized, in the same way that technology and business culture were standardized, according to the specifications of imperial powers.

Indeed, the history of the spread of the English language throughout the world is inseparable from the history of the spread of English and American imperialisms. This fact is important when we consider the place of English in formerly-colonized multilingual societies. The imposition of English effectively tied those societies to a world imperialist culture which was to impose, almost permanently, severe limitations on those countries' ability to make independent linguistic choices at the moment of independence. We have since heard much about how practically all of those countries ostensibly took the "pragmatic" decision to choose English as the *lingua franca*. How can we fail to notice that an historically predetermined "pragmatism" has been transformed, by the metropolitan culture, into an act of choice on the part of subject cultures and then praised as the very essence of wisdom? How can we fail to note that the supposed decision-makers were, structurally speaking, captive native functionaries of the colonial imperial powers? In reality, the functionaries merely responded to the call of necessity at a given point in time: the necessity of limited choices. After all, when you want to use an electrical gadget in Africa, hadn't you better purchase a plug that meets specifications standardized in the western world?

It is not too difficult to see how English as a language became tainted with imperial interests at that time in the progress of western imperialism when the need for the standardization of technology prompted the need for the standardization of language. In fact, I would hazard a guess that the very concept of an international, or world, language was an invention of western imperialism. In any case, the language chosen was destined to be English, with French fighting hard for the title. Consequently, the spread of English went parallel with the spread of the culture of international business and technological standardization. From there, the jump towards the standardization of international thought becomes easy to make. Today, the link between English and the Western corporate world is stronger than ever.

As far as South Africa is concerned, even Professor Butler notes how "major international corporations are pouring money into black schools, frequently with the specific aim of improving English."[3] Beyond that, the British Council, too, continues to be untiring in its effort to keep the world speaking English.[4] In this regard, teaching English as a second or foreign language is not only good business, in terms of the production of teaching materials of all kinds (a service-business sector that increases the numbers of possible consumers of British and American commodities throughout the world), but also it is good politics. The Commonwealth, after all, is an alliance of historically captive users of English.

Now, English-speaking South Africans are, inevitably, heirs to the history of the English language. In South Africa they constitute an English language outpost that is expected to do its historical duty to the imperial heritage of that language. For example, in the article already alluded to, Professor Butler, while altruistically denying to the English-speaking South Africans an ethnic interest in the English language, since the language really "belongs to all," evokes that very interest when he asserts that "White English-speakers must enlarge their constituency;

they can only do this by enlarging the influence of their language."[5] This necessarily follows from how Professor Butler imbues English-speaking South Africans with a patriotic duty to help teach English in South Africa and to teach it well. "The importance of good models of spoken and written English cannot be over-emphasized," asserts Professor Butler. Consequently, "English should be taught effectively as it used to be in the old mission schools, in which there were always devoted English-speaking models." Indeed, they were devoted! Furthermore, it is "particularly important that future teachers of English in black schools should be educated and trained in institutions where a significant number of the staff use English as a mother-tongue or are highly proficient speakers of it."[6] Clearly, we can see here a permissive attitude that goes hand-in-hand with the prescription of standards. Let us call it a prescriptive open-mindedness.

All of which goes to indicate that the role of English in South Africa is a matter the complexity of which goes far beyond the convenience and correctness of its use, for that very convenience, and that very correctness, are, in essence, problematic. The problem is that recourse to them is fraught with assumptions. Recourse to them begs fundamental historical, cultural and political questions on the assumption that everyone knows what issues are at stake. But, in fact, we cannot assume the validity of premises that have not themselves been scrutinized carefully. This latter tendency not to be critical about premises is pervasive in South Africa at the moment when all kinds of scenarios of the future are being drawn up in the hope that the oppressed will be dazzled by their brilliance. This problem is so important that we need now to look at the problem of English from a national context.

If we look at the testimony of many white organizations on the question of change in South Africa, we shall immediately discern a pattern of thinking and attitude that seems to typify what the average white person, the traditionally privileged, thinks about the central problems of change. These organizations fall into three general categories:

First, we have organizations whose interest in a future dispensation is determined almost entirely by their economic interests. For example, I am thinking in particular of an organization such as the Association of Chambers of Commerce of South Africa (ASSOCOM). Recently, ASSOCOM commissioned Professors J. A. Lombard and J. A. du Pisanie to provide "academic help" in drawing up an ASSOCOM memorandum called "Removal of Discrimination Against Blacks in the Political Economy of the Republic of South Africa."[7] This memorandum was to be prepared for "submission to the Cabinet Committee on the political future of Urban Blacks." The memorandum is important not so much for what it says, but for the package of assumptions that provide an uncompromisingly nonnegotiable context for the memorandum's submissions.

Central to the memorandum's position is the following starting point:

> Believing that REFORM should be governed by (a) adherence to sound PRINCI-PLES of statehood and (b) EVOLUTIONARY rather than revolutionary changes, it is proposed that the acceptable basic elements of the existing order be identified, recognised, and extended.

> It is suggested that these basic elements are to be found in the COMMON LAW of South Africa, with particular reference to the norms governing (a) personal freedom, (b) freedom of property and contract, and (c) personal culpability. A DECLARATION OF RECOGNITION by all negotiating parties of these norms would be a necessary condition for further progress in negotiations. To these three common law norms should be added a formal recognition of (d) the basic rules governing the maintenance of a sound national currency and (e) the principles governing the right to tax.

> It is further suggested that the PHILOSOPHY BEHIND THE COMMON LAW NORMS which currently govern the basic character of the private enterprise economic system of South Africa, be extended to form the basis for the new POLITICAL STRUCTURES within which blacks will participate on equal terms with other citizens of the Republic of South Africa.[8]

Behind the evident posture of reasonableness in this passage are pitfalls that can trap the unwary. The memorandum, for example, offers a negotiating position while subtly positing, at the same time, nonnegotiable principles. The signposts of these nonnegotiable factors are there: "*sound* PRINCIPLES of statehood"; "*acceptable* basic elements of the *existing order*"; "*sound* national currency." Behind such words as "sound" and "acceptable" are firm assumptions about what is desirable. They hide the ideological anxieties of their users. Behind such seemingly objective virtues of efficiency are such unstated declarations as that "we must preserve our way of life as we know it" and "all those who are reasonable and privileged enough to think like us will see the value of our position"; consequently, there is an implied strategy that "we may have to educate the opposition." In this latter regard, the last paragraph in the above quotation is more explicit: the "basic character of the private enterprise economic system of South Africa" must be left intact. The legal philosophy behind that system must be "extended" so that its specifications can also cover black people. This implies that the concept of "human nature"[9] may need to be distributed more widely to include black people. Indeed, the memorandum refers to black people as "the prospective black citizens of the Republic."[10]

It seems to me that the more appropriate title for the memorandum should be "The Protection of Capital in a Rapidly Changing South Africa." In this regard we may not fail to notice the significance of the fact that ASSOCOM is an "Incorporated Association not for Gain." It may not be "for gain," but ASSOCOM is clearly interested in creating a climate that can maintain conditions for maximum gain for its members. Fundamentally, the qualification regarding gain is a kind of deceptive propriety.

The second category of organizations includes those groups which have attempted to produce all kinds of scenarios for the political future of the country. They include, of course, such groups as the Progressive Federal Party, and, yes, today, the Nationalist Party. The latter has produced a set of scenarios that have led to the kind of constitutional tinkering that has resulted in the Tricameral Parliament. Of course, nothing illustrates more dramatically than this parliament the futility of reform politics. Indeed, these acts by the Nationalist Party should properly be called "the modernization of the methods of maintaining white domination."[11] *That* is the hidden definition of "reform."

More significantly, however, is how some highly influential organizations in this second category are to be located in universities where they draw upon the aura of objectivity associated with university research. Perhaps none is better known than Professor Schlemmer's ill-fated Institute of Social Research based at the University of Natal, Durban. There is much intellectual tinkering that takes place in the context of such institutes which derives its authority not necessarily from the ideologically biased findings of research (although the intellectual practitioners involved will proclaim their objectivity), but from the backing of those findings by an intellectual hegemony based on the rituals of research, statistical data and evaluation, the presentation of findings at seminars and the dramatic press release. The politics of academic research is no more glaring than in such a situation. Always lacking is the sense of genuine conviction in the necessity of a future that accommodates the intuitions of the oppressed, for the oppressed themselves have been reduced into being a mere "factor of analysis" among other factors. Nevertheless, when the history of South Africa is finally updated, it may be found that the country has never had so many political theories thrown up for discussion.

Lastly, there have been diverse cultural interests to whom the challenge of the future has involved the need to open up cultural and educational centers to all races. Missing in these admirable acts of good-will is an accompanying need to alter fundamentally the nature of cultural practice itself. It is almost always assumed that, upon being admitted, the oppressed will certainly like what they find. The opening up of white private schools, for example, is a good illustration of the strategy of containment through absorption. Where there has previously been the absence of freedom, the mere exercise of making facilities available may easily be mistaken for the presence of freedom. That way, a dominant hegemony that has been in existence is left intact as it gains more supporters from among the ranks of the oppressed.

What is common to all these diverse interests? It is the unquestioned, nonnegotiable primacy of western civilization and its spectrum of values embodied in what has been called free enterprise and the special kind of democracy based on it. There is no doubt that the influence of the West in South Africa is vast, and that that influence has not only rubbed onto all segments of South African society, but also that it is destined to continue well into the foreseeable future. Its active defense, though, is largely a matter of habit, indicative of an entrenched and largely uncritical manner of thinking about the quality of life in South Africa on the part of those who have benefited vastly from it: what has been called "the South African way of life."

Unfortunately, for the vast majority of South Africans, western civilization has not been the glitter that it has been for those who brought it here. For the majority of the oppressed, the experience of western civilization has largely been the experience of poverty, malnutrition, low wages, mine accidents, police raids, selective justice and a variety of other similar negations. Consequently, this majority has not been, as it were, hegemonized to any great extent. For example, thanks to apartheid, they are so largely untouched by much of the discourse of western political philosophy that even at the popular level, buzz words and expressions such as "human rights," "free enterprise," "human dignity," "self-determination" and other standardized political vocabulary have not been absorbed to the extent that they would figure prominently in the people's subjective experience of political language. On the contrary, the relatively few who have been aware of such political vocabulary are those who have experienced it as applying to the privileged whites. Thus "human dignity" was the dignity of whites; and "human rights" were the rights of whites.[12] Hence, black people's experience of western civilization in general has been premised on their exclusion from its perceived advantages, except when, for purely functional or utilitarian reasons, their participation was sought. This kind of functional participation is even more evident today, when it is required in order to legitimize white South Africa's perceptions of "acceptable" change. So that even at that crucial moment of historical transformation, the oppressed have to experience themselves as tools.

In a well-known poem, Agostinho Neto sums up the relationship between most of Africa and western civilization graphically:

Western Civilization

Sheets of tin nailed to posts
driven in the ground
make up the house.

Some rags complete
the intimate landscape.

The sun slanting through cracks
welcomes the owner

After twelve hours of slave
labor.

breaking rock
shifting rock
breaking rock
shifting rock
fair weather
wet weather
breaking rock
shifting rock

Old age comes early

a mat on dark nights
is enough when he dies
gratefully
of hunger.[13]

From the foregoing discussion, it should be clear then that much of the talk about reform and change from the point of view of white South Africa in general is premised not on what the whites of South Africa may have to unlearn, but on what black people, those "prospective citizens of the Republic," need to be speedily introduced to so that they can become "responsible" citizens of the future, so that they can become westerners in black skins. In a nutshell, the entire ideology of reform is based on the "humanization" of the oppressed according to the specifications of South African capital, which, itself, is governed according to the specifications of the international corporate world.

The practical aspects of this modern form of colonial "pacification" imply the implementation of modern principles of business management. In the same way that the scientific attitude in eighteenth- and nineteenth-century Europe influenced the entire spectrum of European thought, today the dominance of international monopoly capital has bequeathed to the world "principles of management." Such an approach to reality has made it habitually difficult for corporate authority, as well as those influenced heavily by that authority, to discern the fundamental causes of human disaffection. "Management principles," in situations where the desire for freedom is as deep as it is among the oppressed in South Africa, are applied like the analgesic that is habitually administered to kill a headache where rest would have ensured a more permanent cure.[14]

For the present, the challenge before the spectrum of white South African interests subscribing to the ideology of reform is the "management" of the irreversible demand by the oppressed for liberation. This "management" attitude began with the Sullivan Principles at the workplace, and was extended to the need for the creation of the African middle class in the context of the larger society. Mirrored in this strategy is the desire to "manage" African aspirations through the intended effect of substituting the technicalities of civic responsibility (the "opening up" of white business areas for blacks, the ninety-nine-year lease, the creation of community councils, abolition of apartheid at the workplace, employee housing and other worker benefits, etc.) for the fundamental desire for freedom.

Clearly, the "management" attitude leaves largely uncomprehended and untouched the reality that the oppressed's call for freedom is premised on the total subversion of the social "biology" of South African repression.[15] This kind of desire for liberation is based on a complete understanding and recognition by the oppressed of the fact that the white ideology of reform is based on the white's "biological" need to maintain a sense of social and individual well-being that is based on a structure of needs validated by the white's oppression of others. The greatest pathology of such a social system is the blunting of the humanistic vision and the constriction of the intellect resulting in the death of the social conscience of the beneficiaries of the system. Consequently, any reformist prescriptions for the future, emanating from the oppressor, are bound to be an inextricable part of the culture of repression. On the other hand, for the oppressed, the pathology has prevented the realization of their human potential. As a result, the oppressed, as the direct victims of such a society, have no vested human interest in maintaining it. This is because the structure of social needs nurtured by such a society is incapable of ensuring a new, more humanistic sensibility that can be the only liberating condition for the birth of new men and women in South Africa.

The inherently subversive quest for freedom by the oppressed of South Africa is even more evident today where their erstwhile demand merely to be allowed to participate in the various structures of government has clearly given way to an insatiable desire to create: to create comparable structures on the basis of a new human sensibility. Where much of the activity of political resistance up to the sixties was not based on a far-reaching, fundamental critique of the nature of government and economic arrangements for the production and distribution of national wealth, later, especially since the end of the sixties, and mainly under the impetus of the Black Consciousness Movement, many black organizations, mainly of a professional nature, were established as alternatives to the system: students, social workers, lawyers, doctors, journalists, workers and other professional sections of the black community established alternative organizations of various kinds in both urban and rural areas. They did this in order to create institutions that were independent of those established by white power, ones which could effectively articulate and project the concerns and interests of the oppressed.

However, there have since been further significant developments. What we are beginning to witness now is a further shift towards the establishment of alternative structures at the *grass-roots level* in various communities in the townships as well as in some rural areas. The establishment of these grass-roots organizations is, no doubt, a response to the intensification of the struggle and the deepening of experience resulting from it. For example, the call for the rendering of the townships ungovernable has given way to the need for their governability, only this time on foundations *rooted in the experience of the people themselves.* Unfortunately, as these significant changes are taking place, whites, in general, are not there. Industry is not there. Yet, what is happening in the townships is bound to have a tremendous impact on the way government will be organized, how the educational system is going to be altered and on the way in which relations of production in the corporate world may have to be rearranged. Here, new forms of democratic participation are being created out of the practical experience of township existence.

This situation must present South African radical intellectuals with their greatest challenge thus far: the emergence of new forms of democracy, of new ways of social thinking, will require not a condescending and manipulative attitude of management, but a deep understanding, the kind that should lead to a radical codification of social thought which results from new forms of social practice. Specifically, some of the challenges may manifest themselves in the following directions:

1. It would appear that relations of power within the African family, particularly in the townships, appear to have undergone a tremendous transformation. For better or worse, there is an increasing tendency towards parent/child consultation. To what extent, then, will this development affect the quality of family life, and in what directions? Whatever the case may be, the practice of democracy in the home is bound to have a marked effect on its practice in the immediate neighborhood, in the first instance, and then, ultimately, in the entire country.

2. One place which will definitely be affected is the workplace. Industry may be compelled to take into account the emergent needs of the evolving African family. What adjustments may need to be made in concepts of production, in the relationship between the factory, the workers in it, and the community those workers come from?

3. Since the aim is not to reproduce old bureaucratic structures of government, which over the years have habituated the mentality of repression, emergent grass-roots democracy may have to be elevated right up to the level of national government. In this regard, what forms of participatory democracy will emerge, which will express the spirit of struggle, of the quest for a new morality?

4. The remolding of the educational system toward one that will inculcate these emergent values and speed up, at the same time, the production of skilled and educated Africans at all levels of the social and economic activity, is at the root of the new day.

Also central to the need for a new education is the recognition that apartheid culture has been a cultural disease that has deformed whites themselves. As has been suggested above, the disease has ingrained in them the habit of experiencing their well-being in terms of their oppression of others. For this reason, it cannot be taken for granted that whatever white South Africans have to offer is inherently valuable. Their blueprints for the future may be tied up with social "biological" needs that can only be met under the old negation. Everything is going to be subjected to the most rigorous scrutiny. In this regard, the reeducation of whites, therefore, should constitute a crucial area of education, for indeed, the educators themselves need to be educated. For example, white children by and large are not participants in the making of the future right now. Tragically, where they participate they come in as soldiers to smother the dreams of their peers. Whatever vision of society determines their actions, it is dead to the future. The social virus of apartheid can be seen to reproduce itself even at that very moment that fundamental change is called for. The white polity, even as it watches with culpable indifference the physical killing of black children, is busy killing the souls of its own children. Of what use can these children be to the future?

5. In concert with new needs, it may be essential to work out new technological priorities.

6. What kind of means need to be devised to facilitate the rapid yet creative improvement of life in the rural areas?

This has been a rather lengthy digression from the question of language. But, in fact, the issue of language should become clearer from the broad social perspective that has just been drawn. From this perspective, one can go on to evaluate the state of any aspect of society. But since our interest, at the moment, is in the English language in South Africa, we shall necessarily go on to focus on it specifically.

Basically, I think that we cannot afford to be uncritically complacent about the role and future of English in South Africa, for there are many reasons why it cannot be considered an innocent language. The problems of society will also be the problems of the predominant language of that society, since it is the carrier of a range of social perceptions, attitudes and goals. Through it, the speakers absorb entrenched attitudes. In this regard, the guilt of English then must be recognized and appreciated before its continued use can be advocated.

For example, Professor Butler, in his very persuasive essay, makes several statements which reflect traditional views on the validity of the English language in multilingual societies, particularly those in Africa. Here is a list of statements made by Professor Butler. They indicate the depth of the problem as I see it:

1. The English language is of vital concern to all South Africans. (p. 164)

2. The English pose no political threat to anyone. Their language, however, is wanted and needed by all. (p. 165)

3. Blacks have not forgotten the quality of those old mission institutions; and they are more determined than ever to have command of English. (p. 168)

4. English, unlike the other languages in South Africa, is not "an own affair" of the ESSAs. It is everybody's affair, because it is indispensable in a way that our other languages are not. (p. 169)

5. In expressing his support for a unitary system of education in which English may have to be the sole medium of instruction, Professor Butler makes a remarkable statement: "Thought, like money, has no colour." (p. 169)

6. White English-speakers must enlarge their constituency; they can only do this by enlarging the influence of their language. (p. 172)

7. The "democratic tradition, and . . . the English language. These are deep in ESSA birthright and tradition, and are open to all South Africans." (p. 172)

I will not discuss these points in turn because I think the context in which they could properly be looked at has already been spelt out earlier in this discussion. The inherent limitations of these statements will now be obvious. But I will briefly sum up my response. We could begin with the remarkable statement that "Thought, like money, has no color."

The remarkable thing about this statement is that it is true. But even more remarkable, for our purposes, is that it is incomplete. It should also be added that "thought, like money, is linked to economic and social class." For example, it has been shown that the corporate world in the United States, controlling vast sums of money, also effectively controls thought in that country, a fact which renders problematic the much-vaunted concept of freedom of speech in that country. Thought, in the public domain in the United States, is canned thought, often selectively siphoned off from solid research and thrown at an impressionable public by sides contending for social, political and economic dominance.[16] It is this canned thought that is then exported to the rest of the world through advertising, through corporate business English, through scientific gadgetry and its accompanying technical English and through the political wisdom of the Voice of America. How could Professor Butler miss this phenomenon?

Of course, one does not want to give the impression that the world community uncritically accepts this kind of American onslaught on the international mind. But in countries where there are constituencies linguistically and culturally tied to American ideals, we should not be blamed when we insist on a rigorously critical kind of vigilance. It is at this point that we return to Professor Butler's call to ESSA's to show their patriotic duty in helping to "spread their constituency" through the teaching of English. How else can they spread their constituency without, at the same time, spreading their social vision through their language? Central to this vision, for example, is their "democratic tradition." Does this tradition include the kind of grass-roots democracy that is flowering in the townships of South Africa at the moment? The implicit ideology sustaining Professor Butler's social and political vision definitely excludes this new phenomenon. Indeed, the link between thought and money is often fraught with intrigue!

I do not mean to suggest a mechanical one-to-one relationship between language and society, but I do want to suggest that before we declare English to be our unquestionable national language, we must be critically open-minded about several possible eventualities:

Firstly, South African English must be open to the possibility of its becoming a new language. This may happen not only at the level of vocabulary (notice how the word "necklace" has acquired a new and terrible meaning), but also with regard to grammatical adjustments that may result from the proximity of English to indigenous African languages.[17]

Secondly, the teaching of English will have to be freed from the functional instruction of corporate English. A dangerous offshoot of this corporate approach to the teaching of language is to be discerned in the SABC(TV)* programs of language instruction. The programs are designed to teach whites selected African languages. Below is a typical teaching segment.

The aim of the lesson was to teach the question "Where are you going?" in SePedi. Three whites each meet an African whom they ask in SePedi: "Where are you going?" The first African is a messenger who replies that he is going to the post office. The second is a domestic servant who replies that she is going to the store, and the third, a worker dressed in overalls, replies that he is going to some similar place of work. The point about these lessons is that seldom do the segments carry situations in which blacks and whites meet as equals. The situations are often ones which involve employer(white)/employee(black) relations. Remarkable about the segments is the functional context of language use. Clearly, the lessons are not designed to promote meaningful communication between humans; rather, they are designed to enable whites to make better use of their black workers. Thus, the psychological approach to language learning is flawed from the word *go*. No doubt, though, the SABC is convinced that it is "bridging cultural gaps."

There is yet another revealing aspect to the situation just described: it is that, structurally speaking, the colonial relationship that existed between European and African cultures in South Africa is duplicated in the relationship that is being perpetuated between English and Afrikaans on the one hand, and African languages on the other hand.

---

*SABC: South African Broadcasting Corporation

231

Where African cultures in the colonial context held, for imperial cultures, only an exotic anthropological interest, now, in the South African context, African languages hold a mainly functional, manipulative interest. They are a means towards a more efficient use of African labor.

The above example of language teaching by the SABC typifies the context of learning that also characterizes the traditional teaching of English to Africans. What may need to be emphasized is that if the recognition that English belongs to all who use it is more than academic, then in multicultural societies English will have to be taught in such a way that the learners are made to recognize themselves through the learning context employed, not as second-class learners of a foreign culture, or as units of labor that have to be tuned to work better, but as self-respecting citizens of the world. The idea of teaching English through the exposure of second-language learners to English culture should be abandoned. If English belongs to all, then it will naturally assume the cultural color of its respective users.

Thirdly, in promoting English in a multilingual society, especially in the South African context, where the dominant culture feels more inherently valuable than the dominated cultures, it may at some point become increasingly and dangerously difficult for us to make a distinction between English and education. At a certain juncture, education appears to have become synonymous with the acquisition of English. That being the case, a fracture between the acquisition of knowledge and the acquisition of English must be brought about. This is in the obvious recognition that the sphere of human knowledge is much wider than any one language can carry. Corporate English appropriates knowledge by equating it with the mere acquisition of language. That English may be spoken universally does not imply that it carries the sum total of the world's wisdom. The sooner the oppressed of South Africa know that, the sooner will they appreciate the immense freedom of choice before them.

Fourthly, it may be said that there are aspects of English that are not tied to any manipulative interest: literature and the world of learning in general, for example. That may be so. But these considerations are seldom at the center of the need to spread the hegemony of English today. Promoting a foreign language in another culture cannot, for the vast majority of the members of that target culture, go beyond the merely functional. That is to say, English is an international language, but it is international only in its functionally communicative aspects. For the rest of the time, indigenous languages fulfill the range of needs that English similarly fulfills for its native speakers. From this point of view, the functional acquisition of English in a capitalist society such as ours can further reinforce the instrumentalization of people as units of labor. So it is conceivable that the acquisition of English, precisely because the language has been reduced to being a mere working tool, can actually add to the alienation of the work force. Indeed, in the same way that grass-roots organizations are meant to protect people from the oppressive impersonality of the state, indigenous languages can be a refuge away from the manipulative impersonality associated with corporate English language acquisition.

As the center of the problem, in fact, is the educative function itself. The humanization of the educative function is a dire need, since South African society still has to produce a viable homegrown humanistic ethical tradition. From the word go, modern education in South Africa was tied to material accumulation. Rampant capital accumulation, such as is characteristic of the times of Cecil Rhodes, meant that the ability to found economic growth on a homegrown ethical culture was severely limited. That ethical culture, particularly for the ESSA's, especially in their moral stance towards the oppressed, became instead no more than humanitarian politics. And it is there, possibly, that we have the origins of that protective benevolence towards the oppressed, associated with this community. It is that similar attitude now that wants to rescue the oppressed from ignorance through the vehicle of the English language.

We have come a long way from my introductory comments. They were not intended to be a direct criticism of the Academy as such. Rather, they were designed to be an analogical approach to my central thesis that uncritical open-mindedness, in this case about the manner in which the English language is being promoted in South Africa today, can be a dangerous form of encapsulation. However, should the Academy feel that the cap fits it, then it is invited to get a firm hold of that cap and wear it. Beyond that I am certain that there are more areas to this topic that I have not touched. The major focus of this paper was to seize the opportunity to present and formulate the problems from the perspective that I have adopted. I can only hope that I have been sufficiently provocative to provide something for the participants of this conference to discuss and debate in the sessions to follow.

---

1. Article in the *Listener* (October 21, 1965). Quoted in *The Critical Evaluation of African Literature*, Edgar Wright, ed. (London: Heinemann, 1973), p. 3.

2. Guy Butler, "English in the New South Africa," *The English Academy Review, 3* (1986), pp. 163–76.

3. Ibid., p. 166.

4. Recently, the British Council began marketing, on behalf of the BBC, a package of audio-visual instructional materials called *Television English*. This package offers, among other things, "interesting collections of carefully selected excerpts from BBC-TV programmes about a wide range of topics including: British life and customs, traditional crafts, medicine and health, new inventions, British institutions, history, people at work, fashion and clothing, leisure activities, food and drink, British countryside, music and art, buildings, British humour."

Furthermore, the package is meant for "intermediate to advanced learners of English around the world who

"* are interested in seeing and learning about aspects of British life, culture, technology, humour, history, etc.

"* would like to watch BBC television programmes in English and learn how to follow them

"* want to study the English the British use when talking to each other using current words and idioms."

5. Butler, p. 172.

6. Ibid., p. 173.

7. See J. A. Lombard and J. A. du Pisanie, "Removal of Discrimination Against Blacks in the Political Economy of the Republic of South Africa," a memorandum for ASSOCOM, No. 3, 1985.

8. Ibid., p. (i).

9. Lombard and du Pisanie declare that the "market economy is the product of human nature and the politico-economic system patronizing the market economy is based on a more realistic and consequently superior understanding of human nature" (p. 20).

10. Lombard and du Pisanie, p. 15.

11. See Heribert Adam, *Modernizing Racial Domination* (Los Angeles: University of California Press, 1971).

12. See note 9, on the need for the extension of the economic-legal attribution of "human nature" to black people.

13. Agostinho Neto, in M. Chapman and T. Voss, eds., *Accents* (Johannesburg: Ad. Donker, 1986), p. 186.

14. For an extensive and most revealing analysis of this manipulative social attitude of modern corporate America see Joel Kovel, *The Age of Desire* (New York: Pantheon, 1981).

15. See Herbert Marcuse, *An Essay on Liberation* (Harmondsworth, England: Pelican Books, 1972). Note Marcuse's use of the term "biology": "I use the terms 'biological' and 'biology' not in the sense of the scientific discipline but in order to designate the process and the dimension in which inclinations, behaviour patterns, and aspirations become vital needs which, if not satisfied, would cause dysfunction of the organism. Conversely, socially induced needs and aspirations may result in a more pleasurable organic behaviour. If biological needs are defined as those which must be satisfied and for which no adequate substitute can be provided, certain cultural needs can 'sink down' into the biology of man. We could then speak, for example, of the biological need of freedom, or

of some aesthetic needs as having taken root in the organic structure of man, in his 'nature,' or rather 'second nature'" (p. 20).

16. See Noam Chomsky, "Thought control in the USA: the case of the Middle East," in *Index on Censorship*, Vol. 15, No. 7 (July/August 1986).

17. Marcuse, pp. 41–43, in which Marcuse shows how the struggle for liberation also takes place in the field of language itself. See also Mothobi Motloatse, ed., *Forced Landing* (Johannesburg: Ravan, 1980). Motloatse is very forthright: "We will have to *donder* ["beat up on"] conventional literature: old-fashioned critic and reader alike. We are going to pee, spit and shit on literary convention before we are through; we are going to kick and pull and push and drag literature into the form we prefer. We are going to experiment and probe and not give a damn what the critics have to say. Because we are in search of our true selves—undergoing self-discovery as a people.

"We are not going to be told how to re-live our feelings, pains and aspirations by anybody who speaks from the platform of his own rickety culture."

Photograph by René Weideman.

The Black Afrikaans Writer: A Continuing Dichotomy[1]

Hein Willemse

For a biographical note on Hein Willemse please see page 180.

I

Language is usually a highly charged issue. It is axiomatic that "the linguistic is always at base the *politico*-linguistic, a sphere within which the struggles of imperial conqueror with subjugated state, nation-state with nation-state, region with region, class with class, are fought out."[2] The case of Afrikaans is not dissimilar. Afrikaans is so embedded in the political arena of present-day South Africa that any final projection as to its ultimate position should really be suspended until we have won our political emancipation (and/or until the last Afrikaans speaker has died). For many South Africans Afrikaans is anathema; for other South Africans Afrikaans is the language of their bread and butter; for many other South Africans Afrikaans is the language of their most intimate experiences. And many of these South Africans are black.[3]

This paper represents a personal account. Hence the often personal tone and style. And may I dedicate it to three fellow South Africans who have struggled and striven towards the realization of the whole South African nation:

1. Dikobe wa Mogale—poet, jailed in 1984 to ten years' imprisonment for alleged terrorist activities; and to the memory of:

2. Alex la Guma—novelist, veteran exile who died in Havana, Cuba, on October, 13, 1985.

3. Benjamin Moloise—poet, executed on October 19, 1985, for the alleged slaying of a policeman.

Their case histories exemplify the position of the creative personality in South Africa more powerfully than any paper or treatise. This is an indication of the extreme anger, anguish, determination and resolve of the South African oppressed. The fact that they wrote in English is peripheral. What is relevant, however, is that their lives, their writing, were completely intertwined with that of the South African freedom struggle. Let no one underestimate the extent of their example on future generations of writers.

Afrikaans is known primarily as the language of the Afrikaner. The language of the oppressor. Many people still recall the numerous plac-ards in Soweto, June 1976: "No Afrikaans," "Away with Afrikaans," "Afrikaans stinks." The motorial cause for that extensive period of unrest, it is generally accepted, was the enforced teaching of science subjects in Afrikaans:

> To an educational system already subject to severe strains was added the doctri-
> naire ruling on the use of Afrikaans mathematics and social studies. This was
> objectionable on several grounds: few teachers were qualified to use the language,
> proficiency in English was popularly regarded as a prerequisite for clerical employ-
> ment, and Afrikaans was unacceptable for ideological reasons.[4]

Ideologically, Afrikaans equals Afrikaner rule. It was (and *is*) an identifi-able element of the everyday repression and inconveniences of black South Africans' lives. To scorn Afrikaans is to symbolically declare your abhorrence of the present political dispensation.

The events of June 16, 1976 sparked nationwide protests, acts of subversion and deaths. Black Afrikaans-speaking students like myself were drawn into various political activities: the layout, printing and distribution of pamphlets; organizing of political meetings; and the arrangement of cultural forms of protests. And frequently I read my poems. In Afrikaans. That year many deaths occurred across the coun-try. In the Western Cape, black working-class areas like Guguletu, Nyanga, Elsie's River, Ravensmead and Heideveld bore the brunt of the police fire. Ironically, in a series of upheavals that started out as a reaction against Afrikaans, many Afrikaans-speaking people (primarily those in the three last-mentioned areas) were killed. This juxtaposition may appear to be melodramatic but it represents rather graphically the dilemma of the black Afrikaans writer.

So many atrocities are perpetrated in the name of "Law and Order," many of these *in* official Afrikaans. Given the generally high level of bilingualism in South Africa, some black Afrikaans writers may expediently opt out and write in English, in the process avoiding the suspicion of being less committed and literarily in cahoots with Afrikaner rule. Personally, however, this would have meant the premature death of my creative endeavors, and the beginning of an unbearable language schizophrenia. The task now is to continue writing in Afrikaans and to be constantly aware of this dichotomy: the oppressed writing in the language of the oppressor. One also has to accept as fact that Afrikaans is at once the language of the conqueror and the language of the oppressed. This, furthermore, implies that the black Afrikaans writer must constantly be in pursuit of a literary commitment *in Afrikaans* which is overtly counter-hegemonic.

II

I propose to address the following: a short overview of the debate on the origins of Afrikaans; Afrikaans as language of Afrikaner nationalism; Afrikaans as language of the oppressor; Afrikaans as language in the current insurrection.

Afrikaans has a very short history. As a written language it is less than two hundred years old. As a spoken language it probably developed during the ensuing years of frequent contact between the European colonizers and the aboriginal Khoikhoi and San people:

> The Khoi . . . were among the first to change the Dutch language by adapting it to their own tongue and pronunciation. They consequently altered the grammatical structure of Dutch and progressively developed the Afrikaans language. The Dutch colonists, caught up in this creolization process, consciously and unconsciously adapted the simplified Dutch.[5]

With the importation and indenture of slaves from Angola, Java, Madagascar and Malaysia, the creolization of Cape Dutch or proto-Afrikaans received further impetus.[6]

The genesis of this new pidgin, Afrikaans (literally: from Africa, Africa's), has for years been the terrain of exhausting ideological battles.[7] Opposed to the above almost logical, linguistic interaction theory, Van der Merwe, from a diachronic purist position, concludes:

> it is clear [that] no non-whites as a group or as individuals influenced Dutch to such an extent that it changed to Afrikaans . . . We recognise non-white influence with regard to our vocabulary, nothing more.[8]

238

According to Van der Merwe, these loanwords are negligible, not affecting the grammatical and syntactical core of Cape Dutch. He asserts that Afrikaans "has its origins in and from the spoken language of the Whites" who "spontaneously" developed latent tendencies of their Western Germanic dialects.[9]

Afrikaans has, since the rise of Afrikanerdom around the turn of the century, been closely identified with the Afrikaner. Afrikaans, vulgarized Dutch, became the valued possession of the Afrikaner. Afrikaans has been usurped and used as a prominent ideological vehicle in the Afrikaner's ensuing battle for political hegemony (c. 1890–1948). The close affinity between Afrikaans and the post-1948 South Africa became more pronounced. Consider the renowned Afrikaner writer André Brink's evaluation of the relationship Afrikaans/Afrikaner-rule:

> More and more, the Afrikaans language of apartheid became eroded by newspeak, by the necessary distortions imposed by the adherence to an ideology which has to shape the world to its own image. In simplistic terms, the language of apartheid, colonized by the imperialistic activities of politicians, has now become the Language of the Lie . . . Because of the power it wields . . . . the establishment's voice is the one that resounds in the world. And so Afrikaans has become identified, more and more, in the mind of the world, with the apartheid ideology.[10]

Not only "in the mind of the world," but also in the experience of the majority of South Africans, Afrikaans equals apartheid and repression. Afrikaans is the language of the *baas* (boss):

> Morning Baas,
> Baas,
> Baas Kleinbaas says,
> I must come and tell
> Baas that,
> Baas Ben's Baas says,
> Baas Ben want to see
> Baas Kleinbaas if
> Baas don't use
> Baas Kleinbaas,
> Baas.[11]

Compare also this scene from *Woza Albert!*:

PERCY: En nou! En nou? Who is this? Who is sitting around eating lunch with my kaffirs? That's why you're getting cheeky, hey? Ja, you sit around and have lunch with terrorists!

MBONGENI: Hau! He's not a terrorist, Baas! He's a big man from heaven![12]

Wa Ntodi's poem reveals the suzerainty of the *baas* over the worker. This servility is convincingly illustrated on the level of dialogue:

> Afrikaans (unlike English) marks the distinction between the polite and the familiar second person prenominal form—*u/jy*. But in racist South Africa, in the contact between coloniser and colonised, boss and labourer, even the polite *u* is not sufficiently distanced. The flexibility and economy of the syntactical shifter are lost and nouns and proper names (all Afrikaans in this poem) are retained. The consequence is an enormous clogging up, an enormous redundancy of information. The poem enacts, ironically, at the level of dialogue, the inefficiency, the opaqueness of apartheid colonialism.[13]

Afrikaans is the language of the riot policeman *sjambokking* students. It is the language of the ill-mannered shop attendant. It is the language of the eviction notice. Afrikaans is the language in which a former minister of police, Jimmy Kruger, said on the death of Black Consciousness activist, Steve Biko: "Dit laat my koud."* Given this proven legacy of callousness, inhumanity and brutality, and then certainly not only at the level of language, is it any wonder that black people demonstrated so forcefully their rejection of apartheid and Afrikaans?

Afrikaans Literature, the Afrikaner's canonized cultural goods, has in essence been a faithful bedfellow of Afrikaner nationalism and Afrikaner identity. Especially during the earlier decades of this century. D. F. Malan,[15] in a speech in 1908, exemplifies the attitude which nurtured this proximity:

> Elevate the Afrikaans language to a written language, make her the bearer of our culture, of our history, our national ideals and with that elevate the *volk* [literally: nation; here it refers exclusively to the Afrikaners], who speak it . . . . The Afrikaans Language Movement is nothing more than an awakening of our *volk* to a feeling of their own value and to the call to take up a more dignified position in the world civilization.[16]

It is against this background of close affinity between Afrikaans, Afrikaans Literature and Afrikaner Nationalism as well as the ideological maneuverability of the language that the position of black Afrikaans writers must be considered. They participate in a literature tightly bound by Afrikaner identity. With these odds it is no surprise that the overall production of black Afrikaans writers is rather scanty. Since

---

*"It leaves me cold."

240

1944 only fourteen black Afrikaans writers, mostly poets, have published their work.

May I overburden you with a note on the use of Afrikaans? Afrikaans,
in large parts of the Cape, Transvaal and Orange Free State, has to a
significant extent been the language of the impoverished underlings: the
farm laborers, the fishermen, the general populace of the barren hinterland. The upwardly mobile and the career-minded consciously chose
English. This is material in understanding the political and social inser-
tion of black Afrikaans poets. The majority of them are of rural extraction with late teenage introduction to urban life, usually due to the
furtherance of their scholastic careers.

Given the rural extraction of some of the earlier black Afrikaans
writers, and the overall political and the structural organization of
the essentially colonialist society, some of these writers succumbed to
what Frantz Fanon called the processes of assimilation. To illustrate, I
will compare the rather interesting cases of Peter Abrahams and S. V.
Petersen.

In Abrahams's book of poetry, A Black Man Speaks of Freedom (1940),
there are some revealing poems: especially on the relationship of the
poet vis-à-vis the community. In "Self," the poet sees himself as representative of the people:

> I'm a poet
> And through hunger
> And lust for love and laughter
> I have turned myself into a voice,
> Shouting the pain of the people
> And the sunshine that is to be

In "Laughter," Abrahams's militant and even revolutionary proclivities
surface. Stridently he rejects Christianity and the religious acceptance of
fate:

> I have learned to love
> Burningly
> With the fiercest fire;
> And I have discarded my humility
> And the "Will of God"
> And the stories of my wise teachers
> Arming myself with the wretchedness
> In every plain man's life,
> And all the tomorrows my soldiers
> I battle on behalf of Freedom
> That will restore the laughter of man

Petersen wrote at about the same time. His reaction to similar circumstances is self-scorning and, as opposed to Abrahams's strident call for freedom, a curious contradiction manifests itself. In a poem, "By Seweweekspoort," he contemplates:

Versonke in myself,	Lost in myself,
—'n swerweling, oplaas tot rus	—a wanderer, finally chained
geboei, gebind—	to repose, bound—
het ek vrede hier gevind	I have found peace here

In another poem, "Aand op Riversdal," he says:

En so het ek die land aanskou,—	And so I behold the land,—
Self tot rus gebind, geboei . . .	myself bound in repose, chained. . .
Dit was aand,	It was evening,
Aand op Riversdal	Evening in Riversdale

This specific yearning for peacefulness and tranquility—and eventually for broader societal freedom—is contradicted by the imagery, namely that of peacefulness in fetters. Petersen's notion of freedom is limited and the expected representative voice of the oppressed collective does not appear in his work. Petersen's concern is more with the personal outreach of a particular individual. This intense and well-nurtured individuality of Petersen is indeed a salient feature of his poetry. Unlike Abrahams, he never really establishes or attempts to establish a close rapport with the black mass. Petersen's relationship with the dominant cultural order is pronounced, and it influenced his relationship to that of the oppressed. His call is for the recognition of his blood relationship with the Afrikaner, or if you prefer, the oppressor. That's as far as my illustration goes.

It is not uncommon for black Afrikaans writers to go through a phase of denial and questioning their decision to write in Afrikaans.[19] Especially after 1976 no black Afrikaans writer can be spared the intellectual anguish of rationalizing his choice of language. My decision to continue writing in Afrikaans has been profoundly influenced by an incident in Namibia.

As a member of a dramatic troupe, I went on a nationwide Namibian tour. Lüderitz, a small fishing town on the Atlantic coast, was our first stop. We were to play three or four one-acts—among other things, an English-language play, Inkululeko. We arrived at noon, to be met by the president of the local branch of the organizing Students' Organisation. He spoke English—rather haltingly, until he overheard an Afrikaans conversation among some of the players. And then he said something like: "My goeie God, ek't gedink julle praat net Engels. Ek't nie geweet hoe om vir julle te sê dat daai Engelse stuk nie hier gaan werk nie. Almal praat hier net Afrikaans." ("Good God, I thought you only spoke English. I didn't know how to tell you that that English performance wouldn't work here. Everyone here speaks only Afrikaans.")

And although I knew that Afrikaans was the *lingua franca* in Namibia, it struck me for the first time that we had a very real problem of communication. We realized that *Inkululeko* (the Xhosa for "freedom") could not be performed, whatever its message. After much discussion, it was clear that the political message was too important to cancel our performance. The only viable option was to translate the work into Afrikaans. Five hours later we had—in verse—a tentative Afrikaans equivalent of *Freedom*. For the next week we rehearsed incessantly and polished the Afrikaans translation while traversing the meandering dirt roads in a cramped Volkswagen. For the whole of that tour we never once performed *Inkululeko* in English. There are times when one cannot deny one's experience. That was such a time.

In a country where many writers describe their roles as functionaries engaged in popular struggle, they must consequently demonstrate their affinity with society. They must speak, in more ways than one, the language of their audience:

> Any pupil who spoke Afrikaans was treated with contempt by some teachers and most pupils. So naturally one attempted as far as possible to hide the fact that you were Afrikaans-speaking. On leaving high school I decided never to speak Afrikaans unnecessarily. This was my protest against the Afrikaner government; the *volk* and the system in this country. Later in my development I came to realise that workers on the farms speak Afrikaans. Workers on the Cape Flats and elsewhere speak Afrikaans. I became aware of the fact that if I wanted to identify with the struggle of the working class I had to speak, understand and write the language we all know.[20]

This *raison d'être* for writing Afrikaans may be severely criticized by conservative and reactionary critics as utilitarianism at variance with Literariness and Literary Exclusivity. And very little of this literature for/about/by working-class people may be considered acceptable in the Afrikaans canon. I really doubt, however, whether acceptance into the ruling-class culture is at all the objective. It is obvious that we have here a cultural activity created under trying circumstances, the writing of embattled people searching and struggling for a comfortable niche.

In recent political movements the message of liberation, in some areas, is rendered in Afrikaans. The language being consciously part of the message. During the recent and still-continuing struggles in this part of the country, the Western Cape, school children are singing these battle songs:

PW is 'n terroris (x3)	PW is a terrorist (x3)
Le Grange is 'n murderer, (x3)	Le Grange is a murderer (x3)*
Ma, ek wil 'n Casspir hê, (x3)	Ma, I want a Casspir (x3)
Ma, ek wil 'n Buffel hê. (x3)	Ma, I want a Buffel. (x3)

Or:

Die mammas, die pappas,	The mommies, the daddies,
die boeties, die sussies,	the brothers, the sisters,
die uncles, die anties,	the uncles, the aunties,
die hondjies, die katjies,	the doggies, the kitties,
is almal tesame in die struggle.	are all together in the struggle.

Or the trade unionists sing:

Klim op die wa (x2)	Climb on board the wagon** (x2)
Klim op Cosatu se wa	Climb on board COSATU's wagon
Almal wat Cosatu lief het,	Everyone who loves COSATU
klim op Cosatu se wa.	Climb on board COSATU's wagon.

These are evidence of a more relaxed attitude towards the use of Afrikaans in practical political activity. Also, in organized political groups there is a sensitivity to prevent the situation where, in oppositional discourses, elements of the upcoming classes are suppressed and marginalized. Profoundly at work is the development of a counter-hegemony. Currently the political organizations are sensitive to working-class demands and value working-class acceptability. This sensitivity also extends to the sphere of language.

For the black writer to write in Afrikaans is an overtly political act. He cannot ignore the Afrikaans literary heritage. Afrikaans literature has in essence always been directed to one particular portion of this country: the Afrikaner. The need of black Afrikaans writers is to take as their audience the whole of the South African nation, "to learn how to speak," in the words of Jeremy Cronin, "with the voices of this land."***

---

*P. W. Botha is State President of South Africa; La Grange was Minister of Law and Order.
**The ox wagon is a symbol of the Voortrekkers, the Afrikaans settlers, and therefore of Afrikaans nationalism. Here the symbol is turned against the Afrikaaners.
***See page 81.

244

The basic historical fact for the black writer is that blacks have not yet attained their political emancipation. The writer finds him-/herself in continuous contestation with the ruling order in South Africa. In this sense it is paramount for the black writer to contribute towards a visible counter-hegemonic literature—a literary voice that continues to be the embodiment of a people engaged in political and social struggle.

The need for a visible counter-hegemonic literature extends into the area of publication. This implies, for example, that all the major Afrikaans publishing houses are off-limits. The political and economic interests of the South African government and these publishers are decidedly coterminous. To publish with one of these publishing houses would lead to an unavoidable compromise.[23]

The position of the black Afrikaans writer is indeed overburdened with extra-literary issues. For many observers these concerns may appear to be peripheral, not really affecting the essential craft of writing. The materiality of writing, especially language, however, cannot be ignored when it forms such a prominent part of the power struggles in one's society.

---

1. This paper was read in its original form by the author at the University of Iowa, Iowa City; the African Studies Association conference (November 23–27, 1985), New Orleans; and at a writer's forum at Dora Falck, Muizenberg, May 1986.

2. Terry Eagleton, *Criticism and Ideology* (London: Verso, 1976), pp. 54–55.

3. Although the majority of the Afrikaans-speaking blacks would be classified "colored," i.e. mulatto, in South Africa, I know from personal experience that there are other so-called "African" classified people who have as their first language Afrikaans. See also Elsa Joubert, *Poppie* (Johannesburg: Jonathan Ball, 1981), p. 14: "Everybody spoke Afrikaans, even the Rhodesian Africans and Xhosas and Sothos living there."

4. Tom Lodge, *Black Politics in South Africa Since 1945* (Johannesburg: Ravan, 1976), pp. 54–55.

5. Kenneth Jordaan, "The origins of the Afrikaners and their language, 1652–1720: A Study in Miscegenation and Creole," in *Race*, Vol. 15, No. 4 (London, 1974), p. 462.

6. Marius Valkhoff, *New Light on Afrikaans and "Malayo-Portuguese"* (Louvain: Editions Peeters Imprimerie Orientaliste, 1972), p. 65.

7. For English overviews of these debates see Jordaan and Valkhoff.

8. H. J. J. M. van der Merwe, "Die ontstaan van Afrikaans," in *Afrikaans: sy aard en ontwikkeling*, ed. H. J. J. M. van der Merwe (Pretoria: J. L. van Schaik, 1972), p. 29.

9. Ibid., p. 50.

10. André Brink, "The future of Afrikaans," in *Leadership S.A.*, Vol. 3, No. 2 (Johannesburg, 1984), pp. 34–35.

11. Motshile wa Ntodi, "South African Dialogue," in *Century of South African Poetry*, ed. Michael Chapman (Johannesburg: Ad. Donker, 1981), p. 347. [This English-

language poem uses the Afrikaans word "Baas," which means "boss" but is associated with white Afrikaans dominance, hence the noun "baaskap," "boss-hood" or "boss-ship." In this poem, the worker uses "Baas" to address the middle-aged employer and "Klein-baas," "little boss," for the employer's son. – *Editor's Note*]

12. Percy Mtwa, Mbongeni Ngema and Barney Simon, *Woza Albert!* (London: Methuen, 1983), pp. 50–51.

13. Jeremy Cronin, " 'Laat ons ranks vassa' – African poets and the use of Afrikaans," in *Swart Afrikaanse skrywers*, eds. Julian Smith, Alwyn van Gensen and Hein Willemse (Bellville: U.W.C., forthcoming).

14. Oswalk Mbuyseni Mtshali, "The removal of our village – Kwa Bhanya," in *Fire-flames* (Durban: Shuter & Shooter, 1980), p. 43.

15. In 1948 Malan's Nationalist Party came to power on the apartheid election ticket.

16. Quoted in Hermann Giliomee and Heribert Adam, *Afrikaner mag: opkoms en toekoms* (Stellenbosch: Universiteits – uitgewery, 1981), p. 80, translation by Hein Willemse.

17. Hein Willemse, "Die wrange klag, die satire en opstandigheid van die kleurling: towards a critical reconstruction of the intellectual history of black Afrikaans poets," *The Political Economy of Race I*, ed. Wilmot James (Bellville: U.W.C., 1984).

18. See the following instructive quotation from Richard Rive, *Writing Black* (Cape Town: David Philip, 1981), p. 6:

I grew up in an atmosphere of shabby respectability, in a family chafing against its social confinement to dirty, narrow streets in a beaten-up neighbourhood. Our hankering after respectability became obsessive. We always felt we were intended for better things. The family spoke Afrikaans, as the youngest I was spoken to in English. We were members of the Anglican church.

19. S. V. Petersen and Adam Small, for instance, published respectively *Meditations on the Brink* and *Black, Bronze, Beautiful* (Johannesburg: Ravan, 1975). Small's *The Orange Earth* and an English translation of *Kanna hy kô hystoe* (*Kanna, He Is Coming Home*) and Peter Snyders's *Violations* have been performed.

20. Beverley Jansen, "Poësiepaneelbespreking," in *Swart Afrikaanse skrywers*, eds. Julian Smith, Alwyn van Gensen and Hein Willemse (Bellville: U.W.C., forthcoming).

21. Jeremy Cronin, *Inside* (Johannesburg: Ravan, 1984).

22. For analysis of the influence of apartheid on literature see V. A. February, *Mind Your Colour* (London: Routledge & Kegan Paul, 1981); G. J. Gerwel, *Literatuur en Apartheid* (Bellville: Kampen, 1983); and R. M. Kavanagh, *Theatre and Struggle in South Africa* (London: Zed Press, 1985).

23. This is not a shared or representative opinion. The majority of black Afrikaans writers still publish with the major Afrikaans publishing houses.

An Artist Is Struggling with Chains

Text and linocuts by John Muafangejo

John Muafangejo was born in Angola in 1943. He studied in South Africa and now lives in Namibia. He is one of the region's most celebrated graphic artists, with much of his work depicting South African as well as Namibian subjects. Below is a transcription from his linocut work entitled "An Artist Is Struggling with Chains," in which Muafangejo gives an account of his history in his own words and punctuation.

An Artist is straggling with chains in order to tear it from the stem. OMALAMUANDI) where I dwelt untill I looked After goats, calves and milked the cows. I was lovely son in my father out of 9 sons because I was obeyed son more than Muafangejo's sons although I was the fiveth son in my father and the sixth son in my Mother. 1)I thanks to my ex-Bishop Rt. Robert H. Mize who was sent me to Art College in Natal on the 11–01–1967. 2)I thanks to my friend Rt. Rev. C.S. Mallory who was told the Dr. A.L. Spencer-Payne in England to pay my two years Art course from 1968 to 1969. All 2 Bishops are Americans. 3)I thanks to my Bishop C.O. Brien Winter who was helped me for 3 years open my small Studio at our Mission and the first employed me for teaching art here for 4 years. 4)I thanks also to Rt. Rev. R. Wood who was helped me last year to my refresh course at Rorke's Drift and employed me for temporary teaching while I wait my answer to come for overseas further study Art. I hope, I will be the first professional African Artist in S.W.A. in feature if Gods will. Together with Mrs Olga Livinson the S.W. Africa Art Association, the President of Art Education who was paid my refresh course last year. 5)I thanks very much for Oshikango Police men those helped me in my troubles sickness. They sent me to Engeld Hospitality treatment for free of change. 6)I was in chains both arms and legs for 7 days without question me. I have no work and no money salary. I do care because I am not born with work or money. 7)I am 33 years old unmarried man. Does n't mean that I dislike women but I am friendly to them. Those I met five ladies are Love greement breaker. I am happy, enjoyable man in his Art work daily. There are just two great human needs: Light on the Mystery of life and Life for the Mastery of life. I am with God.

*   *   *

House for the Leader our old house for the owner of Mission. The Anglican old fashion building was burn up by Night owl or by master nobody while the Anglican Artist was arrested in 9th of August in 1975. Artist was tied arms and legs with chains by somebody and sent me to Onekuaja Kuanjama Witch doctor to give me some medicine for 7 days, in 16–8–75. They were said that John was sick for mad but they were just worried me too much and I was talking too much most reading Bible, singing and Praying because I was lonelyness. They were talking lie to say I was mad man. I was worried. The house was burnt on 14 of August 1975 during the night between 12.00 to 1.00 at Night while I was at Onekuaja. This house is the biggest house more than all building sleeping houses in the Anglican houses in the Mission. You Christians must the Anglican Churches remember this room in your prays and you can give the collections for Rebuild it.

My own short story about the Anglican First Famous Artist John Muafangejo in the whole of S.W. Africa. I am the Kuanjama tribe who was born in Angola in 1943 at (ETUNDA LO NGHADI).

St Michael Church in Windhoek

©1985 John N. Muafangejo.

Death of a chief. Manduma the Ovambo Chief being decapitated by Lt. Tom Marony (docter) before his death in action on 6th February 1916. Mandume the great Chief amongs the OVAMBO chiefs in Ovamboland. We remember him in our n...

ANGLICAN SEMINARY BLOWN UP: The seminary blown up by bombing by Master no body. This building was destroyed by un known people on Thursday 18-6-1981 at 1. a.m. It is near the border of Namibia and Angola. This destruction is the 3rd of St Marys buildings those were same about like that one.

(1) House of Archdeacon in 1975. (2) House of Priest, Engineering for litehouse and carpentery work shop in 1414. The Eighth Bishop Rt. J.H. Kauluma was preaching in saddness togethur with his Archdeacon Revd. P.H. Shilongo for the destroyed houses of Odibo Mission. Bishop will be Rebuild them one day but we are Anglican Christians; let us thing when we will got same helpful to our Bishop beause it is not new fhing. It is old action which was going slow by slowly. If we are truly Christian faithy. We must give 10% of our Properties to Bishop when he will ready for Rebuild the three deferents builds. Please. As what ANGLICAN NAMIBIA ARTIST FULFIL like AMEN. JOHN 7:37-45.

(OMUBISOFI WA TUCK:

audita nuluhodi unene molomile ei. Vakuetu ovaholike tupasukeri o'e si Pamba kue Lilongikida Omolon anjonauno etu. Ohele ei Jaudpalala kalunga. Esi osili osikolo savame velihonga no vapita most Marys Odibu. Eisho longhenda la Pamba Kalunga otafale no neni kuvo omutenja no ufiku. Ep jlo, lange kunje oleli ile Elombuelo kunje janajeni sa Omaongato a eso andja modibo ku bish. Cfi wongeleka jai Agilikana okukuafela oku tu ngulula c aturigilo u dibo ose si ojo inaja ngeleka adiseMowambo sandj koufareki wakelera.)

(SHRI T.N. NJAPA VY: JO. C Eimbula 112)

New ARCHBISHOP DESMOND TUTU ENThroned At

St. Georges Cathedral C Town in 7-9-1986.
OUR Namibia → We was Praying and Plodding for our
New ARCHbishop DESMOND TUTU of CaPe TowN
Father hear our Prayers, Bless him and Keep him in
our mind, HoPe, and Be Strong, Peaceful, Kindness
ARCHbishoP in defficlt time but god will helP him.
© 1986 John N. MUAFANGEJO

Oral Performance and Social Struggle in Contemporary Black South African Literature

Kelwyn Sole

For a biographical note on Kelwyn Sole please see page 164.

In a class on African *orature* recently, I was discussing the use of forms of oral expression—jokes, proverbs, the telling of stories—in Soweto with a group of black post-matriculants. "You still hear them among people in the train," one student said. "Some people," another chipped in. "Who?" I asked. "The people in the third-class carriages." "And the people in the second-class carriages, what are they doing?" "Reading newspapers and magazines."

It is frequently forgotten that, even today, large numbers of people in South Africa are nonliterate or at best only semiliterate. A study carried out in 1980 estimated that the number of those not adequately literate in their first language might be as high as a third of the total black population over the age of fifteen; and the problem is compounded by a subsequent unavailability of English (widely regarded by political organizations as the *lingua franca* of a future post-apartheid South Africa) to an even larger number of people.[1] This fact is, obviously, a crucial one to bear in mind when reading South African literature and assessing its social significance and political relevance.

Popularizing the Political: the Dilemma of Black Consciousness

After the Sharpeville massacre and the banning of black political organizations in 1960, many of the writers of the so-called "Drum" generation of the previous decade were jailed and fled into exile. The grip of apartheid laws tightened. Stricter censorship was enforced, and all but a few city venues were barred to black performers and audiences, which effectively curtailed the easy production of multiracial musicals and plays. Black musicians found themselves removed by the government (in connivance with the white musicians' union) from white hotels and nightspots, an important source of their revenue. Although some multiracial theater continued to exist on the peripheries, black dramatists, musicians and directors found themselves by the mid-sixties in a position where they were forced to play in township halls whether they wanted to or not.

The most noticeable effect of this was a tailoring of theater to suit a popular township clientele. Dramatists such as Gibson Kente and Cornie Mabaso, who had been part of the multiracial Union of Southern African Artists in the previous decade, struck out on their own. While a number of more intellectual plays (by Anouilh, Pinter and so on) were still performed, Kente and another playwright/director, Sam Mhangwane, evolved a successful formula to attract township audiences. Traveling around the townships in combis with impromptu sets, they performed a melodramatic and spectacular form of drama which highlighted the use of more accessible oral forms such as music, song and dance. Episodes in everyday township life were presented, and a number of stereotyped characters (the gangster, the venal priest, the policeman) were introduced for audience recognition and amusement. Some characters spoke in the tsotsitaal patois* endemic to the townships.

Both Kente and Mhangwane enjoyed a great deal of commercial success playing for black audiences. Generally speaking, Kente

> knows what the people want. He knows they want an escape. A simple story with lots of sadness and laughter. The central character must be someone everyone can identify and feel for . . . . He knows also, and this by now is largely his fault, that the audience doesn't want to be taxed, made to think, listen too hard and, above all, self-criticise. All the hardships (and these must be heavy) must be blamed on someone else. And there must be a ray of hope—that all will be well one day, without our having to do anything about it.[2]

Thus, while reflecting accurately many of the hopes and frustrations of township life, this theater tended to remain politically quiescent.

This form of popular theater has stayed a feature of township life right up until the present time. However, by the late sixties a new, politically assertive ideology was on the upsurge among black university students,

---

*tsotsitaal patois: street slang

intellectuals and theologians: the ideology of Black Consciousness. Basing itself on principles of black pride, self-determination and self-worth, Black Consciousness had a strong "back to Africa" cultural tendency. Rejecting white expertise and values as potentially corruptive, the young black artists who adopted this philosophy insisted on political messages in their art and consciously directed their work to black audiences and a black readership.

Significantly, the forms initially given prominence in this new cultural movement were drama and a poetry to be actualized in public performance. While some poets continued to publish their works—the success of Oswald Mtshali's first volume *Sounds of a Cowhide Drum* (1971), among, it was alleged, a largely white readership caused a minor sensation—the emphasis turned more and more self-consciously towards performance media. In a situation where publishing and the media were in the hands of the white establishment or liberal white patrons at best, performance came to be seen as a way to have immediate political effect on a black audience in a manner which, due to its ephemerality, could at the same time evade the stringent limitations placed on political utterance. Frequently, plays did not exist in written form at all, but were created in a workshop situation and altered as the situation and audience demanded.

A variety of cultural groupings emerged around the country dedicated to pursuing these ideological and formal goals: the Cultural Committee of the South African Students' Organisation (SASO), the Theatre Council of Natal (TECON), the People's Experimental Theatre (PET), the Mihloti Black Theatre Group and the Music Drama Arts and Literature Institute (MDALI or, more commonly, "Mdali") are among the best remembered of these. Not only students but also older black artists and writers began to be attracted to these groups, as well as those who had skills important to performance art, such as the musicians-cum-poets Lefifi Tladi and Molefe Pheto.

Literature and drama were used as a means of political and cultural communication and *conscientization*, an attempt at "dynamic communal discussion" by artists determined to inform all sections of black society of their position as blacks in South Africa, to give them encouragement and to awaken, unify and mobilize them under the rubric of their black identity. As an example of this attempt at direct communication, when Khaya Mqayisa of Port Elizabeth mounted his play *Confused Mhlaba* (about an ex-Robben Island prisoner who finds his people apathetic and self-seeking on his release) at Mofolo Hall in Soweto in the mid-seventies he used a small stage within touching distance of the audience, gave them flowers and chatted with them during the course of the play in his attempt to "become a member of the audience," in the words of one reviewer. Another Eastern Cape playwright, Mzwandile Maqina, adapted the Kente format for his play *Give Us This Day* in an effort to popularize its political content among as wide an audience as possible.

Language was increasingly considered as only part of the expressive vocabulary of performers. Music, dance, comedy, mime, gesture and other visual devices were stressed in various attempts at popularization and to evoke an immediate display of emotion. At the same time, Black Consciousness took on a combative if fluctuating position vis-à-vis other forms of theater about or for black people. White-directed and ethnic-influenced shows such as *Ipi-Tombi* and *kwaZulu* were regarded as anathema because of their distortion of traditional rural life, their frequent government sponsorship and tendency to portray blacks as uncomplicated, smiling children. Black Consciousness reviewers pointed out also that theater which made use of indigenous languages but played before mainly white audiences in South Africa and overseas, such as Welcome Msomi's "Zulu Macbeth" drama *uMabatha*, relied more on spectacle than meaning for its success. Even political theater by blacks which included some white influence or help was derided by extreme exponents of Black Consciousness: Mongane Serote's slanging of the blacks in Workshop '71 as "non-whites, schizophrenics, guinea-pigs" is a famous example.[3]

The popular township theater of Kente and others was also slammed for its lack of political message and content: there is a noticeable tension in the comments of Black Consciousness playwrights between the impatience displayed at this theater for its lack of commitment and the envy implicit at the audiences it managed to attract. To spread their influence, Black Consciousness groups presented festivals of drama and poetry, poetry readings, and cultural events. The South African Black Theatre Union and Mdali held art festivals. PET and the cultural group Shiqomo collaborated in a program of poetry readings and music called *An Evening of Black Thoughts* in 1973, as did TECON in the show *Black Images* the same year; poets gave public readings at venues such as the segregated University of the North, and Lefifi Tladi's music group Dashiki performed a reading of Aimé Cesaire's West Indian epic *Return to My Native Land*, dramatized and with musical accompaniment. At these festivals, poetry and drama by local artists rubbed shoulders with speeches by Baldwin and Fanon, poetry by Senghor, Baraka and Diop, and works by overseas dramatists such as Peter Weiss and Ed Bullins.

This movement towards oral performance and popular participation remained contradictory. The attitude of political and cultural activists at the time fluctuated between extolling "the people" and criticizing them

257

for their lack of politicization. Sloganeering, polemics and a rather vague gesturing towards a romanticized and abstract "Africa" dominated, at times, at the expense of any sympathetic portrayal or dialogue around the concrete problems and attitudes of black working-class people. Audiences occasionally did not extend beyond an already *conscientized* educated minority. A black critic criticized the second Mdali Festival of the Black Arts held in Soweto in 1974 for not going beyond

> a small group of conscious brothers and sisters, most of them would-be graduates who go to a play expecting their imaginations to be stirred to thrilling extremes by hair-raising slogans . . . . Where were all the thousands who go to Gibson Kente's plays and set the walls rocking with their responses? Big question. And if Mdali can find the answer, they will be a success.[4]

Although traditional precolonial Africa was used as an exemplar for social and cultural behavior, the dislike these radical urban black artists felt for the white government's ethnicizing policies was reflected at the time by an ambiguity and suspicion amongst many of them that traditional culture and the use of African languages would be all too readily amenable to apartheid and tribalism. Some attempt was nevertheless made to use indigenous languages in their productions and poetry readings (the poet Sipho Sepamla reports that some black audiences at the time had already taken to shouting "khulumani isiZulu — speak Zulu!" when they did not follow the action of the plays).[5]

The South African government seems to have originally hoped that Black Consciousness would be amenable to the segregationist aspects of apartheid, but was quickly dissuaded from this misconception. From 1973 onwards cultural and political figures became subject to continual harassment. Saths Cooper, Strini Moodley and other TECON members were jailed for nine years in 1975 on a variety of charges; Pheto and Tladi were detained and later fled the country; PET was listed as a subversive organization in 1975; Mqayisa was banned and other poets and playwrights detained and questioned by the Security Police; and even Gibson Kente was detained and harassed for a period after 1974 when his plays became for a while more political.

Speaking to "The Dispossessed": the Effects of 1976

Black Consciousness had by the middle of the decade begun to spread outward from its student base into a wider stratum of urbanized, more articulate members of the black community at large. Community and worker organizations were set up, although these tended to remain fairly small. The discourse in which a great deal of mobilization continued to take place was that of the need for unity of all blacks in racial terms, irrespective of their social position. When SASO and the Black People's Convention initiated worker organizations in 1972, for example, they put forward programs which stressed leadership and recreational programs, black dignity and the "role and obligation" of black workers towards "black development."[6] Only a few activists, such as the poet Mafika Gwala, spoke of the danger of class differences within the black community itself. Where class antagonism in South Africa was spoken of at all, it tended to be in strictly racial terms—all blacks were workers, irrespective of their position in society. Such a position obviously appealed least to the less-privileged classes in black society, the black working class and marginalized groups in the rural areas. Moreover, although some cultural activity aimed at incorporating black workers rather than merely preaching to an undifferentiated mass of people about their shared blackness occurred—a night of committed poetry recited to music and drums presented by Mdali in conjunction with the Black Allied Workers' Union in Soweto in 1973 is a case in point—such activity was peripheral to the central thrust of the cultural revolution taking place.

It can be argued that there were signs of a radicalization away from these terms in SASO in the two years prior to its banning in 1977. Nevertheless, the single event which spread the seeds of political fervor further into the black community than all previous efforts was the uprising which began among Soweto schoolchildren in June 1976 and which quickly spread to other inhabitants of the urban townships throughout the country. In this process of direct and dangerous confrontation with the state, cultural means were used and emphasized. The audiences at poetry readings, art exhibitions and plays within the townships soared, with school students and younger people well to the fore. An increased desire to participate in literary and artistic production was evinced: Medupe, a writers' organization started in Soweto in early 1977 with twenty members, had within six months incorporated over two hundred active writers and performers, and played an important role disseminating "read-poetry" to live audiences (the young poet Dumakude ka Ndlovu observed: "Read-poetry is for the People. It gives them a message to take home. It is simpler than written poetry, so that even the layman can understand it").[7] Oral techniques in presentation became increasingly sophisticated. The use of drums, flutes and other musical instruments became almost obligatory in the reading of poetry.

Mime, gesture and variants in voicing were used in flamboyant and effective ways by dashiki-clad poets and musicians who performed at funerals, commemoration services and cultural evenings to support and give voice to the mood of the times, in amongst the speeches and the singing of freedom songs. Groups of people performed symbolic portrayals of emotionally-charged events such as the death of Steve Biko in 1977, the execution of freedom fighter Solomon Mahlangu and the shooting of Hector Petersen, the first victim of Soweto 1976. Despite experiments by some radical poets with quieter, more reflective styles of presentation, a mode of performance which stressed a ritual of group solidarity and heroism in the face of adversity predominated. In addition, the stress on performance in front of an audience which could attest to the authenticity of the poet's or dramatist's experience, and participate in these rituals of identity and assertiveness, was such that some younger poets during the years immediately after 1976 were suspicious of any poet who published at all.[8]

Despite the banning of Medupe in 1977 and the continuing state harassment of writers and performers, this activity burgeoned. The poet Ingoapele Madingoane was perhaps the preeminent of these performers who instilled his readings and his audience alike with such emotion. His long epic poem "Black Trial," about the ravages of colonialism and the cultural rediscovery of Africa, was so popular in the late seventies that some younger poets could perform it from memory. Madingoane and other Soweto poets traveled the country, performing and inspiring.

In the period after 1976 writers' groups mushroomed throughout black South Africa. Groups such as Mpumalanga Arts in Natal, PEYARTA in the Cape and Guyo Book Club, Bayajula, Khauleza and the Creative Youth Organisation in the Transvaal created literature on the page and in performance, sculpture, painting and other forms of political art. Poetry, music and drama were often welded together into cultural spectacles lasting for several hours, both in the townships and in city venues (after a number of such venues had become available to black performers at places such as The Market in Johannesburg and The Space in Cape Town from the middle of the decade). The Witwatersrand-based magazine *Staffrider*, set up in 1978 to cater to this cultural upsurge and a prose revival which was beginning to take place, reflects in its pages some of the excitement and popularity of literature in this period.

Perhaps better known to audiences outside of South Africa, though, is the work of young playwrights who first came into prominence during this period. At the end of the seventies and in the early eighties Matsemela Manaka, Maishe Maponya and Zakes Mda wrote, workshopped and performed plays which attracted a great deal of attention. They, Manaka especially, emphasized the need for their theater to create a unity of "the dispossessed"—that is, to focus its creative energy and attention on the life of less-privileged black people. As Manaka noted in the preface to his play *Egoli*, which dramatized and extrapolated from the lives of two black mine workers:

> Through our eyes we have seen the sufferings of the people. We have seen them being moved from fertile lands to barren areas, we have seen them starve in squatter camps. Through our eyes we have seen the life of our people assume various shapes of humiliation and suffering. Thus the continual struggle to create "Egoli" . . . we felt committed to focus our creative thoughts on the plight of the workers.[9]

The impatience that was expressed with nonpolitical black art earlier in the decade remained a constant theme. Maponya observed in 1980 that "we find amongst our playwrights those who are involved in theater for art's sake; to amuse themselves, make mockery and fools of our people."[10] Dramatists like Maponya and Manaka presented their plays at a variety of venues, at places like The Market on the one hand and garages, community halls and township churches on the other. They continually stressed the need to perform at venues accessible to ordinary township residents and have even performed and improvised at weddings and funerals. They have dealt with areas of working-class life as well, setting some of their plays in mine compounds, white farms, villages and so on. Their plays attempt to alleviate language problems by using a mixture of English, Afrikaans, Zulu and Sotho.

They have, moreover, continued the tradition of workshopping plays in rehearsal rather than starting from already-fixed scripts, a technique used to great effect by white and black dramatists such as Athol Fugard, Barney Simon and Workshop '71 before them. This has allowed to some extent a group rather than an individual experience to be presented: Manaka, for example, has remarked that, as his plays are based on the experiences of his actors and himself, he generally casts his plays before he scripts them. They, and several other playwrights, have also adopted the familiar episodic structure of township theater, intermingling naturalistic and symbolic modes to achieve their overall effect. Consequent to this, it can be argued, is a movement in their plays between depictions of the actualities of life among less-privileged black people and the use of such themes as a symbolic metaphor for racial oppression: a strong Black Consciousness emphasis and ideology interweaves with the plays' demonstration of the processes of exploitation at work on plantation, mine compound and mine. To some extent at least they are "optimistic trage-dies" (in Mda's words), showing suffering and insisting that it can be overcome by political means, which carry the familiar message that blacks must unite racially and workers politicize themselves to achieve a changed South Africa.

However, by the end of the seventies the hegemony of Black Con-sciousness, although still strong in the arts, was challenged and in many areas broken by the reemergence of the nonracial programs and ideol-ogy of the exiled African National Congress. Today, in reality, national-ist aspirations are mingled in many black cultural productions with an emphasis on the role of the working class and an admiration for social-ism. In current Black Consciousness organizations, too, the rhetoric used has become very much directed to these goals, although these organizations are still not amenable to the presence of whites in their ranks in leadership positions. On the other side of the political fence, the 1983 launching of the United Democratic Front (a coalition of liberal and left-wing organizations) acted as a spur to a cultural creativity which, while maintaining and transforming many of the themes and preoccupations of previous black literature and performance, placed less emphasis on racial factors and more on the immediacy of the liberation struggle and a striving for a nonracial, democratic country. At present a widespread overt political culture exists throughout South Africa, which has incorporated and directed many artists' imaginations – at funerals, political rallies and on other occasions young activists sing freedom songs, perform militant dances such as the *toyi-toyi* and hear poetry performed by well-known UDF poets such as Mzwakhe Mbuli and Jeremy Cronin.

Artistic preoccupations are often similar to what has gone before: the need for a "national culture" of resistance to be built up inside the country, the need for an art which focuses on unity and political ques-tions, and the desire to forge a political and popular consciousness by artists and writers who alternatively listen to and direct "the people."

"Controlling our Creativity": the Role of the Trade Unions

One of the results of a noticeable and growing militancy among working-class blacks since 1973 and a subsequent growth in trade-union organization and activity towards the end of that decade has been an increased visibility in South African life of a welter of cultural forms that less-privileged people have created for themselves to use. To give examples, one need only think of the choir and *mbaqanga* music popular among organization and activity towards the end of that decade has been an increased visibility in South African life of a welter of cultural forms that less-privileged people have created for themselves to use. To give examples, one need only think of the choir and *mbaqanga* music popular among urbanized and semi-urbanized people, the *isicathamiya* choral singing-cum-synchronized group dancing of proletarianized migrant workers, and many other forms. Interestingly enough, it is these migrant workers who are still by and large in contact with their rural roots who use and transform traditional forms of expression and culture to new concerns. They still find their creative identity to some degree in the rural areas from which they come, although many of them spend their lives mainly in the urban centers and exhibit a consciousness which contains elements of class, racial and ethnic concerns. Known as the "people between" (*amagxagxa*), they play a significant role in a number of recent cultural developments taking place—as they assimilate and mould elements of their own Western and urban township life-styles into something which has meaning for them.

It must be stressed that these cultural forms have been developed and altered throughout the history of the urbanization of blacks in South Africa. In this process the presence of an overweening commercial commodified culture has also had its effect, since the development of a recording industry for black music in the thirties and the advent of a state-controlled black radio since the early forties. It is only now, however, that these forms are being afforded more prestige as activists and literati have become aware of the importance of "working-class culture" for political mobilization. Commercially-oriented and defined music such as *mbaqanga* has generally been held in least regard (as evinced in the remark of writer and scholar Njabulo S. Ndebele in 1972 that "*mbaqanga* cannot make one think seriously about life,"[12] but neo-traditional forms of singing and dancing have also previously been ignored for their lack of political content and proximity to ethnic consciousness. Now, at trade-union social evenings and general meetings, in among the slogans and freedom songs, one finds praise poetry and dances performed where tradition and ethnic roots are mobilized for new purposes. More privileged performers have also been increasingly attracted to the use of these forms, and the vagueness of the earlier "back to Africa" call is being tempered by a more concrete and wholehearted appropriation of tradition. One playwright, for instance, has spent time studying the Chopi xylophone: and this movement has not been without its gentle ironies, as urbanized black students have responded enthusiastically to any opportunity they may get to study traditional *orature* and performance, while denying at the same time that they have ever been alienated from its influence.

Many of the forms of cultural expression used by lower-class people are at present overlaid with political content. Religious hymns are, for instance, resung with political words. A transformation of the most highly-valued traditional oral poetic form, the praise poem, has also taken place. With its direct relationship to political power, praise poetry—previously mainly directed at traditional rulers or modern-day demagogues such as Matanzima—has filtered through to populist movements such as Inkatha and working-class trade-union organizations. Although several poets now perform at trade-union functions, perhaps the best known is Alfred Temba Qabula, who began his career as praise poet and dramatist while working as a forklift driver at the Dunlop factory near Durban.* Hailing originally from the Flagstaff area of rural Transkei, Qabula has a wide knowledge of traditional oral forms on which to draw for his performances, during which he comments on and praises events in trade-union and wider political life.

In the last five or six years working-class black people have also begun to transform drama to a political use specific to them. Although some examples of the use of dramatic expression by less-privileged people were existent by the late seventies—*Imfuduso*, the play created by the women of Crossroads squatter camp near Cape Town would be an example—the appearance of the play *Ilanga Lizophumela Abasebenzi* (*The Sun Will Rise for the Workers*) in 1980 marked the inception of a new type of worker drama. This development is all the more remarkable when one realizes that migrant workers often have scant knowledge of drama in the Western sense of the word, seeing it as a form of spectacle akin to soccer matches and the ilk, and that urbanized working people appear to be more familiar with the escapist and morality theater of the Kenti and Mhangwane pedigree. In fact, *Ilanga* evolved from a situation where a white lawyer asked workers who had been fired from a foundry near Boksburg in the Eastern Transvaal to act out the story of their strike and subsequent assault by the police, because their accounts conflicted.

This trade-union theater uses a variety of languages—with English rather less foregrounded—and sometimes appears to the outside eye extremely improvisatory and even crude. Problems in workers' lives in the home and on the job are frequent themes used, as are labor disputes in the factory, the drudgery of wage labor and the relation of workers to

---

*See Qabula on pg. 276 ff.

those who manage and profit from their lives. Very few of the actors in these plays have previous acting experience, and those who do usually have worked with directors like Kente and Msomi.[13] There is consequently a degree of expertise present in the shape of white and black actors and trade-union officials who help to workshop and develop these plays.

Interaction with the audience is an important focus of performance, especially when these plays are performed in front of trade-union audiences. *Ziyajika* (*The Turning Point*), for example, depicts a hard-won process of unity taking place among workers from diverse backgrounds and ends on a high note with a successful strike and the singing of worker and freedom songs by the actors, with the audience usually spontaneously joining in. In the Dunlop play, the audience on some occasions is invited to submit demands to a labor dispute taking place on stage. The emphasis in these plays is basically a supportive one to the message of trade unionism, putting forward situations and conflicts which worker audiences can identify with, and interpreting the underlying structures of oppression and exploitation for the audience. Simon Ngubane, one of the actors in the play *The Long March* (developed by workers who had been fired from the British-owned firm Sarmcol near Howick in Natal), comments:

> We started the play last year and its aim is to show the real struggle about what happened at Sarmcol. It makes a great difference if you see what's happening rather than just hear about it from other people.[14]

Furthermore, there is a movement in these plays away from presenting black political aspirations and experiences of life in South Africa as a noncontradictory, seamless whole. In their dances, songs and these plays, workers express a combination of religious, regional, sexual, class and other identities, and pay attention to their political concerns with an admixture of ethnic, nationalist and socialist sentiments. An awareness of class antagonisms within, and outside, the black community is among the concerns expressed: *Ilanga* for one contains strong criticism of a black manager who talks to the striking workers of their common brother- and sisterhood. There is an awareness, too, of the fact that the creativity of lower-class black people in South Africa has always been marginalized and considered unimportant. The Durban Cultural Group connected to the trade-union federation FOSATU noted in a 1985 interview that "[our cultural work] takes a step, a small step, towards pushing workers to start controlling their creative power. So far this power has been used by everybody in power and with money, for their own purposes . . . a lot of people with a *tickey's** worth of education have a superior attitude towards us. They speak a language we don't understand. Our task is to take our rich or poor heritage and make it satisfy working people, their families and any other suffering people in South Africa."[15]

In Conclusion: Writing, Performance and Power

It can be seen, then, that oral performance and musical accompaniment have widened the scope and aspirations of black South African literature considerably in the last twenty years. Drama has, perhaps, always been a form which can and does assimilate spectacle, speech, gesture and other modes of expressivity in a manner not possible to other forms of literature only amenable to the printed page. Thus, among the less literate audiences in South Africa, these nonverbal aspects of presentation are often used to make the plays more acceptable to them. The performance-poetry developed in South Africa in the seventies also attempts to direct an oral immediacy into what has become primarily a written form, in an effort to reach a wider black (rather than white or overseas) audience. Such intermingling of written and oral forms can take varied and surprising shapes: recently the launching of a book of poetry in Johannesburg was accompanied by the oral performance of one of the poems in the volume by a drama group!

Black South African literature has been created mainly by an overlay of middle-class people who could read and write but who came from a racial background where oral forms of culture predominated. Early black writers such as Sol Plaatje, Samuel Mqhayi and Benedict Vilakazi still had an immediate knowledge of oral tradition at the same time as they assumed, to a degree, the values and standards of European literature and art. By the forties and fifties this dual knowledge is much less in evidence among the urbanized, English-speaking writers of the time who are still the best known in the rest of the world today.

This trend away from an African culture has been partly reversed in the last fifteen years among more-privileged black South Africans, initially among that group of people least in contact with their cultural roots — the urban stratum of students, intellectuals and political activists who have perhaps felt this alienation most keenly. In the face of apart-

---

*tickey: a no-longer-used coin of small denomination

heid's hostility to any form of cultural assimilation or interplay between racial cultures, and in the face of the continuing oppression of blacks within the country, the urge by middle-class people to return to and identify with their own people became a necessity.

There is a huge upsurge of "political culture" taking place in South Africa at the moment. At funerals and political meetings, a combination of poetry, dance and freedom songs renders palpable the determination felt by people for political liberation. It is easy to romanticize or be teleological about this upsurge, however: there are previous examples of a politicization of culture produced by expectations of freedom in this country which were unfortunately not sustained. An example from history would be the cultural activity around the populist-cum-trade union organization the ICU (Industrial and Commercial Workers' Union) in the late 1920's, particularly in the Durban area. It is not culture, finally, that changes political realities: although in South Africa cultural and literary means have often been used to achieve or enhance political organization in a meaningful way.

Underlying political slogans are forms of culture which are little known outside of the country, which are expressive of the everyday lives and hopes of people and which have come to contain political attitudes. The choral group Ladysmith Black Mambazo, as an example, has been overwhelmingly popular among black audiences for years in a way no writer can hope to emulate—but it is only through their presence on Paul Simon's recent *Graceland* LP that the way has been opened up for wider recognition. There is a realization in South Africa that working-class people's everyday activities are as important politically as any amount of slogans and rhetoric, and are a force to be reckoned with. This growing awareness is in stark contrast to a previously-held attitude among activists that workers were in essence underpoliticized and unequivocally in need of guidance and education from their more privileged counterparts. Njabulo S. Ndebele,* possibly the most influential figure in South African literary studies at the moment, has commented at length in a 1984 article published in *Staffrider* that black writers should concentrate on telling stories (thereby emulating the anonymous story-tellers on buses, trains and in the streets) that describe the quality of everyday life rather than rely solely on overt political sloganizing:

> The matter is simple: there is a difference between art that "sells" ideas to the people, and that whose ideas are embraced by the people, because they have been

---

*See pages 32 and 217.

made to understand them through the evocation of lived experience in all its complexities. In the former case, the readers are anonymous buyers; in the latter, they are equals in the quest for truth.[16]

The reworking of oral culture for literary purposes does not mean that written literature itself has been assigned to a back seat. Black workers are aware that, in a very real sense, literacy and education are power, and that much of the country's politics is still conducted at a level of language and in a language which is the property of the educated and articulate. The current crop of black "worker poets" writes *and* performs orally, seeing both as legitimate. As Qabula says, "People must write. They must take out their pens and paper and write. It doesn't matter if it is good or bad—the voice of the workers must be heard." A certain amount of creative literature is starting to appear from writers in the townships who are not directly connected to worker organizations but are part of this tendency, of whom Bheki Maseko,* a driver from Soweto, has so far had the most impact.

Despite the aversion to print literature which was particularly noticeable in the mid-seventies, poets have published throughout the last fifteen years in Black Consciousness journals such as the *SASO Newsletter* and also intermittently in small literary magazines such as *Ophir* and *Donga*. The rise of alternative publishing houses in the early seventies inside South Africa allowed political writers a degree of space to publish that was previously practically unavailable: and *Staffrider* magazine has since 1978 made a plethora of South African writing available to a wider public who would otherwise never have seen it.

In the face of commercial culture and control of the mass media by the government, a constant theme has been the battle for publishing space, performance venues and facilities. Black playwrights still complain of a lack of venues for alternative theater outside of a few playhouses such as The Baxter in Cape Town and The Market: there is some antagonism to be found among more radical actors and dramatists in the townships to what they refer to as "market plays," which they believe are still mainly tailored for the white, educated and overseas market. Attempts have been made in the last fifteen years to set up black publishing houses—of which BLAC Publishing House and Skotaville Publishers have been the most productive and enduring. Frequent calls have also been made to set up viable trade unions which could alleviate the exploitation of all black and/or political artists, from sources as politically diverse as Gib-

*See page 143.

268

son Kente, Medu Art Ensemble and the Black Consciousness-inclined federation of trade unions, CUSA (Council of Unions of South Africa).

Finally, the role of whites and the use of language are still a constant source of debate in South Africa. The presence and influence of whites were anathema to early Black Consciousness adherents: and there is still a strong Black Consciousness tendency among many of the better-known black writers, even though the nonracial UDF is more popular among ordinary black South Africans. Mdali, with its strong Africanist sympathies, was revived in 1979 and almost immediately ran into conflict over the presence of whites at one of its meetings in Cape Town; the African Writers' Association (formed after the demise of the South African PEN branch in 1981) and Skotaville Publishers also direct their attention exclusively to blacks. Writers and artists closer to the UDF and the trade unions take a different attitude to this subject. Indeed, a number of white performance-poets close to the latter organizations are now to be found, of whom Jeremy Cronin, Keith Gottschalk and Ari Sitas* are the best known.

The debate over the advantages and disadvantages of writing and performing in English or African languages continues unabated over a decade after the subject was first brought up in writing circles. Many performers attempt to solve this problem by using an admixture of languages in their productions. This debate has recently been further extended by the beginnings of a black Afrikaans literary movement in the Western Cape, an area of the country where Afrikaans is in everyday use among "colored" people.

It can be seen that, instead of the uniform "black experience" which is often projected by South African literature to readers overseas, the cultural and literary life of South Africa is rich and diverse. In a situation where oral forms are often more popular and more immediate to a great number of people, the hegemony of the written page and of proficiency in English has come to mask the cultural and political complexities which inform all literary activity. Creative artists who use oral expression have found it difficult to break out of the straitjacket of this hegemony: Ingoapele Madingoane's *Africa My Beginning*, for one, loses most of its emotional appeal and nuances of performance on the printed page, even if the printed page may be better than nothing. Recently the UDF poet Mzwakhe has tried to sidestep some of these strictures by making his poetry available on the cassette tape *Change Is Pain*, where he performs with reggae-based musical backing.

---

*See pages 71, 177 and 275.

Disagreements over how to democratize culture, over what types of culture are politically viable and over what comprises "good" literature are always taking place in contemporary South Africa. In a situation where international audiences for South African literature and experimental theater are in many cases more readily amenable than local ones, performers and writers continue to stress that the popularizing of their work in the local community remains one of their crucial tasks. In an article in *Drum* magazine in 1984, Matsemela Manaka castigated German critics who "rave about bad productions from this country. They don't hesitate to label a mediocre play as a masterpiece," and further pointed out that such an idolatrous attitude was superficial, patronizing and eventually unhelpful to South African artists.[19] It can only be to the good of South African literature and performance that a more critical, exploratory and demanding attitude to creative work is, it would seem, starting to appear.

---

1. Linda Wedepohl, *A Survey of Illiteracy in South Africa* (Cape Town: Centre for Extra-Mural Studies, University of Cape Town, 1984), pp. 9–10.

2. Robert Kavanagh, "Gibson Kente '74," *S'ketsh* (Johannesburg, Summer 1974/75), p. 24.

3. Mango Tshabangu, "Mihloti Newsletters Vol. 2, No. 1," *S'ketsh* (Johannesburg, Summer 1973), p. 45.

4. Anonymous, "The Mdali Festival of the Black Arts 11," *S'ketsh* (Johannesburg, Summer 1974/75), p. 33.

5. Sipho Sepamla, "The Black Writer in South Africa Today: Problems and Dilemmas," *New Classic* 3 (Johannesburg, 1976), p. 20.

6. See Bennie Khoapa, ed., *Black Review 1972* (Durban: Black Community Programmes, 1973), pp. 27, 123.

7. Dumakude Ka Nalovu, "Somebody Is Dead," *Donga* 6 (Johannesburg, 1977), p. 6.

8. See Anthony Emmett, "Oral, Political and Communal Aspects of Township Poetry in the mid-Seventies," in Michael Chapman, ed., *Soweto Poetry* (Johannesburg: McGraw-Hill, 1982), p. 181.

9. Matsemela Manaka, *Egoli — City of Gold* (Johannesburg: Ravan, 1980), back cover.

10. Ken Maishe Maponya, "Scribe speaks out on black theatre," *The Voice* (Johannesburg, October 22–28 1980).

11. Zakes Mda, "Commitment and Writing in Theatre: the South African Experience," *The Classic*, Vol. 2, No. 1 (Johannesburg, 1983), p. 15.

12. Njabulo S. Ndebele, "Black Development" in Steve Biko, ed., *Black Viewpoint* (Durban: Black Community Programmes, 1972), p. 27.

13. Ari Sitas, "Culture and Production: the Contradictions of Working Class Theatre in South Africa," *Africa Perspective*, Vol. 1, Nos. 1–2 (Johannesburg, 1986), pp. 90–91.

14. Pippa Green, "A Place to Work: Sarmcol Worker Co-ops," *South African Labour Bulletin* (Johannesburg, 1986), p. 19.

15. Durban FOSATU Cultural Group, "Culture and the Workers' Struggle," *South African Labour Bulletin*, Vol. 11, No. 2 (Johannesburg, 1985), pp. 72–73.

16. Njabulo S. Ndebele, "Turkish Tales, and Some Thoughts on South African Fiction," *Staffrider*, Vol. 6, No. 1 (Johannesburg, 1984), p. 48.

17. Anonymous, "The Worker Poets," *Learn and Teach* 3 (Johannesburg, 1986), p. 21.

18. See, for instance, Doc Bikitsha, "Poetry in the Vernacular," *Rand Daily Mail* (Johannesburg, February 22, 1978); Risimati j'Mathonsi, "The Less Known Voices," *The Bloody Horse* 5 (Johannesburg, May-June 1981), p. 30.

19. Kaiser Ngwenya, "Artistic vow holds them to their roots," *Drum* (Johannesburg, November 1984), p. 97.

"We All Participate in Every Level of Production" / linocut by Sipho Hlati.

"Vukani Basebenzi" ("Workers Rise") / linocut by David Hlongwane.

From *Black Mamba Rising*

South African Worker Poets in Struggle

Edited by Ari Sitas

Published by the University of Natal
for the COSATU Workers' Cultural Local

Introduction

Ari Sitas

Ari Sitas, born in 1952, studied at the University of the Witwatersrand. One of the founding members of Junction Avenue Theatre Company in Johannesburg, he has been involved in all its major projects since 1982 — such productions as The Fantastical History of a Useless Man, Randlords and Rotgut *and* Marabi. *Since 1980 Sitas has also been closely involved in trade-union activities, as well as an initiator of the workers' theater movement. Following his move to Durban in 1983, Sitas has worked closely with the unions based in the region, and particularly with COSATU, the progressive confederation of trade unions.*

Sitas now lectures in industrial sociology at the University of Natal, and is an editor of the South African Labour Bulletin, *a journal closely linked to democratic organizations within South Africa.*

Alfred Temba Qabula, Mi S'dumo Hlatshwayo and Nise Malange are known by thousands of workers in Natal. They are known for their cultural work: poetry performances, plays, songs and their struggle to create a cultural movement amongst workers in Durban. They see themselves as part and parcel of a growing and confident democratic trade-union movement in South Africa. In 1985 all three of them were central to the creation of the Durban Workers' Cultural Local, whose principles are outlined below. By the end of the year they were responsible for the development of a Trade Union and Cultural Centre at Clairwood alongside the shop-steward council in the area.

The poems in this book have been composed for performance at mass meetings, trade-union and community gatherings, for festive and somber occasions. Save Nise Malange's poems, the rest have been composed in the Nguni (Zulu and Xhosa) vernaculars. Consequently, the poems printed here in translation and outside their context suffer; they lose much of their oral power: the songs, the chants, the ululations, their improvisatory nature and, of course, the popular responses that accom-

275

pany their oration. Despite that, the words here are strong enough to communicate in their own right. What follows is a brief introduction to the three activists.

Qabula

Alfred Temba Qabula was born at Flagstaff, Transkei, in 1942. His grandfather was a transport-rider; his father and his uncles were miners and sugarcane workers. Migrancy and influx controls ruled his area's and his family's life. Seventy percent of the able-bodied men in his area subsist through migrancy.

Qabula was raised under harsh conditions as a child—he was orphaned after his father was poisoned and his mother wilted away very early in his life.

As a young man, barely eighteen years old, he was caught up in the Pondoland rebellion. He survived the conflict by hiding and starving in the forests with his friends. In those days death was stalking the area, and agriculture collapsed. The year 1964 found him on a train bound for Carletonville to start his first migrant contract with a construction company on the mines. For five years he lived in the compounds at night and worked as a plumber in construction gangs during the day. In 1969 one of his foremen started a business at Redhill and lured him away to Durban. There, he lived with his uncle at Amaouti in Inanda Reserve. It is no surprise that Qabula's poems, songs and "praise-pieces" are pained by the "hurt of migrancy."

His immediate family—a wife and three children—remained on the land. His heart, his feelings and his source of inspiration remained with them in their world of the countryside. As he announces in one of his poems, the natural sounds and landscapes there are his sources of inspiration, but also a source of resistance: "From this criss-cross of sounds / and song / Delivered by your creatures / I / get inspiration / to sing / And also to write / And also to ask my sisters and brothers / 'Why are you quiet? / Silent?' . . . is there nothing that tickles you into action / from all this?"

Despite his feelings, though, his experience is of an urban world of ugliness, harshness and noise where "we see the railway tracks / the highways, the buildings and factories / the structures . . . we hear / the trains / the motor cars and machinery / the bombs going off / the sound of gunshot / and you refuse to ask them why they are conducting

276

themselves like that / You don't complain / when they are making so much NOISE! . . ."

In 1974 he entered the noisy world of factory production at Dunlop S.A. (Sydney Road). From then on he had to adjust to the demands of the mass production of rubber products.

Qabula adjusted to his job by creating a unique world: in his head. For the past decade he has been composing songs there about everything that affects his life and the lives of others. He survives the working day by composing songs of redemption or resistance: "I would see something that hurts, that causes me pain and then I would spend the working day making a song about it."

In 1983 he joined the Metal and Allied Workers' Union (MAWU)* and was part of the shop-steward steering committee which organized all the Dunlop workers into the union. That year, he participated in the making of the "Dunlop Play."** In 1984 – dressed in a colorful costume – he started to perform his "Izimbongo zika Fosatu" composition at union meetings. His performances initiated a revival of imbongi*** poetry in union gatherings in Natal and beyond. This oral poetry, thought by many to be a dead tradition or the preserve of chiefly praises, resurfaced as a voice of ordinary black workers and their struggles. Since then Qabula has written more poems, plays and projects within the Durban Workers' Cultural Local. He is now completing a book on his life experiences and together with Hlatshwayo and others he continues to orate his poems.

Hlatshwayo

Mi S'dumo Hlatshwayo was born in 1951. He grew up as an "illegitimate" child in a working-class household in Cato Manor / M'Kumbane – a sprawling shack settlement in Durban. His family's poverty made him leave school by standard seven**** and search for a job. As he told FOSATU Worker News, all his dreams were sunk: "I wanted to be a poet, control words, many words, that I may woo our multi-cultured South Africa into a single society. I wanted to be a historian of a good deal of history; that I may harness our past group hostilities into a single South

---

*This COSATU-affiliated group was founded in 1973.
**A play about worker history devised by Dunlop factory workers.
***imbongi: praise-singer
****Standard seven is equivalent to freshman year in high school.

African history . . . After 34 years of hunger, suffering, struggles, learning and hope, I am only a driver for a rubber company" (*FOSATU Worker News*, No. 35, June 1985).

He continued his self-education by reading whatever came his way: from biology primers to Zulu history books. He learnt about poetry through the *eCibini* (or St John's Apostolic Church), which was famous for its healing rituals. He had joined the church after being healed when he had had a serious illness. In that independent African church of the poor, he experienced for the first time in his life a community of concern and care. He found a church without status distinctions, where ordinary people shared and prayed together. He also experienced in the church's emotional gatherings his baptism in "words of fire": the lay-preachers, men and women who were imbued with a prophetic and messianic vision, and had integrated the *imbongi* tradition of Nguni poetry in their religious sermons. He was discovering there the power of language and poetry — where Christ, sometimes a furious black buffalo, cut through the shrub and gorged to proclaim his victory on earth.

The sense of a caring community he experienced at church he carried over into all levels of life: he started participating in efforts to organize the Clermont community and later joined MAWU when it started organizing at Dunlop Sports where he was working. But, if anything, it was the Dunlop strike of 1984 that triggered him to cultural action. After hearing Qabula perform his *izimbongo* of FOSATU, he realized that one did not need to be somebody from the university to write poetry. In fact, he was schooled through the church in the tradition himself, without knowing it before. He composed *A Black Mamba Rises** to praise the Dunlop workers' struggle. He then joined Qabula and others to form the Durban Workers' Cultural Local.

He has since composed more poems, written and directed plays and initiated many projects. In October 1985 he resigned his job at Dunlop Sports to become the Local's full-time cultural organizer.

Malange

If Qabula is the singer of the hurt of migrancy, if Hlatshwayo is the urban poet of an undying tradition, Nise Malange is the wandering youth of the 1976 generation. She was born at Clovelly near Cape Town in 1960 and

---

black mamba: an extremely venomous African snake. See poem, "The Black Mamba Rises," on page 296.

grew up in a one-room shelter there, only to move to a shack at Vrygrond a few years later. Her father was "African," her mother a "colored" and she somewhere in-between. By 1966 her family moved to Guguletu, where they have been residing since.

In 1968 Nise was sent to a "colored" school at Elsies River and then to a school at Nyanga East—wherever she went she was mocked for not being either a "real" colored or a "real" Xhosa. But at Nyanga East her schooling was disrupted by altercations involving the hostel* population there. Her father decided to pack her off to the Transkei in 1975 whilst she was in standard six, to get her out of dangerous township influences. She lived there through the 1976–77 rebellion, when she was exported back to Cape Town.

In Cape Town, too, she lived through the brunt of the 1977 student rebellion. The war between the witdoeke** from the hostels and the location residents, clashes between youths and police—in all these, many of her generation died. In the same year she was then sent by her family to Sada in the Ciskei to resume her studies. Before long, new protests swept through the school, and there were new hardships and detentions. By 1981 she was out of the Ciskei and back to Cape Town. By 1982 she migrated to Howick, Natal, to reside with other members of the family there. Her life shares all the afflictions experienced by an entire black generation. In 1983 she started working for the trade unions in Durban and now she is an organizer for the Transport and General Workers' Union.

Her involvement with culture started from youth groups in the Cape—making plays, writing poetry and dancing. She has written many poems in Natal, which she recited in many mass meetings. She joined Qabula and others after the "Dunlop Play" to start workshops on a new play: *Why Lord?* Since then she has been directing, writing and reciting many projects in the Workers' Cultural Locals in Durban.

Conclusion

Qabula's, Hlatshwayo's and Malange's work presented here has inspired many workers to start building a cultural movement. As they told the *South African Labour Bulletin* in 1985: "We are involved in this, however

---

*hostels: dormitories for male workers living away from home
**Black conservative vigilantes whose white armbands, or *witdoeke*, gave them their names

hard it is for us after work, because we believe that our struggle is not only there to destroy the oppressive powers that control us. It is there also to build a new world. To do this, we must begin now—at this stage, for every black worker who picks up a pencil and forgets about the bottle, there's a victory. But most of the work is for performance in every place where people and workers meet . . ."

Migrants' Lament—A Song

Alfred Temba Qabula

If I have wronged you Lord forgive me
All my cattle were dead
My goats and sheep were dead
And
I did not know what to do
Oh Creator forgive me
If I had done wrong to you
My children: out of school
Out of uniforms and books
My wife and I were naked—naked . . .
Short of clothing

If I have wronged you Lord forgive me
I went to WENELA*
To get recruited for the mines
I went to SILO**
To work at sugarcane
Oh creator forgive me
If I had done wrong to you
But they chased me away

*The Employment Bureau of Africa, the mine-labor recruiting organization of the Chamber of Mines

**Sugar Industry Labour Organisation, a labor-recruiting organization for the sugar plantations

They needed those with experience
With long service tickets and no one more

If I have wronged you Lord
Forgive me
I left my wife and children
To look for work alone
I had to find a job
Oh Creator forgive me
If I had done wrong to you
I was despairing in Egoli
After months searching for this job
And when I found one
I lost it
For I didn't have a "SPECIAL"*

If I have wronged you Lord
Forgive me
I found a casual job
I felt that my children would be happy
With my earnings
Oh how happy I was!
Oh creator forgive me
If I had done wrong to you
Yes, as my children were happy
And as I was working
The blackjacks arrived to arrest me
So again I lost my job

If I have wronged you Lord
Forgive me
When out of jail I searched again—
Another casual job, happy again
The boss was happy too
And he gave me a letter
To fetch a permit from back home
Oh creator forgive me
If I had done wrong to you
But the clerk said: "I can't see the paper"

---

*Migrant workers for the mines and plantations get a "special" after long service.

And added: "You must go in peace my man"
So I had to buy him beer, meat and brandy
For him to "learn" to read my piece of paper

If I have wronged you Lord
Forgive me
I was working again
But I realized so far for nothing
Oh Creator forgive me
If I had done wrong to you
So I joined the union to fight my boss
For I realized: there was no other way Lord
But to fight with the employer
There was no other way
Now go troublemaker go.

(*MAWU AGM,* * *Curries Fountain Stadium, 1984*)

---

*AGM: annual general meeting

Africa

Alfred Temba Qabula

Oh, I thank the Creator
For molding and placing me
In Africa

When my eye rests on you Africa
You are indeed
A bride on her wedding day
Plumed in all the treasures
Found in you:
The gold, the silver, the copper and aluminium
The diamond, the lead and iron . . .
Recounting them would take us
To infinity

When winter comes
Our eyes touch the mountain peaks
Clad in snow
Confirming you Africa
Indeed a bride on her wedding day
It is then, at such a time
When you look at the trees
Tall trees
Tall trees and short grass
All swaying in unison
Singing a tuneful song
Waving from this side and that

As if singing and saying
"We thank you Africa
For the nourishing rain
For your sun

As it strengthens us against the cold
For stretching our tendons with your winds"

The Tears of a Creator

Alfred Temba Qabula and Mi S'dumo Hlatshwayo

O maker of all things
Grief
Assails you from all sides
Each step forward you take
Brings enmity nearer
What is the nature of your sin?

In the factories
Your enemy suffocates you
On this side: the bosses
On that side: the boss-boys

Attackers and assailants
Stalk you
From all chambers
And channels . . .
Permits and money
Become the slogans
Through which
They pounce on you
What is the nature of your sin?

Your labor power
Has turned you
Into prize-game

For the hunters of surplus
What is the nature of your sin?

In the buses
In the trains and taxis

You are the raw meat,
The prey
For vultures
Are you not the backbone
Of trade?
What is the nature of your sin?

Worker
Your rulers
Have dumped you
Away from the cities.
Now all the misfits and orphans
Of other nations
Can suck you dry

Now
You are a nameless breed of animals
A stock of many numbers
And your suppressor's lust
To suck you dry
Recognizes neither day
Nor night
What is the nature of your sin?
Your hand
Has developed
A drunkard's tremble
It can no longer draw straight lines
To steer you clear
Between the law enforcers and the bandits

Worker
Are you not the economy's foundation?
Are you not the engine
Of development and progress?

Worker
Remember
Who you are;
You are the country's foundation base and block

Oh maker of all things
The world over
Worker
Your capacity to continue loving
Surprises me, its enormity
Touches the Drakensberg mountains.
What is then
The nature of your sin?

Your sin
Can it be your power?
Can it be your blood?
Can it be your sweat?

They scatter you about
With their Hippos
With their vans
And kwela-kwelas*
With their tear gas
You are butchered
By the products of your labor
These are the cries of the creator of all this

COSATU
Woza 'msebenzi,** woza COSATU, woza freedom.

Oh COSATU
We workers
Have traveled a long way here

Yes: we have
Declared wars

---

kwela-kwela: police van
**Woza 'msebenzi*: Hurry up, workers

On all fronts
For better wages

Yet,
Victory eludes us.

We
Have dared to fight back
Even from the bottom of the earth
Where we pull wagonfuls of gold
through our blood.

We have
Come from the sparkling kitchens
Of our bosses.

We have arrived from the exhausting
Tumult of factory machines.

Victory eludes us still!

COSATU
Here we are!

Heed our cry—
We have emerged
From all corners of this land
We have emerged
From all organizations.
We have emerged
From all
The country's nooks and crannies!

We say today
That
Our hope is in your hands
We are ready.

We say:
Let your hands deliver us from exploitation
Let our freedom be born

Let our democracy be born
Let our new nation be born

COSATU
Stand up now with dignity
March forward
We are raising our clenched fists behind you
Behind us
We call into line
Our ancestors in struggle
Maduna and Thomas Mbeki
Ray Alexander and Gana Makhabeni
J. B. Marks and hundreds more.

Where are you ancestors?
Lalelani and witness:
Here is the mammoth creature
You dreamed of
You wanted to create
The one you hoped for
Here is the workers'
Freedom train!

It is made up of old wagons
Repaired and patched up oxcarts*
Rolling on the road again
Back again
Revived!
Once capsized by Champion
The wagon—once derailed by Kadalie**

Here it rolls ahead
To settle account with the oppressors
To settle account with the exploiters.
Here it is:
The tornado-snake—Inkhanyamba with its floods!

---

*See note on page 244.
**Champion and Kadalie were leaders of the Industrial and Commercial Workers'
Union (ICU), a general union for black workers founded by Kadalie in 1919.

Its slippery torso!
Here it is: COSATU
The spears of men
shall be deflected!

Here it is:
The tornado-snake of change! Inkhanyamba,
The cataclysm
Clammed for decades and decades

By a mountain of rules.
The tornado-snake
Poisoned throughout the years
By ethnicity
And tribalism.

Here is this mammoth creature
Which they mocked!
That it had no head!
And certainly no teeth

Woe unto you oppressor
Woe unto you exploiter

We have rebuilt its head
We lathed its teeth on our machines.
The day this head rises
Beware of the day these teeth shall bite.

On that day:
Mountains of lies shall be torn to shreds
The gates of apartheid shall be burst asunder
The history books of deception shall be thrown out

Woza langa*
Woza Federation
Woza Freedom

COSATU
Stop now

---

*Woza langa: Hurry up, sunshine

Listen to our sound

You'll hear us sing
That the rulers
And employers
Are sorcerers!

Do not smile
Do not dare disagree

If that was devoid of truth
Where is the ICU of the 1920's to be found?
Where is the FNETU of the 30's to be found?
Where is the CNETU of the 40's to be found?*
And the others?

They emerged
They were poisoned
Then
They faded!

COSATU
Today be wise!

In the desert
Only the fruit trees
With long and sturdy roots
Survive!

Learn that
And you shall settle accounts with the oppressor
You shall settle accounts with the exploiter
You shall settle accounts with the racists.

---

*ICU grew like wildfire through the 1920's, but was a spent force by the end of the decade.
FNETU—Federation of Non-European Trade Unions, a 1920's federation of black trade unions organizing on an industrial basis.
CNETU—Confederation of Non-European Trade Unions. Formed in the 1940's, it enjoyed a short period of rapid growth and militancy.

Here is COSATU
Who knows no color
Here then is our tornado-snake-inkanyamba

Helele*
COSATU

Helele
Workers of South Africa

Helele,
Transport workers
Helele,
Miners of wealth
Helele,
Cleaners of the bosses' kitchen
Helele,
Builders of the concrete jungle
Helele,
Workers of South Africa
Helele,
Makers of all things

Woza 'msebenzi! Woza COSATU! Woza freedom!

(COSATU launch, Kings Park Stadium, November 1985)

---

*Helele: Praise be!

I, the Unemployed

Nise Malange

I'm here
Living under a black cloud
Here, living in thinning light
Here
Freedom is nailed to a tree
To die.
Here I am living: in a matchbox

I am here dying of hunger
And my country is also dying
My children are dying too
Look at them:
How dull their eyes
How slow their walk and the turning
Of their heads
Nothing for them to eat
Can you hear?
They are crying.

I spit at the sun
Shining on me
Blazing everyday
I am waiting for the rain to come
And I cannot plow this beautiful piece of earth.
Here I am: unemployed

I
the unemployed
I am here but invisible.
preacher-man pray for the rain to come

White collars
In your chrome and brown armchairs
Please brighten up this thinning light
I am appealing to you oppressors
To free
Freedom from the tree.

My face
Buried with anger and sorrow
My stomach
Filled with hatred and pain
I behave like a lunatic
My kids are dying—
Malnutrition, kwashiokor*
There is nothing growing here
And the animals have died.

All I hear now
Is the wind at night
It whirls around
Spelling the agony of a death
I'm dying.

(Curries Fountain Stadium, May Day 1985)

---

kwashiokor: term for "malnutrition"

The Black Mamba Rises

Mi S'dumo Hlatshwayo

The victors of wars
But then retreat
The Builders of nests,
But then like an anteater
You then desert.
Heavy are your blows,
They leave the employers
Unnerved

On your side are your
Brothers even at the new
Jerusalem
Let it be workers! They say,
The heaven above also
Approves.

Ngudungudu, the woman
Who married without any
Lobolo,*
Busy boiling foreigners'
Pots
Yet yours are lying cold.

---

*lobolo: dowry furnished to bride's family

The humble bride,
Affianced without the
Bridegroom's consent
Yet others are affianced
With their fathers' consent,
Even the Japanese have now
Come to be your bridegrooms,
So! Bride why are you entwined by chains,
Instead of being entwined
With gold and silver like the others?

The Black mamba that shelters in the songs
Yet others shelter in the trees!

Ancestors of Africa rejoice,
Here are the workers coming like a flock of
Locusts,
On rising it was multi-headed,
One of its heads was at Mobeni,
Njakazi, the green calf of
MAWU can bear me out
Another of its heads was at baQulusi
Land at Ladysmith,
On rising it was burning like fire

Even Sikhumba*—the leather that
Overcomes the tanners,
Sikhumba who knows no race
Who stabs an old man and
A young man alike,
Using the same spear
Who stabs a man's bone,
Inflicting pain in the heart

But he is now showing a
Change of heart
Here is the struggle,
Sikhumba and Mgonothi are mesmerized,
Asking what species of old mamba is this?

---

*Name used metaphorically to designate the factory manager.

Dying and resurrecting like
A dangabane flower.
It was stabbed good and proper during the
Day,
At Sydney Road right on the premises,
To the delight of the impimpis,*
And the delight of the police
There were echoes of approval there on the
TV at Auckland Park saying:
Never again shall it move,
Never again shall it revive
Never again shall it return
Yet it was beginning to tower with rage.

The old mamba that woke up early in the
Morning at St. Anthony's
Let's sit down and talk, he
Now says

The spear that thundered at
Dawn at St. Anthony's,
The spear that devoured the father and the sons
And the daughters
Then the men came together,
Devouring them whilst singing
Yet the songs were just a decoy.

Rife are the rumors,
That those who defied the
Unity have sunk,
To the throbbing hearts of the
Employers

You black buffalo
Black yet with tasty meat,
The buffalo that turns the
Foreigners' language into
Confusion,
Today you're called a Bantu,

----

*impimpi: "sell-out," spy, traitor, etc.

Tomorrow you're called a Communist
Sometimes you're called a Native.
Today again you're called a Foreigner,
Today again you're called a Terrorist,
Sometimes you're called a Plural,
Sometimes you're called an
Urban PUR*

You powerful black buffalo,
Powerful with slippery body
The buffalo that pushed men
Into the forest
In bewilderment the police
Stood with their mouths open

Rife are the rumors
That those who defied
Being pushed into the forest
In exile they are,
One Smit is in exile across
At the Bluff,
One Madinana is in exile across
The Umgeni river,
Both can bear me out.

Praise poets, messengers
Observers,
Run in all directions,
Stand on top of the mountains,
Report to Botha at Pretoria
Report to our heroes on the
Island,
Report to the angels in your
Prayers,
Say unto them—here is a
Flood of workers,
The employers have done what
Ought not to be.

_____

*PUR: Permanent Urban Resident—term used in The Koornhof Bills

Why tease the mamba in its
Century-old sleep?
The writing is on the wall,
No stone shall stand on top
Of the other till eternity,
Tell them—the borrowed
Must be given back
Tell them—the chained
Must be chained no more
Tell them—these are the
Dictates of the black mamba,
The mamba that knows no
Color,
Tell them—these are the
Workers' demands,
By virtue of their birthright
Dunlop workers I'm taking
My hat off,
I'm bowing to you with
Respect.

(Dunlop Strike, St. Anthony's, November 9, 1984)

Interview with FOSATU Cultural Group*

South African Labour Bulletin *staff*

SALB: How important is cultural work? Why are you involved in the area?

FCG: This question must be asked of people who have been exposed to the work we do. For *us* it has been important in three ways: (a) it takes a step, a small step, towards pushing workers to start controlling their creative power. So far this power has been used by everybody in power and with money, for their own purposes. Brother Mi Hlatshwayo will be talking about this at the July workshop:** how we have been culturally exploited and impoverished; (b) it creates a better sense of unity amongst workers: poems, songs, plays, etc., and the struggle to make them available to our brothers and sisters, enriches us. We are not united because of need or hunger alone; (c) it educates people about our struggle and puts across a true picture of things—our picture. You see, we are involved in this, however hard it is for us after work, because we believe that our struggle is not only there to destroy the oppressive powers that control us. It is there to also build a new world. To do this, we must begin now.

SALB: What is the future direction of cultural work to be?

FCG: We cannot predict the direction it will follow. But we would like to see some developments like: (a) the work must be deepened, for the

---

*Reprinted from the *South African Labour Bulletin*, Vol. 10, No. 8 (July/August 1985).
**Annual cultural workshop prohibited by the 1985 State of Emergency.

workers to gain more skills in the factory, and at the local and community levels—this is a lot of work for us to do so the work can happen smoothly; (b) we must think seriously of the correct spaces and venues for it to happen; (c) more care should be spent in making the work reflect our moral vision—for example, it should be democratic; it should attack division on lines of color and rank; it should actively encourage women to come to the fore; it should communicate better. . . .

SALB: Are there any organizational gains from cultural work?

FCG: On this you must ask the Dunlop or the Frame shop stewards. If it awakens the need for unity and the need for justice, if it educates correctly, then it is a help to organization.

SALB: Do you see your work as having a specifically working-class character? How does this contribute to, or conflict with, the wider tradition of black cultural resistance and protest?

FCG: There are very strong cultural traditions: we are schooled in them from childhood. But at the same time, there is no *one* tradition—there are many. Of course, it has many political elements from the past. But it also has many new ones. Where it gets its character is quite simple: it starts from our experience and our unity. So it has to draw a line against any exploiter in the factory or the townships; against impimpis; against white and black politicians who betray us; against divisions. It also differs from a lot of black creators who have a patronizing attitude to us: a lot of people with a tickey's worth of education have a superior attitude towards us. They speak a language we don't understand. Our task is to take our rich or poor heritage and make it satisfy working people, their families and any other suffering people in South Africa.

SALB: What are the implications of a move from "performance" to written work? Will this make your work less immediately accessible to a broad audience?

FCG: It is not true that our work is mainly becoming pieces of paper. No, there are a small number of us who *also* write. But there are hundreds performing. At this stage, for every black worker who picks up a pencil and forgets about the bottle, there's a victory. But most of the work is for performance in any place where people and workers meet.

SALB: How does management view these plays—where they are often the subject of attack or ridicule?

FCG: Management has not seen much of the work. There were some tensions about the Dunlop Play. But, overall, some of them are irritated because they hear they are ridiculed.

SALB: Thus far the plays have clearly acted to reinforce the work of the unions. No union can be perfect. Can plays also have a critical role, highlighting problems in order to discuss and improve the working of the union? Perhaps to confront areas of division or potential division?

FCG: Criticism is what happens every day between workers and shop stewards, shop stewards and trade-union officials. Cultural workers as well are involved in criticizing conditions—it cannot be otherwise. Either you tell the truth or you might as well become laughable. The difference is that we don't criticize in order to divide workers but rather to do the opposite: to strengthen the unity of workers, and make the leadership accountable to us. The imbongi's role, remember, was always to praise and criticize.

SALB: Are you aware of the articles written on working-class culture in the *SALB*? What do you feel about them?

FCG: Yes, some of it. The culture issue made us think a bit. There are two criticisms: (a) none of the people we know, like in music, was discussed—also the exploitation of black and worker creators was not discussed; (b) there was no challenge to the work we do, so we can sit down and think carefully about mistakes. But overall it was O.K. because our friends and families now can see as well that we are serious (*laughter*).

SALB: How far has this cultural work been taken up by other workers and become generalized?

FCG: A lot of cultural activity is just taking off spontaneously. People see things happening and want to do things themselves. At every union AGM another group springs up. Now we need to give coherence to all this energy. This is not just entertainment, it is a weapon. We have to work collectively, but also allow space for individuals to develop. So with the plays—some have been written by one person, others have been workshopped by all the participants. There has been more emphasis on individual writing recently—as we see in the pages of *FOSATU Worker News*.

The cultural work is important in breaking down barriers between different unions and groups of workers—and also between workers and their families; and between the factory and the community. Much of the recent work shows a concern with these broader social issues.

Two Excerpts from
A Sport of Nature

Nadine Gordimer

Nadine Gordimer, born in Springs, Transvaal, is one of South Africa's most celebrated and prolific writers. Her work has included volumes of short stories, novels and criticism. She has, during the course of her career, become increasingly outspoken in her rejection of the apartheid system, and in recent years has contributed a number of important essays on the issue of culture and politics.

Gordimer's fiction has always been awaited with keen interest, and has won critical acclaim both locally and abroad. Among other awards, she won the Central News Agency (CNA) Prize in 1979 for Burger's Daughter *(New York: Viking, 1979) and the Booker Prize in 1974 for* The Conservationist *(Viking). Her uncompromising prose has led to the banning of two of her novels,* The Late Bourgeois World *(1966) and* Burger's Daughter, *both of which have subsequently been unbanned.*

Gordimer's most recent works are July's People *(Viking, 1981),* Something Out There *(Viking, 1984) and, with photographer David Goldblatt,* Lifetimes: Under Apartheid *(London: Cape, 1986). The following excerpts are from her latest novel,* A Sport of Nature, *which was published this spring by Knopf.*

Intelligence

Tamarisk Beach in the late afternoons was the place of resurrection. Those who had disappeared from their countries while on bail, while on the run, while under house arrest; that noncriminal caste of people from all classes and of all colors strangely forced to the subterfuge of real criminals evading justice—they reappeared on foreign sand in swimming shorts and two-piece swimsuits. While they swam, their towels, shoes, cigarettes were dumped for safety in numbers under the three etiolated tamarisks for which the British colonial families had named the beach once reserved for their use. Now hungry, raucous local youths hung about there all day, acrobatically light-fingered. If those of the new

---

caste—big men, some of them, cultivated on distant soccer fields—
looked warningly at the boys, they jacked themselves swiftly up palm
boles and laughed, jeering from the top in their own language, that not
even the strangers who were black as they were understood. Sometimes
a coconut came down from there like a dud bomb, unexploded, from
the countries left behind; the local boys fought over it just the way the
scorpions they would set against one another in a sand arena fought,
and the victor hawked it round for sale.

There was no respite from heat in weeks passing, months passing. Like
exile itself, a sameness of time without the trim and shape of home and
work, the heat was unattached to any restraints of changing seasons.
Only in the late afternoons did something stir sameness: a breath blew
in under it, every afternoon, one of those trade winds that had set
history on course towards prehistory, bringing first the Chinese and
then the Arabs to that coast. It brought to Tamarisk Beach the men
from alley offices with unpaid telephone bills and liberation posters,
from the anterooms of European legations where they waited to ask for
arms and money, and from the comings and goings between taken-over
colonial residences and ex-governors' offices where rival political groups
struggled to keep their credentials acceptable to their host country,
lobbying, placing themselves in view of the powerful, watching who in
the first independent black government there was on his way up to
further favor, and worth cultivating, and who was dangerous to be
associated with because he might be on his way down.

The exile caste came to the beach for air. And then the original
impulse—to breathe!—became part of a social ritual, a formation of a
new regularity, a necessary ordering of a place where other needs that
cannot be done without might be met. Many had experienced this kind
of formation even in jail. On Tamarisk Beach they strolled through the
colonnades of palms, avoiding or meeting each other, eyeing across a
stretch of sand faces separated by the distance of alliances dividing
Moscow and Peking, East Germany and the United States, or the desert
distance of solitary confinement and the stony alienation that succeeds
screams in those who have known torture since last meeting. They
paused to pick tar and oil-slick from the soles of their feet, and scratched
the hair on their chests, smoked, shook water from their ears—just for
those hours in the late afternoon could have been holiday-makers anywhere. There were some women among them, political lags, like the
men, and defiantly feminine, keeping up with curled, home-tinted hair,
ingenious cut of local cotton robes as sundresses, and cheap silver-wire
jewelry from the market craftsmen, the high self-image needed to defeat

the humiliations of prison. There was sensuality on Tamarisk Beach. It came back with the relief of a breeze; it came back with the freeing of bodies from the few clothes thrust into a suitcase for exile and worn in the waiting rooms and makeshift living quarters of exile. It became a pattern of human scale made by strollers in the monumental arcade of palms and swimmers dabbling in the great Indian Ocean at the edge of a continent.

There were hangers-on, at Tamarisk. Not only the thieving urchins, but friends and acquaintances picked up by the exiles, and the append-ages of love affairs and casual dependencies of all kinds. There were also those who passed as these and were suspected, found out or never discovered to be part-time informers for the governments whose enemies the exiles were. Most of the "beach rats," as they were known, were themselves expatriates—black and white—who had been expelled from or broken with a series of schismatic groups in the exile community; others had become misfits, easy to recruit for pocket-money spying, in a survival of the old European tradition of black sheep. In imperialist times, these whites were "sent out" to the colonies; in the breakup of colonial empires, their counterparts took advantage of transitional opportunities to get by, far away from the censure of home, in some warm place whose different mores didn't concern them. It would have been difficult to distinguish imposters from the genuine, those after-noons on the beach. The tall Jew whose incipient tire around the waist-line was being prodded at by a wobbly-breasted blonde girl—what was there to show, in his mock affront, that the black beard he still wore he had grown in order to escape across a border disguised as one of the White Father missionaries, dangling cross, breviary and all? Who could tell the difference between the credentials of a little beauty with a Huguenot delicacy of face structure, speaking Afrikaans, and the black man, her fellow countryman, talking trade-union shop with her in the same language? Hadn't both served their apprenticeship as jailbirds, back there? Suspect everybody or nobody. Leaning on an elbow in the sand, talking to an intimate, wandering to borrow a cigarette and join this group or that, resting one's back, in sudden depression, against a palm-pillar in this place of littered sand and urine-tepid shallows—gossip and guarded tongues erratically mingled with the long-held breaths expelled by the ocean on a coral reef. Among the regulars, every after-noon, there was a girl who looked as if she had slept in her clothes and hadn't combed her hair. Probably true; many, through obscure quarrels of doctrine and discipline, found themselves not provided for by any liberation movement housed up rotting stairs. This one (a man who was doing his best, without funds, to drink himself to death on local gin) had left his country before receiving permission from his cadre to do so. That one (staring at the sea as if to blind himself with its light) belonged to another organization and had defied its policy: recognized the validity of the white courts by accepting *pro deo* legal defense.

The Afrikaner woman noticed the girl about: she was clean, the hair naturally like that, tangled because in need of a cut—just living through hard times, as everyone was, more or less. She seemed a loner, but not lonely; at least, the men appeared to know that she was approachable. She came by herself to the beach, but as soon as her presence was noted there was always some man, arms crossed over his chest, digging a toe in the sand, chatting to her. The tamarisks cast no more than a fishnet of shade. She sat there beside other people's possessions the way the stray dogs came to settle themselves just beyond cuffs and blows.

When the Afrikaner woman saw the big safety pin that held together the waistband of the girl's jeans above a broken zipper, she had one of the contractions in her chest just where, whatever rational explanation there was, she knew there to be some organ capable of keener feeling than the brain. It was this organ, taking over from all the revolutionary theory she had studied since recruitment at seventeen in a jam factory, that had been responsible for her arrest along with black women protesting against the pass laws, and her bouts of imprisonment as an organizer of illegal strikes and defier of laws decreeing what race might live where. She asked about the girl. The story was doing the rounds, by then: that was the girl who had come with that Andrew Rey fellow, the journalist. The man who had disappeared, dumped her, now. The one who was found to be politically unreliable (the informant was a member of the Command in exile and had the authority to decide such things). As for his girl . . . what was anyone to do with her? She clearly didn't belong to any movement at all; his camp follower, pretty little floozy. But he had misrepresented himself, and she must have moved about with him in all his unacceptable contacts, so she wasn't *their* responsibility, really.

Yet the Afrikaner woman brought her a pair of her own jeans, concealed in one of the straw bags from the market so the girl wouldn't be embarrassed by receiving charity in front of everyone at the beach. As she became accepted—because Rey had betrayed her, too—as one at least by implication belonging to the cause Rey was suspected of double-crossing, the member of the Command was among the men on the beach, far from their wives and likely to be for many years, with whom she slept.

Certainly she had no place to sleep in alone. Not until the Afrikaner woman decided something must be done about her. Christa Zeeder-burg, urged to reminisce at the end of her life, never forgot the safety pin. —Just an ordinary safety pin, the kind you buy on a card, for babies' nappies. That's all she had, then!—

If you have lived your young life with black nannies and cooks to feed you and at worst always an aunt's stipend deposited monthly, it must be difficult to believe there is nothing for you in the houses you pass and the banks in their pan-colonial classical gray stone with brass fittings. For many weeks she was waiting for Rey to come back; that was her status. She was living in their room in an old hotel from British times which now functioned only as a bar; his radio was on the wicker table and his pyjamas were still under the pillows. He had gone on a quick trip to Sweden about a communications development project they wanted him to start in East Africa, or (depending to whom he was talking) to Germany to tie up a television documentary based on a book he was writing. She knew she could not go along. Already there had been problems; when the vehicle that took them from over the South African border arrived at their country of refuge, it turned out that although she had no passport he—quite properly, a professional in these matters—had an Irish one. He went with his companions to the local hotel in the small frontier town; she spent the night in the local jail—well, on an old sofa in the chief warder's office; they couldn't put a white girl in the sort of cells they had. It was quite fun, really; she could sleep anywhere and wake up fresh. Her experience was something they joked about together, next day, all very exciting, like the leopard they saw crossing a red road at dawn. It disappeared into the bush as they themselves were doing, hour after hour, mile after mile, beyond pursuit.

He had taken only half the money she had. He wouldn't hear of taking more than that; he was going to come back with grants that would keep them for two or three years, they were going to look for a flat—or an old house; why not occupy one of the nice old houses with gardens the colonists had fled when independence came to this country? She was in one, once, while he was away. Some people from the beach took her along to a party given by the representative of a European press agency. The agency operated comfortably; there was a telex chattering in what had been a children's playroom, and the agency chief could refresh himself in the leaking swimming pool. She would have written immediately to tell what a good idea it would be to have a house like that from which the development project could be run, and the television documentary planned, but she had no address. She thought of looking round for such a house, in preparation. But the suburb along the sea was a long walk from town, and soon the taxis, reassuringly humble with their missing doorknobs and rust-gnawed mudguards, had become expensive in relation to the money she had left.

Unlike observers, she expected him back any day. She passed the days wandering purposefully about, looking, listening, smelling, tasting. The ancient town was a Mardi Gras for her, everybody in fancy dress that could not possibly be daily familiar: the glossy black men in braided cotton robes and punch-embroidered skull caps; the Arab women with all their being in their eyes, blotted out over body, mouth and head by dark veils; the skinny, over-dressed Indian children, bright and finicky as fishing-flies; the stumps of things that were beggars; and the smooth-suited, smooth-jowled Lebanese merchants touched with mauve around the mouth who sat as deities in the dark of stifling shops. Her watch was stolen in the hotel and she kept track of time by a grand public clockface and the regular call of the muezzins from the mosques. There were no laws—nothing to prevent her going down into the black quarters of the town, here, except the rotting vegetables and sewer mud that had to be stepped through, and the little claws of beggar children that fastened on her whenever she smiled a greeting, not knowing that every day she had less and less to give away. She bought pawpaws and big, mealy plan-tains, more filling than ordinary bananas, down there; cheaper than in the markets. She picked them from the small pyramid of some woman whose stock and livelihood they were, arranged among the garbage, spittle and babies scaled with glittering flies. She ate the fruit in place of lunch and dinner on a broken bench on the esplanade and did not get sick.

Her aunts—Olga, Pauline—even Len, her father—they had never given her the advantage of knowing what to say to someone to whom one owes money and can't pay. The wife of the hotel proprietor stopped her as she came along the veranda where her room was, and broke her silence.

—Going on for six weeks, and rates are strictly weekly, dear. You know that, don't you? We aren't running a charity. We have to pay even the yard boys the fancy new minimum wage this government's set down, I don't know how much longer we're gunna be prepared to carry on, anyway.— A drop of water run down to one of the spiral ends of the girl's hair had fallen on the dry sun-cancer of the woman's forearm. —We have to pay for the water you're using for those lovely cold showers you take whenever you fancy.— From the day that fellow went off with his briefcase, never mind the pyjamas left under the pillows, the proprietor had not been happy about the situation. There'd been bad experiences before with that CCC lot who'd taken over Tamarisk for themselves. That's what the regular white residents from the old days called them: commies, coons and coolies. She looked at this cocky miss who played the guitar in her room as if the world owed her a living, looked in a way that made the girl feel she would be physically prevented, by the barrier of a scaly arm, from getting past her.

—I haven't any money.—

She didn't think of assuring that she was only waiting for "her friend" to come back, of promising all would be set right and paid then—soon. It was only when she knew, quite simply, what to say, that with that truthful statement another became true: she was not waiting. She was now one of the regular coterie of Tamarisk Beach, making out. She packed her bag and hung the room key on the board behind the unattended reception desk. The pyjamas she left under the pillows.

Casualties

At this point in the novel, the same South African white girl, who has fulfilled a number of strange roles in her vagabondage, is married to an African National Congress revolutionary. They are living with their small daughter in exile, in Zambia. The time is 1967.

Yes, she knew them all. Except Mandela and the others with him. Mandela remained the voice on tape heard when she was a schoolgirl. Mandela was in prison down South, off the very last peninsula of Africa, pushed out to an island in the Atlantic by white men who frightened themselves with rhetoric that his kind would cast them back into the sea by which they came. Her old friendship with Tambo dates from those days when she used to serve him tea at Britannia Court and somehow produce enough food to go round whomever Whaila brought home. There hasn't been anything she hasn't profited by, at one period or another; the cuisine at the Manaka flat stood her in good stead, in its day. Oliver Tambo, even then, had the eyes of sleepless nights behind his thick glasses, and the opacity of flesh that, as it did in Whaila, marks the faces behind which decisions must be made: loosed boulders whose thundering echoes a passage, out of sight, into consequences that cannot fully be foreseen. Tennyson Makiwane was one of those who came to Britannia Court, too—another namesake, inheritor of Victoriana—who was there in a Xhosa family who admired Tennyson? Tennyson Makiwane gave Nomzamo a stray kitten he had taken in—Makiwane who outcast himself, years later, from the cause for which, like the other frequenters of Britannia Court, he lived then, a man whose shame was obliterated for him by a traitor's death.

Whaila knew at least an edited version of his young wife's life; she had told him how she had got to Tamarisk Beach with the journalist, Andrew Rey, and when she had expressed wonder that anyone (Rey) who seemed so committed to the cause had abandoned it (she had this wider interpretation of his having dumped her now), Whaila gave one of his held-back sighs that became a grunt. —We'll have them, too. Casualties. And not operational ones . . . There'll always be some who won't go the whole way.—

On the eighth of August 1967, he told her. The little girl had climbed into bed with them, early in the morning. She sat astride her father's chest and he spoke it straight at her, who couldn't understand and couldn't betray. —Umkhonto is crossing the Zambezi today.—

Hillela turned her head to him; he saw her eyes, that were never bleary in the morning but opened from sleep directly into acceptance of the world as it is. —It's begun?—

—It's begun. Two parties. Nothing big in numbers.—

—How many?—

But even in the telling there was some instinct to hold back. — Enough.— The little girl rode him as her mother had loved to ride a playground's mythical bull. —There'd be no hope of getting through with a whole company. I only hope the ZAPU* crowd really knows what they're doing. Ours have to depend on them to find their way hundreds of miles through the bush. It's all the way sticking to Wankie.—

—What about animals? Can you just walk about among lions and elephants?—

—That's not the problem. Lions don't come looking for men and if you sight a herd of elephants you can turn and head the other way for a bit. The danger is running into the Rhodesian army patrols; Wankie's the only route you've got a chance against that.—

The child bounced her laughter into gurgles, thumping him. He lifted her gently under the arms, to regain his breath, gently put her down again.

Hillela sat up with one of her surges of energy, her sunburned breasts juggled between tightened arms. She took his hand, hard. Then she was out of bed and moving about the room as on the morning of some festival. She rushed back to kiss him, holding his head, her possession, between open palms. She rolled on the floor in play with the child and trod by mistake on the kitten. Amid laughter and meowing he watched from the bed the excitement she felt, for him.

While he shaved she lay in the bath trickling water from a sponge onto her navel. Her belly was coming up; the creature in there was beginning to show its presence. She did not ask him, this time, what color he thought it would be; they would be a rainbow, their children, their many children.

—What will happen when they get to South Africa?—

The sound of the razor scraping. —They'll split into smaller groups and operate in different areas. They'll join up with people inside. There are specified targets to go for.—

—In the towns or in the country? Where they cross the border it'll be farmland, won't it? Are they going to attack white farms? Or is it going to be pylons and things like that, in the cities?—

—Military installations, power stations—hard targets.—

---

*ZAPU: Zimbabwe African People's Union

—There won't be bombs in cafés and office buildings, or in the street? I can't imagine what that would be like—

He dried his hands, ridding them of something more than shaving foam. He was aware of her waiting for him to tell her what she should be feeling about the unimaginable. —If the government goes on doing what it does, torturing and killing in the townships, in time . . . well, we'll have to turn to soft targets as well.—

—Soft targets. You mean ordinary people. People in the streets.— Pressing her fingers into her belly, testing for a response from the life in there. She thought she felt a faint return of pressure and he mistook, with a flicker of displeasure, the beginnings of a smile relaxing her lips as lack of understanding of what she really had said.

—Ordinary people? What ordinary people? Our ordinary people have always been the soft targets. Our bodies, hey? Our minds. The police use violence on us every day and white people think they keep out of it, although the beatings-up and the killings are done on their behalf, they've let it happen for so many years. One day the blacks will have to carry the struggle into white areas. It's inevitable. The violence came from there. Violence will hit back there. It must be, we know it. But not yet. Not now.—

—Innocent people?—

—Are there really any innocent people in our country?—

She was communicating in nudges with the third person present, inside her. —And me?—

Down on him came all the sorrow of pain and destruction that his people had endured, were suffering, and would endure no longer, and all the suffering they might have to inflict in consequence, in the knowing horror of victim turned perpetrator. Of course she brought it upon him; he had brought it upon himself by making such a marriage. Sometimes her lack of any identification with her own people dismayed him, he who lived for everything that touched upon the lives of his; there was something missing in her at such times, like a limb or an organ. This secretly felt, paradoxically, in spite of the fact that he saw their own closeness as a sign; the human cause, the human identity that should be possible, once the race and class struggle were won. With her, it was already one world; what could be. And yet he looked at her lying pearly under water, the body prettily shaded and marbled as white flesh in its uncertain pigment and peculiarly naked nakedness is, and had to say what there was to say. —Yes, you too. If you happened to be there. You were born in sin, my love, the sins of your white people.—

But saved. She knows how to look after herself. She climbed out of the bath and he wrapped her in a towel tenderly, as if she had just been baptized.

Through the still heat before the rains men moved as the wild animals moved in the bush where tourists used to follow game rangers' advice about the best areas to find and photograph them. There was silence. Whaila was silent about the silence. The occasional news that came back to the offices behind the tin security fence was confused in a way that did not allow an interpretation that was anything but bad. The maps had turned out to be inaccurate in a territory where the only true maps are the migratory paths of wild creatures drawn by the imperatives of the propagation of life, not the campaigns of war. The two parties lost their way, and the journey took much longer than provided for; they ran out of food. Moving like wild creatures in the bush, they were spotted like wild creatures by game rangers. On the fourteenth of August fighting with the Rhodesian army began. It was easier to hear the Rhodesian version of the combat over the radio than to keep up with how Umkhonto actually was faring. The Rhodesians, who lied so consistently in their own favor about every campaign in their civil war, claimed "overwhelming victories" against the ZAPU and Umkhonto guerrillas. When news did come through from the Freedom Fighters, they claimed victories, too; and after two weeks they were still fighting.

Hillela searched Whaila's face for news each time he entered the flat: still fighting! If certain people had thought her "full of herself" before, what could they have said of her now! She went about with the beginnings of her big African family—the one by the hand, the other swelling her like a bellying sail—in animated confidence that she was escorting the first generation that would go home in freedom. She would deliver what she had heard discussed there at suburban tables, what had been aborted by hesitations and doubts, the shilly-shallying of what was more effective between this commitment or that, this secondhand protest or that. Her blood was up, the color of her skin warmed her eyes, darker with what she saw in the inner eye. —Pregnancy suits you, you're lucky.— Her friend Sela envied her energy, mistaking its source. *Mutter Courage*, as her older friend Udi knew, survived on war as well as survived it.

No one reached home down South. By mid-September there was defeat; most of the guerrillas were either killed or captured by the Rhodesian army, and the few who had managed to get as far as Botswana were imprisoned for illegal entry. But one of the parties had been successful in mobilizing black Rhodesian villages as support bases for future attempts; planning must already have begun for a new incursion. The

317

huge weight of Joshua Nkomo was lowered once or twice onto the cheap furniture at Britannia Court, the little namesake welcomed to sit on whatever space there was between his enormous stomach and knees— he, too, could have been regarded as an old friend, later; but Hillela has never lost her instinct for avoiding losers. Christmas had a significance other than the traditional when the time came; her friend Sela Montgomery invited the Kgomani family to the traditional kind of dinner her English husband would have expected had he been there, with a tinselled tree, presents and plum pudding, but over the wine Hillela grasped Whaila's hand in covenant with another occasion—at the end of December brothers from the camp were going into Rhodesia once again.

Whaila was with Tambo and his other colleagues eighteen hours a day; she saw him, usually, only when she opened her eyes as he came into the bedroom late at night. She did not ask questions but behaved with her friend Sela as if she knew everything and was saying nothing. This empty boast became real when Whaila, in some inexplicable urge to honor the clasp of the hand in the way that his possession of her body could never do, in some certainty of trust that would transform both him and her and their relationship, told her the plans in detail. This time Umkhonto men were a much larger force, and under their own command. —We've learned our lesson. We've gone over the logistics again and again, this time. Nothing left to chance. One of the main objectives is going to be to help ZAPU prepare rural people for an uprising. It's all one struggle. Their war's ours.—

The handclasp held. She had more concealed inside her than a baby; weeks went by and the men in the bush moved about undetected, hidden by the local people down there. The nature of time changed. With each day, each week, it was something gained, not passed. Each morning, when she and the man beside her woke together, their first thought was the same. The intimacy was an entry into one of the locked rooms of existence. No one could ever surprise them there; no one could ever appear in that doorway and look upon them, judge them. He was lover and brother to her in the great family of a cause.

And all around, the marvel of daily life went on weaving continuity as the birds in the rampant bougainvillea threaded shreds of bright cloth, human hair combings, twigs and leaves into their nests. On the twenty-sixth morning in January Hillela smelt the scent of the frangipani as the breath of her own body, the thick pollen in the hibiscus trumpets as her own secretion, as she stretched, the baby inside lifting with her, to hang washing in the old garden of Britannia Court. Whaila came down from the building on his way to the office—that banal summing-up of an ordinary man's day that had so little to do with the row of prefabricated huts behind the tin security fence. He strolled over to say goodbye and they laughed because her belly (her Nkomo, they called it) got in the way of an embrace, and instead he turned her about and crossed his arms over her breasts from the back, bending round her neck to kiss her cheek. His bare arms in a short-sleeved shirt were, for an instant, the black shining arms that had flailed the sea, coming towards her from the shore. She recognized now, in the heady oxygen of a morning after rain, that she had even then noticed that watch he still wore, flashing on the swimmer's left arm.

Ten past eight when he left for "the office." She went to the market in the afternoon. Sela was persuaded to come with her; —But leave Nomzamo at the house, Hillela. You know you'll say you'll only be half-an-hour there, and then you expect that little kid to trail around for two or three.— Sela was right; the smells and colors and sounds of the market were the adornments Hillela wore as brightness and bells of an extended self, and she could not pass any stall or squatting vendor without stopping to finger, admire, question and talk. What she was supposed to have come to buy she forgot, once in among the cloth-hung alleys, the yards with their pyramids of rape, cabbages, oranges, okra, bananas, groundnuts; she could not be kept to any purpose or time limit. They went through the sheds where dried split fish and grasshoppers were laid out neat and stiff as if lacquered. Sela had to ask, for her, the names of roots big as torn-off heads or fanged like drawn teeth. Hillela had dozens of lengths of kanga cloth hooked down from the stallholders' rails and draped them, one after another, over Sela's crêpe two-piece. Wonderful, wonderful: Sela, a Nubian queen! As if she could be persuaded to wear such things; but she was stirred by some old familiarity that afternoon. The questions she was urged to ask on behalf of her friend, in the language she shared with the market people, developed into conversations, laughter and even an insider's scepticism about prices. —No, no. That's far too much; don't give it to him.— Sela was bargaining, with all the pauses of feigned loss of interest, the African organ-note hums, required. Sela's white shoes were splashed with the mud and scales from around the fish-vendors' tables and the spurt underfoot of rotting vegetables studded with flies; a young madman naked except for a sack he held over himself did not beg but rooted in the mess: yet Hillela that day saw only wholeness. —Everything's here. Everything in the world that you really need. Come and see.— There was furniture that delighted her with its parody, in cane and grass, of suburban coffee tables, and its brave approximation of white middle-class ugliness in sofas and chairs

319

covered with acrylic-colored plastic and hammered together, out of the memory of something seen in a white man's house, in the cubist angles of the thirties. She liked best the tinsmiths' section set out under trees with exposed clubfoot roots. —Come and see!— She followed every process of the ancient craft adapted to the waste materials a modern industrial society throws away. Here a man was cleaning the paint off tin containers and drums; there another was hammering them out into sheets. Others were cutting shapes from the sheets as she cut out dresses for her child. Saucepans, pots, funnels, buckets, ladles, braziers for the charcoal most blacks used for cooking were set out for sale. —Those pots burn the food if you put them on electric stoves, Hillela, I'm telling you.— —Oh come and see these funny little things!— Hillela did make one purchase, in spite of Sela's good sense. She held up a tiny object formed as an inverted, hollow pyramid, with a handle like that of a cup soldered to it. —What's this?— —You must have seen the women selling groundnuts in Cairo Road. They're measures—for a handful, when you buy. What will you do with it, Hillela? Don't give it to Nomzamo to play with—these things are not well finished, they've got sharp edges.—

The children belonging to Sela's relatives made a doll out of the namesake and never wanted to part with her. This was one of the many evenings when they wandered back with Hillela to Britannia Court. Hillela taught them the school songs she had sung in South Africa, as they walked home with her past Sandringham Mansions and Avonlea Place; a sunset first stamped out every coarse leaf of the flamboyant trees against translucent lakes of sky and then clotted the black metallic cutouts into a cage of earthly dark. The little straggle of woman and children made their cheerful chorus far beneath, and stumped up the stairs to the flat. When Whaila came home, the streetlight that could be seen from the kitchen window was on, bats circling it like the rings round a planet. He held his little daughter up to look, but she wriggled away to the other children. There was the static of frying behind loud play; Hillela, barefoot in her broad stance of pregnancy, was cooking chips for their supper. The eldest girl had made herself at home with the radio playing monotonous African music; on one of those sudden impulses children have, all scrambled out of the room to some game in the bathroom but the music wound on. The level of noise was raised by a tumble of running water. Neither Hillela nor Whaila was sure, for a moment, whether or not the doorbell was ringing. He said something she didn't catch, where she bent at the open refrigerator to fetch a carton of milk, but she was aware that he had passed behind her to go to the door and she took off the shelves a couple of cans of beer as well—it was the time in the evening when one or another of the men from the office or camp would call in. The door was swollen by summer damp and she seemed to hear all at once the prelude of its scrape along the linoleum, a pause in which she had no time to grasp that there were no greetings exchanged, and then a crack that splintered the thick homely hubbub against the thin walls of the flat. Something fell. As she turned there was another crack and a bolt of force hit the refrigerator door she stood behind. Someone—one, more than one—ran clattering down the corridor of Britannia Court; the doorway was open and empty: and Whaila? Whaila? As she came out from behind the shield of the refrigerator, he was there, on the floor. Whaila was flung before her, red flowing from the side of his head, his neck, under the shirt pocket where his pen still was hooked. His open eyes faced the wall and his lips stretched finely in that expression drawn by his life.

His life running away in red like the muddy filth in the gutters of the market.

There was a wrenching upheaval inside her as the fetus convulsed and turned. The bullet that was lodged in the refrigerator door penetrated her consciousness in the bullets' disorientation of sequence; she felt she was shot. She backed away from death, from death ebbing away Whaila. Backed away, backed away. Her shoulder hit the jamb of the doorway leading to the internal passage of the flat. She opened her mouth to wail but terror blocked her throat and instead of her cry there was the voice of a radio commercial enthusing over a brand of beer. She burst into the bathroom in the path of a plastic duck one child had thrown at another; the children saw in her terrible face grown-up anger at their game. She grasped the thirteen-year-old girl in charge. She dragged her to the kitchen, but when they reached the doorway, she herself turned to the wall and pressed her bent arms tight against her head, screaming.

It was the child who went in, and began to heave small, hard breasts in deep breaths that became sobs, and slowly went up to the dead man who had been Whaila, and touched him.

There have been others since then. They received parcels of death in mail from their home country. It seems that in the case of Whaila Kgomani, one of the first, the agents employed by the South African government might have bungled their mission. It was said in Lusaka that they were meant to kill Oliver Tambo, but came to the wrong address. Seeing a man through the blistered glass door, they did not wait to verify any identity; there is no margin for hesitation in such tasks. Others said the government's instructions were carried out: Whaila was a key man in the planning of armed infiltration. In South Africa itself, of course, the death was reported as the result of rivalry and a power struggle within the movement; as any statements from the organization itself were banned and could not be published, that version became the accepted one for most white people, if they were aware of the assassination at all.

"Unemployment" / linocut by Hamilton Budaza.

Nine Poems

Mazisi Kunene

Born in 1930 in Durban, South Africa, Mazisi Kunene studied at Natal University and became head of the Department of African Studies in the University College of Roma, Lesotho. After leaving southern Africa, he became a founding member of the Anti-Apartheid Movement in Great Britain and has represented the African National Congress in Europe and the U.S.

Kunene now teaches at UCLA, and is well known for his work on the Zulu epic. His book publication includes two epic poems, Emperor Shaka the Great (London: Heinemann, 1979) and Anthem of the Decades (London: Heinemann, 1981); and two volumes of poetry, Zulu Poems (London: André Deutsch, 1970) and The Ancestors and the Sacred Mountain (London: Heinemann, 1982; African Writers Series).

A Note to All Surviving Africans

We erred too, we who abandoned our household gods
And raised theirs with soft skins and iron flesh..
Their priests made signs at our forefathers' grounds
They spoke in a language that was obscure to us.
To win their praise we delivered our children,
But their lips were sealed and without the sacred mark.
Tired of obscurity they invaded our earth,
Plundering the minds of our captured children.
Yet nothing was so foolish as to burn the symbols of our gods.
Then, to follow helplessly the bubblings of their priests
We emulated their ridiculous gestures and earned their laughter.
Now, we dare not celebrate our feast unless purified by fire
Unless our minds are nourished by the Ancestral Song.
We have vowed through the powers of our morning:

We are not the driftwood of distant oceans.
Our kinsmen are a thousand centuries old.
Only a few nations begat a civilization
Not of gold, not of things, but of people.

Ancient Bonds

The strange shadows that nourish the bonds of our past
Greet us as we enter the dancing place.
They open the large wings of a cloud
Revealing a thin crescent of a rising moon.
The Ancestors invite us to the vision of the river
Knowing we have suffered enough;
Through them we float aimlessly on a dream
And yet our names must remain hidden from total joy
Lest through weakness we may succumb
Falling slowly into the depths of mindlessness.
Our love must survive through the ancient flames.
We must congregate here around the sitting mat,
To narrate endlessly the stories of distant worlds.
It is enough to do so,
To give our tale the grandeur of an ancient heritage
And then to clap our hands for those who are younger
        than us.

The Tyrant

Through uncertainty the tyrant imposes his power.
He chooses the gods that speak his own language,
To make us stand before him like cattle.
By his ancestral names he haunts our children.
They must parade at his festivals like slaves
To declaim the glories of his violent prophets.
The enemy boasts the power of the sun,
The beast steals the young from their mother's breast,
The tyrant celebrates, the feast is in his name. . .

Cowardice

I overcame her who was my enemy
Who seized my staffs of courage
And was unkind to my clansmen.
I said to her: Go away,
Go to the worlds of running men
And when you have seen their fallen glory
Turn to the shadows of our ancient mountains.
Listen to the eternal beat of our forefathers,
To them who are older than the oldest mountain,
For they have grasped the continuity of life.
From them we know now:
Whoever foils the violence of evil men
Nourishes the visions of our children. . .

The Prayer of Ramses II

Alone in the battlefield with my brothers
Our enemies had surrounded us
We prayed aloud into the secret dwellings of the great god Ra
We turned to him who has never deserted us
We addressed him who has blessed all our journeys
We said: "Oh father, mother, great one among the great ones
Great spirit among the great creations
Great Eye that sees far into the distant night
We praise your enormous shields
Raise them high and scatter our enemies in all directions
We beg you, great master of our universe
May we return unharmed to our sacred Egypt
Let us once again prosper in the embrace of our children
You who has chosen us to lead the myriad races of the earth
Great father Ra, whose great powers are forever open
Give us protection through the secret bonds of your children."
Thus it was granted to him, the Forefather,
Thus did he route his enemies and destroy the barbarians!

Steve Biko's Anthem

The sun blazes its flames,
Its fierce rays burst open the enveloping night,
From here I see the restless generations to come,
They run wild like the wind, they hold onto the eagle's tail,
They sing the anthems of our forefathers,
They declaim the epics of the Maluti Mountains.
Three hundred years ago
We chose the brotherhood of battle.
The crowds followed us with their song.
Their lips quivered in anger,
They broke the neck of the salamander.
They came to the festival by the dead of night,
They set the cities on fire,
The madams fled in terror through the alleyways.
My children were free to praise their father!
Yet not even dawn could bring peace
The stars fell precipitately from the sky
What was once the Milky Way bowed to our sun!
We are tall, we who are the children of the morning,
We who worshipped at the altar of fire,
We who made the beast flee for its life.
This age is ours, we made it bear the sacred flower,
We planted the seed of our freedom at the mountain-region
To bear fruit for all peoples.
In your name, young man of the river,
You who loved me in my youth
Until I was decrepit with age;
In your name, young man of the sun, let there be rain,
Let there be beautiful songs in our festivals,
Let humanity walk proudly.
You who followed after me, your turn has come!
You must nourish the dream
To make Africa sing from Algeria to the Maluti Mountains.

Final Supplication

The gods set me free,
They annointed my forehead with birth-herbs
To protect me from the whirlwind,
From the poisonous dust of a lost continent.
Long ago, through no fault of ours,
By some freak in the universe,
Something was born,
Something without shape or form
Except to go round and round,
As if maddened by some fear
Asking the question "Why? Who am I?"
Its truth was revealed in the blood of the innocent.

Ah! the gods set me free
After a thousand years in India
After a thousand years in pre-America
After a thousand years of wandering in space
The gods said I was free to go to Africa
To search for my children,
To look for my clansmen.
For such was the legend:
That I was born there.

But how can anyone know
After three thousand years?
Even the old women who bequeath their blessings,
Who reveal secrets from generation to generation
Could not recall.
All they could say: "Yes, there was such a man,
But so many go by that name!"

I recited my lineage from time immemorial,
From our first known ancestor, the Sun.
They laughed still louder,
Proclaiming: "This house has been beset by many such names!"
They led me to a hundred different villages

With relatives of the same name and same family.
Finally I was taken to the far regions of the universe,
Where I was exiled into the endless night of the cosmos,
But the gods came and claimed me!

The Humanity of All Things

A salute to those who are young,
Who see into the heart of darkness,
Whose eyes have entered the deep ocean,
Who shall not abandon our cousins of the forest
Who shall wait patiently through the harsh season.
They shall sing of the strange powers of the morning star.
Then the stone shall turn from its ancient sleep,
It shall greet the traveler.
The friendly bird shall see him.
It shall comfort him with a song,
His thousand eyes shall penetrate into the universe,
He shall see the shadows of the earth,
For all things are part of our truth.
Nothing is superior,
Not even the illusions of our heritage.

The Vision of Life

There is a heritage of wisdom in the sky:
The continuous succession of suns and moons and stars,
The furtherance of life through the convoluted cloud,
The inverted sky tossing out the dust of stars,
The fierce encounters of new earths and old suns,
The splendid rivers churning out the promise of future life,
The earth, our earth, drugged to sleep by time,
Its eyes closed into the darkness of the night,
The green plant growing silently from the dream,
The magic awakening of its eyes, the rainbow colors,
The coalescence of the mountain-winds,
The rediscovery of our clansmen,
The long embrace, the tears of joy . . .

Photograph by René Weideman. (This "stayaway" call actively commemorates the inspirational place of South African school students in the unbroken tradition of resistance which sprang from the June 1976 Soweto conflict.)

Lovesong After the Music of K. E. Ntsane*

Antjie Krog

Antjie Krog lives in a farmhouse in a small farming community near Kroonstad. In 1970, when still a schoolgirl, she published Dogter van Jefta (Cape Town: Human and Rousseau), a collection of explicit and erotic verse which caused a considerable stir in the Afrikaans literary community. Since then, her poetry has continued to provoke much debate because of its sexual candor, and its willingness to confront such issues as the nature of womanhood, racial conflict and Afrikaner aspirations. In 1973 she won the Eugène Marais Prize for Januarie-Suite (Cape Town: Human and Rousseau). Her most recent collection is Jerusalemgangers (Cape Town: Human and Rousseau, 1985, 1986), a cycle of poems in which she creates a community and then explores its tensions and passions.

"Feet, take me and carry me
carry me to the far side**
she shines like an ostrichfeather
like a feather shines its shining vibration
soundlessly to the one who sits alone
alone under the willow she sits at ease."

(Mohlalefi*** stands that side of the river:
across the water he will come to me
for myself I choose not I was chosen
at the high gathering at Mokgatjane****
a whirlwind gathers in the mountains
threads towards me like a needle through a hat)

---

*One of the great Sotho poets
**The poem follows the "rhyme scheme" of Sotho oral praise songs, which is not a rhyming of sounds but a rhyming of images. The poem alternates between the voices of the lovers: Mohlalefi, the man, speaks inside quotation marks, and Moratuwa, the woman, inside parentheses.
***One who knows everything
****Meeting of the tribal elders

"I greet you, Gray One with deep pools
you who cut across the farms of the whites
reptile who bites out dongas* at the borders
when I want to cross you I am unsettled
I remember the days of the ancestors
when they fought for this land."

(Mohlalefi stands that side of the river:
across the water he will come to me
on the bank he stretches his legs
stretches his legs like a bird of prey
he rubs repeatedly at his chest
his heart rises like dough)

"Already I hear the *tjhutjhumakgala*
thing of the whites, millipede that clangs
that smokes pulling chains of smoke behind it
that wears a grass hat wrong side up
that thickens clear air, into the calm
it churns out cloud. It leaves us: pitchblack."

(Mohlalefi stands that side of the river:
across the water he will come to me
my body is charged my skin is light
every sinew glows like a filament
I anticipate your ears against my palms
my body will melt on your mats like butter)

"I greet you Moratuwa. I shall not
take you. Tilane** moves his beard in the grave.
I will glide like a snake. I am bereft.
I am poor. The morninglight over Thaba Tseko
announces the pain of each day. Farewell Moratuwa,
I now become a warrior: *Metsi a pshele re a bona*:
        the water evaporates as we watch."

Translated from the Afrikaans by David Bunn, Jane Taylor and the author

---

donga: small ravine
**Tilane was one of the great Sotho warriors.

From *Senkatana*

S. M. Mofokeng

Sophonia Machabe Mofokeng was born April 1, 1923 near Fouriesburg, Orange Free State, South Africa. He obtained a B.A. degree from Fort Hare in 1942 and three degrees from the Witwatersrand University (1944, 1951, 1955). While teaching botany and Afrikaans, he wrote various works, including a book of short stories, Leetong; *a book of essays,* Pelong ea ka; *and* A Textbook of Southern Sotho Grammar *(1957), which he co-authored with C. M. Doke.*

Mofokeng died in 1957, at the age of thirty-four, after a long illness.

Senkatana, *the play from which the following excerpt comes, was first published in 1952 in the "Bantu Treasury Series" of the Witwatersrand University Press. It is based on a Sotho legend in which the child hero and dragon slayer, Senkatana, kills the Monster that swallowed all the people and their livestock, and all living creatures, and frees them from its dark entrails, the people thereupon unanimously proclaiming him their king. Mofokeng drew strong parallels between this legend and the bondage of the black people of South Africa. But it is today, more than ever, that the aptness of this parallel has attained its greatest starkness, as the black children of South Africa, like Senkatana, are facing the Monster with courage and conviction that justice is on their side, and will prevail in the end.*

This newly-translated excerpt comes from a scene near the beginning of the play, in which Senkatana wakes up from a long sleep under a tree out in the open. The entire scene is in the form of a soliloquy in which Senkatana first admires the beauty of nature, then decides it is the right of everyone to see and admire this beauty. But all the people are in the belly of the Monster.

Act I, Scene 1 (partial)

But where are all the people gone? Where are other eyes
To share with mine this beauty?
Where are other faces, to smile
When they behold the beauty that I see?
Ah, what a calamity has befallen us all!
A misfortune that has no parallel!
This misfortune that separated us!

All the people are in the belly of the beast,
All are confined in a terrible darkness,
Darkness deeper than the deepest ocean,
Darkness that stretches without end!
And from that darkness comes the piercing cry of God's
      creatures,
A cry deeper than the darkness itself,
A cry arising from the depths of their feelings.
[*With a sorrowful voice:*]
All of us suffer, we lack peace;
We yearn for many different things!
They yearned for freedom,
To view all things beautiful that the light reveals;
We too thirst for freedom,
Freedom to be happy and joyful.
Happiness is not complete when denied to others,
We were all born to be free, it is our right!
All were born to live with others,
To view with them all things beautiful,
To rejoice with them and live in fellowship!
Without them our freedom is but a mockery,
It is a cause of sorrow and weeping;
It is not freedom but a terrible bondage!
It is a darkness of unfathomable depth:
Darkness in the midst of light,
Sorrow in the midst of joy,
Weeping in the midst of celebrations,
Hunger in the midst of plenty!

Translated from the Sesotho by Daniel P. Kunene

Three Poems
Patrick Cullinan

Patrick Cullinan was born in Pretoria in 1932, and attended school in Johannesburg and later in England. He completed his academic career (but not his education) by reading modern languages at Oxford, majoring in Italian. He spent many years farming and sawmilling in the Eastern Transvaal but in the early seventies he and Lionel Abrahams founded Bateleur Press in order to publish new South African poetry and fiction. He was also editor of The Bloody Horse *(1980–81), which had the same aims. Three collections of his poetry have been published:* The Horizon Forty Miles Away *(1973),* Today Is Not Different *(1978) and* The White Hail in the Orchard *(Cape Town: David Philip, 1984), from which the second and third poems, below, are taken. He has received the Olive Schreiner and two Pringle prizes for his poetry. He now lives in Cape Town and lectures in English at the University of the Western Cape.*

Homage to David Livingstone
Phakamile Yali-Manisi*

It has always been a little hard
to make it move, to get the drama.
Yet when Bellini drew a saint
receiving the stigmata,
he filled the open spaces
with dogs and hares he copied
from a pattern book.
He knew a miracle
could hold that vulgar stock.

---

*A Xhosa imbongi or praise-singer

Mendelssohn in his symphony,
The Reformation,
finds tunes abundant
in the common store;
he makes a solemn gala throb
with lieder from the street,
and turns to Luther,
converting
A Mighty Fortress Is Our God.

Now hear Manisi in his praising:
the words that circle words.
You have the skill, Imbongi,
And yet this tongue
I hardly understand.
I say you do,
but do not make your song:
your poem calls back.
It is

and is not memory. Your words
beat time, they drum
and circle round each other:
as dancers do who clap to start
and hold a rhythm, known at once
and new. Here is life's rhetoric,
a shape that hovers in the song.
And when it vanishes,
it must be there.

A Dream of Guests

I

When the year came to my broken house
the guests were there bringing their own guest.
They had the long face and poor digestion
of those who had once been rich.
And what was there to eat but sour bread,
the wine as thick and black as mud?

Away from this house with its smell of the unwashed
over the blue sea to their islands,
long since gone my children, leaving no toys
but the doll at the foot of my bed,
the arm torn off, eyes out, its belly gutless;
and this I tell all comers is my wife, long dead.

II

We waste his land and sell his gilded tomes:
his colony of schoolbooks; wordlists and Latin primers
being most in demand. In this house
we all have the same odd pace, the witty eyes
of those who have the death-wish. It is a broken place
and we would like to leave these passages,
derelict with ancient rubbish, modern rage.

No one believes there are harlots in the attic
ready to satisfy our one inane desire;
no one believes there are golden-long vintages
brooding in the cellar.
There are no facts that matter here,
only absurd alcoves reached by a rickety stair,
or porticoes stuffed with sofas piled
to form a hopeless barrier on the way
to flea-infested granaries, not filled.

Swooping at twilight,
we have seen no swallows in the courtyard,
but have observed
other things wounded, broken-backed in the gutter.

III

But with such a host there is no going.
The guests must stay and listen, crossing their legs,
yawning, bored numb by his soliloquies
on travel and the pleasures of a well-stocked mind.
They will hear his rant, his explicable loathing of Pygmies,
again and again. Until he dies they will continue to exploit
his miserable possessions and burn his ancient gifts.
And in the half-shuttered light of the long afternoon
they must listen as he turns to them, defensive and accusing;
as by revenge in a mirror they will watch him step,
pace odd, alive, and the staring back
of witty death-searching eyes.

To Have Love

To have love and then lose it:
the white hail in the orchard
lying with leaves it has stripped
and the storm moving away.

"Dollar Brand" / linocut by David Hlongwane.

Those Jolly Little Beetles

Wilma Stockenström

Wilma Stockenström was born in 1933 at Napier in the Cape Province, where she attended school. She received a B.A. from Stellenbosch University, majoring in drama, and has subsequently worked as a translator and free-lance actress (stage, film and television). She has published poetry, prose and a play.

Her latest novella, Die Kremetartekspedisie *(Cape Town: Human and Rousseau, 1981), has been translated into Dutch, French, Swedish and English. The English translation, by novelist J. M. Coetzee, is titled* The Expedition to the Baobab Tree *and was published in Britain by Faber and Faber (1983). It is at present being translated into German.*

Stockenström's poetry anthologies include Vir die Bysiende Leser *(Cape Town: Human and Rousseau, 1970),* Spieël van Water *(Cape Town: Human and Rousseau, 1973) and* Van Vergetelheid en van Glans *(Cape Town: Human and Rousseau, 1976).*

She is married to Ants Kirsipuu, a linguist/anthropologist, and lives in "hateful Pretoria."

Around the towering heap in the middle of the veld
the mailed treasurers congregate
with stiff coattails polished bright
and knobbly eyes fixed telescopically on the sand pulpit.
Whence speaks with insect-insight, the biggest beetle:

What seems like vain scrabbling, dearly beloved ones, is
intricate ceremonies to the initiate.
Thank the god of bugs and beetles in general,
for my leadership.
I caution you to honor the outward appearance
as traditionally behooves a beetle.
Come let us pray. Oh beetle god,
blessed are we who are not proud,

for luckily, oh beetle god, we realize
that we are nothing
without the shell around our entrails.

Translated from the Afrikaans by Rosa Keet

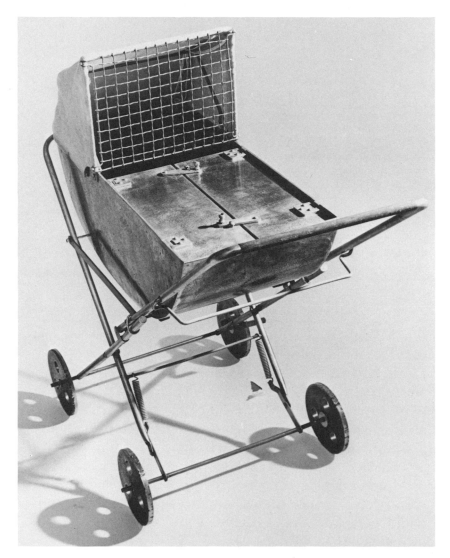

"Riot-Protected Baby Carriage" / sculpture by Gavin Younge.

Easter Transit

Phil du Plessis

Phil du Plessis is a poet and journalist who works as a medical practitioner and psychotherapist at Kalk Bay near Cape Town. During the past twenty years he has published four volumes of poetry as well as literary, art and music criticism for most of the major newspapers. He was founder-editor of Wurm, and editor of New Nation and Izwi, which launched a number of prominent black writers. His published volumes include Geskrifte om 'n houtgesig (Cape Town: Tafelberg, 1970), Die Diep Soet Afgeronde Stem van my Dooies (Cape Town: Tafelberg, 1975), Lyksang (Johannesburg: Perskor, 1980) and Ek Sing Waar Ek Staan (Cape Town: Tafelberg, 1986). "Easter Transit" is from a privately published volume.

Steinkopf 1983

The flanks
of these dire hills
bloom
wax-green.

Do they speak
of atonement,
of death,
of fragrant spring
and blossom
on the hyssop,
do they speak
of another
autumn?

On this journey
I go in the night,

into the night
while a dry wind
escorts the moon
and me,
and roughens
the ridges.

Ahead on the road
the slaughterhouse truck:
and I
smell wool and dung and blood.

Translated from the Afrikaans by Patrick Cullinan

Photograph by René Weideman.

Coronach at Cave-Rock

Douglas Livingstone

Douglas Livingstone was born in Kuala Lumpur, Malaya, in 1932. At the age of ten he came to South Africa. He was educated in Natal and in Zimbabwe, where he trained as a marine bacteriologist. Since 1964, Livingstone has been in charge of marine bacteriological research at the Council for Scientific and Industrial Research in Durban.

His first significant anthology of verse was Sjambok, and Other Poems from Africa *(London: Oxford University Press, 1964). Since then he has published a number of collections, which have won important awards, including the Olive Schreiner Prize (for a radio play) and the Central News Agency (CNA) award for his* Selected Poems *(Johannesburg: Ad. Donker, 1984).*

Driftwood. A small, silent piece, cluttered with lichen,
transfused by years at sea, evading – at first – shape:
the holster-stock of a machine-pistol issued
to U-Boat crews. Then, Gothic in wood, a number
a name: A VON WEBERN. Certainly not *that* one –
gunned down at Mittersill in 1945.

(I am Anton. As in   Chekov. The unscripted
who prefer melodies   to content, to form, add
syllables, aspirates   Not many understood.
Even now I care naught   for such dense cluttered lives.
I touched my pencils to   varihued manuscripts:
spare beauties in profile   like these Austrian peaks.

Trapped by time, arranging   after my dear masters
Bach, Beethoven, Schubert   Mahler – gentlemen who
left out nothing, yet I   am presently of them.
For me, my bagatelles   enfolded essences:
variation and space   counterpoint and silence
never developing   beauty parenthesized.

347

Strings touched with a feather   the electric shiver
up the dangerous stairs   of a crumbling mansion
tiptoed emanations   the boiling of plasmas
the unspeakable sounds   of music from my skull:
an abrupt lightning flash   blurt of depth-charged thunder
—I transposed none of these   but they are of me, there.

I survived the Terror   declining to depart
knew Kokoschka, Berg   Adler and Schöenberg. Then that
wry final cantata   a GI fusillade.
"The *pensato*-scorer"   let them mock as they will
—the notes so delicate   they can only be thought.
Twelve tones temper my world   My small pieces will live.)

Stuck upright—my move—the piece stands to: half-a-cross,
mere weathered bagatelle, short armless monument.
Long-lived notes make more durable headstones than most.
Maybe you, too, were an indignant pacifist.
A conscripted detail, sure, you raged in the throes
as your crumbling essence drowned in blood or water.

Two Poems

Keorapetse Kgositsile

Keorapetse Kgositsile was born in Johannesburg in 1938. A journalist by profession, he is one of the sixties political exile community. In the mid-seventies Kgositsile worked with the Columbia University Writing Progam, and later with Black Dialogue Magazine *in New York.*

Kgositsile taught for ten years at the University of Dar Es Salaam, the University of Nairobi and the University of Gabarone. In 1985, when South Africa invaded Botswana, where he was then living, he moved to another front-line state, and remains in exile.

His more recent volumes of poetry include My Name Is Afrika *(1971) and* The Present is a Dangerous Place to Live *(1975). These poems are from his collection,* Herzpuren *(Heartprints), which was published in Germany by Schwistinger Galerie-Verlag in 1980.*

For Billie Holiday

Lady Day, Lady Day,
Lady Day of no happy days,
Who lives in a voice
Sagging with the pain
Where the monster's teeth
Are deep to our marrow.

Lady Day of no happy days,
Carried in a voice so blue
She could teach any sky
All about blues.

Lady Day of no happy days,
Mrs. Scag still roams

The treacherous ghetto streets
Of white design wasting
The youngbloods who think
Themselves too hip to learn
From your hurt.

Lady Day,
Them that got power,
Wealth and junk
Are still picking your pain
For profit and fun.

Lady Day, Lady Day
Of no happy days,
The willow still weeps for you
Though now we should know
That all tears are stale,
Though now we should know
That tears ain't never done nothing
for nobody.

Song for Ilva Mackay and Mongane

Hear now a sound of floods
Of desire of longing of memories,
Of erstwhile peasants who can
No longer laugh downhill. My brother
Knows there is no death in life,
Only in death. That music is native,
So I sing your name.

You are child of your tongue,
You will be born with gun
In one eye and grenade in the other.
You are Tiro: There is no such thing
As escape or sanctuary in life where
All things come to pass when they do,
Where every bloodstain is a sign
Of death of life.

You are Mandela, You are all
The names we are in Robben Island,
You are child of sound and sense
You can look the past
Straight in the eye.
To know this season and purpose
You have come from yesterday
To remind the living that
The dead do not remember the banned,
The jailed the exiled the dead.
Here I meet
And this way I salute you
With bloodstains on my tongue:

I am no calypsonian
But this you have taught me.
You could say you were from Cape Town
Or Johannesburg, Accra or Bagamoyo,
New York, Kingston or Havana.
When you have come from tomorrow
We shall know each other by our bloodstain.

Train Churches

Text and photographs by Santu Mofokeng

Santu Mofokeng was born in October 1956. He studied photography as a darkroom assistant for Die Beeld, *an Afrikaans newspaper, became a photographer's assistant with Thomson's Publications in 1984, and returned to* Die Beeld *in 1985. Later that same year, he joined Afrapix, the photographers' collective of which he is now a full member. Throughout this period, Mofokeng recalls, he was aided and encouraged in his photographic career by David Goldblatt, who provided him with criticism and training in photojournalism. His work has been widely published in most of the main newspapers in and around Johannesburg, as well as in the* Weekly Mail *and* Pace. *He is married, has a son, and lives in Soweto.*

Early-morning, late-afternoon and evening commuters preach the gospel in trains en route to and from work.

The train ride is no longer a means to an end, but an end in itself as people from different townships congregate in coaches—two to three per train—to sing to the accompaniment of improvised drums (banging the sides of the train) and bells.

Foot stomping and gyrating—a packed train is turned into a church.

This is a daily ritual.

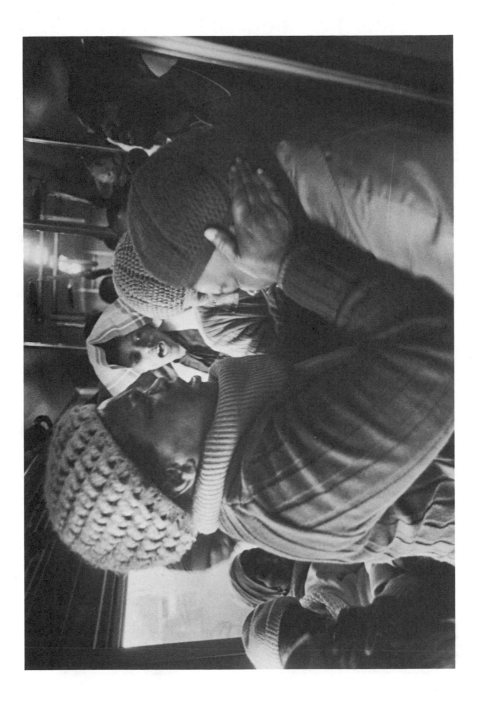

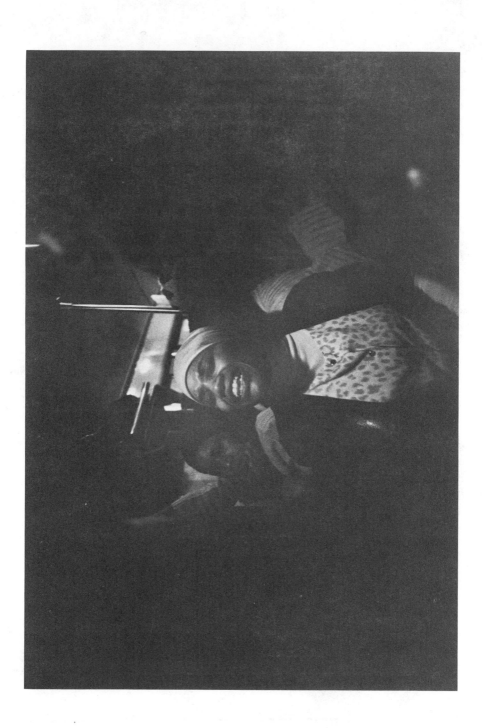

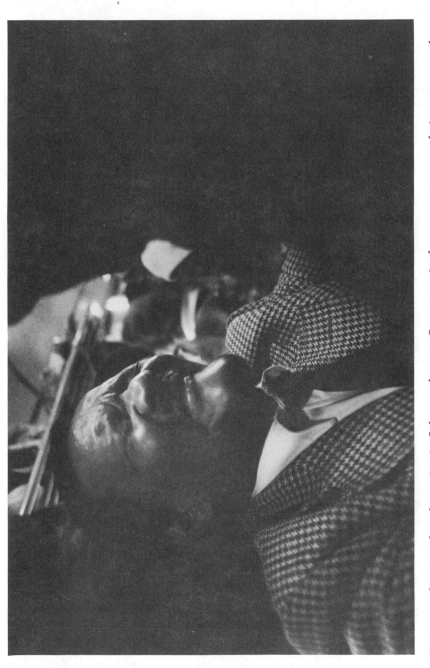

Priest conducting church service in Johannesburg-to-Soweto train for commuters on their way to work.

People running in circles and chanting before dispersing for work.

Park Station, Johannesburg. Singing continues onto platform before people go off in different directions to work.

From the Introduction to *Salutes and Censures*

Dennis Brutus

Born in Harare, Zimbabwe in 1924, Dennis Brutus was educated at Fort Hare and the University of the Witwatersrand. He was imprisoned on the notorious Robben Island, a political penal colony off the coast of Cape Town, for his active opposition to the apartheid regime. He is a past-president of the South African Non-Racial Olympic Committee, which was responsible for having South Africa excluded, because of its racial policies, from the Olympics.

Brutus has made a significant contribution to South African poetry: he was recipient, with Arthur Nortje (see page 382), of the Mbari Poetry Prize in 1962. His most celebrated collections of verse are Sirens, Knuckles, Boots *(Mbari Press, 1963) and* Letters to Martha and Other Poems from a South African Prison *(London: Heinemann, 1968). His most recent collection is* Salutes and Censures, *originally published in 1982 and due out in 1987 (from Africa World Press) in a new edition for which he has written the unpublished introduction excerpted here.*

A former Northwestern University professor, Brutus is currently chairman of the Department of Black Community Research and Development at the University of Pittsburgh.

I am not one for large pronouncements about the role of the artist or the poet: I am not given to pontificating, and I am not given to prescribing how others ought to write. Yet, at the same time, I must recognize that the way I write implies a statement about writing, and about the judgments I make of others, those I like and those I dislike, those I admire and those I dismiss. These judgments imply certain standards which I have adopted for myself. What I have not done is to attempt an elaborate defense of such judgments. No "apologia." What I would say is that there is no obligation to be a committed poet, any more than there is an obligation to be a committed sculptor or painter. However, for me what is not relevant to society, what is purely abstract, is generally simply boring and often seems an evasion of reality. I have no problems with the statement that the artist should not merely depict the world but should transform the world.

Clearly, my concern is more ambitious than merely social representation. I'm interested in social transformation. But as I've said many times in other places, I do not see any obligation on the artist (*qua* artist). What I *do* see is an obligation on every human being to be involved in humanity and therefore through whatever one does, as a politician, as a poet, as a plumber, as a philosopher. I think what one is about as a human being is the human condition and one must address this. Not all the time, not boringly, but certainly, inescapably, at times.

* * *

Of course, I come out of the African tradition and I think one does not discover the tradition and then decide to adopt it and live within it. That's not how the process works. One grows up surrounded by the tradition, a tadpole in a pond, and in that pond the climate is of commitment. I must be careful not to exaggerate, because one has to separate two things here. Firstly, there was my discovery, as an adult, of an African tradition as articulated by critics. Further, there was that African tradition of the commitment of the artist as a social being, who derives his inspiration from the community and returns his creative product to the community. Certainly that's the theoretical framework.

What I grew up with (and this is curious because there was a clear schizophrenia or dichotomy here, as there was in other parts of my life), was very much the English, mainstream poetic tradition through my mother and through my schooling in missionary schools. It was the tradition of William Wordsworth, but also of Longfellow's "Excelsior," certainly of Tennyson's "Sir Galahad" poem. But it was a tradition which also included poems like the "The Slave's Dream" by Longfellow, which speaks of a hunger for freedom, and also Scott's "Lay of the Last Minstrel," which had a strong influence on me and which carries those memorable lines: "Breathes there the man with soul so dead,/ Who never to himself hath said,/ This is my own, my native land!" Implicit in those lines is a statement of patriotism taken for granted, and a statement *for* patriotism which I assumed I was entitled to make; therefore, an assumption that South Africa was and always would be my native land. And then there was that marvelously simple, jingly lyric which I liked so much that I memorized it and then set it to music of my own (much to the irritation of my brother Wilfred, who was always an astrigent critic rectifying my sentimental and romantic effusions):

Higher, higher do we climb
Up the path of glory
That our names may live through time
In our children's story.

I cannot recall where that is from and I doubt very much if I will be able to track it down. My recollection is of a school reader that I read at 15 Brock Square, Dowerville, Port Elizabeth, that little segregated township—by some reports the first segregated housing scheme for colored people in the history of South Africa, and certainly of the Cape Province, and most certainly of Port Elizabeth. A segregated township of one hundred homes—which has now become an all-white township, if it exists at all—from which I was excluded by law once I had come out of prison. Although I remember defying that prohibition and traveling through it with Omar Cassem, my old ally, and seeing how run-down it had become, taken over by an extremely poor working-class section of the white population, many of them rural workers coming into the city for the first time and adapting slowly to the industrialized environment around them.

*   *   *

So there is that English mainstream poetic tradition which includes the two elements of *mere* or *pure* lyricism, pure narrative. Wordsworth's Lucy Gray poems and "The Daffodils" and "I Wandered Lonely as a Cloud," but also Longfellow's "The Slave's Dream" and "Excelsior," with their moral and political patriotic statements. On the other hand, I grew up in an African ("colored," if you like) tradition of involvement in society. I remember my mother's social commitment: the church choirs, the relief work, the helping of poorer members of the community, and, because of her somewhat better education, teaching in a ghetto school. Teachers were very highly regarded. They were the leaders in a society where there were no political leaders. So I remember all her work and all her concern—some of it excessive to my selfish eye, because her concern for the less fortunate somehow led to a diminished concern for the well-being of our own family of four children. Or so it seemed to me at the time.

My father's social concerns were even larger. He was unfortunately a rather isolated and, I think it not unfair to say, arrogant man who felt himself intellectually perhaps, and educationally certainly, above most of those in that little ghetto. Not that there weren't other teachers. One of them was a Mr. Rademeyer, principal of the school where my mother taught; but my father looked at him with disfavor. He had come into the city from a small country-town and therefore was thought to be a bit of a bumpkin. (The decision to appoint him had not been made by the community, but by that mysterious body that presided over our educational lives called the "School Board" and which consisted of anonymous white persons sitting somewhere in the city where we could never penetrate. But that is an aside.) There was also Jimmy Davidson, the brilliant young man whom I first knew as a high-school student and subsequently as a teacher. He taught me Afrikaans for a while, as I had been badly handicapped by my education in a missionary junior school where the nuns were either English or Irish, and not equipped to teach Afrikaans. I believe that Jimmy Davidson was a strong influence on Arthur Nortje, the fine young man whom I taught and whom I still regard as the finest poet to come out of South Africa and probably out of Africa.

There is, then, this concern with society. My father followed attentively the politics of the Middle East, the Balfour Declaration, the struggles for independence in Africa. The complexity of South African politics he followed as if he were still a participant. He may have been among those few who had what was called the *Cape Franchise*, which was subsequently taken away.

My father was consulted by others in the community and was regarded as well-informed. There were also the occasional conversations in the family (I think they were more frequent when I was a small boy — somewhere perhaps between the ages six and ten. Later, tensions between my parents increased until they led to an eventual breakup.) From these I became aware of the political debates, got to know the personalities and the antagonisms between them, without yet knowing what the issues were at bottom. Of course I was aware of interracial conflicts and divisions. Certainly we were not white, and out there were the white people who controlled our destiny. Some of us felt, alternately, aggressive and subservient. There were also the Africans, the "natives" who lived even further out on the edge of the city and who passed through our area, or the outskirts of it, on the way to their area, each morning going to work and each evening coming from work.

* * *

I grew up knowing vaguely of resistance. My mother talked of the days of slavery, of how her mother had in fact known slavery, may have been a slave herself. She was of African descent, but of mixed heritage: an English family called Webb, apparently. She had told my mother of how slaves had been tied to the large wheel of an ox wagon and whipped. So there is that.

My mother used to recite the poem "The Slave's Dream" to her children. She had memorized it and I certainly had memorized most of it at one time and can even quote in part from it now.

> Beside the ungathered rice he lay,
> His sickle in his hand;
> His breast was bare, his matted hair
> Was buried in the sand. . . .
>
> He saw once more his dark-eyed queen
> Among her children stand;
> They clasped his neck, they kissed his cheeks,
> They held him by the hand! . . .

Then, toward the end of the poem,

> The forests, with their myriad tongues,
> Shouted of liberty . . .

It may be that line which stayed with me through all the years of my impressionable boyhood and into my adulthood.

Around this time, too, I became acquainted with Byron's poem "The Dying Gladiator":

> I see before me the dying Gladiator lie:
> He leans upon his hand—his manly brow
> Consents to death, but conquers agony . . .

Again this was, for me, an image of someone defeated but indomitable, unsubmitting in defeat. The image fused with memories of resistance to colonial repression, resistance to the Afrikaner, resistance against those who have conquered the African or the "nonwhite." Much of this was referred to in a kind of shorthand because people understood each other. I learned about and understood it without quite catching all the details. The tradition of resistance was there, and was with me years later when I organized parents in parent-teacher associations to protest against the Group Areas Act and the forced removals of people from their homes in the cities. Such government policies created the ghettos and townships outside of the city, as Port Elizabeth became all-white.

I had no commitment to the protection of property. But I had a commitment to protecting a right, and the right was the right to live where you pleased and, certainly, the right not to be moved because of your race. That was the struggle in which I became involved.

Ping-Pong: Excerpt from Hearing of the Case of Dennis Brutus in Immigration Court

Transcribed by Y. B. Holly

The tape excerpted here was supplied by the U.S. Immigration and Naturalization Service office in Chicago (where the hearing was held) and transcribed by Y. B. Holly, who lives in Evanston, Illinois, and is secretary of the Dennis Brutus Defense Committee and The Africa Network.

SG*: Professor Brutus, you referred several times to your activities in the area of sports in South Africa. Would you please give the court one specific example of your activities with regard to the organization of the sport of table tennis?

DB: With the question of table tennis, there existed in South Africa two bodies. One was an exclusively white organization and the other was an organization open to all South Africans. I was an official of the latter.

SG: And what position did you hold in that organization?

DB: It varied. Initially, representing a club to a regional union, and finally to a national organization.

SG: What was the name of that organization?

DB: The nonracial one was called "South African Table Tennis Board." The exclusively white one was called "South African Table Tennis Union."

---

*SG: Susan Gzesh, Dennis Brutus's attorney

SG: When you refer to your holding positions in that organization, what general time period were you in office?

DB: As early as 1948 onwards until 1961, when it becomes illegal for me to be in a sports organization.

SG: How did you first get involved with table tennis?

DB: Playing it myself, then becoming the coach of the team of the high school and organizing a team there, and representing that team in the Union.

SG: What communications did the national organization that you were part of have with the international?

DB: A world federation had been formed and it was accepting membership from national bodies. In the case of South Africa, it had two teams—a body open only to whites and one open to all players on the basis of nonracialism. Ultimately, the world body decided to reject the application of the all-white body and to give membership to the nonracial body.

SG: We heard Mr. Lapchick* testify that that took place in 1956. Is that correct?

DB: That is correct.

SG: Was there any response from the government of South Africa to the exclusion?

DB: There was a statement from the South African government made by the minister in charge of sport, who was called the "Minister for the Interior," in which he describes the action of those who got the white body excluded as a form of treason and announced that people will be prosecuted for supporting treason.

SG: Professor Brutus, what had been your personal role in relation to getting the all-white table tennis union excluded from the International Table Tennis Federation?

---

*Dr. Richard Lapchick was an expert witness who had written his dissertation on racism in sport, and who was acquainted with Dennis Brutus's work.

DB: As the vice-president of the national board, and as the person assigned to conduct much of the international correspondence, I had a major role in it.

SG: Was your role publicly known?

DB: Publicly.

SG: Will you please list for the court, briefly, what other sports organizations you were involved in during the 1950 to 1958 period?

DB: Yes, they included athletics, track-and-field, boxing, cycling, swimming, weight lifting, table tennis, judo and football and soccer, where we had about 47,000 players. My role was to coordinate the different sports and to set up a single organization that could act on behalf of roughly 60,000 athletes.

SG: During that period, were sports officially segregated by law in South Africa?

DB: Yes, but in fact when the National Party came to power in 1948, you get an intensification of that. It becomes much more severe and athletes are arrested and tried for playing in the wrong group area so that a black playing in a white area or a white playing in a black area could be arrested and charged with a violation of the Group Areas Act.

SG: You've just described the formation of a national organization of other sports. What was the name of that organization?

DB: South African Sports Association.

SG: Could you describe briefly for the court the events leading up to the founding of the South African Sports Association?

DB: We began by publicizing the need for a coordinating body, and I wrote an article in a liberal journal that was circulated widely, announcing a meeting for such a purpose. And as a matter of fact, this article was used by the Secret Police to intimidate other people to stay away, by saying that they were aware of the intentions of such a meeting. At the first meeting in East London the Secret Police attended. Subsequently, it was the material of this organization which was confiscated by the Secret Police.

SG: What was your personal role in organizing that meeting?

DB: I was a sports official who was later elected secretary.

SG: Was there anything illegal about sponsoring activities?

DB: Nothing at all.

SG: What organizing was done by you in South Africa during this period with respect to the Olympics?

DB: I collected the statements of ministers of the government and others on their determination to enforce racial segregation in sport, and mailed these to Chicago to Avery Brundage at 10 North LaSalle Street. He was at that time president of the World Olympic Committee and I brought to his attention the racism of the team, as enforced by the South African Olympic Organization.

SG: Did the public acknowledge the South African Sports Association as a legal organization?

DB: Yes, there were reports of it in the press.

SG: Approximately what year was that?

DB: From 1958 onwards to 1961.

SG: Did you carry on your correspondence with Mr. Brundage during this period?

DB: Mr. Brundage often declined to answer the letters. Sometimes when he did we would receive only empty envelopes, with no contents.

SG: Why did you receive an empty envelope?

DB: I think it was a deliberate attempt to intimidate me, to let me know that the Secret Police were aware of the dissidence going on.

SG: Do you believe that the Secret Police were opening the mail?

DB: I do.

SG: Will you please tell the court what "SANROC" is? Mr. Lapchick already mentioned that organization in regard to your activity.

DB: One of the reasons Mr. Brundage gave for declining to pay attention to our correspondence was that he only accepted correspondence from Olympic Committees. As long as we were called the South African Sports Association, he did not have to pay any attention to it. When we reformed SASA, the South African Sports Association, and created the South African Non-Racial Olympic Committee, in contrast to the official Olympic Committee, which was a racial one, we were then in a position where he could no longer ignore our correspondence.

SG: Professor Brutus, was there in the Olympic Charter a basis for the organization's activities?

DB: It was extremely important, as it stressed laws in the organization of the Olympic Games. What is known as Fundamental Principle One was there: that any country that was guilty of discrimination on the basis of race, color or religion or politics must be excluded from the Olympics.

SG: Professor Brutus, prior to your banning in 1961, was there any other official response to your activities?

DB: In what regard?

SG: With respect to your employer. You were a government employee, were you not?

DB: I was teaching in a government school and I received warnings—from an official from the Education Department—which were directed, I think, primarily at the fact that I was still teaching a regular syllabus, declining to teach children of a black school that they were inferior or giving them an inferior education. But it did include a warning about my political activities as well.

SG: Approximately what year did you receive that warning?

DB: Nineteen-sixty.

SG: What political activities were referred to in that warning?

DB: I think they were primarily about my protest against racism in education, but also my protest against the Group Areas Act, Forced Removals and the denial of political rights through the Suppression of Communism Act.

SG: Professor Brutus, you stated before that you were banned from teaching in 1961. How did you make a living after you were banned from teaching?

DB: For a short while, I worked as a journalist, but an additional law made it a crime for me to write anything for publication or a criminal act for any editor to publish anything I wrote. So it became impossible for me to continue to work as a journalist.

SG: Were you also arrested in South Africa for violation of your banning order?

DB: Yes.

SG: And could you please describe the circumstance of your arrest?

DB: In May of 1963, I was arrested in the offices of the South African Olympic Committee. Avery Brundage had sent someone to South Africa to investigate racism in South African sport and since the person who was doing the investigating would meet only with officials of the white Olympic Association, I made an effort to supply information about other athletes. I went to the meeting not intending to attend the meeting, but only to deliver this information. While I was there, two members of the Secret Police arrested me, and I was charged, because of attending this Olympic Committee meeting, with contravening my banning order.

THE ARTS

A healthy architectural playfu

A new glossy architectural magazine, ADA, mixes a healthy eclecticism with maddening trendiness, writes IVOR POWELL

I DON'T think I'm being overly generous when I say that the study of architecture tends to be approached in a far more enlightened, imaginative and holistic way inside the teaching institutions of this country than most of the other so-called creative disciplines.

At a recent national congress of architecture students, for example, papers delivered covered topics as diverse as the politics of colonialism, musical form, graffiti, geomancy, and painting; all these were construed as being of some relevance to the business of putting up buildings. Such eclecticism in a time which has not yet shrugged from its back the thin spectre of Modernist specialisation is obviously as healthy as it is refreshing.

At the same time — and perhaps the two things are not entirely unrelated — the study of architecture tends as often as not to be an insufferably groupie affair, self-conscious, trendy, self-congratulatory, exclusivist.

ADA (Architecture Design Art), the new magazine put out by a group of unaffiliated architecture-related people in Cape Town, reflects both tendencies in more or less equal proportion. The contents of the first issue include: an interview with Cape Town artist Manfred Zylla; a feature on Cape Town architect Peter Amm's rather gorgeous new home near Camps Bay; an interview with Cape Town composer John Simon; a piece on oddball Cape Town bicycle designer John Stegmann; a complementary if somewhat insubstantial article on bicycle decoration as a phenomenon in black culture; some pictures of rather silly

RESTRICTED

Images of Soweto, '76, in Manfred Zylla's drawing 'Bullets and Sweets', a double-page spread from ADA

little post-Modernist soufflés by Cape Town sculptor Angela Ferreira; as well as various little bits of variously trivial trivia. The selection of material then suggests a certain

The architect turns artist

THERE is no shortage of criticism, derision even, of "modern" architecture, and most of it is justified. One of the reasons for its unsatisfactory nature may be found in the inability and unwillingness of the majority of contemporary architects to practise or, for that

EXHIBITION: Letters and Postcards from Home: works in pen, ink and watercolour by Allan Schwarz Cassirer Fine Art Gallery

culminating in "about 348 portraits of the

degree of cultural agility and a certain lateral and very welcome playfulness.

This on the one hand — and let me say here that I don't object to the exclusive focus on Cape Town culture in itself; God knows Jo'burg has done that often enough. I'm merely noting it in relation to a magazine which purports to be "about Southern African creators and their creations".

On the other hand — and often enough on the other face of the page — there is discernible in ADA a kind of trendy arrogance that is exemplified in the inclusion — opposite the

Surreali
narcissi

In its
irritatin
is perni
are refl
Nowhei
unfortu
fittings i
home n
mildest
doubt or
that life,
general,
in this
teeniest
role of
country
These d
involvec

Sure, i
service t
South A
saying..
only put
to comm
where 1
resultin
spontan
environ
spontan
where tl
perceptic
history o

It gets
Simon, t
respondi
the deatl
from ta
commitn
context,
abstract
politics?
governm

Of all
magazin
Zylla wl
begins t
country,

Boys from the Border; Sweets and Bullets

Manfred Zylla

Manfred Zylla was born in Germany, and was apprenticed in the printing trade in Augsburg. His involvement with South Africa began in 1970 when he first traveled to Cape Town. In 1974 he met and married a South African woman. After 1976, he, his wife and daughter returned to Germany for a brief period but were soon back in Cape Town.

In the years which followed, as the level of urban protest escalated, Zylla became an increasingly important documentarist, political satirist and teacher. Living in the so-called "colored" community of Athlone, Zylla was witness to numerous scenes of police violence, and recorded these in his work. He was involved with the Community Arts Project (CAP). A series of his works depicting characteristic white South African "types" (such as businessmen, farmers, soldiers) was exhibited at CAP. Zylla invited members of the community to paint over and scrawl on his works. The event was filmed and documented in a booklet; the booklet was immediately banned.

In 1985 a young relative of his wife's was slain by the police in the notorious "Trojan Horse" episode (see Chronology, *page 486).*

Zylla is at present in West Germany.

*   *   *

Boys from the Border (1985), is a series of eight pencil-on-paper drawings, four of which immediately follow. The next work, Sweets and Bullets (1985), is a "pencil-watercolor," with the candies along its top and bottom borders appearing gaily multicolored in the original.

Four Poems

Arthur Nortje

Arthur Kenneth Nortje (1942-70) was born in Oudtshoorn, a town best remembered not for its poet but for its caves and its ostrich farming. He was educated at the University of the Western Cape which, at that stage, was not a fully recognized university but a university college for so-called "coloreds" created by the apartheid machine. Nortje won a scholarship to Oxford in 1965. After completing his degree, he taught for two years in Canada. He returned to Jesus College to further his studies, but died suddenly in Oxford under mysterious circumstances. The coroner returned an open verdict.

In 1962 Nortje was, with Dennis Brutus (his teacher and friend), co-recipient of the Mbari Poetry Prize. His posthumously published volumes are Dead Roots (London: Heinemann, 1973) and Lonely Against the Light (New Coin, 1973). A copy of his Notebook is housed at Northwestern University, Evanston. In 1982, an anthology, Somehow We Survive, edited by Sterling Plumpp (New York: Thunder's Mouth Press), made available some unpublished poems, edited from the manuscript.

Nortje's poetry provides perhaps the clearest articulation of the physical and psychological brutality of grand apartheid in the sixties and seventies.

The following poems are previously unpublished.

Horses: Athlone*

I mite am watching at the street-end
horses drag to a huge standstill.
Hoof's iron slipped on damp cement
is hard luck to the animal.
Curse which thunders to the cocked ears,
raping whip of rubbish chief,

---

*a suburb of Cape Town

hoots and jeers of armored monsters,
these are wisdom's steel and proof.

One pony only screamed the anguish,
bladed open all the old scars,
bristles in flared nostrils tinder.
He whistled wishes to the ashen stars,
spunk among the brutes. Fat lash
fried him crisp in the hungering air.

July 1963

Exit Visa

There were evils in the road.
I ate acorns.
Lands where rumored honey flowed
lay barbed covered with thorns.
But I acquired stronger boots,
sharpened my teeth on bitter fruits.
For that Strongman's prowess
was long unable
to crush my spirit

Nor was his genius equal to
though he was blond & I black
removal of the sun from me cement-celled
I had seen and spoken to the light
though at any time he could call the darkness back

Evils accumulate,
Perils that patiently lie in ambush
at every crossing would snare my progress
had He and His Praetorian henchmen
had their way.
After marching orders
they laughed about my wintering in cold climes
beyond those golden borders,
With a lump in the throat
I took my gypsy leave.

November 1970

From the Way I Live Now

From the way
I live now
in a foreign winter
of centrally-heated freedom
no longer the watchman finding
nutriment in the glow of an African fire
but merely a mouthpiece
dried of wonderful ghostly tales
may be inferred
a timely escape from inhuman coils
by those who entertain me to tea.

Or I have seen in a room of sipped sherry
holding a medium cream
the lips of gentility move
which would certainly be above
hints of even the minutest cowardice
in this young and so
admirable South African
though afterthought aforethought
with some would indicate
here walks a radical manqué.

Unjustly do
I live the way I do now,
accepting smiles & favors for my buried ones.

O under the broiling sun
convict me for my once burning ideals
my brothers

October 1970

[Untitled]

The spacious days pass into the neutrality
of naked trees from which the winds have shaken
a golden burden. Frail the harvest fluttered
to earth & gutter, lapped up by the rains.

On wet leaves, large with sadness, fall my feet
lithe in rubber. As I move to tackle
this appointment I ponder autumn's desuetude,
as I walk to handle that engagement

My hands clog the pockets of an overcoat
& after supper & the music elsewhere
Inside: rooms, by electric fire, bookshelves
Continues academia in extraordinary mildness

I find myself upon the street in safety
going back to a thought procession
resisting the littered desk with its expectations
for a propped posture in an unmade bed.

And thus I munch a windfall apple,
smoke cigarettes, adjust a bookmark, do not open
my mind upon the point where it left off,
Stare at the mirror & walls, write verse

November 1970

The Amanuensis
(from *Dreamwork*)

Wayne Assam

Wayne Assam was born in 1961. His collection of short stories, Dreamwork, *has a thematic and stylistic unity. The stories are crafted with a high degree of verbal precision. It is thus not surprising to learn that Assam's primary love is poetry, and he is at present working on this, as well as on a novel.*

In 1985, together with T. Zambonini, he translated Salire *by Maria Negri from the Italian into English. He and Zambonini are at present translating the Afrikaans poets N. P. van Wyk Louw and D. J. Opperman into Italian.*

This is the first of Wayne Assam's stories to be published, and it is with great pleasure that we introduce his work here.

It has long been a source of surprise to me that, even in the present age of progress at any cost, a scientific defense of prejudice has yet to see the light.

The eminent philosopher and thinker Dr. Y at last agreed to grant me an interview. I hope it is good form to say philosopher *and* thinker. Since making the acquaintance of that great man I have become more heedful of contradictions, paradoxes, neoplasms, pleonasms and tautologies. Not that I, of course, an unworthy dilettante, presume to distinguish among these mysteries with the histological punctiliousness of the deep doctors of metaphysics.

May I say, doctor, I said as I shook his hand, what an honor it is at last to meet you, so to speak, in the flesh. He grimaced and at once withdrew his hand, impatient, I suppose, of the body, as no doubt befits a great spirit. It was a spectacle awesome, humbling and surprising, such as is not given one to witness every day. Confirmed at last, in my own experience, was a phenomenon which I, as a common man among common men, would not otherwise seriously have imagined possible. Though with me grossly, in the body, he had, in the mind or spirit—assuming that they are one and the same—taken flight. How many of us can afford such luxuries?

I coughed. This proved inefficacious. Might we not begin? I ventured. He seemed lost within himself, if that adequately expresses the facts. I repeated myself. Fortunately the room did not echo. I consoled myself with the silence.

It appeared he would be thus withdrawn no little while. I seized upon this opportunity to examine a great man's room at my leisure. It was remarkable, the room, for a combination of roominess and sparse furnishing that did not however communicate to one—I mean to me—an atmosphere of empty isolation, a clear sign, this, I supposed, of the uncluttered efficiency of the philosopher's mind. Let me hasten to add that I am well aware of the present anti-hermeneutical vogue. I think I may say, however, that, in this instance, I was provoked.

What can I do for you? said Dr. Y. I must have looked puzzled. *I* should be the one to look puzzled here, said he severely. The nature of your business? You have an appointment? Well, in that case. He waved me to a chair.

His secretary entered with some tea. See that we are not disturbed, said Dr. Y. She nodded, and left as quietly as she had come. I thought that injunction unfortunate. Even my first impressions of her were favorable.

Now then, he said, pouring. You have some questions? How many sugars? Sweet tooth, I see. Fire away then.

I thought it best to have a sip of tea before beginning. Yes? he said, yes? How is it, I said, beginning, that science has not kept step with the march of prejudice? Metaphors come in very handy to people like me.

I was not in the least insulted when he flung himself backwards into his chair. But the answer, the answer, said Dr. Y., is locked in the very terms of the question. I remained in the dark, anxious for illumination. Examine if you will, said Dr. Y, your terms. Take science, there's a term for you. I don't doubt it, my dear Dr. Y, said I, but I remain firmly in the dark. I am, my dear fellow, said he, drawing himself erect, a philosopher, not a candlemaker. I resume. Would you not say or rather incline to the proposition that science consists in selecting, from a multitude of possible causes of a particular phenomenon, that cause or conjunction of causes—or shall I say rather reasons, causes having fallen, in our age, mysteriously into disfavor—Where am I? Er was all I could manage. Ah yes, said he. Which accounts for it with the greatest symmetry and economy? I saw no immediate advantage in dissent. And would you not denominate the faculty which performs this act—I intend no frivolous dramatical allusion—would you not designate it, said he, to make an end, judgment? If pressed, I said, I would. Science, then, said Dr. Y., is a question of judgment.

The secretary entered for the tea-things. What a stroke of luck! I was just able to gulp down my last drop. I was able, also, to note, in passing—that is to say as she passed—her stirring figure and entrancing gait.

A question, said Dr. Y, of judgment. Consider, now, with me, prejudice. I am speaking of the word. Attend very closely, now, while I give a demonstration of the modern analysis.

My alarm must have been evident. He tried in vain to reassure me. However, I lacked not only pen and paper but also that well-known mechanism for projecting abstractions upon some inner screen. Dr. Y dismissed my fears, as I recall, with a swish of his tie. Even if I myself were unable to follow, he would, he said, so to speak, bring me back word of any discoveries he might make. I was desperate and this reassured me. He waited courteously a moment while I dug myself into my seat, and began.

The point I wish to make, said the doctor, becomes clear when we generate from the substantive "prejudice" an hypothetical transitive variant form "prejudge." He paused, and continued. Now "pre-" means "before"; it signifies antecedency. He invited me to ponder, for my own edification, a sprinkling of confirmatory examples from personal experience. I thought of "prestidigitator," "premonstratensian," "preputial," "pretzel" and "prestissimo." Accordingly, said Dr. Y, we now have—if I may appropriate a much-vaunted metaphor from contemporary mythology—the two atomic forms "pre"—equivalent to "before"—and "judgment." Now these two forms, as separate particles, suggest no sure meaning to the mind. From this fact we infer that what we have before us here is no less than a missing third term, a preterition, a conceptual elision—the law, in short, of the excluded middle.

I sat silent, blank and breathless. I confess I considered excusing myself, as I used to do many years ago at school when it all got beyond me, under pretext of ill health. But the good doctor had a look of such intellectual delight that it would have convulsed me with guilt to abandon him.

We are now in a position, said Dr. Y, to survey, in schematic form, our present position. I cannot deny I was extremely glad of the chance to take my ease, as it were, at last, and survey the aforementioned position. He scribbled the following schema high on the topmost sheet of a thick wad of notepaper:

$$\begin{aligned}
\text{Let "pre" + "judge"} &= 0 \\
\text{then } 0 &= \text{"pre" + "judge"} \\
\text{but this is absurd} & \\
\text{therefore "pre" + "judge" + "x"} &= \text{non-0} \\
\text{this yields:} & \\
\text{"pre" + "x" + "judge"} &= \text{non-0}
\end{aligned}$$

I hope sincerely that I have remembered well. I was never one for symbols, there may be omissions. Perhaps there was a Q.E.D. All the same, I must say, without meaning to boast of it, that I do read rather well upside-down. The way in which I acquired this little art is quite detaining. But perhaps some other time.

My schooldays seem distant to me now. I have a vague memory of the image, in a textbook, of some ancient ponderer deep in meditation, with a moving finger in the mud or sand. In those days, I suppose, writing-pads were harder to come by. It is charitable to assume that he had a bath or wash afterwards. At any rate, I endeavor still, even at this late date, to emulate his expression of sublime oblivion, so far as I am able, in memory or imagination, to reconstitute it.

That is all very well, said Dr. Y, but let us now ask ourselves what it is exactly that precedes judgment, since that is the point we have reached. He repeated the question. I, enchanted once again by sandcastles and mudbaths, heard its echo dreamily within. Ponder it at your leisure, urged Dr. Y, mull it over. What is it that might and very likely does precede judgment?

I had not reckoned with such demands upon my concentrative faculties. That which is not judgment? I ventured in desperation. Excellent! cried Dr. Y, excellent! My dear, dear fellow! Ah, the austere satisfaction of clarity and logical thinking, the inexorable march of reason valiantly onwards against the citadel of comprehension!

I am a man of no great gifts, I say it without shame. It is merely a piece of ill-fortune, I hold no one accountable, least of all my forebears, whom well I might. And yet, I may say truly that I have tried time and time again, by availing myself of every opportunity to acquaint myself with the works of men and women my superiors in intellectual and imaginative power, as well as by such independent thinking as a man of my modest courage and capacities is capable of, to, to—I say it with some trepidation—to better myself. However, this matter is delicate and by no means to be rushed.

Dr. Y buzzed for his secretary. Yes, doctor? she said. A glass of water for my guest, said he. I drank it down in one great gulp. She really seemed a most delightful creature.

I think, said Dr. Y, that a second interview would be quite in order. Next week? Make a note, my dear. The same day and hour? In that case goodbye.

And he bent to his work.

*   *   *

When the time for the second interview had come I found myself much fortified after a week of Scrabble and crossword puzzles. If I mention this it is only that those inclined to sneer at such pastimes might bethink themselves.

The secretary led me in. No occasion had, so far, arisen for me to learn her name. I admit I considered throwing propriety to the winds. But the very sensuous austerity which attracted me to her left me, for the moment, utterly, utterly—how shall I say?

Dr. Y regarded me warily as we shook hands, but I kept my lips sealed. Perhaps smiling would have lessened the effort. Sit down, sit down, my dear chap, said Dr. Y. You are well? Much better, I said. No thank you, my dear, said Dr. Y, that will be all, for the moment.

What a superb figure! It seemed to me she had noticed my interest and, what is more, so I felt persuaded, was not displeased by it. She closed the door softly after her.

Ah yes, said Dr. Y, looking up from his notes, ah yes. Now then.

Is it likely, I said, dear doctor, that science might, one day, provide evidence that prejudice is a fact? Oh it undoubtedly exists, he said. Ah, ah, I see what you mean. No, no, I deem it improbable.

I rose, thinking the interview at an end. But to my surprise he went on.

You remember our previous discussion of course? I remembered vaguely, from my schooldays, from my classical lessons to be exact—unless I am greatly mistaken—the figure of the rhetorical question. But I am reminiscing.

It will do no great harm, nonetheless, said Dr. Y, to speculate upon the matter. It seemed a capital idea. A paronomasiac, I see, said Dr. Y distantly. But do sit down, won't you, my dear chap. Let's not stand on ceremony. I expressed my concurrence in action.

It *is* odd, at any rate, to resume, this, how shall I say, said Dr. Y, deficiency, call it that, of or in science. I waited quietly in polite ignorance. When you consider how long it has been among us—I refer, said he, to prejudice—you might almost call—that is to say denominate—it by the designation tradition. It was at this point in particular that I remember being struck by the good doctor's peculiar originality of conception. The more I think about it, said Dr. Y, the more I am almost persuaded that progress such as we know it would have been inconceivable without it. I agreed and begged him for an illustration. I am a philosopher, sir, said he, not a draughtsman. I craved his pardon. After a moment of silence he went on.

Consider if you will the following. Would you not say that there exist— let us, for convenience, leave out of account the outer nebulae and confine ourselves to our own—I intend a secular sense—parish—that there exist, to make an end, persons superior, to other persons, in, for instance, artistic dexterity and intensity of feeling, in bureaucratic ambidexterity and professional condolence, in analytical profundity and a capacity for sustained concentration? It was painful, but I saw no way to deny it. Is concentration, however, I begin to wonder, a faculty in its own right? But that is merely by the way. Accordingly, said Dr. Y, we are blessed as it were with fine painters, composers, writers, even, with great administrators and military tacticians, with superb thinkers—which includes, I suppose, the mathematicians and logicians—and, last but by no means least, with—I speak in all humility—outstanding philosophers.

Would you not say, then, doctor, I said, that as in individuals, so, too, in nations? Your formulation, said he, is obscure, or perhaps merely clumsy, or indeed, perhaps, the one on account of the other. Which shows that everything is related. To everything else, I mean. But I think I take your meaning. The nature of things being what it is and not, so far as the present state of knowledge enables us to ascertain, otherwise, I express myself, on this question, in the following manner.

You admit, of course, said Dr. Y, that there have been, on the tellurian sphere, at various times, battles and wars, and that these have been fought and waged between and against different nations, alliances apart? So, roughly, I had always been taught. And that there have been, in these engagements, both victor and vanquished, master and maimed, dead and living? I hesitated. He was gracious. I make no apologies for my constitution. However, eager to continue, I ventured, Doctor, may we not *assume* the affirmative, and see what follows? Ah, my dear fellow, said he, my dear, dear fellow, you have begun at last to imbibe the true philosophical spirit. I thanked him for his kindness, and, returning the favor, bade him resume.

I resume, then, said Dr. Y. Now it is clear that he who is victor is victor, in many instances, by virtue of superiority, to him who is vanquished, that is. Even if we admit destiny I cannot see how this would change or rather permute anything. For it is patent that destiny would of necessity select only superior agents to transmit its intentions.

I was glad he mentioned destiny, an enigma I have never been able, if you will permit me the expression, to penetrate to my satisfaction. Dr. Y, however, spoke no more of destiny.

But do not for a moment think, said Dr. Y, that I imagine or would have you imagine victory to be merely a question of keeping one's fingers crossed. Oh no, my dear fellow, said he, you must, in addition, mark you, be constantly on your toes. At any rate, the fact remains that there necessarily exist, as a convincing working hypothesis, superior and inferior races.

Yet are there not those who say, said I, not that I say it, that in reality it is all but a single great race? By Blunderbuss! cried Dr. Y, what a rash assumption! Will they insinuate, without a shred of evidence, that we were all going in the same direction to begin with? He rose to the full height of his great argument. Let us, said he, have an end at last to all such and suchlike lunacies, and concern ourselves with the facts. And where the facts are as yet undisclosed or misconceived or, indeed, unspeakable, let us fix our gaze in consolation upon the great eternal truths!

The secretary entered with the tea. How enchanting she looked as she bent over and set down the tray! Dr. Y raised his eyebrows. Perhaps I did, too, in sympathy. Why three? said he. Professor Q is here, said she. Why then show him in, said he. Professor Q entered quietly behind her. But, doctor, she began. Desist, said Dr. Y, he is among us. Ah! what a glorious—She shut the door.

Professor Q drew up a chair in eager anticipation. Dr. Y signaled to him from the eminence so far attained, tracing the path of discovery that had led to it. I hope I may be pardoned for such figures. We are not all of us intelligent enough to think without their aid.

I see, said Professor Q in quiet rapture, I see, I see. Yes, said Dr. Y from a great distance, yes, yes. Shall I pour? I ventured. I poured regardless. We sipped in silence, save for the sound of the sipping.

And yet how is it, cried Professor Q, spilling his tea, how is it that there irrefragably exists a class of entities M, such that the proposition p "the members m', m'', m''' . . . of class M are constituted such that an impartial observer O, at a coign of vantage C, fixed by a set of coordinates (Θ, ϕ, h), would, in surveying a random section of M, experience that section not as particulate, but as a continuum" is, in many instances, completely satisfied? The good doctor and I agreed that it was incomprehensible.

Professor Q withdrew a large pipe, blew down its shaft, filled and lit it, and sat back vaporously in his high chair. Dr. Y produced from a drawer in his great desk a silver box richly ornamented with curious designs. I am trying to give up, thank you, I said, declining a cigar. Sheer hypocrisy—I abhor smoking.

Yes, indeed, cried Professor Q, puffing, what we require above all are clear distinctions. Precisely, said Dr. Y, spitting. Where there is distinction, said he, there also will you find classification. Quite so, cried Professor Q, together they constitute one of the hallmarks of our great democracy. Yet how, I ventured, might any distinctions hold where all are equal? The two great scholars shuddered behind a pall of smoke.

I see here, do I not, cried Professor Q, an affinity with the matter—if you will forgive me for being obvious—with the matter of smoking, in our day, among the young. Dr. Y drew deeply at his cigar. I thought with nostalgia of my schooldays. I allude of course, cried Professor Q, to the question of blurred distinctions. Hence the affinity. I see what you're driving at, said Dr. Y. I waited politely in silence, lost in a fumy haze.

The secretary entered and left at once, coughing and clattering away charmingly upon her high heels. I myself took full advantage of this opportunity to cough once or twice unnoticed.

For consider, cried Professor Q, childhood is all very pleasant and so forth, a kind of abandoned idyll sought once more in vain in song and sermon. But we outgrow it, do we not, we attain, in time, to be brief, the raised plateau of maturation. You say how is the precise moment of this attainder—that is to say attainment—to be recognized? I say again, consider. We deploy once more our great fleet of distinctions, we gird our loins for war and victorious conquest, we await a wind of inspiration, and analysis is once more in full swing.

Now, cried Professor Q, what is thus revealed? Dr. Y withdrew delicately his cigar. Briefly, cried Professor Q, this. There exist, do there not, at the poles of childhood and adulthood, the—if I may thus express myself—the lollipop and the cigarette. Naturally, I pass over here in silence, for the sake of symmetry, convenience and refinement, the maternal breast and other succedanea. I resume. Thus do we find in the sweetness of childhood much that is rotten, whereas—

But are you not, my dear Q, said Dr. Y, are you not now wandering just a little? My dear Y, cried Professor Q, am I not, as are you, a wanderer, an explorer, a voyager, a journeyman of the intellectual realm, the noetic sphere? Indeed, said Dr. Y. Well then, cried Professor Q. Quite, said Dr. Y.

Whereas the smoker in his maturity draws into himself, so that they are borne in him much like tremendous problems, the customary inhalations, and then after a moment's thought, releases them once again into the nameless void. Dr. Y nodded in approval. I began to wonder whether I was not out of my element, or at least out of my depth. Indeed, it is only thanks to an ingenious cassette-recorder concealed on my person that these interviews can be given here, for the edification and instruction of posterity, more or less in their original form, as close in tone and wealth of incident as was possible in transcription. But of this more later.

I confess I fail entirely, my dear professor, I said, to recognize the precise affinity to which you have alluded, if you will forgive my ignorance. I am a scientist, cried Professor Q, not a saint. However, consider if you will the following.

Smoking is everywhere adjudged by those qualified to do so, to wit smokers, a mark of superiority, elegance and good breeding. This is not the moment for going more deeply into the sound and sundry reasons for such a judgment, adumbrated earlier on in my lecture. Now, and here we find ourselves at the crux, the core, the—how shall I say?— heart, the hub, the nub, the very *noli me tangere* of the matter—how is classification on this head to retain its precision, when, in our age, regardless of years, sex or race, all the world and his wife have begun to smoke?

Dr. Y drew desolately at his cigar. The inference, said he, though manifestly fallacious, that people are today maturing far more rapidly than they used to, seems inescapable.

While the two majestic savants drew and puffed in silent anguish I began, despite myself, to consider these matters more closely. The following hypothesis, which, I have since learnt, I did not originate— though this will trouble only those of primogenitary humor—occurred to me. It still seems to me now, upon mature reflection, to have retained its first appeal. I see in it the clear elegance, the symmetry, the ordered inevitability, of a simple though unifying fundamental truth. Moreover it is entirely reasonable.

But what are the facts? Let us contrast civilized man with the primitive races.

We observe, first, that, among us, generally, men show facial hair.

Next, that, among them, generally, men lack facial hair.

And, again, that universally, with few exceptions, boys lack facial hair.

The inference is clear. Thus is the general validity of our theory conclusively demonstrated.

Let me not, however, deny that several asymmetries have since, in this connection—entirely involuntarily, I must emphasize—occurred to me. Among these is the fact, very probably no less so than any other, that, universally, women of advanced age, so far as circumstances enable them to attain it, display, on occasion, facial hair. Concerning the precise effects of vanity and modern technology upon the frequency of this phenomenon I do not pretend to be qualified to pronounce an opinion. Indeed, if truth be told—and I am one of those who hold that it must, in many cases—I have been unable to resolve this entire perplexity to my satisfaction. Who is so bold, however, as to declare it wholly beyond the ingenuity of man?

But I come now to a grave difficulty. Those rash enough to oppose the General Law enunciated above will perhaps endeavor to prove it wrong by, say, *reductio ad nauseam*. They might, accordingly, reason as follows.

You say that pilosity is a mark of civilization.

And yet the ape is distinguished by hirsutism.

Reply.

I will not deny that this argument carries a certain force. But I intend to show that such cogency as it has it borrows more from sentiment than logical acuity. I see no more advantage in denying the hirsutism of the ape than in denying the pilosity of civilized man. Accordingly, I shall deny neither. However, let me say this to our opponents, and let them never forget it, that—or rather, since I have digressed horribly, let me resume this matter at the earliest opportunity.

Nothing could be seen but smoke, nothing felt but a stinging of the senses and the urge for flight. I was far too desperate to seek reasons for my going. Finding the door at last I opened it a little, but no light penetrated the haze. I slipped out and, without fear of disapprobation, coughed to my heart's content.

The secretary sat, as it seemed to me, with an air almost of expectancy at her typewriter. The smoke, I gasped, pointing, coughing, adjusting to the oxygen. She offered to type up my notes. I revealed to her my ingenious machine. We arranged to meet later at her flat, where we would transcribe together quietly over a light meal and some good wine.

A superb woman in many respects. In all, very probably. I myself think her unique, in the sense—how shall I put it?—in the sense that there is, in the world, so far as my experience goes, none other quite like her.

Her influence upon me is certainly growing. Soon, perhaps, she will suggest that I dispense with my slaves. What should I say? What do? What right have I now, at this late date, I ask you, to change the whole course of my life? And does not even she, now, enjoy, through association with me, benefits whose provenance she might well—how shall I say?

I trust these are not frivolous questions.

It cannot now be long before at last I learn her name.

Sweetness

Sheila Roberts

Born in Johannesburg, Sheila Roberts was educated in Potchefstroom, and then at the University of South Africa and Pretoria University.

Her first collection of short stories, Outside Life's Feast (Johannesburg: Ad. Donker, 1975) won the Olive Schreiner Prize, the first of a number of awards she has received. Her other books include a volume of poetry, Dialogues and Divertimenti (Johannesburg: Ad. Donker, 1985); two novels, He's My Brother (Johannesburg: Ad. Donker, 1977) – recently unbanned in South Africa and published in New York as Johannesburg Requiem (Taplinger, 1980) – and The Weekenders (Johannesburg: Bateleur Press, 1981); and her most recent collection of stories, the well-received This Time of Year (Johannesburg: Ad. Donker, 1983). She is currently a professor of English at the University of Wisconsin, Milwaukee.

Sheila Roberts is perhaps best known for her ability to recreate the petty hopes and great anxieties of the suburban South African living in a racially divided society. "Sweetness," which was first published in Contrast magazine (No. 59, July 1985), won the Thomas Pringle Award for prose from the English Academy of South Africa in 1986.

After keeping her mother four days in capricious labour, Clare chose to be born on January 29, 1914, the very day that Gandhi chose to leave South Africa for India, never to return. So on the night of January 29, Clare's mother, a sturdy eighteen-year-old, slept the sleep of exhaustion and disillusion, and General Smuts, rid of a troublesome mystic, slept the sleep of relief.

Clare's mother was Dutch, *her* mother, she always boasted, having twice met and talked with Queen Juliana of the Netherlands. The grandmother, the acquaintance of a queen, could substantiate her grandeur by showing her possessions: some fine old pieces of jewelry and crystal and a set of beautiful Dutch stamps, all of which, she said, she was saving for Clare. To Clare's unremitting disappointment and to her young mother's secret jealous satisfaction, a loitering miner out on strike stole the valuables from the grandmother's bedroom on the night of

March 15, 1922, having first tied up the grandmother with her own Lyle Thread stockings. At eight years old Clare received her first intimation that her childlike conviction of a foreordained distinction awaiting her might be misconceived.

Clare's father was a skinny Englishman with tired-lidded eyes and a cleft chin, a kind of watered-down working-class Douglas Fairbanks. He had come to Johannesburg to find a job on the mines, had married the stalwart Dutch girl several years his junior, and had proceeded to give her a baby every two years for the next twenty years, starting with Clare, who had not wanted to be born. In return for these unwelcome favors, the Dutch girl perpetually fulminated and stormed at him, beat Clare cruelly with a rawhide whip kept hanging behind the kitchen door for that purpose, threw cups and saucers at the walls, and on occasion was known to dump her husband's warm plate of dinner in his lap. He died (when the tenth child was five), emaciated and disoriented, having been slowly strangled by the black lung contracted underground. Clare had loved her father. He never beat her unless her mother forced him to. She remembered once that he had spilled some sugar he was putting into his tea and how, under her mother's raucous impatience, he had winked at Clare and whispered, "It's good sometimes to spill a little sweetness."

Clare remembered that miners' strike of 1922, when her inheritance was stolen. When in 1984 the SABC ran a docudrama about it, Clare, now shrunken and ill, had felt herself to be more than usually tremulous. She suspected that the SABC was showing the movie for her specifically—that a public acknowledgement of her experiences might be the long-awaited distinction. She attended very closely to the TV images, would not allow her husband to talk during the show and waited for the telephone to ring so that someone could question her on the veracity of something. Of course the phone did not ring, and of course Clare had known and knew very little about that huge disturbance. All she did recall was wandering out in the street when she heard shots in the distance and banging and shouting a few doors down. She saw Mr. Koekemoer and Mr. Luyt throw old furniture and wood slats into the street and thought they were angry. But when she saw Barnie Koekemoer and Boetie Luyt come out to help their dads, she was able to distinguish between violent ill-temper and urgent strategy. She went to help. Later, her mother, furious because Clare had "interfered" with the neighbors, tied her right leg to the kitchen table with a length of rope and kept her there for two days, declaring that *that* would teach her to wander. For two days Clare had to crouch under the table at mealtimes and eat her food from a plate on the floor like a dog, keeping her eyes watchfully on the many legs surrounding her like jail bars in case someone inadvertently or on purpose kicked her.

As things turned out, there was no fighting on their street, but an unexploded bomb was dropped into their back garden, smashing several ripe pumpkins into a vast pink, sticky, pitted obscenity.

At seventy, trembling, Clare watched the SABC's show, but would not admit to herself that the colors and significance of history had evaded her.

By the time she reached adulthood, Clare knew that the distinction she believed life would bestow on her would not come in the form of a grandmotherly gift, nor in the form of expansive motherly love, nor from her own energetic action, for her flesh and bones had been infused with a timidity akin to embalming fluid. Or rather, having lived for twenty-four years in the path of her mother's siroccos, her possible leaves and branches of enterprise had become sclerotic.

In 1938, hearing on the wireless names like Rhineland, Sudetenland, Czechoslovakia, and an infinite repetition of the opinions of Germany, Britain, France and Russia, she grew to suspect that her distinction might come through travel, though each time she stared at a tiny hazy newsprint map she would feel the sensation of a rope tied round her right ankle. But she fantasized that someday someone would put a boat ticket into her hand, help her on board and send her off somewhere.

That geographically expansive year of 1938 she met a daring blond young gold-miner, the owner of a monstrous Harley-Davidson, part animal, part machine. Every Saturday, Wally the miner took her on the back of his bike to the bioscope and bought her a bag of chocolate creams. She would eat them all, not saving any for her gray-haired but still raving mother and her noisy siblings. And as the last one melted between tongue and soft palate, she would think, *Sweetness, Sweetness.* In 1939 Wally and Clare married and Clare felt (only momentarily, but not for the last time) that her bond with Wally might be her distinction. When Wally joined the army in 1942 to be part of the South African contingent of "Tobruk Avengers," Clare realized enviously that she was still waiting for her own miraculous chance to travel—imaginary rope or no imaginary rope.

Wally returned from North Africa and Italy in 1945 an enthusiastic and unashamed drunkard. Brandy, sugar and water was his staple, the bread-and-butter of his imbibing, but he constantly experimented with other liquors and liqueurs, particularly on weekends. At one time it was eggnog and kirsch that he mixed while extolling their strengthening properties, another was vodka laced with Kümmel, and for several months he went for "kleiner-kleiners," which are a shot of brandy swallowed fast, followed by a more leisurely pint of beer. When he was trying out unusual mixtures or when he took to wine for a time, he would insist that Clare taste the drink to learn appreciation, and later offered the glass to the children, three little girls born in 1939, 1942 and 1946. In Italy, he maintained, the children drank wine and it was good for them. When the Nats got in in 1948 he made them all drink Van der Hum in celebration, even the two-year-old, who then amused them all by dancing giddily.

The extended families on both sides deplored Wally's drunkenness openly. They all took turns to nag, coax, cajole and threaten, and tried to shore up the sagging boughs of Clare's passivity so that she would stand against Wally's addiction. But she merely listened to their indignation, nodding and murmuring, but could not oblige them. What she did, however, was turn to the little girls. At bedtime she would tell them stories of her childhood and youth, of how her mother had mistreated her, and how neither happiness nor anything of distinction had ever come her way. She spoke slowly and softly. Hardly understanding her, the girls were nevertheless moved to a deep childish pity, and as the years went by they took more and more of the household tasks off her hands. And more and more, Clare discovered she had headaches, wonderful dank headaches that sent her to lie on a bed that metamorphosed into a darkened cave smelling of vinegar.

Her one consolation during those years of Wally's rowdiness and the wasting of his wages on drink was the vaguely bitter distinction she achieved by being the wife of a man of lost potential. Wally's family started the story that grew into an indestructible legend: that Wally had been a clever lad and a bright young man, one who had been going to make a success of something some day, but that he would never do it now because of the drink. "Wally could have been a fine man and a good provider," they would say to Clare, whereupon she would feel a mantle of dignity settle on her shoulders. Again she would nod and murmur, as if she had known all along of the potential, as if she had chosen her husband with acute discrimination.

As soon as they were old enough to get jobs, the three girls (variously glutted from having had to serve as parents to their parents) left home in turn. Out in the world they hoped to rid themselves of a confused inner weightiness and to grow young, light and easy. Eventually the eldest left for England and the two younger ones for Australia.

When the last girl left, Wally gave up drinking, not out of grief over losing his children but because he had been shocked sober by Prime Minister Verwoerd's assassination. He felt that the country now needed his full attention. He started learning Afrikaans—belatedly and badly. Clare, now fifty-two, found an uninebriate, politically muddled but verbose Wally very tedious. She hated to have the editorials from *Die Volksblad* read out to her in a halting Afrikaans, which she did not understand even when it was unhalting.

She retreated more frequently into subterranean headaches. She also began answering more diligently the letters from her daughters. She suggested with increasing directness that she should visit them in turn, but either they did not comment on her suggestion or they kept pointing out that they had no place for a guest in their one-room apartments. Noleen, the eldest, salved her conscience each time she did not take up her mother's self-invitation by sending home parcels of good English chocolates. The word *Sweetness* still came to Clare as she ate them all, alone and methodically, but not as mellifluously as before. When her insistence that mothers and daughters should not be separated for too long became strident—she even underlined the words on the page—she merely succeeded in delaying her daughters' replies. Every day she visualized herself in a neat beige suit, carrying a fine leather overnight bag, boarding a large plane for London or Sydney. She saw herself as distinguished, even beautiful, as she crossed the expanse of an air terminal.

Over the years Clare grew smaller and more simian, though she was unaware of this. Whenever Wally took photos of her to send to her daughters, she would write behind them: *Supposed to be me! Supposed to be me!* Several times she argued that Kodak had sent back the wrong photos. During those years she once again enjoyed that dubious distinction of being married to the fittest old man in the neighborhood. Wally had diverted all the enthusiasm he had felt for alcohol into personal-fitness programs. He had trimmed down, firmed up and put on a healthy glow to his relatively unlined face. His once-blond hair had turned a brilliant admirable silver, and his long brisk walks around the neighborhood earned him many acquaintances. Even the dogs seemed to like him. People she had never met stopped Clare at the shops, saying, "Your husband is wonderful!" The family all said behind their hands, Hasn't Clare aged?

By 1976, when the Soweto riots broke out, the two daughters in Sydney had given Clare seven grandchildren between them, children she had only seen in bad reciprocal photographs, the sun in their eyes, all frowning, all blond, all looking alike. Noleen in London had remained single, having had her fill of what Americans call nurturing (a word absurdly suggesting that human beings are as pleasant as gardens). Clare grew obsessed with the idea of visiting Noleen. As time passed, Noleen's spinsterhood made her age unnaturally in Clare's mind's eye until Noleen seemed her contemporary. She visualized them as two lone elegant women together in London. In the shops. In the parks.

In 1976 Wally gave up fitness for target practice. He also bought a thoroughbred Alsatian which he named Lucia after a woman he had known in Italy. He had her spayed when she was still pre-estrous, to make her wild, and took her to killer-training school. Clare hated Lucia. One day in 1979 Clare tripped over a rucked mat and fell, startling Lucia, who promptly bit Clare several times in the head. The doctor who was called in to stitch the wounds was so appalled by the length and depth of the gashes that he notified the police. A magistrate ordered Wally to have Lucia destroyed, but Wally's lawyer managed to get the sentence commuted to defanging. With a defanged Lucia back in the house even before Clare's bites were healed, she felt the first stirrings of an indignation rendered quiescent almost sixty years previously by her mother's rawhide whip. This little sprout of indignation pushed her to pack a suitcase and keep it in readiness under her bed.

By 1984, when the SABC broadcast its program on the 1922 miners' strike, Lucia had been run over and Wally had had to have his bottom lip removed because of cancerous growths. He looked a little dog-like himself without the lip, but was still spry and shock-haired. He nattered all day in Afrikaans about two things only: the Great Depression and how he had retained his job, and his experiences in Cairo and Rome during the war. Clare never listened. But the two daughters from Sydney did visit that year, frightening Clare. They had both grown into stocky loudmouthed women, both uncannily like Clare's own mother. She would become dumb and wide-eyed in their presence. But her indignation was growing.

One spring morning, still in 1984, Clare went into town by bus. She withdrew a large sum of money from the savings account. Then she went by taxi to the South African Airways office and bought a return ticket for London. She had no intention of returning, but, not wanting to get into a debate over legitimacy and sponsorship, she paid the fare. Using the same waiting taxi, she returned to Eloff Street, where she bought an expensive beige suit from an exclusive boutique. Two weeks later she left the house silently at dawn while Wally was still asleep in his bed, and walked to the corner phone booth. There she phoned another taxi. As she was about to climb into the vehicle, she fell. She seemed to lie hazily on the pavement for a long time, but then, with a lightened sensation and the awareness of bright sunshine, she was lifted up and driven away. She enjoyed gliding over the smooth tiles of the airport and with quiet excitement boarded the aircraft. There was a momentous roaring as it taxied down the runway. She was a little startled, however, when the stewardess who had been offering her candy to chew for takeoff changed her uniform for a white coat and drew a syringe out of the air. Clare fell asleep with the strong sensation that there were ropes tying both her feet. When she woke much later and was introduced to a sweet-faced middle-aged woman named Noleen, she was convinced she had arrived.

"Domestic Worker" / linocut by David Hlongwane.

Blood Relatives

Daniel P. Kunene

Daniel P. Kunene was born in 1923 in Edenville, Orange Free State, South Africa. He has received degrees from the University of South Africa and the University of Cape Town, and has taught at the latter university, as well as at UCLA. His books include Heroic Poetry of the Basotho *(Oxford, England: Clarendon, 1971); two books of poems,* Pirates Have Become Our Kings *(East African Publishing House, 1979) and* A Seed Must Seem to Die *(Johannesburg: Ravan, 1981); and a collection of short stories,* From the Pit of Hell to the Spring of Life *(Johannesburg: Ravan, 1986).*

Kunene is currently a Professor of African languages and literature at the University of Wisconsin-Madison, having left South Africa in 1963 for political reasons.

NakaMandla stood alone on the platform. She had just seen the train disappear round the hill not far from the village and the station. Her son, Mandla, was in that train. The people from the village who had been on the platform with her had left. There had been the rather visibly pregnant young woman holding the hand of a toddler son in one hand while with the other continually caressing her distended stomach. She went to the station whenever the *bombela* train was coming, either with its new recruits from farther south, or with the weary returned ones who had just completed their *joyini* of twelve months or more. She looked at every male face hanging from the windows or getting off. Then, without talking, she would turn around and go back to the village. Then there was the man with the wooden stump, who was in his middle years. The children had nicknamed him *Malabulabu* because of the rags he wore. Malabulabu would start at the far end of the platform and beg his way down to the tail of the train holding his cupped hands close under the faces of the passengers leaning from the windows. The only other conspicuous person was an old man with a pure white head of hair and a very dark face. His sight was not very good, but he would genially nod his head to everyone around while flashing his broad, toothless smile. Finally there were the odds and ends of nondescript people who had one thing in common: they all looked like the earth which clung to any exposed parts of their bodies, as if to remind them where they had come from and where they were going. That was it, except for the stationmaster or guard or whatever they called this man who wore a heavy black serge uniform on hot or cold days alike and waved a green flag to make the train go. *He* did not look like the earth. His chubby face was red and it glistened with the sweat of contentment, which he kept wiping with a white handkerchief.

NakaMandla had been only peripherally aware of these people, as her whole attention was on her son, Mandla, who was leaving in the *bombela* that day. And now she was left alone. How long the other people had been gone she could not tell. A fresh breeze blew rather whimsically this way and that, and her tattered dress obeyed, wrapping itself around her legs according to the wind's direction. I must go, she said to herself. I will go to Mandla's father. He must talk to me today. He must say what I have done to be punished like this.

The village, which comprised shelters made with every conceivable piece of material, but largely rusty sheets of metal and pieces of cardboard, lay directly ahead of her as she stood on the platform. By contrast, the latrines, which stood in a neat row like soldiers at attention, were made of brand-new corrugated iron sheets. As she left the station, NakaMandla did not go to the village. She could not bear to think of her little hovel without Mandla. Her beautiful Mandla. Now the only sound that would greet her would be the lonely drone of a fly. No, she would go to Mandla's father first. That would make things a lot better.

She walked towards the hill behind which the train had disappeared. She was humming a tune which seemed to lighten her step. She would have worn her shoes to the station, but they were so torn, and that unreliable Zwelonke had never come round to fixing them, though he always promised to. She could hardly blame him, though, because he had lost the only awl he had when he was moved from his last temporary settlement. To have attempted to mend shoes without his awl would have been an affront to his professional pride. But at last he had promised her, as a personal favor, that he would use a thatching needle. Poor man. It did not matter, though, about the shoes. She would have worn them simply in deference to the solemn occasion of her son's departure. The soles of her feet had become thick and tough from habitual walking, summer, winter, all seasons.

Ah, SekaMandla, don't try to stop me, she said to herself as she came upon a tree trunk that lay across her path as if placed there on purpose. I am coming, no matter what. The trunk was obviously too heavy. Too much trouble to try to move it. So she walked around it. There were also a few rocks, bushes, mounds like anthills and other obstacles of that sort which she skirted easily like one walking in familiar surroundings. A woman must never step over sacred places and objects, or over a man's legs, she kept reminding herself. SekaMandla will hear me today, she said, as if to strengthen her resolve as she rounded the last obstacle and knelt down. A large boulder completely concealed her from the village. The railway line passed on the other side of the hill. Leaning her body forward so that she was in a half-crouching position, and holding her hands together in an attitude of humility, she began to speak:

"SekaMandla, I have come to worry you again. The child, *our* child, is gone. Mandla. He just left a little while ago. The train that passed here, he was in it. He is going to Goli to look for work. Pray to the ancestors to help us. Now there is no one left. The house is empty.

"There is no food, SekaMandla. That cow you left for me, it had become so thin that it had a very hard time when it was calving. It nearly died. But it didn't die. The calf died. We tried to eat the meat, but it was too slippery. We threw it away. I feel like vomiting even now when I think of it. When the cow was still a little strong, I sometimes lent it to the neighbors and I would get a handful of mealies in return. But it became weaker and weaker. This place, SekaMandla, has no water, as you know. None for people, to say nothing about animals. It got weak and I thought it was going to die. So I sold it. Are you listening, SekaMandla? I *sold* it, that cow. They gave me almost nothing for it. Just a little bit of money which got finished even before one month had passed.

"I am suffering, SekaMandla. But I know things can be much better if you like, if you just forgive me. You *know* it was not my fault, Seka-Mandla. You were away very long in the mines. I did not even know if you were still alive. That *joyini* was longer than any other that I have ever known. But I was hoping all the time, and waiting and waiting. But waiting and hoping are twins. When hope died, waiting withered and eventually died also. It was so dry here in this place, so dry, and I was alone trying to dig that little plot they gave us. I asked you to forgive me before, and I am asking you again because this man. . . . It was just a temptation. He helped me to dig my field. And I was confused, not knowing whether I was a widow or not. I am only a person of flesh and blood, just like you. Furthermore, SekaMandla, I know you too are a human being, a person of flesh and blood, just like me. And all those years. Those gold mines are like death. When a man disappears there, you must forget him. He dug my field for me.

"You remember, SekaMandla, they moved me and our child Mandla, together with a lot of other people, just before you were expected to come home after you had worked one year at Deep Level Mines. Well, you know how it is. We just saw the army trucks stopping outside and they told us to take everything and load quick-quick because we were going away. You only found me four years later. By accident. And then I knew (Oh God!) you had been looking for me all that time, your heart never willing to give up. I still see the pain in your eyes when you saw my condition, and you coughing like that. Since then the frown of anger and agony on your forehead has never become smooth again, especially when you looked at me. I was afraid you would kill me. Also, your eyes made me feel a chill in my blood because they were so cold and accusing. But how cruelly I had killed you, I could not even begin to imagine. That was why I went to my uncle's place so that the child should be born there, far away, where you would never have to see it.

"Remember, SekaMandla, when I came back you were more sick and you could not even walk properly, and Mandla would sit behind the rocks over there and when he came back his eyes would be swollen from crying? Remember? The neighbors were always coming and going. Comforting us. Bringing this and bringing that, just to help us. And when you went away, they continued to stand by me, a little bread, a little milk, a little word of comfort. Calabashes came to my house and went away. Always when I returned them my heart bled because they were empty, except for my thanks. But they understood.

"But I really came to tell you about the children. The one born at my uncle's place, they called him Velaphi, for they said 'We don't know where he came from.' He is still at my uncle's place. He never left there. He is quite grown now. *Our* son, Mandla, just left in the train, as I said. I am alone. But I know he will come back. He will come back and change all this, my son Mandla. Your son too, SekaMandla.

"Now, I say, you must talk to me, SekaMandla. You must say something. Tell me what to do . . . wait, I will go home and make you something to drink. I have a handful of corn. I will grind it and make some gruel and then come back so that we can drink it together before the sun goes down. I wish I could brew some *mahewu*, but that would take too long."

NakaMandla got up and shook the dust from her clothes. But before turning to go, she stooped and picked up a small flat piece of wood lying on the ground near where she was kneeling, saying, "It seems the *nsika* fell off. I'll fix it. I'll replace the *nsika* so that it can stand firm again. Don't worry, I'll bring it back." She wrapped it with a piece of cloth and then put it gently between her breasts, underneath her clothes.

As she walked towards her house, she passed two neighbors talking. They looked like scarecrows, she thought, and she struggled to stop herself from bursting out laughing. She finally came level with them and then said, without stopping, "I just spoke with SekaMandla. Things will be all right now. I'm going to make him some gruel. He's so thirsty." After she passed, the scarecrows looked at each other and laughed, exposing pink, toothless gums. They shook their heads and then, after a moment's silence, continued their conversation.

When she got home, NakaMandla took a dishful of grain, knelt by the millstone, put on it a measure of corn she had scooped with both hands and then began grinding vigorously. Beads of sweat soon formed on her face, but she was lost in the rhythm of her back-and-forth strokes and the sound of the crushing maize. Suddenly she stopped, took out the piece of wood from between her breasts, unwrapped it, put it tenderly on her lips before laying it on the ground beside her. On its face was scrawled, with a careful hand like that of a child learning to write, the words:

Petros SekaMandla Kuzwayo, he born 9 of March 1930, he die 27 of November 1970 because he cough too much, r.i.p.

She began to grind again.

The Fly

Andrew Martens

Andrew Martens has been involved in theater for many years. A graduate of Rhodes University in Grahamstown, he completed a B.A. in English and drama and an honors degree in drama. He subsequently completed a master's thesis on South African playwright Athol Fugard, and has also been involved in a number of theatrical projects.

The short story which follows is due to appear in a publication of the End Conscription Campaign (ECC).

"What can they do to you for disobeying orders?" the youth thought, standing limply against the wall with tired red eyes and jaw hanging loose, the sound of a slammed door echoing into the recesses of his head. "Will they keep me in a dark hole until I see the light of their logic?" He examined his world. The ceiling was surprisingly high, about twelve feet. The floor area of the cell was about fifteen feet by eight, and in the wall opposite the door there was a small window, about a foot square. It was too high to see out of. There was a pile of rough blankets, a sanitary bucket with several bloated iridescent flies crawling sluggishly around the rim, and a grimy enamel pitcher of water. Something seemed out of place, but he could not put his finger on it.

The youth lay down full-length on the thin lumpy mattress and stared at the ceiling. The concrete floor was cold and smooth, rubbed down by the long line of criminals who had stood, walked and slept on it. At least they had left him his watch. It kept good time. It reassured him. He looked at it now. The flickering quartz digits told him that it was 5:10:10. The double ten pleased him. Symmetry and harmony in numerals always pleased him. He allowed his eyes to drift up along a sunbeam which was sloping slightly downwards through the window and burning a bright square just above the door. Inside the square was

411

the dark shadow-cross of the bars. He could see dust particles swirling through the light, moving dreamily, aimlessly, as if in water. "And all that dirt gets into your lungs," he thought vaguely. One of the drowsy flies took off from the sanitary bucket and launched itself into space, buzzing laboriously through the heavy air. As it wandered into the molten stream of sunlight, its green abdomen flared in a tiny moment of glory before it settled on the dull metal of the prisoner's viewing-hole. It was then that the youth realized what had seemed out of place in the cell. There were twelve blankets in the pile at the foot of his bed. It seemed unreasonable that in this place of bare necessities there should be twelve blankets when one or two would have sufficed. He stared at the bright patch above the door as his mind drifted. He remembered a song which had been playing over the radio in the car which had brought him to this place. He could not remember the words, but the clattering little melody spun through his head and then faded into repetition. He remembered how the two military policemen sitting on either side of him had stared unflinchingly ahead as they tapped out the beat of the song on their knees.

The light bulb was housed in shatterproof perspex,* he noted. And over the perspex was a wire mesh. He wondered why the light was so carefully protected. Surely no one would wish to break it. Sitting in a well-lighted cell was surely preferable to sitting in darkness. As he pondered this the youth became aware of the patch of sunlight dwindling into a thin, bright strip. The dust particles faded into anonymity, as the cold gray twilight seeped in. He sat on the mattress and pulled off the heavy constrictive army boots and the coarse nutria trousers, but kept his shirt on. The cool air on his feet was pleasant. Then he fetched three blankets from the pile. One he wrapped around the mattress and the other two he spread over the top. As he crawled underneath the blankets he felt a limp sense of relief. The waves of exhaustion washed over him, but still his mind was too busy to relax into sleep. It was not long before the light clicked on and the pale evening was banished by the dirty yellow glint of the electric light.

What was it about the boy's face that had made him do it? He remembered that uncanny moment of utter silence. That had been the morning before, about thirty hours ago, he calculated, and still he had not slept. He kept seeing the boy's face, and he kept remembering the frozen moment which would always be a hole in his life, because nothing could be measured in it. It was the smile on the boy's face which haunted him.

---

*perspex: clear plastic

It had been only his third day in the township. At first he had imagined that township duty would be a welcome relief in the endless stream of ennui of which his job as a guard at the ammunition dump had consisted, but it had not turned out that way. In the guard tower overlooking the ammunition dump he had at least been free to dream, to absently count the procession of hours till it was time to sleep, and while he counted he could watch the glittering patterns which the searchlights created as they moved over the rolls of barbed wire. In the township it was different. There were people there, a sea of sullen black faces that stared at him in dumb insolence as he looked out of the gun holes in the side of the truck.

Then they had received orders to bring in a community worker for questioning. They had not been told why. When they reached the man's shanty, the captain went inside with one other soldier. The youth and three others waited in the truck. He watched through the gun hole as group of potbellied children emerged from a neighboring shanty to stare with blank-eyed curiosity, standing there with their hands idly linked, their little pointed black penises jutting out from beneath their swollen bellies. He waited in the bleak morning sunshine. His companions were talking about the possibility of blonde women having black pubic hairs. One of them was licking the melted remains of a chocolate bar from its plastic wrapping. The youth watched the strange dedication with which the pale glistening tongue probed the folds of the plastic.

Their dull silence was abruptly interrupted by a gunshot. They jumped up and crowded around the gunholes in time to see the door of the shanty flung open and two teenaged boys burst out into the sunlight. They stared frantically for a moment at the truck and then bolted up the road, quick and lithe as cats. The youth saw it at once: one of the boys had the captain's rifle gripped to his chest as he ran. The soldiers simultaneously exploded into action. They tumbled out of the back of the truck, taking off their safety catches as they moved. The youth heard a voice, cracked and falsetto with excitement, yelling, "Skiet hulle, skiet hulle!"* He glanced towards the shanty and saw the captain standing in the doorway with blood streaming from a bullet wound in his shoulder. It was all too quick for thought, for decisions, or even for feelings; the youth lifted his rifle in a familiar and habitual movement to his shoulder. The screaming all around him receded and seemed to be coming from very far away, from the other end of a long tunnel. All he was conscious of was the thick blood thump in his head. He saw the

---

*skiet hulle: shoot them

distant figures of the two boys as they reached the end of the street. He saw one bobbing torso wavering in his sights. He shut his eyes, and as he did so, he gently squeezed the trigger. The sound of the gunshot pulled him back from the end of his tunnel. He opened his eyes as the flat echo rolled away across the township. His target was down. There were two more gunshots from one side, but the other boy had escaped around the corner of the house at the end of the street. The boy who had been hit was still moving. He seemed to be trying to crawl away. The youth broke into a run. Still he was not thinking. He heard the babble of voices around him, and was vaguely conscious of his companions clustering around their captain, who had collapsed on the ground outside the shanty. All he could feel was an overwhelming desire to get to the fallen boy. He did not know why. He did not know whether he wanted to finish him off or help him, or simply prevent him from escaping. He just knew that he had to be there. He ran and his feet felt heavy and dream-retarded as they kicked up puffs of dust in the road. His breath rasped and the sweat soaked through the armpits of his uniform.

He reached the boy and stopped a few yards from him. The boy lay propped up on one elbow, struggling to breathe. The sweat was rolling into his eyes, and he blinked feebly at its salty sting. The bullet had passed straight through the right side of his chest and the blood was welling steadily out of the wound, staining his ragged T-shirt a shocking sticky red, before dripping onto the parched dust. He stared up at the youth with sad, moist eyes. The youth remembered a cat he had once seen which had been run over by a car. In the cat's eyes there had been the same bottomless darkness, that same unfathomable final confrontation between life and death. In the end it was not important whether one was black or white, or even whether one was a cat or a human, all that was left was that mysterious struggle in impenetrable darkness. Silence descended upon the youth. The world disappeared and all that was left were two eyes in a black face, two liquid gateways to another dimension of unguessable darkness, with no time and no distance. He did not feel the rifle slipping from his hands and falling to the ground where it lay next to the boy's life blood.

Afterwards they told him that he had disobeyed an order, and that he had endangered the lives of his fellow soldiers. They told him that his companions had come running to help him, and that the boy, even as he lay dying, had lifted the rifle and fired it at them. However, weakened as he was from his fatal wound, his aim had not been steady and the shot had gone wide. Still, the fact remained that the youth had stood by impotently not four yards away as the boy had fired the shot.

414

The youth didn't remember any of this. He tried to, but all he could remember was that the boy had died with a smile on his face. It was very difficult to place that smile. It was the sort of smile one might give when one has done something incorrectly, but realizes that it is unimportant anyway, the sort of smile which might be called rueful, and which consists of equal measures of sadness and scorn, the sort of smile which sees the final absurdity of death. But now the fact remained that he had failed in his duty. And yet he felt no trepidation. They had already questioned and shouted at him for many hours. They had slapped his face, thrown him to the floor and poured virulent insults upon him. They had called him a coward as if it were the lowest level of animal life. A lesser evil of which he had been accused was a lapse in patriotism. But of course it was cowardice which really rankled their sense of manhood. Cowardice was after all the trigger which had caused him to neglect and betray his fellow South Africans. He felt no trepidation because he knew they would let him go in the end. They would see that it had only been his third day in the township, and that he had never shot anyone before, that he had never particularly distinguished himself as an exemplary soldier during training; they would see all these things and sooner or later they would send him back. Naturally, because sooner or later they would need him again. For the present they would make life unpleasant for him. They would deprive him. They would remove any human contact from his life, except for the cold words of his accusers. He would lie motionless in a hole until he saw the pure light of their logic, a logic which told him that, in order to preserve a society in which people lived in harmony, he had to ignore his own yearning for harmony and pull the trigger which took a life. He had to do this with his eyes open in the bright sunlight.

In the morning he realized why the light bulb was so well protected. The night had been punctuated by fitful bouts of wakefulness. He had drifted in and out of fragmented dreams filled with images of the boy's smiling face. The light had stayed on all night, as he realized it would every night. He would never be in darkness while he was in that cell. He couldn't pretend he was somewhere else, he couldn't wake up not remembering where he was, he couldn't even retreat into seeing nothing and existing nowhere. He had come to understand why a prisoner would want to smash his light bulb.

The prison was a small one, because it was a small town, so there wasn't a separate section for nonwhites. The white cells were at one end of a corridor and the nonwhite cells at the other end. Far away in the cold clear winter dawn he heard men singing, a deep and soothing bass lament. It was a gentle sound, a song that wept and rose, and then faded into silence, leaving the dawn to the yapping dogs in the street once more. For a while there were no noises in the prison; then he heard slow hollow footsteps gradually approaching his door. The key turned rustily in the lock and the door swung open. An old man, so old that his eyes could barely be discerned among the wrinkled flaps of skin, stepped inside. His uniform was threadbare and ill-fitting, but it was spotlessly clean. He was carrying a tray on which was a plate of food: two greasy toasted sandwiches and two boiled potatoes. He stood silently in the doorway, his gnarled hands gripping the tray, his face inscrutable. The youth stared blankly back at him. At last the old man seemed satisfied with his inspection, and, nodding agreement to himself, placed the tray next to the youth. "Have you got a cigarette?" the youth asked. Without saying anything, the old man reached into an inner pocket and brought out a tattered bag of tobacco. Methodically he tore off a strip of newspaper and rolled a crude cigarette in it. He then produced an ancient flint-operated paraffin lighter with which he lit the cigarette. He drew deeply on it before handing it to the youth. The tobacco was harsh and dry. It tasted of dust.

The youth lay back on his mattress as the old man's footsteps receded down the corridor. Above him the light bulb clicked off, but the dank morning light had been dominant anyway, so it made very little difference. He stared at the patch of blue sky through the bars. He worked out that the cell was facing west, since the setting sun the evening before had cast a beam directly across the length of his cell to the door on the other side. He watched his smoke curling upwards and disappearing. He thought again about that sunbeam of the evening before, how the flies had shimmered through it, how the dust had seemed like Jacob's ladder climbing up through the bars. When he finished the cigarette, he tossed the stub into the sanitary bucket, and lay huddled in his blankets.

It turned out to be an icy winter's day. The wind whipped and fluttered through the bars of the window. Later in the morning he was visited by a legal officer, who, he learned, was going to represent his defense at the court-martial. The legal officer was a guiltily apologetic graduate who announced that he understood the youth's position, that he himself had been grudgingly forced into military service, and that in similar circumstances he himself would have reacted in the same way as the youth. He too would have dropped his weapon in horror at what he had done. He explained that he was lucky in that his law degree allowed him duties which exempted him from actual combat. He assured the youth that the court-martial would be nothing but a formality, that the court would definitely let him off with a mild spell in detention barracks if he pleaded guilty. He asked the youth some questions, filled in several forms, and left with a nervous handshake and a final assurance that all would be well if he were to throw himself on the mercy of the court.

The cold seeped under the door and the floor was a slab of ice. Far away down the corridor he heard a babble of voices which grew in volume and continued for several minutes, a distant grumble of discontent. Something was upsetting the crowd in the nonwhite section. The commotion ended suddenly. Somebody must have come to shut them up. There were one or two strained shouts, and then silence. Half an hour later the singing started again; this time it was a loud, vigorous song which continued for about an hour and then abruptly stopped. The youth felt cold, so he took another blanket from the dwindling pile at the foot of his bed, and wrapped his feet in it. There were now six blankets left in the pile. He stared at the ceiling and wondered what he could do to pass the time. He started counting the bricks, but lost count some way past five hundred. He paced the length of his cell wrapped in blankets, and felt his nose grow raw and cold. He lay down again and watched the window. Once a starling flew past, but otherwise there was nothing but the cold, dirty sky. He curled himself into a ball under his blankets and thought of home.

At precisely one o'clock the old man came with his lunch. Toasted sandwiches, potatoes and some soggy rice. He also brought another sanitary bucket to replace the old one, whose smell was now beginning to pervade the cell. While the old man was rolling a cigarette for him, the youth asked a question: "What's going on down there?" He gestured towards the nonwhite end of the corridor.

"The kaffirs say they are cold, that they want more blankets. But they are just trying to cause trouble." The old man pursed his lips sourly and spat into the sanitary bucket.

"Oh," said the youth, and thought for a moment. "Can't you give them some more blankets?"

"We haven't got any more. We're waiting for stock from Pretoria." The importance of the problem drifted away from the youth.

"Have you got anything for me to read?" he asked.

"Nothing for the prisoners to read. Only the Bible." With that the old man turned on his heel and swung the heavy door shut behind him. However, shortly afterwards he brought the youth a Bible as well as three grubby old copies of the *Farmer's Weekly*.

The youth spent the afternoon poring over the magazines. There were pictures of black men in overalls, holding enormous rams for the camera. There were pictures of burly white men in short pants and long socks, fat women posing graciously beside lush beds of flowers. There were articles on how to combat pests and diseases, hunting stories and a survey of stud farms in the Karoo with pictures of magnificent, sleek racehorses. The youth stared at these pictures, trying to work out where they fitted in. As he thought, he became aware of a bright spot on the edge of his vision. He looked up and his first thought was that it must be five o'clock, because just above the door there was a thin strip of sunlight. The watery clouds must have moved on, and the pale but crisp sun had emerged. He laid the magazines aside and watched the imperceptible growth of the bright patch above his door. Suddenly an idea thudded into his head. It caused a quick smile to break over his face. He sat a moment longer, watching the dust swarm through the slanting sunbeam, then he stood up. He picked up the six blankets from the foot of his bed, folded them up as small as he could. Then he did the same with the blankets on his mattress. He placed them all in a pile at the bottom of the door and climbed carefully onto them, balancing his arms against the wall. He lifted his head slowly and was struck full in the eyes by the glowing sword of light. After the brooding darkness of the past day in the cell, it was like stepping into another world; it was like Moses confronting God on the mountain. He shut his eyes and watched the burnt, swirling colors of his eyelids. He stayed there, motionless, his arms braced against the doorframe, wandering his gaze around the bright center, never quite directly, until the sun set over the lip of the window and the cell was suffused in a pale, lilac glow. He slid down until he was sitting on the blankets. He was blind. The cell was a dark presence on the fringes of his consciousness, and he felt as if his head were radiating like a flaming torch. He imagined that on his face had been branded the dark shadow-cross of the bars. His thoughts were silent. The sun had given him this gift of blinding light, but now there was only darkness once again as the bright cold of day stiffened into the sharp cold of night. The sky was clear. There would be a heavy frost. He waited quietly.

He was cold during the night, but he didn't take another blanket. He lay curled as tight as he could on the mattress with his hands squeezed between his legs to keep them warm. He lay quietly, listening to the singing from down the corridor. It was so deep and continuous that the resonance seemed to fill the air in the prison with soft, warm vibrations. He wondered if it kept them warm. Sleep came to him gently, and despite the cold, he slept well for the first time in three nights. Just before dawn he had a strange dream. He dreamed that his head had swelled to enormous proportions and that his arms and legs shrank out of existence. He became a huge, bloated head. His eyes grew larger and larger and became like two bottomless pools. People from his life gathered around him. His mother scolded him for not brushing his hair. He tried to tell her that he had no hands with which to do it, but the words wouldn't come. A smiling black boy poked him playfully with a rifle and laughed. The corporal shouted at him to get up and run with the rest of the platoon. They were all around him, all talking at once, all telling him to move, so he concentrated as hard as he could and began to rock back and forth, but that only made him fall over. He lay there, forced to stare up at the sun. Deep inside the glowing ball he thought he could see the shadow-cross. He heard the rumble of approaching thunder. It grew louder and louder so that his giant head was filled with its throbbing intensity. He wanted to scream that he didn't want the thunderclouds to come and blot out the sun, but no sound came. He opened his eyes and woke to find himself staring into the light bulb. The singing had stopped and the dawn had come.

With the dawn came a realization. The people at the other end of the corridor had too few blankets, and he had too many. He felt that he ought to give them his excess blankets. He was not sure why. It was something to do with their song. He felt a strange yearning for the power and the harmony which he perceived in those sad, disembodied voices. They were cold. They were so cold that it hurt them. He could hear that in their song. They didn't have blankets, but they had a song. He had no song, and too many blankets. His sense of logic wished for things to be evened out. There was only one other factor to consider: if he were to give away his surplus blankets, he would not be able to build a ladder to his patch of light when five o' clock came. He would not be struck full in the face by the blinding light. He pondered this as he waited for the old man to come with his breakfast. "I am a prisoner here because I failed to act," he thought. "We are all criminals in this prison." He made his decision.

When the old man put his plate of porridge in front of him, he was ready with his questions. "How many people are there in the cells down there?" he asked, nodding his head towards the other end of the corridor.

"The kaffirs, you mean?"

"Yes, how many?"

"Nothing to do with you."

"But just out of interest, how many?"

"Why are you asking these questions?"

"Well, what I thought was, that if they're cold because they've got too few blankets, maybe they could have some of my extra ones." The old man stared incredulously at the youth for a moment, as if there were a joke which was beyond his grasp and which he was struggling to comprehend. Then his eyes narrowed with suspicion and distrust.

"Listen, are you looking for trouble? Because you'll get it for sure."

"I only thought . . ."

"Well, don't think. These blankets are for the white cells, and until we get stock from Pretoria, the kaffirs can lie together to keep warm." The old man stopped speaking. His mouth contracted inwards with his irritation so that his jowls puckered into a fine network of wrinkles. He spat violently on the floor next to the youth's mattress and left the cell. There would be no more rolled cigarettes.

The youth understood that there was no point in arguing. He spent the day listlessly staring at the ceiling, staring at the sky through the bars, paging once more through the *Farmer's Weekly*'s. He even read Luke's gospel in Afrikaans. When five o' clock came and the first razor-thin strip of sunlight appeared above his door, he rolled each of his blankets into a ball and one by one he tossed them up through the bars in the window. It was not easy because the gap between the bars was not large, so it took some time for him to get nine of the blankets through so that they fell down outside. He wondered how long it would be before they would be found. It did not seem important. Three would be enough to keep, he thought, enough to keep away the pain, but also enough to feel the cold. When he had finished, the sunbeam was filled with the swirling dust he had stirred up. He lay back on the mattress and watched while it faded away. Soon they would take him to his trial. Maybe they would give him a desk job afterwards. He laughed at the thought.

A Little Cloud
Out of the Sea,
Like a Man's Hand:
From the Experiences
of an Afrikaner Housewife
in the Bosom
of a Nuclear Family

Ingrid Scholtz

Ingrid Scholtz (a.k.a. Lettie Viljoen) was born in Johannesburg in 1948. She completed a B.A. (fine arts) at the University of the Witwatersrand and then an honors degree in Afrikaans/ Nederlands. Scholtz obtained an M.A. for her work on the poet Breyten Breytenbach, and now lectures in fine arts at the University of Stellenbosch. She has published two novels, Klaaglied vir Koos (Emmarentia: Taurus, 1984) and Erf (Emmarentia: Taurus, 1986). She is widely regarded as one of the most innovative and significant new Afrikaans writers. She lives in Stellenbosch and has a daughter.

I

1) To hell with fabrication. What I write is true. Except perhaps for Fien and Betty, the monstrous and deceased white twins, whom I include together with some oddments of their bleached imagination. And Koos, from the same painful era.

   The fate of white Fien and Betty is a metamorphosis. As they lived by the cunt, so will they die by it.

   The white twins Fien and Betty, should I press their boisterous memory to my breast or suffocate it with damp cottonwool?

   Their saga forms a counterpoint of blindness.

2) Autumn approaches. Everything is charged. Everything has a threatening aspect, the slumbering, smoldering aspect of mortality. I get up, open the windows and the shutters. The ground is wet. The leaves fall. The beauty is faultless.

   I argue with my husband. I look for loopholes. My brain lies like a fungus in its hollow.

   Perhaps one should make a list of what art has attempted to do, from the human excreta in cans (*merde rouge*, a friend describes it as follows: you eat pink paint and shit a pink stool) to Harrison's complex indoor micro-systems. Then you consider your own alternatives. What are the possibilities for coming to terms with the mounting violence? But clearly also more than that.

My husband talks to me in the kitchen. It is a characteristic of our useless life that we think in circles, he says. If (material) objects get in our way, he says, we must get rid of them.

(The other women, my white contemporaries in town, supporters of amongst other things the doctrine of Christ, their homes are like the stems of plants—filled with sap. They do not waver, they are not irresolute. We are fighting a holy war on our borders. The prognosis is good. Order will remain with us, it will be with us and our fenced-off properties, forever and after, amen.)

3) Fien and Betty recall in an unguarded moment how the skin of his upper eyelids, where it starts off to the left and right of the nose, began to resemble the ridge of the penis. And the ridge itself could slice the tongue like a tableknife. They also recall how once there was no sound, but how every leaf on every tree was perfectly visible, even the grain of the wood, and every vein on the leaves of the plants, and the slow lice on the veins, perfectly camouflaged, and the microscopic animal life on the lice, and all the titles of the books.

4) The revolutionary consciousness has to be mobilized from inside, it cannot be enforced from the outside. In the car, between point A and point B, my husband mentions some of the facts. He mourns the fact that in his white lifetime he will probably never have the chance of living for some time in a black area like Soweto or Crossroads. Our child delicately picks the moss off the walls. He plays on the pavement with a little stick. We eat with our friends. Braised stuffed shoulder of lamb, herbed carrots and rice. Crêpes aux mandarines for dessert, coffee. These facts speak forcibly enough for themselves.

In bed my husband curses, speaks in hushed tones, speaks with even greater urgency about the necessity of caches for weapons, speaks intimately, as if he is planning a special journey for us.

There is a song that says when you are with me, I am like flowers that bloom in summer.

5) I read more from Jack Burnham's *Great Western Salt Works*, essays on the so-called post-formalist art. It was written in the seventies.

Harrison made an ecological environment in 1973, an indoor micro-system, a tank of eight-by-ten-by-three feet, containing approximately 1,500 gallons of water. It simulates an estuarial pool at the equator. High-intensity lamps function in twelve hourly cycles, like the sun. The ground forms a gravel filter; day and night temperatures differ by three degrees. Inside this pool there are crabs. Harrison and his wife feed these crabs themselves, because their natural food is not available. In this way the human transaction becomes a substitute, Burnham says, and a metaphor for nature. He observes these crabs carefully. He gets to know their habits. He feels that he becomes a substitute for nature if he looks after the crabs on their own terms. Eventually he and his wife want to reclaim a utilitarian function for art, on a highly refined level. Make of art the nonverbal communication system that it once had been.

6) I could have started this section with a text—Gramsci, Marx or even a father of the nation. Gramsci says, the individual can change very little, considering his frail power. But when the individual associates himself with other individuals who want to bring about the same change, he becomes multiplied to an impressive extent. And if the desired changes are rational, a change can be brought about which seemed impossible at first.

What are the alternatives (my husband says it is a characteristic of unserious thought that it dares to be flippant): translating Lenin into Afrikaans, setting Marx to music—in this way the unsuspecting listener may unwittingly receive a small guide to a (cultural) revolution through the otherwise-unwilling ear.

There are many choruses, while you polish your floors. The chorus of protesters through letters to the newspapers, the chorus of objective and cynical outsiders, the chorus of passionate doubters, the chorus of procrastinating Afrikaners, the chorus of Afrikaners with contented hearts, the chorus of missing Afrikaners (very small), the chorus of white Leninists, and the chorus of maimed Afrikaners—expanding ominously.

Then I rest my body, so fastidious about its comforts.

My husband remarks, on the road between here and the Strand, that Lenin was right, the Permanent Force should be abolished.

I look out of the car window. The valley is lined with terraced flanks, it reveals a close relationship between crustal structure, rock quality and surface form. The high flanks are built of krans-forming gray quartzites, which overlie the softly rounded, shrub-covered slopes further down. The valley (through which we are traveling) is straight for nearly thirteen kilometers towards the southeast and remarkably asymmetrical in cross-section. The kranses of Table Mountain quartzites slope down onto the southwestern flank, and are resumed at a much greater elevation on the northeastern flank. The twin peaks are carved from this high-lying part of the quartzite roof. This roof spans the valley's end near the second waterfall, although the quartzite beds have visibly moved down on the western side. We arrive at our destination, and swim in the shallow, flat, calm sea.

Early in the morning, when the birds start singing and the curtains are slightly lifted by the wind, you dream about a painless process of change, where the role of ideology consists of prescribing the forms and methods of the political struggle.

II

1) Till here. Then suddenly.

I relapse into a fucking black silence. What do I care? I am dead and history. My uncle by marriage was shot through the head on the border. I am history in a similar way. My fleshly pleasure is history. I have milk in my breasts and horrors in my head. Every day I experience violence, in so many refined (praise almighty God!) forms. I am turned in on myself like a well. As in my dream the woman lies in a dark tank full of water. My own sex between my legs, fucking mute. I have a husband and what can I offer him? My unwillingness, my shortsightedness, my fear. A trivial personal history, and a trivial destiny, smaller than tjimpritja, the rockfish. And bigger in my enormous personal lust, which has little to do with bodily pleasure, my enormous irresponsibility, my blind claims for survival, fulfillment, comfort, which make me fill the room like a trailing plant, grow, brood at night, dream, count and wait: a walking, fleshy time bomb.

My husband in my arms, is he kissing a clanging cymbal? My flesh is without nuance, without warmth, without shelter; my thought is without coherence. I can say no more except that I shout from my bottomless well, a small sound, without consequence. But I preserve my awful nature. I keep a low profile, although I grow and fill the room and swell portentously. It is night. My child breathes inaudibly next door. It is a night filled with beauty.

It will have to be even blacker. My guilt is also without consequence. My mouth is shut. As if it matters, what I say. If I could speak about the stars and the heavenly bodies. If I could speak about the geological formations of the whole Cape. If I could have done with the old person, and take up the new like a bed, to whom the cause of liberation lies closer to the heart than self-preservation or neurosis. We do not fall within the circumference of grace.

I shout Kaffir. shit. fuck. help.

To maintain your sanity you think about small footprints of animals in sand, somewhere.

My husband says it is a pity that the Jamaicans (the young township blacks refer to themselves as such) are politically so passive. I do not look at the young black, our guest, who sits opposite me, but eat my rice and minced meat.

2) I start making cards. On them I write down lists of things. Lists of plants. Lists of birds. Lists of animals. Lists of eras. Lists of heavenly bodies. Lists of friends. Lists of places of refuge. Lists of swear words.

A buck, a mongoose, a thing that scratches, that digs in the ground. Something that burrows like a mole. Something which is blind under the ground as well.

3) Drag in all the characters now. What has happened to white Fien and Betty, the two mute girls. Probably unaware to the last round. Koos burst through the undergrowth, then. Now pulls back in isolation, aimlessness, an insatiable (private) (white) (male) licentiousness. Inside his head there are larger-than-life pinups and a helpless Jesus. And Sem drinks at the breast of a Jungian foster-mother. He drinks himself to his fill without guilt. The northwestern districts which we visited once have burnt so small. Reduced to a photograph. All the eloquent stones, all the silence. Stare at it, see if you can decode, on the photograph.

4) I am not interested in a story. Only in ruthless progression, or call it regularity. If you want to read a story, read the history of the ANC, or the history of the house of Phalo.*

---

*house of Phalo: an eighteenth-century Xhosa dynasty

(On home ground nothing is left of art anyway. The house is burning, and art fondles itself in the bathroom. Or am I mistaken?)

White Fien and Betty, their domain was the bed. In those days the bed was as good a domain as any other, one would have thought. Can one forgive them their monstrous ignorance? Koos burst through the heavy undergrowth, and that *was* good, wasn't it?

5) I take out my cards. I read on the card with the names of trees:

> Bastard cobas
> African pencil-cedar
> Karoo boer-bean
> Baboon grape
> Baobab
> Outeniqua yellowwood
> Quiver tree
> Camphor tree
> Silver tree
> Stinkwood
> African poison oak
> Marula
> Olifants River euphorbia
> Transvaal Bushman's tea
> White karee
> Red stinkwood
> African rock fig
> Barberton cycad
> Small bitter-leaf
> Ironwood olive
> Tamboti

I put my cards away. I am catering for the dead again.

I would have liked to recount an anecdote from the life of my forefathers. I get carried away and lose perspective. But Fien and Betty, and even mentioning them gives them a weightiness they don't deserve. Therefore I take out my cards with the animal names and I read: mongoose. badger. jackal.

God help me that I should rather think about the animals than about the pining and decomposing whites of then and now.

III

1) A young black visits us from the townships. Our child asks, what is the color of his cheeks? Sometimes he brings a friend. Under our roof, they say, it is heaven. They can listen to music and shower for a long time (where they come from there is no hot water). For the duration of his visit, the black man says, he is exempted from his daily fears.

 We are connected to the townships by the thinnest strand of mucus.

2) I must not cry. Wait, I must think carefully. What do I want? I do not have to cry. It is pleasant here. The colors are beautiful. There are many books. I can plant the garden full of plants. The country is still making economic progress, my husband says with wonder. We have time, we can move about, we have enough warm clothes, blankets and shoes for winter.

3) Fien and Betty, come and sit with me. What happened? What went wrong? Your faces resemble the folded/creased visage of a five-week-old embryo. What has gone wrong, tell me while we have tea and cake.

 You do not come, you do not talk, you do not know. You do not remember. You mutter inaudibly, or is it untenably? Do I imagine you to be saying, spinning, spinning, spinning towards a fascist ending?

 So much to integrate. My husband encourages me. My resolutions swell like fruit.

 No. No wait. You want to say something. I am not sure that I want to hear. I have a headache and my eyes burn. I close my ears. You shout: bend his head back and put your tongue down his throat! Whose names are we calling! The STAG deodorant sits coolly on the windowsill! I do not want to hear anything of your muddled whisperings. It is over. You say you have not remained unpunished.

 But Fien and Betty shout in such a swelling chorus that I can hear nothing else. They shout: we have eaten of the poisonous plants and now we shall die! We have been peeled, cut open and eaten, and who were we that we would not have suffered the humiliation!

 Enough of outpouring. I have compassion with you, even if it is too late.

4) The black man who connects us to the townships by a thin strand of mucus, has infected us with an eye virus. We are the only people in this (white) town suffering from an eye virus.

But slowly I grow again in strength. I gather my forces. I shall display my true colors yet and they will be marvelous. By day my eyes glow with the virus. The doctor puts orange-colored drops in to determine whether the eye surface has been damaged. My eyeballs turn green. Green tears well up in my eyes. I cannot read. I try and rethink, reshuffle and order everything. I walk through the house with glowing eyes and decide which of my possessions are too valuable for me, because I shall have to free myself from them. I attempt to plumb my middle-class nature, to isolate it and tie it off like a wart.

My eyes are very painful the first night. It feels as if they are covered with fine gravel. I cannot sleep. I am cold. At four in the morning I make myself some tea and eat something with it. The next morning I regret ever having opened my eyes. They are sticky with a yellow secretion and it now feels as if there are bits of glass on the surface. I lie in bed the whole day with my eyes closed after I have been to the doctor. I do not sleep. I try and grasp things— behind my phosphorescent eyelids—but they evade me, nothing has substance, only outlines.

As soon as I start getting better things become more dense, move back and jell in their old patterns.

5) I am well again. I walk through the OK Bazaars. I touch the materials. I finger the corduroys. I might be saying goodbye. I fear discomfort and privation. What are our chances for survival; we have lost our taste for subsisting on termites. How shall we survive then? Better to be scratching out words in sand with sticks, or to write on leaves or against tree trunks. Please understand—this does not concern an individual I; I am one of a sort. I get up, have breakfast, prepare food, I conserve my white flesh exquisitely, touch the materials in departmental stores, etcetera. Like others of my kind, elsewhere, in all the homes throughout the Republic with its outstretched wings, its eagle, and its lovely promises of law and of order.

6) I have not forgotten my cards.
    I press them to my breast.
    I read: jackal. hare. badger. Somewhere where sand is hot and it is

isolated, where small mammals dig, burrow; noiselessly, a nonhuman existence.

I read my cards because I am scared of forgetting.

7) I start writing facts to memorize on my cards. These facts I must learn off by heart. I learn the facts of the rubbish in the streets of the townships. I learn the facts of the absence of sidewalks and gutters in the townships. I learn the facts of the size of the houses in the townships. I learn the facts of the evacuated plots with old car wrecks, the absence of parks, playgrounds, lawns and trees in the townships. I memorize how the wind blows through the streets, how it blows the bits of paper. I memorize the whole landscape, how it looks when the wind blows, when it rains, when the sun shines.

And what does it help me.

8) On a small card I write:

Mangesi
I belong to the house of Phalo.
I am black.
I shall overcome.
I have it in me.
I shall scratch it out on the trees.

9) If I can scratch it out on the trees, or with a stick on the banks of the dam, how I am harassed by images of membranes being cut in small, quick strokes.

10) In the heart of winter I join a group of women of other colors. My life now consists of drinking wine and eating fine food with our last white friends, and of attending meetings with the women of other colors to fight the rising bread price. And sometimes I see Fien and Betty as they swim past me, but they blow so many bubbles in the water that I cannot hear what they have to say.

IV

1) THERE ARE TWO CAMPS.
In the one camp are those *for* the STRUGGLE.
In the other camp are those who are not for the STRUGGLE.
There are only these two camps.

2) There are four women.
   They rise up like a flame.
   They say: a person is only against us if he gives evidence against us in court.

3) I read what the (unknown, black) artist says: blue makes the eyes attractive. It is halfway between red and black. It is not as visible as red and not as dark as black. It is cool and clear to look at.
   The artist says: kékí-lines are bold
                     gòmbó-lines are soft
                     Èfọn-lines cut the flesh of the cheek open like a fruit.

4) Fien and Betty come to rest at last. They float in a canned-fruit bottle like two poisonous homunculi. They stand on a shelf. Maybe someone will take them off that shelf someday. Perhaps they will perish as even canned-fruit bottles must do. They might even stand on someone's shelf in the new republic: the Republic of the people. Then they will stand on a shelf in a house in which living people move, with histories, who paid for the house with their blood.
   Now only the four women remain. They are living women. (There is a shift here, a change.) They are not preserved and in bottles. They each have a personal history and an impersonal history because they say the personal life must be made subservient to the demands of the organization.

5) I am old now.
   Although my young child grows boisterously.
   I do the same things every day.
   In the morning I open the shutters and the curtains.
   I let the black servant in.
   I have breakfast.
   At intervals throughout the day I walk from window to window. At every window I stop and see how the grass grows more rankly in the garden. It is the kikuyu grass which I planted a long time ago against my husband's advice. Where the kikuyu doesn't grow, dried grass and weeds grow. In one spot red geraniums flower between the long, dried grasses.
   Every evening I close the shutters and the curtains.
   I am alone now. Because my husband has gone off to fight. Per-

haps it is he moving tonight with nearly a hundred heavily-armed men through the thick bush past Tsumeb in the direction of Grootfontein. How am I to indicate that he is moving *with* the enemy?

Here I could have ended with a misguided prayer to a discarded God: protect him, protect them, protect us.

I remind myself that the era of the Great Chalk Seas is long past, but that the earth preserves its memory like that of all her other eras.

In the meantime the earth is more beautiful this year than ever before. Perhaps because everything is so desperately and mysteriously balanced. Behind my eyes violent images flash continuously. (Some are portents too dark and unthinkable to consider for much longer than the batting of an eyelid.) How must I keep them at bay? I still have my cards. I think about the animals, about the geological eras. How can I do otherwise but notice daily the heap of wet leaves, the firmness of the plants?

6) The wonderful mountains still surround us. The wonderful valley reveals the close relationship between the crustal structure, rock quality and surface form. Various rocks and soil types are exposed to the observant eye, and everywhere there are signs of deep weathering and staining from red oxides and iron. The deep ground-layers have been formed on the granite subsurface, while the ground-layers formed by crushed slate and conglomerates are much thinner, with a much paler color. In places spots of pale, bare rock surface are visible on the higher, sloping ridges, under cover of the massive Table Mountain quartzites. And God knows what has happened to Koos in the presence of these pale rifts.

7) I talk to the black man on the telephone in a genial, confidential tone. We talk like old friends or confidantes.

There is only one way: a complete surrender to the facts.

8) I do not want to be a human being anymore. Want to go back into wormholes; burrow like an animal. Lie against the brown banks. Make hollows. Suck the small stones. Listen to the silky ants, the soft flies. See how the air flaps. Crawl back into the Free State of the past.

I receive news that my grandfather is dying somewhere in the Orange Free State. He is delirious, he says: Nena, Nena you were like my own child. Somewhere else or close by in the same place under a heap of earth lies my maternal grandmother. She was legal wife to the dying grandfather.

I imagine myself to be held by my husband still, while the Cape plovers shriek and he whispers himself hoarse on his damned social message. But time has ceased. I cannot remember where I am, it feels like the room in which the grandmothers slept when I was a child; it is death, it is the same time.

Who is this man with whom I sport at night, he wants to break my body with his passion. I press my unborn children like pillows against my body and I forget that I have forgotten what true erotic community is. The birds at night. Everything dead quiet at the dam during the day. Only the flapping of the water suddenly as I look up at the Free State sky, clear above the Table Mountain quartzites. I do not have that much time left to choose between the fruitful and the unfruitful life, pluck it out roots and all. Every thought, every deed, every breath consistent and in the service of liberation – to share with others food, shelter, warmth, responsibility. The development of a politicized life and culture.

9) I sometimes long for my husband.

I scan the TV screen anxiously for signs of him amidst the pieces of wreckage and the rubble.

No news of him has reached me yet.

I stay behind with my cards and canned-fruit bottles.

The cards are handy because my memory is failing.

One day I stand high above the town, on my way to the dam, to go and lie on the warm banks. I look down on the sports fields. Only after some time do I realize that the sports meeting is not for normal people, but for paraplegics of all colors.

Cruel, I think, and walk on.

Translated from the Afrikaans by the author

"Nkomati" / sculpture by Gavin Younge, one of a series which take their name from the many small border posts between South Africa and the frontline states— "Nkomati" referring to the South Africa/Mozambique border. (The South African Defence Force has repeatedly crossed these borders in so-called hot-pursuit operations against ANC allies and bases.)

Six Drawings and a Sculpture

Dumile Feni

Dumile Feni was born on May 21, 1939 in Worcester, South Africa. Remembering the cave paintings of his ancestors seen as a child – paintings which still inspire the style and sensibility of his work – Feni says, "I am amazed by one thing that I'm glad never left me – that is the beauty of the line, the fine lines." In the fifties, he learned about casting through an apprenticeship at the sculpture, pottery and plastics foundry of Block and Leo Wald in Jeppe, Transvaal, and exhibited in several group shows in Johannesburg.

By the sixties, Feni had two one-man shows running concurrently, and his works began to be shown overseas. By the end of the decade, he came under increasing harassment by the South African Government. The authorities disliked the attention he gave such figures as Nobel Prize-winner Chief Albert Luthuli and resented the anti-apartheid sentiment evident in the titles he gave to his sculptures and drawings. He was also an active sympathizer of the banned African National Congress. After being in and out of prison, and often in hiding, he was finally forced into exile.

Despite the hardships of exile, Feni has struggled to develop and expand his wide artistic interests. Though he considers himself to be a sculptor first, he has made posters, murals and calendars for the cause of South African liberation and served as a visiting lecturer in the College of Fine Art at UCLA and the Massachusetts College of Art.

Mother and son

Statements . . .

Statements . . .

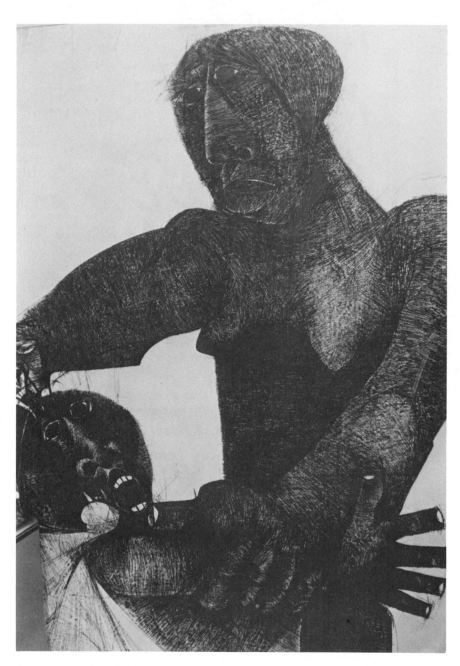

Homage to the children

The path for the children: An acknowledgement

For Tim Sutcliffe (1914 – 1986), Headmaster, Clifton Preparatory School, Durban

Peter Sacks

Peter Sacks was born and raised in South Africa. He now lives in Baltimore, where he is an Associate Professor in The Writing Seminars and English Department at Johns Hopkins University. He is the author of The English Elegy: Studies in the Genre from Spenser to Yeats *(Baltimore: Johns Hopkins University Press, 1985) and of* In These Mountains *(New York: Macmillan, 1986), a collection of poems.*

Although it's more than twenty years, and though
two weeks had passed before I got word
of your death, there's always been enough
to draw on—working backward

to the image of you shepherding our parents
on Speech Day—then still an all-whites
school for boys, pre-adolescent
stock of wealthier Durbanites—

a class ritual, you very much Headmaster,
large, flushed with the heat, by choice
wearing your Oxford gown, Brasenose, the war,
a radio actor's vivid cast of voice:

"Ladies and Gentlemen, Boys, I'm happy to . . ."

Inevitably how you flogged me,
the whistle and burning impact of the cane,
I doubled over one arm of an easy
chair, my mouth pressed hard against

the floral pattern of upholstery.
The worst was for disrupting *Hamlet*
at the old Alhambra: had it been only
bravado, the fulfillment of a bet,

or more the overflow of tense desire,
even the fury of self-recognition
that possessed me to yell "chicken-liver"
when he couldn't stab the king?

Or earlier still, with *Caesar*, how
beneath your voice the world first disappeared
to language—classroom, desks, the glow
of morning light in from the yard

obliterated by the fall of words
that shattered everything except themselves.
You'd clambered dangerously upon two boards
propped on a desk we thought would shelve

beneath your swaying bulk—two hundred pounds
packed sweating in a tight safari suit,
like some colonial general in the far bounds
of the tropics. One hand held out,

as if only for balance (since you
hardly looked at it), your copy
of the play, a small blue
Clarendon edition waving open

far above our heads, to Antony
alone with the still-bloody corpse
of Caesar. That slow voice of stony
grief and climbing rage forced

me straight into the dark,
as if someone had thrown a switch—
near-blackout as the current struck
and filled the room.

And do I fix on this, the sheer spell
of annihilating words regardless
of their sense, because an elegy must tell
again the child's first hapless

reaching for the stammered syllables
that lie between us and our loss,
the word between our death and quick renewals
in a language not our own?

Or did I know already why
you chose that speech—the year
of Sharpeville: how the rhetoric of Antony
worked free of time or ideology to bear

the form and pressure of our history?
Hadn't we practiced hiding under desks
the day the crowds marched on the city
carrying stones and sticks,

as if white children might be victimized at last?
Hard now to disentangle fear
from conscience—had the news passed
by me, just how many had been killed

outside Johannesburg? What was the object
of the anger darkening the room—
the mutilated corpse of Caesar,
or the unarmed children shot down in the road;

the bloody hands of Brutus,
or the men with guns? Was it the frenzy
of *all* civil war, contagion of the blood about us
with the prophecy of Antony already

shadowing the land? "O, pardon me,
thou bleeding piece of earth, that I . . .
am meek and gentle with these butchers"
the utterance pouring out like blood indeed,

more than a turn of phrase, now flowing
in the room, already gathering, brutal,
eloquent, unstoppable to the appalling
fury of the curse, the spirit calling

for revenge "with Até by his side
come hot from hell" (by now you'd worked
inside the raging ghost) "shall in these confines
with a monarch's voice cry 'Havoc!'

and let slip the dogs of war. . . ."
—Impossible to say now what was understood,
how much was sense and what was naked terror
moulded only later into sorrow,

conscience, rage—with fear still
at the heart. Twenty-five years since,
that same fear draws me back to school—
that and desire for the mastery of voice

now that you're gone. An old urge
to replace our first authority?
Is this why I remember dramas
of tyrannicide; or is it that our country

always bred desires of that kind?
Besides, what would I take from you—
weren't you preparing "leaders of the land,"
a white colonial school, however true

to generous ideas, however quick to integrate
in later years? Or is it power after all
I would inherit, if only that of speech
so worded I can't tell possessor from possessed,

a voice beyond this impure reaching
to say rest where you are beyond
the red trench of our land;
leave us what you once gave—

if not the power to revenge (since I
still lack all courage for the knife,
and vengeance in itself is only blood),
then strength to name

those whom to curse,
and those for whom to save our hearts—
to carry as if out of war
towards an unknown peace.

Ministers can give permission

WEEKLY MAIL REPORTER

IF you want to discuss anything that falls within the Emergency regulations, you had better phone the authorities for permission.

The Emergency regulations now hold up the threat of 10 years imprisonment, with or without the option of a R20 000 fine, for anyone who "whether orally or in writing, makes any subversive statements or causes such a statement to be made".

This means you could be in trouble if you make such a statement at the dinner table, in casual conversation or even in private notebooks.

And you will have to be careful. Illegal statements now include:

●The fact that a detainee has been released or even the circumstances of his or her detention;

●The effect of a consumer boycott on business performance;

●Date, time, place and purpose of a gathering that has been restricted;

●Certain words of any of the scores of people served with Emergency restrictions.

The only way you can talk about such issues is if you get permission from a cabinet minister, deputy-cabinet minister, the Bureau for Information or a government spokesman.

So, if you want to talk about these things, we suggest you phone one of the numbers given on our front page and ask for permission.

Since all those people listed are public servants, whose salaries are paid by the taxpayer, we are certain they will assist with any reasonable request from citizens not wishing to break the law.

WEEKLY MAIL, December 12 to December 18, 1986

The Prime Minister Is Dead

Ivan Vladislavić

Born and raised in Pretoria, Ivan Vladislavić moved to Johannesburg about ten years ago. He now works in the city as an editor for Ravan Press.

Vladislavić has had a number of stories published in literary magazines in South Africa, but this is the first time that his work has appeared in a major publication. He has just completed a collection of short stories which includes "The Prime Minister Is Dead."

The Day They Killed the Prime Minister

They killed the Prime Minister during the winter.

I was ten years old. That year my parents and I moved to a house in a new suburb. Granny moved with us. Grandfather said he was too old to move, so he stayed behind in the old house. He gave us a post box and two plastic numbers for the gate, and wished us everything of the best in our new home.

It was an ordinary place. Three bedrooms, a lounge, a dining room. No gnomes. No crazy paving. A reasonable path of solid cement from the front gate to the veranda steps. Laying the path was the first major task my father and I undertook.

When we moved in, the house still smelt of raw wood, fresh paint, putty. There was much to be done: the floors would have to be sealed, the fingerprints cleaned off the windowpanes, splatters of paint scraped off the tiles in the bathroom and the kitchen.

The garden was veld. The builders had simply fenced off a rectangle and cleared a patch big enough to put the house down on. The way to

447

get the grass out is to attack the roots. You can't skoffel* with a spade—it grows back. You have to work a fork in around each tuft, loosen the earth, stick a hosepipe in among the roots, turn it on full-blast, blow the soil away. Then you pull on the grass until it comes out, roots and all, like a plug. Knock out the remaining soil against the ground, pile all the grass in the wheelbarrow, push it around to the compost heap at the back.

That's what my father and I were doing on the day they killed the Prime Minister. I was loosening the soil and my father was pulling the grass out. He was wearing his old army uniform, as he always did when we waged war against the garden. Granny was in her rocker on the front veranda, crocheting one of an endless pile of woolen squares which would eventually be herded together into a lopsided blanket. She was listening to the radio, silently, through a small earphone.

I was pushing a wheelbarrow full of grass around to the back. As I passed Granny the rocker lost momentum, stopped. A brightly-colored square dropped to the floor. She hefted her large body out of the chair and stood swaying solemnly, still joined to the radio by the coil of flex. Then she bellowed: "The Prime Minister is dead! Some madman chopped him up with a panga!"**

I carried that thought with me, like a peach pip in my cheek, as I pushed the wheelbarrow round to the back and tipped the grass into the hole my father and I had dug the weekend before.

I see now that the death of a Prime Minister has many consequences.

When my grandfather died he left us a suitcase. There was something in it for each of us. My father got a suit that was too big for him and a pair of pruning shears. My mother got some newspaper clippings and some photographs, old and cracked like leather. I got a pair of lucky nail clippers given to my grandfather by an Italian prisoner of war.

When the Prime Minister died he left us a compost heap, on which practically anything would grow. Mealies grew there once, all by themselves. Granny speculated that Lazarus, who sometimes worked in the garden, must have thrown away the sweet corn that she'd given him for lunch.

Once the Prime Minister was dead they started renaming streets after him, and stations, and schools, even pleasure resorts. Then they renamed our suburb after him. They wanted us to live in a monument. It was a new suburb, and no one minded.

---

*to *skoffel*: to hoe
**panga*: a broad, heavy bush knife

When I came back around to the front with the empty wheelbarrow my father was standing to attention and my mother was holding a glass of sugar water to Granny's lips. She had unplugged Granny from the radio and turned it up so that we could all hear.

Granny finished a blanket that evening, during the seven o'clock news.

The Day We Buried the Prime Minister

We buried the Prime Minister in the spring.

My father and I were planting the orchard on that day. There were thirty trees in all. Three rows, ten trees in each. A platoon of trees, my father called them. The holes we dug were deep and perfectly round. We marked them out with a compass made of two nails joined by a piece of sisal string eighteen inches long.

My father loosened the earth with a pick and I shoveled it out of the hole. The ground was very hard and we had to soak it with water from the hosepipe. Soon my hands and feet were covered with mud. As the hold got deeper the color of the earth would change.

My father said he had desert sand in the turn-ups of his khaki pants, left over from the war. "Come," he would say to me, "hold your dixie here." Then I would cup my hands next to his hairy calves, and he'd peel back the turn-ups so that a trickle of sand flowed into my hands. "Dyed with the blood of patriots," he said, if the sand was red, and "Bleached white as bone by the desert sun," if it was white.

Granny was sitting in her rocker, under a beach umbrella, with the radio on her knees. We were listening to a rugby match, but at three o'clock they were going to cross live to the funeral. We would have a running commentary of the whole procession from the church, through the streets of the city, to Heroes' Acre at the cemetery.

"Numero Uno!" Granny shouted. "Rotting in the soil. A piece of meat. Shame. He leaves a wife and six children."

"He leaves more than that," my father said. And then to me: "Get in the hole, Private."

The holes for the fruit trees had to be four feet deep. I was the measuring stick: when I stood in the hole the ground had to be level with the top of my head. We put rocks in the bottom of the hole for drainage, then compost, then a layer of sand sieved through an old mesh gate. Then smaller stones. More compost and more sand. Each layer of sand had to be thoroughly watered. When the hole was almost full we

449

chose one of the saplings that stood ready in the shade next to the house. We left the name tag on each tree so that we would know which was which until they bore fruit.

All the trees grew except for the fig tree, third from the right, in the back row. It didn't die either. It just stayed exactly the way it was when we put it into the ground.

My grandfather came once a year after that to prune the trees. Each time he would stop before the stunted fig tree and shake his head. But he said that it was good that one tree failed: the earth should never be too kind. It spoiled people.

After he died we let the trees grow wild. We were sick of peaches and plums, and chutney, and jam. We let the weight of the fruit snap the branches and we let the fallen fruit rot into the ground.

"I'm pleased the old man isn't here to see this," my mother would say.

At a quarter to three my mother brought out tea and a plate of biscuits.

"You know," she said when we were drinking the tea, "this funeral is a big occasion. We're not likely to see another like it in our lifetimes."

"Unless they kill the new Prime Minister," my father replied.

"Don't speak like that in front of the child," Granny said sternly.

"It won't harm him if it's true," my father said. "They're pulling out all the stops on this funeral. Massed bands, tanks, a fly-past of jets. Every citizen issued with a flag, every building draped in crepe. A twenty-one gun salute. Now if they kill the new Prime Minister, and I think this is not unlikely, they'll have to do the same, won't they? It wouldn't do if they gave the next Prime Minister a halfhearted send-off."

"That may well be so," my mother said, "but the point is that we shouldn't think that way. You can't go through life taking the great events of history for granted. When one comes along you've got to grab it with both hands."

My father put down his teacup, took the beret out of his epaulet and shuffled it back onto his head, catching up the hair that spilled forward onto his forehead. "What are you getting at?"

"I think it's our duty to let the boy be part of today's ceremony. Look." She took a page of the newspaper from her apron pocket and spread it out on the ground. There was a map with a dotted path running through it, and she traced this route with her finger. "The procession's passing by just here in about thirty minutes. It's a short walk away. Why don't the two of you clean yourselves up and then you take the boy down to have a look."

Just then Granny let out a terrifying scream.

My father stood. "All right men," he said to me, "you've got thirty seconds to wash your hands and feet. Then I want you formed up and ready to move out."

"You should wash up decently and put on some proper clothes," my mother protested.

"Nonsense," my father said. "In times of war we dispense with formalities. We'll go as we are, stained with combat and proud of it."

I washed my hands and feet under the tap, then fell in. My father inspected me briefly. Then he ordered me to climb into the wheelbarrow, passed me the newspaper, took up position between the handles, and we set out. Just before we disappeared around the side of the house I looked back. My mother was packing the teacups onto the tray. Granny waved.

The metal wheel of the wheelbarrow clattered on the tar. The sound seemed very loud, because the streets were so quiet and empty. Sometimes as we passed a house I could hear the muted voice of a radio. But there was none of the usual Saturday bustle. No children playing, no one washing a car or working in the garden.

We did not speak for several blocks. When we came to Theo's café, the limit of my world, my father stopped. He took the map from me and studied it. Then he asked me to hold one corner and with his stubby fingers, the nails still caked with mud, he showed me the way. "We have to go south now for three blocks. Then we have to turn west for another four, and we're there." We went on.

Now there were fewer houses, more shops and office blocks. The streets began to fill with people, all walking in the same direction we were. They were dressed in suits and church dresses, and they walked along in silence. Some of the men wore black armbands. As we approached the older part of the city the buildings became grayer, gloomier. Here huge columns supported stone pediments. Old statues, the flesh blistered and corroded, stared down at us.

When the tar gave way to cobbles the clanking of the wheel grew even louder and now several people stopped to stare at us. I leaned back in the wheelbarrow so that I could look up at my father. His jaw was as set and craggy as a statue's. His eyes looked stonily ahead. The hair that curved back from under the beret could have been cast in bronze. Then I too looked ahead and tried to mold his hard expression to my face.

We stopped soon at a kiosk, where we each received a little flag. Then we rattled on, and at the end of the block I could see a jostling wall of black cloth, splashed with color—the colors of the flag—and many pale profiles all facing to one side. Some of these faces looked back, annoyed, as we approached. We parked behind the wall of people and my father hoisted me onto his shoulders. Then he climbed carefully onto the barrow.

"We're right on time," he said.

The wall had absorbed all color and sound, but now that we rose above it we could see the bright, gleaming procession, hardly a block away, and hear the music.

The procession drew slowly closer. In front was a phalanx of traffic officers, the sun flashing from the windshields of their motorcycles and their black leather boots and gloves. Then came the drum major, shrouded in leopard skin, and the band, all its pipes and tappets bristling. Behind that another machine, a company of soldiers, slow-marching. And then came a truck towing the Prime Minister, in a box covered with a ceremonial flag, on top of a gun carriage, as if he was a secret weapon captured from the enemy. Behind him another squad of soldiers, and behind that tanks, and behind that more soldiers as far as the eye could see.

This solemn movement, this stirring music, hemmed in on either side by the frozen waves of mourners.

When the first company of soldiers had almost passed us, my father raised his arm in a rigid salute. I waved my flag. The men around us swallowed and stared ahead. Some of the women dabbed at their eyes with the little flags. A child started crying.

Then, as the gun carriage drew level with us, the truck suddenly coughed, jerked and came to a halt. A cloud of black smoke poured from the exhaust pipe. The soldiers behind faltered. The front ranks began to mark time. Those behind marched slowly and solemnly into those in front. A few of the men dived for cover under the gun carriage.

The band and the first soldiers marched on. Between them and the stalled truck a fascinating gap began to open.

The driver of the truck climbed hurriedly down and opened the bonnet, tinkered with the engine. Behind, the soldiers stumbled and coughed in the smoke. The gun carriage was now completely obscured.

My father snapped out of his salute, jumped down from the wheelbarrow and squatted so that I could climb from his shoulders.

"Private, we must do what must be done."

He took up the wheelbarrow and, as if they understood our mission, the people parted to let us through.

The box was heavy. The soldiers were already half a block ahead of us. We set off in pursuit, my father pushing the wheelbarrow while I held the box steady. The crowd waved us on. Once the flag got caught under the wheel and the box was almost jerked from the barrow. My father was breathing heavily by the time we caught up with the soldiers and adjusted our pace to the slow rhythm of the music.

I looked back and saw that the crowds that had lined the streets had surged together behind us and were following. On the dark surface of that wave the flotsam of the flags and their faces bobbed.

Outside the cemetery a man in white gloves waved the band and the soldiers off to one side into a parking lot. He directed us straight ahead, through the wrought-iron gates, along the stone walkway that led to the grave. On either side the stone faces of the men in the history books looked down from their columns, unblinking, unmoved.

The grave. The black figures clustered together, the man with the book clutched under his arm, the brass railings. They stood as people do on the edge of a cliff.

My father's stride lengthened. I had to run to keep up with him. The box bucked violently. My father began to run. I stopped, panting, and stared after him. He ran towards the hole. The mouths of the people at the graveside opened. The man with the book held out his pale palm like a traffic officer.

My father ran on. At the last moment, on the very lip of the grave, he dug the metal prow of the barrow into the earth and heaved.

Two Interviews with J. M. Coetzee, 1983 and 1987

Tony Morphet

John M. Coetzee was born in Cape Town in 1940. In the intervening years he has spent periods in Britain and America, but Cape Town is once again his base. He is Professor of General Literature at the University of Cape Town.

Since the appearance of his first novel, Dusklands *(1974; reprinted by New York: Penguin, 1985), his writing has received considerable critical attention. In the Heart of the Country (1976; reprinted by New York: Penguin, 1982) has won the CNA and the Mofolo-Plomer Prizes; Waiting for the Barbarians (1980; New York: Penguin, 1982) was awarded the CNA Prize, the Geoffrey Faber Memorial Prize and the James Tait Black Memorial Prize.* Life & Times of Michael K *(1983; New York: Viking, 1984) won both the CNA Prize and the Booker Prize, Britain's prestigious literary award.*

Foe, *Coetzee's latest novel, is a recasting of Defoe's* Robinson Crusoe.

Tony Morphet teaches in the Adult Education Unit of the University of Cape Town.

The first of these two interviews is surprising in at least one respect: it carries no mention of the Booker McConnell Prize awarded for the novel Life & Times of Michael K. The reason is simple. The interview was conducted, in writing, in 1983 before the South African publication of the book and before the award of the prize. The intention was to publish the interview at the time of the novel's appearance but it failed to find an appropriate forum. It is published here for the first time in the U.S.

Q: The most immediately striking fact is the omission of "the" from the title. I have puzzled over this, not without pleasure, but I cannot find a substantial answer to the riddle. Do you have any comment?

COETZEE: To my ear, "The Life" implies that the life is over, whereas "Life" does not commit itself.

Q: The location of the story is very highly specified. Cape Town—Stellenbosch—Prince Albert—somewhere between 1985-1990. This puts it very close to us, closer than any of your previous work. Were you looking for a more direct and immediate conversation with South African readers? Or is it part of another strategy?

COETZEE: The geography is, I fear, less trustworthy than you imagine—not because I deliberately set about altering the reality of Sea Point or Prince Albert but because I don't have much interest in, or can't seriously engage myself with, the kind of realism that takes pride in copying the "real" world. The option was, of course, open to me to invent a world out of place and time and situate the action there, as I did in *Waiting for the Barbarians*; but that side of *Waiting for the Barbarians* was an immense labor, and what would have been the point, this time round?

Q: How did you "find" Michael K? Where did he come from and how and why did he make his way into your mind as an heroic figure?

COETZEE: I don't remember how I found Michael K. I have no recollection at all. I wonder whether the forgetting is deliberate.

Q: Did you at all feel that you were taking big risks by placing Michael at the center of your fiction? He has a very limited consciousness and it seems that it is for that reason precisely, that he becomes the central figure. It seems a very austere and risky procedure for a novelist to adopt. Are you happy with the result?

COETZEE: Yes, I certainly saw that I was taking a risk by putting K at the center of the book, or at least at the center of most of it. But then it didn't turn out to be a book about *becoming* (which might have required that K have the ability to adapt, more of what we usually call intelligence) but a book about *being*, which merely entailed that K go on being himself, despite everything.

You must not forget the doctor in the second part of the book. He is by no means a person of limited consciousness. But where does his consciousness get him?

Q: Would it be fair and accurate to say that the novel is built on the structural opposition between "*the camp*" in all its hideous variety (from Huis Norenius through Jakkalsdrif, Brandvlei and the Kenilworth Race

Course to the implied horrors of the penal camps), and "*the garden*," principally Michael's cultivation of the land around the pump in the Karoo, but including also De Waal Park and the Sea Point room?

COETZEE: I suppose you might say that there is an opposition between camp and garden. But I wouldn't lump De Waal Park and the Sea Point room with the garden in the Karoo. Nor, I think, should one forget how terribly transitory that garden life of K's is: he can't hope to keep the garden because, finally, the whole surface of South Africa has been surveyed and mapped and disposed of. So, despite K's desires, the opposition that the garden provides to the camps is at most at a conceptual level.

Q: Michael's harvest of, and feast upon, the pumpkins provides us with something relatively rare in your work – a powerful positive celebration. It is a very moving and beautiful scene. Did you have anything like the ceremonies of the first fruits in mind when you composed it? Is there anything further you would like to say about it?

COETZEE: K discovers or recreates some of the rituals of agricultural life, if only because he has to live by the cycle of the seasons. As for positive celebration, isn't there a fair amount of celebration (of elementary freedoms) in *Waiting for the Barbarians?*

Q: The great "given," or "taken-for-granted," fact, in the story is the war. No South African reader will be able to take his eye off the details which the story gives. Did you see it as an important purpose of the novel to take South African readers into the knowledge of what war here will mean?

COETZEE: I am hesitant to accept that my books are addressed to readers. Or at least I would argue that the concept of the reader in literature is a vastly more problematic one than one might at first think. Anyhow, it is important to me to assert that *Michael K* is not "addressed" to anyone. But the picture of war given in the book is, I would hope, a plausible picture of what a state of war might be like.

Q: The narrator in Part Two – the pharmacist turned medic at the Kenilworth camp – mythologizes Michael. He sees him as Adam, the gardener of paradise and in fantasy he follows Michael away from the camp, pursuing him for his "meaning." Is this figure the crisis-ridden liberal of the time? He participates in the camp system but does what he can to alleviate its horrors and stupidities. He is burdened with guilt and with a complex consciousness but he is unable to act on his understanding. He is important to the development of meanings in the novel but his fate is to be swallowed by the facts of war and the camps. Would you like to comment on this figure?

COETZEE: You say that the doctor is "unable to act." But of course he does act, all the time. He heals people, he helps people, he protects people. Does it matter that his actions don't satisfy him? Maybe the world would be a better place if there were more people like him around. Maybe. I put the question, anyhow.

Maybe it isn't helpful to think of the doctor *primarily* as "the liberal." First of all he seems to me a person who believes (or wants) Michael K to have a meaning. I don't think that K believes (or wants) the doctor to have a meaning.

Q: The closing sequence in Sea Point seems in some ways gratuitous — particularly the sexual incidents. Michael's own interpretation that this is people's "charity" is unconvincing. Can you throw further light on your purposes in this sequence — leaving aside the wonderful closing pages in which Michael characterizes himself as a mole or an earthworm.

COETZEE: If the closing sequence doesn't work, that's a pity. Obviously it would be a cop-out for the book to end after Part Two. It is important that K should not emerge from the book as an angel.

Q: The image of the teaspoon and the windmill shaft is so specific and potent that it is almost emblematic with the effect that it tends to displace the density of the preceding sequences. Did you feel you were taking particular risks in using it?

COETZEE: I thought that the prose had been subdued enough for 250 pages to earn that last gesture.

Q: The novel clearly speaks to a range of literary texts — your own books first and foremost but also obviously through the letter K to Kafka. Would you like to comment on your use of Kafka?

COETZEE: I don't believe that Kafka has an exclusive right to the letter K. Nor is Prague the center of the universe.

Q: The story resonates powerfully within the context of your own writing. To explore just one line of inquiry, can we focus on the mind/body split. In *Dusklands* in particular this is a powerful theme in which the mind is dominant. Jacobus Coetzee and Eugene Dawn each in their own way are engaged in raping the world to satisfy the imperatives of the mind. In *Life & Times* you appear to be reversing the dominance. Michael complies in his mind to the demands of the war/camp system—it is his body that will not submit. It yearns for its food—the food of "the garden." It is this dumb imperative which gives his claim to being a gardener such force—even to the point where the camp medic's invocation of paradise seems trite since Michael's experience with the pumpkins is the experience of which the Garden of Eden is an image. He is an ingester of the earth—literally an earthworm, whereas Jacobus is an exploder of the earth. The radical and profound nature of these fictions (if I am not wholly mistaken) imposes great pressure on your readers. Do you pursue the logic of the fiction for your own sake or your readers?

COETZEE: I hope that I pursue the logic of the story for its own sake. That is what is means to me to engage with a subject.

Q: Setting your story in the near future will inevitably draw comparisons with Gordimer's *July's People*. I do not like her work but I wonder whether you were conscious of the comparison and what it meant to you.

COETZEE: Fortunately Michael K had been born and was living his own life by the time I read *July's People*, so I didn't have to worry about questions of influence. Also, Gordimer writes about a Transvaal which is practically a foreign country to me. I don't recognize important similarities between the books.

Q: Does it make any sense to you to recall Marvell—the poet who in the midst of civil war wrote consistently of both the war and gardens?

COETZEE: I had forgotten that about Marvell.

Q: Would you describe your work as structuralist and, if so, what meanings would you want to attach to the term?

COETZEE: No, I wouldn't describe my work as structuralist, mainly because I prefer to give a quite strictly delimited meaning to the word "structuralist." But obviously I have learned a lot from contemporary French thought about the mediations that systems of signs provide.

Q: Your fiction is, you must be aware, vulnerable to critique from both the political right and left. Both are in effect saying "Don't interfere — allow us to finish our tasks and there will be a time for what you want later. The making of a society is a fierce and brutal business and requires conscience to be silent." How would you answer such a joint voice?

COETZEE: Yes, my work is certainly open to attack from right and left, though how vulnerable it is we have yet to see. But would the right really join the left in expressing the sentiments you have attributed to it? I think there are more telling attacks that might be made. But the question remains: who is going to feed the glorious opposing armies?

Q: The left, which in one or another form shares with you a common perception of the life of "camps," is likely to be especially angry at Michael's implicit answer to the guerrillas "in the mountains":
"There must be men to stay behind and keep gardening alive, or at least the idea of gardening; because once that cord was broken, the earth would grow hard hard and forget her children."
The left will charge you with furthering the liberal fantasy of the politics of innocence and so obstructing progressive action. They will, possibly, question the final clause of the quotation most closely, "How will the earth forget her children?," and accuse you of mystificatory categories. Do you have a sense of how you will answer the objection?

COETZEE: I have no wish to enter the lists as a defender of Michael K. If war is the father of all things, let the objection you voice go to war with the book, which has now had its say, and let us see who wins.

Q: You have always taken unusual care in creating your reader and in managing your relations with him. (The double death of Klawer is not easily forgotten.) Whom are you seeking to create as the ideal reader of *Life & Times*? And has your sense of the readers changed as a result of achieving such widespread international recognition?

COETZEE: I wasn't aware that I have ever taken care over my readers. My ideal reader is, I would hope, myself. But I know something of the insidious pressures faced by South African writers to simplify and explain for a foreign audience.

Q: Did you conceive of the novel as in any way a task presented to you by history – the history of South Africa specifically?

COETZEE: Perhaps that is my fate. On the other hand, I sometimes wonder whether it isn't simply that vast and wholly ideological superstructure constituted by publishing, reviewing and criticism that is forcing on me the fate of being a "South African novelist."

Q: If we can take it that *Dusklands* records the interior imagination of colonial conquest, *The Heart of the Country* the intricate ferocities of the master-slave relationship, *Waiting for the Barbarians* the mind of an empire in decline, *Life & Times of Michael K* the meaning of war and resistance, then your total project appears to record the drama of the ruling South African consciousness. Would you accept this description?

COETZEE: I don't know. It sounds very grand, the way you put it. There never was a master plan, though obviously certain subjects get written out and one has to move on. But then, meaning is so often something one half-discovers, half-creates in retrospect. So maybe there is a plan, now.

I don't know what you mean by "the ruling South African consciousness." Is it meant to describe me? Is that who I am?

Q: As a writer you are working in cultural terms. Your fictions however, as we have them, present a puzzling double face. They articulate intensely within themselves, and to each other, but they also have a dramatic referential capacity. Sometimes the impression is that you write to satisfy cruel and exacting "internal" criteria and that any references external to the work are arbitrary and the creations of chance – at other times, especially in *Life & Times*, one gains the sense that you are conducting a very precise dialogue with the South African reality. Would you like to comment?

COETZEE: You have half-asked the question before, in a different form.

I don't know what "the South African reality" is, but I suspect that you are unlikely to discover it by reading newspapers, if only because what

460

you read in a newspaper (of whatever "orientation") has been mediated through the epistemological framework called "news." I have never found anything about Michael K in the newspapers. If I was conducting any dialogue in *Life & Times*, it was with Michael K.

Q: Which came to you first—the "camp" or the "garden." Why? And how did the opposite term construct itself?

COETZEE: –

Q: At points in the story—particularly for some reason when Michael is taken to work on the railway—it seems that you are writing your own way out of an intolerable realization. The structure of the book builds this sense. The opening sequences are exceedingly painful to read because one cannot deal with Michael's vulnerability to the horrors around him. But as the story proceeds, one begins gradually to realize the extraordinary strength and submerged purpose in Michael. As the terms "camp" and "garden" begin to deepen and clarify one realises that at a particular and intense cost there is a meaning deeper than, beyond, and ultimately more powerful than "the camps." Are you in a sense writing yourself (and your readers) into a future?

COETZEE: There is a sense in which Michael K cannot die.

Q: Do you see yourself as exploring the deep structures of the South African imagination? (I can't think of a better phrasing to capture my sense of the meanings of *Dusklands*, *Heart of the Country*, *Waiting for the Barbarians* and *Life & Times of Michael K*.)

COETZEE: The imagination is my own. If not, I am really in the soup.

*   *   *

This interview took place in February 1987:

Q: *Foe* might be seen as something of a retreat from the South African situation. Certainly one, if not the major, interest of the book is the nature and the processes of fiction—of words and stories. Would you comment on the prominence of this theme in the book?

461

COETZEE: *Foe* is a retreat from the South African situation, but only from that situation in a narrow temporal perspective. It is not a retreat from the subject of colonialism or from questions of power. What you call "the nature and processes of fiction" may also be called the question of *who writes?* Who takes up the position of power, pen in hand?

Q: Your attitude to stories has always been ambivalent—they create and bestow meanings but they also construct false worlds (Crusoe's island with its cannibals!). In *Foe* you sharpen the critical side of this ambivalence by constant references to the market in books ("Their trade is in books not truth").

How do these reflections bear on your own position as a successful author?

COETZEE: "Successful author" is a barbed phrase here, a highly barbed phrase. Foe in the book, or Daniel Defoe in "real" life, is the type of the successful author. Am I being classed with Foe, though my interest clearly lies with Foe's foe, the *un*successful author—worse, author*ess*—Susan Barton? How can one question power ("success") from a position of power? One ought to question it from its antagonist position, namely, the position of weakness. Yet once again, in this interview, I am being installed in a position of power—power, in this case, over my own text.

Q: Part of the pleasure of the book is tracking the detailed divergences between Susan's narrative and Defoe's book. There are two features, though, which stand out with especial prominence: Susan herself and Friday. Would you like to say something about your choice of narrator—the begetter of the story? Is there a feminist point here?

COETZEE: I would hate to say either that there is a feminist point or that I *chose* the narrator. The narrator chose me. There is a flippant way of saying that, and a serious way. The book deals with choosing in the serious sense.

Q: Friday has no tongue. Why?

COETZEE: Nobody seems to have sufficient authority to say for sure how it is that Friday has no tongue.

Q: He is an uncomfortable presence but he is more potent as an absence. Is the absence directly related to his blackness—his African-ness?

462

COETZEE: In Robinson Crusoe's story, Friday is a handsome Carib youth with near-European features. In *Foe* he is an African. Whether Friday is potent or not I don't know. What is more important, Susan doesn't know.

Q: You have Susan say that "the true story will not be heard till by art we have found a means of giving voice to Friday." Does this describe the effort that you make in the very surprising closing section of the book, where we are taken, first into Defoe's rooms, and then to the undersea wreck, into Friday's "home" where "bodies are their own signs"?

COETZEE: Since the question is such a perspicacious one, I hate to have to reply: Yes and No. Further than that, I wonder only whether Friday is not beyond the help of art.

Q: In these sequences Friday's "voice" seems to be the voice of nature itself—not of culture or history. Is this a fair reading of the very moving final paragraph?

COETZEE: I'm glad you like the final paragraph. But I would be traducing the book if, from my present position, I said that Friday's voice is the voice of nature. In fact, I would be suspicious of anyone who suggested that one could return to nature by having one's tongue cut out. This may seem to contradict my response to your last question, but the contradiction is only a seeming one.

Q: Friday appears to be a close relative of Michael K's, as well as of a number of other figures in your work—the barbarian girl, for example, in *Waiting for the Barbarians*. Would you comment on the recurring presence of this "family" in your writing?

COETZEE: You have pointed out this "family" to me before. I am intrigued by its existence, but I don't think it is in my best interests to look too deeply into it.

Q: In *Dusklands* you describe Jacobus attempting to reach into the interior life of a stone by cracking it into pieces. There is no interior because at each splitting he is faced with yet another surface. I read this as an image of resistance and it seems to me that Friday (and his relatives) embody a similar form of resistance to efforts to comprehend their interior "meanings." Is that a fair and reasonable reading? Would you like to comment further on the importance which you attach to the notion of resistance?

COETZEE: Yes, it is a fair and reasonable reading. I hope that a certain spirit of resistance is ingrained in my books; ultimately I hope they have the strength to resist whatever readings I impose on them on occasions like the present one.

Q: To return to South African issues. Your writing seems to me radical in the sense that it goes beneath the specific phenomena of history and culture but also deeply conservative in that it throws into doubt the whole significance of created meanings. Would you accept the implication that your work contradicts the idea of a "master narrative"— whether religious or socio-historical—and that therefore human-meaning making can only appear as a series of arbitrary games played out against the innocence and unconcern of nature or being? Susan and Foe against Friday and Crusoe? And where then is Art?

COETZEE: Your questions again and again drive me into a position I do not want to occupy. (But what legitimacy has that "want"?) By accepting your implication, I would produce a master narrative for a set of texts that claim to deny all master narratives. Let me therefore simply say that certain things get put in question in my novels, the notion of arbitrariness being, I hope, one of them.

The Body Is a Country of Joy and of Pain

Douglas Reid Skinner

For a biographical note on Douglas Reid Skinner please see page 41.

A Door to the Soul

If this was a dream, then it was dreamed each week
in a waking sleep, a woman seeing her children
running in a cloud of cries and expectations
along the corridor towards her until the moment
just before they would reach her waiting arms
when the hidden guards would release an iron door
that would fall with a crash between them,
and the children would run headlong into it,
and she would hear their small hands beating
once, twice against it as they dragged her away
and back to the cell where they would watch her,
hour after hour, sitting and weeping and beating
her own arms until they ached and she imagined
them filled with the bustle and noise of the children.

One Sunday in November

They removed all of his days and left him with
hours. Then they removed all of his hours
and left him with minutes. Then they removed
all of his minutes and left him with a silence

that had no line or horizon, and time vanished
into the walls around him. After two years
they gave him one day of faces and voices,
words and the touching of hands and of lips.
And then once more they left him with the hard
pebble that his fingers had worn smooth.
And when no one was left who remembered him
they left him to blink through his tears at the
impossible brightness of the sunlight as he
stepped into an empty street filled with people.

A Flight of Birds

One after the other they entered the room
and forced open her legs, grunting and sweating,
slamming into her, slamming, one after the other,
unbuttoning and unzipping, forcing into her,
one after the other, turning her over and forcing
into her as she screamed, the pain and fear
blurring, without stopping, all night and all
of the following day, the room filled with blows
and laughter, the smells of tobacco and alcohol.
And years later, sitting in her kitchen, she
lays down her knife and fork, and her shoulders
shake as she begins to weep, and the small hands
of her child fly out like birds through the air
to console her, but she cannot stop, and is gone.

A Question of Ownership

For the promise of his body, he said, he would
tell them anything they wished to know.
But slowly and methodically, piece by piece, they
removed it from him. And when they had finished
he could no longer recognize the penis that he
held each morning to urinate, nor the toes that
entered sock and shoe when he dressed, nor even
the rough feel of hands that trembled as he
raised up a cigarette and drew smoke in.

It seemed as if everything belonged to another.
And for eight years he would search everywhere
and not find it, and would go on living a life
as someone else, someone who walked with a limp
and who was deaf, and who could not speak.

"Woman in Detention" / linocut by David Hlongwane.

A South African Photographer in Zimbabwe

Text and photographs by Paul Weinberg

For a biographical note on Paul Weinberg please see page 120.

Zimbabwe – A Turning of Time

This essay was constructed during a period of Zimbabwe's coming-of-age, as it prepared for, and hosted, the Non-Aligned Movement Summit. I could not but puzzle over the fact that only seven years ago the country was in the middle of a violent civil war.

I suppose that is why I was so much more aware of the contradictions that began to unfold as I experienced the disquieting peace of Zimbabwe.

Harare Airport.

Zimbabwe police demonstration.

Harare school boys.

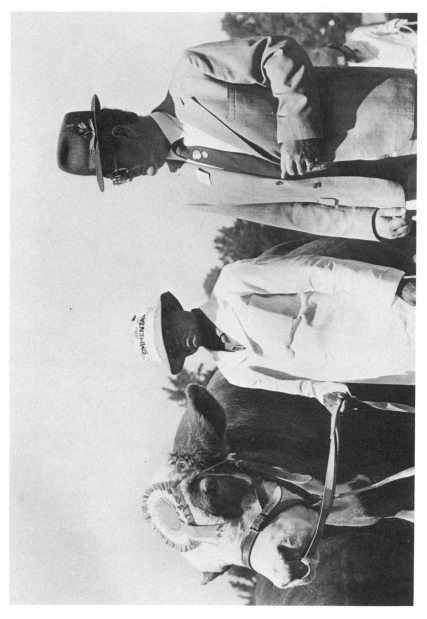

Harare show.

Farmer and workers, Karoi district.

Worker outside Sheraton Hotel, Harare.

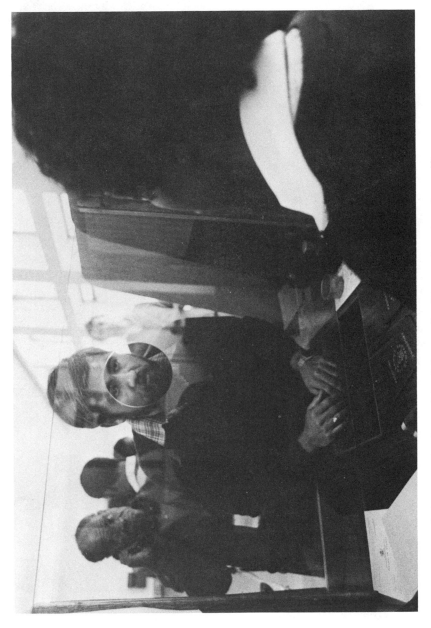

Returning Zimbabwean checks on his rights at the Harare immigration office.

Tobacco farmer and workers.

Non-Aligned Movement celebrations. Harare Airport.

THE EMERGENCY MADE SIMPLE

Should you intend discussing any of the following topics:

- Security force action
- Boycotts
- The treatment of detainees
- The release of any detainee
- 'People's courts'
- Street committees

Simply phone these numbers to ask for permission:

PW BOTHA (State President)	(021) 45-2225	BAREND DU PLESSIS (Minister of Finance)	(012) 26-0261
PIK BOTHA (Minister of Foreign Affairs)	(012) 28-6912	DANIE STEYN (Minister of Economic Affairs and Technology)	(012) 266-568
CHRIS HEUNIS (Minister of Constitutional Affairs and Planning)	(021) 45-7295	WILLIE VAN DER MERWE (Minister of Health and Population Development)	(012) 28-4773
MAGNUS MALAN (Minister of Defence)	(012) 26-6718		
ADRIAAN VLOK (Minister of Law and Order)	(012) 323-8880	BUREAU FOR INFORMATION	(012) 21-7397 (012) 21-7529 (012) 21-7396 (012) 21-7528 (012) 21-7528
KOBIE COETSEE (Minister of Justice)	(012) 323-8581		
STOFFEL BOTHA (Minister of Internal Affairs and Communications)	(012) 26-8081	NEIL BARNARD (head of the National Intelligence Service)	(012) 323-9761
GERRIT VILJOEN (Minister of Development Aid and Education)	(012) 28-5171	PW VAN DER WESTHUIZEN (Secretary of the State Security Council)	(012) 325-4780

Section 3(4)(a)(i) of yesterday's new Emergency Regulations authorises any minister, deputy minister or government official to allow discussion of these forbidden topics. See PAGE 3 for details.

WEEKLY MAIL, December 12 to December 18, 1986

Sequence for South Africa

Dennis Brutus

This poem, although originally published in 1975 in South African Voices *(University of Texas), remains a central expression of the pain of South African exile. It was first reprinted in* Somehow We Survive: An Anthology of South African Writing, *edited by Sterling Plumpp (Thunder's Mouth Press, 1982). For a biographical note on Dennis Brutus, please see page 363.*

I.

Golden oaks and jacarandas
flowering:
exquisite images
to wrench my heart.

2.

Each day, each hour
is not painful,
exile is not amputation,
there is no bleeding wound
no torn flesh and severed nerves;
the secret is clamping down
holding the lid of awareness tight shut—
sealing in the acrid searing stench
that scalds the eyes,
swallows up the breath
and fires the brain in a wail—
until some thoughtless questioner
pries the sealed lid loose;
I can exclude awareness of exile
until someone calls me one.

479

3.

The agony returns;
after a crisis, delirium,
surcease and aftermath;
my heart knows an exhausted calm,
catharsis brings forgetfulness
but with recovery, resilience
the agony returns.

4.

At night
to put myself to sleep
I play alphabet games
but something reminds me of you
and I cry out
and am wakened.

5.

I have been bedded
in London and Paris
Amsterdam and Rotterdam,
in Munich and Frankfort
Warsaw and Rome—
and still my heart cries out for home!

6.

Exile
is the reproach
of beauty
in a foreign landscape
vaguely familiar
because it echoes
remembered beauty.

From A Tough Tale

Mongane Serote

Mongane Serote has long been one of the most emphatic opponents of apartheid, and is a veritable oracle of the anti-apartheid movement in South Africa. He was born in 1944 in Alexandria Township, near Johannesburg. He received an MFA degree from Columbia University while studying in the U.S. on a Fulbright grant. He has published several books of poems and a novel, To Every Birth Its Blood, *and has worked with the Mebu Art Ensemble in Gaborone, Botswana. He currently lives in England. These excerpts are from a long poem published in 1987 by Kliptown Books (London).*

we part with wives, sons, daughters, lovers
we part with comrades
men, women, young and old
whose laughter
or tears
or little things they did which make them them
remind us
we were just a little too late
we did not walk out the door in time
or our long partings held us just a little too long
while laughing
or talking
reading or phoning
maybe too long in an embrace with one long missed
we overslept
or slept at the wrong minute
and thus gave the enemy a moment
to calculate and time to reach us
Then, I must admit—
our sorrow is as red as blood

the silence comes
the quietness holds us, with its chill
it cuts then, painfully, between the mind and the heart

*   *   *

They come young
motherless
they speak of rubber bullets and birdshots
they speak of young fresh blood spilled in the streets
these children of a restless hour
now unfold
peel off
they wear steel threads for nerves
can you hear their rolling footsteps
can you hear their songs
their youth which is enraged by oppression
is the blood of struggle
these children are ageless
women and men
some had not as yet finished being children
others though long ripe, are unable to be mothers or fathers
wives or husbands
they've responded, body and soul to the restless hour
to turn its unlivable moments
to a livable present
through their flesh and blood
by shattering ignorance
and by pain of sleepless nights
step by step
stone for stone
minute by minute
we pierce the mind once woolled by oppression
we tear apart poverty and squalor
and we search for the new man and the new woman
in us—
for my country must be rebuilt.

*   *   *

This is not and must not be a sad tale
it cannot be
it is a song whose strength like strong wind

can blow and reveal our weaknesses
for that we must know.
remember
and this lovers must know better
how
when a heart is broken the mind searches and searches
for something to hold on to
to rest its weariness
and so gather strength for the broken heart
yes
even that has to be done with skill
find the strong branch to hang from for the weak one can break
and where, where would the poor heart be?
we know all this and more
and yet this time asks: *really?*
yes we do
for our future is a poem which says so.

Linocut by Hamilton Budaza.

Heroes of the Day

Sipho Sepamla

Born in Krugersdorp in 1932, Sipho Sepamla is the Director of the Federated Union of Black Arts (FUBA), and the editor of New Classic *and* S'ketsh. *His poetry is powerfully urban, and it seeks to depict the particular experience of the black South African living under apartheid. There is also present in the verse a celebration of the resilience of the oppressed, their will to self-determination. Sepamla's volumes include* The Blues Is You in Me *(Johannesburg: Ad. Donker, 1976),* The Soweto I Love *(London: Rex Collings; Claremont, S.A.: David Philip, 1977) and* Selected Poems *(Craighall: Ad. Donker, 1984). In 1976 he was co-recipient of the Thomas Pringle Award. He has also published a number of short stories, as well as the novels* The Root Is One *(1979),* A Ride on the Whirlwind *(1981) and* Third Generation *(Johannesburg: Skotaville, 1986).*

His poem, "To Whom It May Concern," and the linocuts of Billy Mandindi that were inspired by it, appear on page 66.

O! carry me on the wings of the times
to the site of a modern-day burial

    I want to sing
    I want to dance
    I want to celebrate
  Heroes of the day

O! let me be one of the comrades
Who set aside one day's burdens

    To let their voices shout
    To let their voices cry out
    To let their voices chant all day long
  Songs to the glorious heroes

I want to stamp my foot so hard
that the earth cries dust clouds
that rise and clash in harmony with songs of hope

I want to raise my arm so high
that the fingers touch at will toes of the gods
that they too can dance to the rhythm of the new songs

    Let me say it humbly
    For there is sadness in all this
    There's hope in this dying

Woodcut by Cecil Skotnes.

Appendices

Chronology

This selective chronology begins approximately at the start of this century; it deliberately focuses on the past two years.

1899:   Anglo-Boer War begins.

1902:   Anglo-Boer War ends. Treaty of Vereeniging establishes British rule.

1907:   Gandhi leads civil rights campaign in South Africa (hereinafter, "S.A.").

1909:   The Union of South Africa established, with Louis Botha as Prime Minister.

1912:   The African National Congress (ANC) founded in Bloemfontein.

1913:   The Land Act deprives Africans of the right to own land in S.A. outside of reserves.

1918:   The founding of the *Broederbond*, a right-wing Afrikaner "secret society," to look after and ensure Afrikaner group identity and supremacy.

1920:   Twenty thousand black mineworkers strike for higher pay. This is the last major black miners' strike until 1946.

1922:   The "Rand Revolt." Twenty-five thousand white miners strike partly in protest against a Chamber of Mines' move to replace white miners with black.

1939:   S.A. joins in World War II on the side of the British. This is a furiously debated move because: 1) Britain is the traditional enemy of many white South Africans; 2) There is support for national socialism in certain sectors.

1944:   The Youth League of the ANC is formally constituted.

1946:   India severs trade relations with S.A.

1948:   The Nationalist Party wins the white General Election and
         Dr. Daniel Malan becomes Prime Minister.

1950:   Hendrick Verwoerd appointed Minister of Native Affairs.
         Passing of the Bantu Authorities Act.

1952:   June to October. The Defiance Campaign, a period of passive
         resistance. In these months about 8,500 convicted for such
         offenses as using amenities reserved for whites only.

1955:   "Freedom Charter" adopted at Congress of the People.

1956:   Sixty thousand so-called "colored" voters struck from the vot-
         er's role in the Cape Province.
            August: Twenty thousand women demonstrate at the
         Union Buildings (seat of government in Pretoria) against
         passes for women.
            December: Police arrest the leaders of the Congress Alli-
         ance. One hundred and fifty-six are arrested. The Treason
         Trial lasts for the following five years. All are acquitted.

1958:   Verwoerd, the "architect of apartheid," becomes Prime Minis-
         ter.

1959:   The Pan Africanist Congress (PAC) founded.
            Verwoerd pushes through parliament the Promotion of
         Bantu Self-Government Act, which conceives of eight
         national units for African peoples. This signals active begin-
         ning to "homelands" or "Bantustan" policy.

1960:   March 21: Sharpeville massacre. On this day at Sharpeville, a
         township in the Transvaal, police open fire on passive resisters
         taking part in a public demonstration, burning their pass-
         books in defiance of pass laws which restricted freedom of
         movement for blacks. Sixty-nine are killed and 150 wounded.
         The slayings are received with outrage both locally and inter-
         nationally. Sharpeville Day is a day of mourning and com-
         memoration for South Africans of conscience.
            ANC and PAC are banned.

1961: Union of South Africa becomes a republic.

1963: Political leadership of the ANC arrested at Rivonia, a suburb of Johannesburg. Leadership, including Nelson Mandela, tried and convicted in a notorious trial.

1966: Verwoerd stabbed to death by a white parliamentary messenger while sitting at his desk in the House of Assembly. Balthazer John Vorster becomes Prime Minister.

1969: Dockworkers strike in Durban. All summarily fired.

1975: The Front for the Liberation of Mozambique (FRELIMO) wins Mozambican independence, after 500 years of colonial rule.

1976: June 16: The Soweto Students Representative Council holds a meeting to protest the compulsory use of Afrikaans as a teaching medium in black schools. Police confront school students on their way to Orlando stadium where a mass rally is to be held. By the end of the day 100 students have been killed and townships across the country come out in support of student demands. The day is an annual memorial day, to commemorate the dead and to reassert the role of students in the restructuring of society. June 16 is seen as a turning point.

1977: Black Consciousness leader Steve Biko killed while in police detention.

1984: Government establishes the Tricameral Parliament in an attempt to seduce "Indian" and "Colored" communities by offering them a puppet role in which they could have a say in issues relating to "own affairs."

The United Democratic Front, a massive coordinating body which unites workers' groups, unions, women's movements, anti-conscription groups, et al., is established initially to campaign against the election of members of the House of Representatives, the Colored and Indian flank of the Tricameral Parliament. The UDF and its affiliates begin to play an increasingly important role, as civil disobedience is employed as a strategy throughout South Africa.

Bishop (now Archbishop) Desmond Tutu is awarded the Nobel Prize for Peace for his work in South Africa.

November 5: General stayaway strike in the Transvaal, as nearly one million respond to the call of unions and community organizations.

1985:   July 20: Over 60,000 attend funeral of assassinated leaders in Lingelihle, Cradock.

July 21: State of Emergency declared in thirty-six magisterial districts.

August 11: Twenty Duncan village residents killed in township protests.

August 17: Beaufort West consumer boycott begins.

August 20: Consumer boycott spreads to Western Cape.

August 29: In Cape Town, seventeen die in clashes with police during march on Pollsmoor Prison to demand the release of Nelson Mandela.

October 6: Government closes 460 schools in the Western Cape after continued clashes.

October 15: Cape Town. Three youths die in "Trojan Horse" killings, in which armed police hide in boxes on a truck and open fire on a crowd of stone throwers.

November 21: General stayaway strike in Mamelodi, Pretoria. Thirteen die as 50,000 march on development to demand the troops be removed from the townships.

December 1: National launch of Congress of South African Trade Unions (COSATU).

1986:   January 5: Twenty-three thousand National Union of Mineworkers (NUM) members fired at Gencor's Impala Platinum, Bophuthatswana, after striking for one week over wages and recognition.

February 15: Mass resistance breaks out after disruption of funerals in Alexandra Township. Forty-six people killed in four days.

March 31: In defiance of police ban, 20,000 attend memorial service for Moses Mabhida, general secretary of the South African Communist Party, who died in exile in Mozambique.

May 19: Crossroads squatter camp attacked by vigilantes. Thirteen killed, 20,000 homeless.

June 9: Squatter camp near Crossroads attacked by vigilantes. Eighteen killed, 20,000 homeless.

June 12: Second State of Emergency in two years. Massive detention of activists around the country.

October 1: Thirty thousand miners stage one-day strike to protest deaths in Kinross mining disaster.

October 19: Samora Machel and thirty-two Frelimo officials die in mysterious plane crash.

October 27: Thirty-five thousand mineworkers strike at Gold Fields mine. They return to work three days later as owners agree to negotiate.

1987: January 8: Some twenty South African newspapers run a full-page advertisement marking the 75th anniversary of the founding of the ANC and calling on the government to legalize the group. Police say they will investigate whether the papers have broken any laws by publishing the ads, which had been placed by anti-apartheid and church groups.

April 5: A black police trainee is killed and sixty-four of his colleagues are wounded by a hand grenade thrown into a crowded police parade ground in Soweto. The attack is part of a sharp upsurge in violence and civil unrest preceding the May 6 general election, in which only whites will vote.

April 16: Archbishop Tutu and forty-six other Anglican clergymen disobey new emergency restrictions by asking President P. W. Botha to either free detainees or put them on trial.

April 22: Police shoot six blacks to death during street battles at a Johannesburg railroad station and at union buildings in Johannesburg and neighboring Germiston, after the government-owned railroad fired 16,000 striking black workers. The fighting is the worst in Johannesburg since the government imposed a nationwide state of emergency June 12, 1986, in an attempt to quell unrest against apartheid.

April 24 and 28: In two rulings, the Natal Supreme Court overturns key aspects of the government's emergency censorship provisions that curb the press and outlaw protests and appeals on behalf of people detained without charge, stating that President Botha had exceeded his authority by delegating powers to the police commissioner in a December 1986 decree. The Government states it will appeal the rulings to the Appeals Court in Bloemfontein.

April 27: Police open fire with birdshot during an hour of

running battles with about 350 protesting students on the University of Cape Town campus in violence that followed a student meeting to protest a recent South African military raid into Zambia.

May 4: South African riot police arrest 120 students and fire tear gas at about 50 faculty members at the University of the Witwatersrand in Johannesburg as the students and teachers protest the upcoming whites-only election.

May 6: White voters shift sharply to the right in parliamentary elections. Workers, meanwhile, mount what is called the largest protest strike in the nation's history as some 1.5 million of them stay home from work in the second day of a two-day "stayaway," amid reports of dozens of incidents of stone throwing and arson.

Bibliography

Writings on South African Politics and Literature

Adey, D., R. Beeton, M. Chapman, E. Pereira. *Companion to South African English Literature*. Johannesburg: Ad. Donker, 1986.

Alexander, Neville. *Sow the Wind*. Johannesburg: Skotaville, 1985.

Badsha, Omar ed. *South Africa: The Cordoned Heart: Twenty South African Photographers*. Cape Town: Gallery Press, 1986.

Biko, Steve. *I Write What I Like*. London: Heinemann, 1979.

Boesak, Alan. *Black and Reformed: Apartheid, Liberation and the Calvinist Tradition*. Johannesburg: Skotaville, 1984.

Bozzoli, Belinda. *Town and Countryside in the Transvaal*. Johannesburg: Ravan, 1983.

Callinicos, L. *Working Class Life 1886-1940: Factories, Townships and Popular Culture on the Rand*. Johannesburg: Ravan, 1986.

Chapman, Michael, ed. *A Century of South African Poetry*. Johannesburg: Ad. Donker, 1981.

Clingman, Stephen. *History from the Inside: the Novels of Nadine Gordimer*. Johannesburg: Ravan, 1986.

Copelan, D. *In Township Tonight*. Johannesburg: Ravan, 1985.

COSATU Worker's Diary 1987. Johannesburg: Ravan, 1987.

Daymond, M., J. Jacobs, M. Lenta. *Momentum*. Pietermaritzberg: University of Natal Press, 1984.

Foster, D., and D. Sandler. *Detention and Torture in South Africa*. Cape Town: David Philip, 1987.

Gordimer, Nadine. *The Black Interpreters*. Johannesburg: Sprocas-Ravan, 1973.

Gray, Stephen, ed. *The Penguin Book of Southern African Stories*. New York: Viking Penguin, 1985.

Gwala, Mafika. "Black Writing Today," in Mike Chapman, ed., *Soweto Poetry*. Johannesburg: McGraw-Hill, 1982.

Hirson, Baruch. *Year of Fire, Year of Ash*. London: Zed Press, 1979.

Kavanagh, Robert Mshengu. *Theatre and Cultural Struggle in South Africa*. London: Zed Press, 1985.

Kuzwayo, Ellen. *Call Me Woman*. Johannesburg: Ravan, 1985.

Lodge, Tom. *Black Politics in South Africa Since 1945*. Johannesburg: Ravan, 1983.

Mandela, Nelson. *No Easy Walk to Freedom*, Ruth First, ed. London: Heinemann, 1965.

Manganyi, N. Chabani. *Looking through the Keyhole*. Johannesburg: Ravan, 1981.

Mda, Zakes. "Commitment and Writing in Theatre the South African Experience," *The Classic*, Vol. 2, No. 1 (1983).

Modisane, William (Bloke). *Blame Me on History.* Johannesburg: Ad. Donker, 1963, 1986.

Mphahlele, Es'kia. *Afrika My Music: An Autobiography 1957-1983.* Johannesburg: Ravan, 1984.

Ndebele, Njabulo S. "Turkish Tales and Some Thoughts on South African Fiction," *Staffrider*, Vol. 6, No. 1 (1984).

————. "The Rediscovery of the Ordinary: Some New Writings in South Africa," *Journal of Southern African Studies*, Vol. 12, No. 2 (1986).

Ndlovu, Duma, ed. *Woza Afrika! An Anthology of South African Plays.* New York: George Braziller, 1986.

Opland, Jeff. *Xhosa Oral Poetry: Aspects of a Black South African Tradition.* London: Cambridge University Press, 1983.

Paton, Alan. *Towards the Mountain: An Autobiography.* Cape Town: David Philip, 1980.

Platzky L., and C. Walker. *The Surplus People.* Johannesburg: Ravan, 1985.

Plumpp, Sterling D., ed. *Somehow We Survive: An Anthology of South African Writing.* New York: Thunder's Mouth Press, 1982.

Sole, Kelwyn. "Culture, Politics and the Black Writer," *English in Africa*, Vol. 19, No. 1 (1983).

Stadler, Alf. *The Political Economy of Modern South Africa.* Cape Town: David Philip, 1987.

Tlali, Miriam. "Remove the Chains: South African Censorship and the Black Writer," *Index on Censorship*, Vol. No. 6 (1984).

Tutu, Archbishop Desmond Mpilo. *Hope and Suffering: Sermons and Speeches*, 1984. Johannesburg, Skotaville, 1984.

White Landeg, and Tim Couzens, eds. *Literature and Society in South Africa.* Harlow, Essex; New York: Longman, 1984.

Some Important South African Literary Journals

Contrast / Cape Town
Ekapa / Cape Town
New Classic / Johannesburg
New Coin / Grahamstown
Sesame / Johannesburg
Staffrider / Johannesburg
Standpunte / Cape Town (ceased publication: see page 19)
Stet / Johannesburg
Upstream / Cape Town
Vakalisa / Cape Town
(and various little magazines produced by unions)

For Background on S.A. Politics and Literature (Journals and Weekly Newspapers*)

Architecture Design Art (ADA) / Cape Town
Critical Arts / Durban (University of Natal)
Die Suid Afrikaan / Stellenbosch
English in Africa / Grahamstown
Index on Censorship / London (England)
Journal of Commonwealth Literature / Leeds (England)
Journal of Southern African Studies / Cambridge (England)
Leadership SA / Cape Town
*New Nation** / Johannesburg
Race Relations Survey / Johannesburg
SA Review I, II, III, IV / Cape Town
Sash (journal of the Black Sash) / Johannesburg
Social Dynamics / Cape Town
*South** / Cape Town
South African Labour Bulletin / Johannesburg
South African Journal of Human Rights / Cape Town
Transformation / Durban
*Weekly Mail** / Johannesburg
Work in Progress / Johannesburg

Glossary of Place Names

Alexandra—one of the oldest black "townships" on the outskirts of Johannesburg.

Bophuthatswana—so-called "independent homeland," within South Africa (hereinafter, "S.A.").

Cape Province—largest province in S.A. Southwestern quarter of the country.

Cape Town—judicial capital of S.A. One of two main ports, and an important holiday resort.

Ciskei—so-called independent homeland on coast between Cape and Transkei. Recent site of bloody clashes between Ciskeian militia and activists.

Crossroads—perhaps the most famous squatter camp on the outskirts of Cape Town. Residents resisted removals for years. Site of bloody fights between activists and reactionary vigilantes known as "witdoeke."

District Six—area near central Cape Town. Site of flourishing "colored" city later bulldozed to ground when its inhabitants were moved to an apartheid township. Only the mosques remain.

Drakensberg—highest range of mountains in S.A. In Natal.

Durban—the major city in Natal; also chief coastal holiday resort for white South Africans.

Guguletu—black township outside Cape Town.

Johannesburg—the largest white city in S.A. Sometimes referred to as Egoli ("the place of gold").

Langa—township outside Cape Town.

Lesotho—neighboring state. Government recently toppled with rumored South African complicity.

498

Mamelodi—township outside Pretoria.

Namibia—often incorrectly referred to as "South West Africa." Arid region on S.A.'s northwestern border. Occupied by South African troops in defiance of a UN resolution. South West African People's Organisation (SWAPO) opposes South African presence.

Natal—subtropical climate. Contains area known as Kwa Zulu, stronghold of Zulu *Inkatha* movement, headed by Chief Gatsha Buthelezi.

Orange Free State—central province of S.A. Largely farming districts, but also vast gold, coal and diamond fields. Often popularly associated with conservatism.

Port Elizabeth—large coastal town in Eastern Cape. Auto manufacturing center.

Pretoria—administrative capital of the country. Mainly Afrikaans populace.

Sharpeville—near Vereeniging in the Transvaal. It was at Sharpeville in 1960 that S.A. police opened fire on a crowd of unarmed protesters, killing sixty-nine.

Soweto—acronym for "South Western Townships." Outside Johannesburg. Home of over a million black workers employed on the Witwatersrand.

Sun City—resort in the so-called independent homeland known as Bophuthatswana. Created by South African entrepreneurs, Sun City is symbolically associated with apartheid's decadence and recently has been the target of anti-apartheid artistic expression in the U.S.

Transvaal—northernmost province and beginning of bushveld vegetation usually associated with savannah Africa. Major towns are Pretoria and Johannesburg. Most populous region of S.A.

Witwatersrand—(literally, "ridge of white water")—chief gold-producing belt; site of major gold mines and towns such as Springs, Germiston, Johannesburg, Krugersdorp. The latter towns are particularly associated with white working-class conservatism.

Zimbabwe – formerly "Rhodesia." Country to the north of S.A. Prime Minister: Robert Mugabe.

Glossary of Acronyms

ANC – African National Congress
ASSOCOM – Association of Chambers of Commerce of South Africa
CAP – Community Arts Project
CNA – Central News Agency
CNETU – Confederation of Non-European Trade Unions
COSATU – Congress of South African Trade Unions
CUSA – Council of Unions of South Africa
ECC – End Conscription Campaign
ESSA – English-Speaking South Africans
FNETU – Federation of Non-European Trade Unions
FOSATU – Federation of South African Trade Unions
FRELIMO – Front for the Liberation of Mozambique
FUBA – Federated Union of Black Arts
ICU – Industrial and Commercial Workers' Union
MAWU – Metal and Allied Workers' Union
MDALI – Music Drama Arts and Literature Institute
NUM – National Union of Mineworkers
PAC – Pan Africanist Congress
PET – People's Experimental Theatre
PUR – Permanent Urban Resident
SABC – South African Broadcasting Corporation
SACHED – South African Committee for Higher Education
SASO – South African Students' Organisation
SILO – Sugar Industry Labour Organisation
SWAPO – South West African People's Organisation
TECON – Theatre Council of Natal
UDF – United Democratic Front
ZAPU – Zimbabwe African People's Union

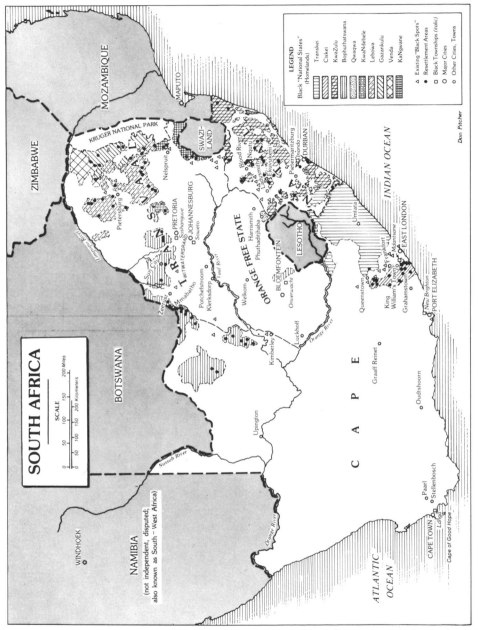

SOUTH AFRICA

SCALE

0   50   100   150   200 Miles
0   50   100   150   200 Kilometers

ATLANTIC OCEAN

NAMIBIA

(not independent, disputed;
also known as South – West Africa)

WINDHOEK

Nossob River

Orange River

Orange River

Upington

Oudtshoorn

Graaff Renet

C A P E

Paarl
Stellenbosch
CAPE TOWN
Lorag

Cape of Good Hope

BOTSWANA

ZIMBABWE

MOZAMBIQUE

MAPUTO

KRUGER NATIONAL PARK

Nelspruit

Pietersburg

SWAZI-
LAND

PRETORIA
Soshanguve
JOHANNESBURG
Soweto

Klerksdorp
Potchefstroom

Zeerust
Mmabatho

Sun City

TwitWATERSRAND

ORANGE FREE STATE

Harrismith
Phuthadijhaba

Welkom

BLOEMFONTEIN
Onverwacht

Kimberley
Luckhoff

Queenstown

King
William's Town
Grahamstown

Umtata

Ladysmith

Pietermaritzburg
DURBAN

LESOTHO

Newcastle

EAST LONDON

New Brighton
PORT ELIZABETH

INDIAN OCEAN

Don Pitcher

LEGEND

Black "National States"
(Homelands)

Transkei
Ciskei
KwaZulu
Bophuthatswana
Qwaqwa
KwaNdebele
Lebowa
Gazankulu
Venda
KaNgwane

△ Existing "Black Spots"
● Resettlement Areas
□ Black Townships (italic)
○ Major Cities
○ Other Cities, Towns